Studies in Regional and Local Hi

General Editor Jane Whittl

Elizabeth Griffiths, May 2016, at Causeway House near Hadrian's Wall.

Managing for Posterity

The Norfolk gentry
and their estates *c.*1450–1700

Elizabeth Griffiths
edited and with an introduction by Jane Whittle

University of Hertfordshire Press
Studies in Regional and Local History

Volume 21

First published in Great Britain in 2022 by
University of Hertfordshire Press
College Lane
Hatfield
Hertfordshire
AL10 9AB
UK

British Library Cataloguing in Publication Data
A catalogue record for this book is available from the British Library

ISBN 978-1-912260-44-7 hardback
ISBN 978-1-912260-45-4 paperback

Design by Arthouse Publishing Solutions
Printed in Great Britain by Henry Ling Ltd

In memory of Joan Thirsk (1922–2013),
historian of rural England – for her unfailing help and support.

Contents

Figures

Tables

Acknowledgements

Elizabeth and I had been good friends and research collaborators since at least 2001, so it was a real pleasure to read her lively prose once more and follow the path she picked through the archival riches left by the Norfolk gentry in the process of preparing this book for publication. I am enormously grateful to Peter Griffiths and Elizabeth Rutledge for their help in recovering Elizabeth's notes and illustrations for the chapters and providing editorial oversight, as well as to Kristopher Harper of the Norfolk Record Society for digging up digital copies of the illustrations for *Her Price is Above Pearls*. Sincere thanks also go to Paul Warde as editor of the *Agricultural History Review* and Alan Metters as honorary secretary of the Norfolk Record Society for giving permission to reproduce previously published research in chapters 7 to 10 of this volume. Elizabeth was actively involved in both the British Agricultural History Society and the Norfolk Record Society and is much missed by the members of both organisations. The publication of this volume would not have been possible without the help of Michael Meakin and Charles Le Strange Meakin who allowed Elizabeth to see documents and paintings privately owned by the Le Strange family, as well as those held at Norfolk Record Office, with permission to reproduce them here. Norfolk Record Office helped to locate document references and provided digital reproductions. A generous grant from the Aurelius Trust made publication of the book in the Regional and Local History series possible. Jane Housham and Sarah Elvins at UH Press provided valuable assistance and encouragement at all stages.

Previous titles in this series
Founding Editor Nigel Goose

Volume 1: *A Hertfordshire demesne of Westminster Abbey: Profits, productivity and weather* by Derek Vincent Stern (edited and with an introduction by Christopher Thornton)

Volume 2: *From Hellgill to Bridge End: Aspects of economic and social change in the Upper Eden Valley, 1840–95* by Margaret Shepherd

Volume 3: *Cambridge and its Economic Region, 1450–1560* by John S. Lee

Volume 4: *Cultural Transition in the Chilterns and Essex Region, 350 AD to 650 AD* by John T. Baker

Volume 5: *A Pleasing Prospect: Society and culture in eighteenth-century Colchester* by Shani D'Cruze

Volume 6: *Agriculture and Rural Society after the Black Death: Common themes and regional variations* by Ben Dodds and Richard Britnell

Volume 7: *A Lost Frontier Revealed: Regional separation in the East Midlands* by Alan Fox

Volume 8: *Land and Family: Trends and local variations in the peasant land market on the Winchester bishopric estates, 1263–1415* by John Mullan and Richard Britnell

Volume 9: *Out of the Hay and into the Hops: Hop cultivation in Wealden Kent and hop marketing in Southwark, 1744–2000* by Celia Cordle

Volume 10: *A Prospering Society: Wiltshire in the later Middle Ages* by John Hare

Volume 11: *Bread and Ale for the Brethren: The provisioning of Norwich Cathedral Priory, 1260–1536* by Philip Slavin

Volume 12: *Poor Relief and Community in Hadleigh, Suffolk, 1547–1600* by Marjorie Keniston McIntosh

Volume 13: *Rethinking Ancient Woodland: The archaeology and history of woods in Norfolk* by Gerry Barnes and Tom Williamson

Volume 14: *Custom and Commercialisation in English Rural Society: Revisiting Tawney and Postan* edited by J.P. Bowen and A.T. Brown

Volume 15: *The World of the Small Farmer: Tenure, profit and politics in the early modern Somerset Levels* by Patricia Croot

Volume 16: *Communities in Contrast: Doncaster and its rural hinterland, c.1830–1870* by Sarah Holland

Volume 17: *Peasant Perspectives on the Medieval Landscape: A study of three communities* by Susan Kilby

Volume 18: *Shaping the Past: Theme, time and place in local history – essays in honour of David Dymond* by Evelyn Lord and Nicholas R. Amor

Volume 19: *Lichfield and the Lands of St Chad: Creating community in early medieval Mercia* by Andrew Sargent

Volume 20: *Histories of People and Landscape: Essays on the Sheffield region in memory of David Hey* edited by R.W. Hoyle

Studies in Regional and Local History

General Editor's preface and introduction

For volumes in the *Studies in Regional and Local History* series I normally write a general editor's preface. This book is rather different: here I am acting as editor and provide both an introduction to the book and an outline of the author's life and work. Elizabeth Griffiths became seriously ill and died in April 2020 before she could complete the book *Managing for Posterity: The Le Stranges of Hunstanton and their Estates 1604–1919*, which was to be published in this series. She had already sent me the first five chapters in good draft, but another was incomplete and six remained unwritten. The chapters already completed were lively, well written and important, outlining the rise of the Le Strange family as prominent Norfolk gentry, comparing them with their cousins the Hobarts and showing how the Le Stranges grappled with controlling and improving their estates in the first half of the seventeenth century. It seemed essential that this research was not lost to posterity. As a consequence, we pressed ahead with publishing a rather different book. It combines Elizabeth's new research on the Le Stranges in the first six chapters, with four chapters based on previously published work to which it is closely related. It is not exactly the book Elizabeth intended, but, nonetheless, it offers a unique window into the lives and work of Norfolk's seventeenth-century gentry in a way I hope she would have appreciated. Three families in particular were the focus of Elizabeth's research: the Le Stranges of Hunstanton, who take centre place in this book, together with the Hobarts of Blickling and the Windhams of Felbrigg, on whom Elizabeth based her PhD. These families' innovations in agriculture, estate management and record-keeping predated the more famous Norfolk innovators of the eighteenth century such as Coke of Holkham, and were just as far-reaching in their implications. Elizabeth Griffiths was the unrivalled expert in their histories. The remainder of this preface outlines Elizabeth's life and work as a historian and assesses the significance of her research, before saying a little more about the themes and structure of the book.

Elizabeth Griffiths went to the University of East Anglia as a mature student, graduating with a first-class degree in History in 1980, before training as a teacher and then undertaking a PhD, which was awarded in 1987. Her thesis, supervised by B.A. Holderness and examined by Joan Thirsk, concerned the management of two east Norfolk estates, Blickling and Felbrigg.[1] It was an important step forward in our understanding of the history of agrarian Norfolk, the most agriculturally precocious of England's counties. Her research tracked the fortunes of these two exceptionally well-documented estates, belonging respectively to the Hobart and Windham families, through the economic and political turmoil of the seventeenth century, beginning in 1596 and finishing in 1717. The main argument, and one that also features prominently

---

1   Elizabeth Griffiths, 'The management of two east Norfolk estates in the seventeenth century: Blickling and Felbrigg', PhD thesis (University of East Anglia, 1987).

in this book, was firstly that historians had mistakenly overlooked the significance of agrarian change in the seventeenth century and secondly that that transformation was most evident in a number of well-documented Norfolk estates. As Elizabeth wrote, 'In Norfolk, economics and political events clearly combined to make the seventeenth century, or more accurately the period from the 1580s to the 1720s, a formative and distinctive period of estate management and landownership.'[2]

Towards the end of her period at the University of East Anglia, Elizabeth also worked as a researcher with Hassell Smith on the history of the Norwich Freemen. This led to her first publication in 1987, *'Buxom to the Mayor': A History of the Norwich Freemen and the Town Close Estate*. It was an interest she would pick up again in 2014, leading the team that made the Norwich Freemen's records available online and writing a history of the freemen for the website.[3]

From 1987 to 2002 Elizabeth lived first in London and then in Kent, teaching history at various schools before becoming head of history at Reigate Sixth Form College. While in Kent Elizabeth strengthened her friendship with Joan Thirsk, who lived there during her retirement. Joan encouraged her to publish and continue with her research, and Elizabeth prepared several publications developed out of her PhD research. The first explored Henry Hobart's role as a seventeenth-century agricultural improver and was published in the *Agricultural History Review* in 1998.[4] The second was a Norfolk Record Society volume on William Windham's remarkable Green Book, published in 2002. The introduction to this appears here in abridged form as chapter 9.[5] Another, examining the impact of adverse economic circumstances on estate management in the later seventeenth century, appeared in an edited collection in honour of Joan two years later, and is reprinted here as chapter 10.[6]

In 2002 Elizabeth moved back to Norfolk and began a new phase of her life as a full-time historical researcher. She embarked on two new research projects, one on sharefarming and the other on the records of the Le Strange archive. Historians had always argued that sharefarming, also known as sharecropping or *métayage*, was absent from England's agricultural regime in the early modern period due to England's precocious capitalist development. Yet during her PhD research Elizabeth had found that sharefarming agreements were relatively commonplace in Norfolk in the second half of the seventeenth century and were associated not with backwardness but with agricultural innovation. Her knowledge went further than this, however, as she had

---

2   Griffiths, 'Management', p. 14.

3   Elizabeth Griffiths and A. Hassell Smith, *'Buxom to the Mayor': A History of the Norwich Freemen and the Town Close Estate*, Centre for East Anglian Studies (Norwich, 1987); and see <http://www.norwichfreemen.org.uk/tracing-our-history/>, accessed 10 September 2021.

4   Elizabeth Griffiths, 'Sir Henry Hobart: a new hero of Norfolk agriculture?' *Agricultural History Review*, 46/1 (1998), pp. 15–34.

5   Elizabeth Griffiths (ed.), *William Windham's Green Book 1673–1688*, Norfolk Record Society 66 (Norwich, 2002).

6   Elizabeth Griffiths, 'Responses to adversity: the changing strategies of two Norfolk landowning families, *c.*1665–1700', in Richard W. Hoyle (ed.), *People, Landscape and Alternative Agriculture: Essays for Joan Thirsk, Agricultural History Review*, supplement series 3 (Exeter, 2004), pp. 74–92.

encountered such agreements at first hand when farming in New Zealand in the mid-1970s. After presenting a number of conference papers on sharefarming in the late 1990s Elizabeth obtained funding in 2005 to lead a project on the topic, with Mark Overton and Michael Winter as co-investigators. It innovatively examined sharefarming in the long run from the medieval period to the twentieth century. The findings of this project were published as *Farming to Halves: The Hidden History of Sharefarming* in 2009.[7] At the heart of this book were three chapters on the seventeenth and eighteenth centuries, drawing on evidence from the Windham, Hobart and Le Strange archives, as well as new evidence from the Townshend family's archive at Raynham Hall.

The sharefarming project overlapped with another focused solely on the Le Stranges of Hunstanton.[8] At the annual British Agricultural History Society conference in 2001 she and I had begun chatting about the early seventeenth-century household accounts in the Le Strange archive, which I had recently looked at for the first time. These meticulously detailed accounts, written very largely by Lady Alice Le Strange, run in a continuous series from 1607 to 1653, filling hundreds of neatly written manuscript pages. They seemed worthy of a research project in their own right. Elizabeth enthused not only about the accounts but about the larger Le Strange archive of which they formed but a small part. She had investigated the archive as a possible third case study when researching her PhD, but had concluded it was so voluminous and rich that it required a study of its own. We thought we would make a start, and formulated a project based on the household accounts. Elizabeth worked full-time on this project from 2003 to 2005. The results were published as *Consumption and Gender in the Early Seventeenth-Century Household* in 2012.[9] This was only the start of Elizabeth's research on the early seventeenth-century Le Stranges, however. In the following years she published an analysis of the notebooks and library of Sir Hamon Le Strange,[10] a collection of the estate and farming documents of Lady Alice Le Strange[11] and an exploration of the exploits of their son, Nicholas Le Strange, in draining Norfolk marshland.[12] These second two pieces appear here as chapters 7 and 8, while the research on Hamon Le Strange underpins chapters 5 and 6.

It was natural that this research would expand into a book, which Elizabeth prospectively titled *Managing for Posterity*. The book was never envisaged as merely

7   Elizabeth Griffiths and Mark Overton, *Farming to Halves: The Hidden History of Sharefarming in England from Medieval to Modern Times* (Basingstoke, 2009).

8   There was also a short diversion into the Boleyns of Blickling: Elizabeth Griffiths, 'The Boleyns at Blickling, 1450–1560', *Norfolk Archaeology*, 45/4 (2009), pp. 453–68.

9   Jane Whittle and Elizabeth Griffiths, *Consumption and Gender in the Early Seventeenth-Century Household: The World of Alice Le Strange* (Oxford, 2012).

10 Elizabeth Griffiths, '"A Country Life": Sir Hamon Le Strange of Hunstanton in Norfolk, 1583–1654', in Richard W. Hoyle (ed.), *Custom, Improvement and the Landscape in Early Modern Britain* (Farnham, 2011), pp. 203–34.

11 Elizabeth Griffiths, *Her Price is Above Pearls: Family and Farming Records of Alice Le Strange, 1617–1656*, Norfolk Record Society 79 (Norwich, 2015).

12 Elizabeth Griffiths, 'Draining the coastal marshes of north-west Norfolk: the contribution of the Le Stranges at Hunstanton, 1605 to 1724', *Agricultural History Review*, 63/2 (2015), pp. 221–42.

a descriptive history of the Le Stranges and the management of their estates; it was always something more. Developing out of ideas about sustainability, Elizabeth was fascinated by the record-keeping and archival practices of gentry families that effectively allowed them to survive over time, from generation to generation. The Le Stranges survived as lords of Hunstanton from the fourteenth century to the late eighteenth century in the direct line, and indirectly to the present day. As she discusses in chapter 1, accumulating knowledge and preserving evidence was not just a by-product of being a gentry landlord, but a strategy that allowed them to maintain and increase their wealth. In the Le Strange archive in particular it is evident that documents were not merely preserved but read and annotated by successive generations. Alice Le Strange learned to keep accounts partly by reading the accounts kept by the early sixteenth-century Le Stranges. Sir Nicholas Le Strange (1661–1724), one of several heirs in the family who inherited as a minor without parents to guide him, carefully read the notebooks written by his great-grandfather Sir Hamon Le Strange in the first half of the seventeenth century.

The work of Elizabeth Griffiths has made three significant contributions to how we understand the changing economy of rural England in the seventeenth century. First, she revealed the richness and potential of estate archives from the sixteenth and seventeenth centuries. These archives can seem dry, with their concern for legal titles, rents and tenancy agreements, and byzantine in their arrangement: certainly off-putting to the uninitiated. Elizabeth made them come alive and showed how their contents could be used to address a wide range of issues. Second, she demonstrated conclusively the extent of agricultural innovation in seventeenth-century Norfolk: Norfolk's eighteenth-century 'agricultural revolution' was not really a revolution but a continuation of trends and strategies that had begun in the late sixteenth century and developed during the seventeenth. Third, and perhaps least obviously, she offered a new way of viewing the gentry in this period. While historians have often portrayed the gentry's involvement in politics, intellectual pursuits and leisure, the gentry are rarely seen as workers. Elizabeth's point was that to benefit from their inherited wealth and to stand a chance of increasing it the gentry had to be actively involved in the management of their landed estates. They were not simply passive rentiers collecting money from their tenants: they had to run their estates like businesses. Thus, the gentry had to defend their legal rights to property and find ways to adjust to changing economic circumstances, such as fluctuating corn prices or the falling value of fixed rents due to inflation, to avoid the value of their inherited estates being reduced.

These active policies were known as 'improvement' in early modern England. Of course, they did not necessarily represent improvement from the perspective of tenants, who saw their rents rise or tenures become less secure. When I challenged Elizabeth on her tendency to see these issues from the gentry's point of view, she wrote another excellent essay titled 'Improving Landlords or Villains of the Piece?'[13] This, again, drew on her knowledge of Norfolk archives and showed how in the late

---

13 Elizabeth Griffiths, 'Improving landlords or villains of the piece? A case study of early seventeenth-century Norfolk', in Jane Whittle (ed.), *Landlords and Tenants in Britain, 1440–1660: Tawney's Agrarian Problem Revisited* (Woodbridge, 2013), pp. 166–82.

sixteenth and early seventeenth centuries rising land values and corn prices led to adjustments in the relationship between lords and tenants. Yet the most effective landlords avoided conflict where possible and worked with their tenants to bring change about. Tenants were not powerless, and costly lawsuits were one of the many pitfalls that landlords sought to avoid.

The first six chapters of this book present a history of the Le Strange family and their estates. Chapter 1 is Elizabeth's original introduction to the book she planned, but has been slightly edited to remove references to the unwritten chapters, although some of the text has been kept as an epilogue that outlines the fortunes of the Le Stranges of Hunstanton between the eighteenth century and the present day. Chapter 2 takes the story back to the medieval period, examining how the Le Stranges established themselves as Norfolk landowners. Chapter 3 examines the situation Sir Hamon Le Strange found himself in when he inherited the estate in 1604 after a long minority. Chapter 4 steps back from the Le Stranges and draws comparisons with two other families, the Cleres and the Hobarts. The Cleres of Blickling offer an example of a gentry family that failed, selling up to the very successful Hobarts. Both examples put the modest stability achieved by the Le Stranges in perspective. Chapter 5 returns to the Le Stranges and examines how Hamon and Alice Le Strange created a 'knowledge economy' with careful and innovative record-keeping that allowed them to run their estates more effectively. These chapters (2 to 5) appear as Elizabeth wrote them, with only very light editing.

Chapter 6 was left unfinished, and thus had to be slightly reshaped. Originally intended as a broader exploration of how Hamon and Alice, and the Le Stranges who came after them, applied the knowledge accumulated in their family archive to the estate, it appears here as a study of building work carried out on the estate, and particularly on Hunstanton Hall itself.[14] This fascinating story takes the history of Hunstanton Hall up to the present day: it still survives, although unfortunately much damaged by fires in the nineteenth and twentieth centuries. These six chapters are accompanied in this volume by four closely related pieces of research. Chapter 7 is an abridged version of Elizabeth's introduction to *Her Price is Above Pearls*, and looks in detail at Alice Le Strange's work as an estate manager, overseeing the Le Strange sheep flocks and rationalising her inherited lands in Sedgeford.[15] Chapter 8 reprints an article from the *Agricultural History Review* that focuses on Nicholas Le Strange, Alice and Hamon's son and heir, and his activities draining land in the coastal marshes of Hunstanton and Heacham.[16] These are topics that Elizabeth had intended to include in the planned volume. The other chapters of the planned book, tracing the history of the Le Stranges after the deaths of Hamon, Alice and Nicholas in 1654–6 up to 1919, were unwritten, although the archival documents necessary to do this are at the Norfolk Record Office for future researchers to explore, and the epilogue outlines what is possible. Instead, this book provides two further chapters focused on the later seventeenth century. Chapter 9 is an abridged version of the introduction Elizabeth

---

14   The unwritten parts of the chapter aimed to deal with agricultural techniques and legal battles.

15   See fn. 11 above.

16   See fn. 12 above.

wrote to William Windham's Green Book.[17] It tells the story of a young landowner trying to make the best of his estate in a period of low corn prices and failing tenancies. These are very similar to the challenges faced by Nicholas Le Strange (1661–1724), who would have been the topic of chapter 8 in the original plan. Finally, chapter 10 returns to the comparative perspective and compares William Windham's performance with that of his near-neighbour Sir John Hobart, reprinting an essay first published in 2004.[18] As such, the new chapters and the previously published pieces form a coherent whole, focused on the issues Elizabeth had intended to address.

Finally, I would like to note that, just as it was important for Norfolk landlords to keep good records so as not to lose their rights to land, so it is important for historians to keep records of their research so that it is not lost to future researchers. Lizzie's record-keeping allowed this book to be published, ensuring it was not lost to posterity. While her lively discussions, innovative ideas, expertise and endless enthusiasm are much missed by her academic friends, her research can and will live on.

Jane Whittle
Exeter, 2021

---

17 See fn. 5 above.
18 See fn. 6 above.

Chapter 1

The Le Strange family
and their records

Securing the status and long-term survival of the family has always been the principal concern of the English aristocracy and gentry. Central to that ambition, at least until the late nineteenth century, was the successful management of their landed estates. Failure to perform this somewhat tedious task could spell ruination for the family. Unfortunately for them, the task became much more difficult from the late sixteenth century as price inflation reduced the value of their rents and placed new demands on their management skills. By the 1600s estates in Norfolk were changing hands rapidly as the unlucky or simply incompetent failed to grapple with the issues, while the astute and enterprising capitalised on their misfortunes. When Sir Hamon Le Strange inherited the family's ancient estate at Hunstanton in 1604, after a long minority, the outlook was bleak; 'he was left neyther household stuff nor stock and his Chief House halfe built and his farme houses in such decay, so he hath built most of them out of the ground', as his wife Alice later recalled.[1] Typically, such estates were snapped up by the great lawyers, notably Sir Henry Hobart of Blickling, who amassed huge portfolios from the profits of high office and exploited their local connections.[2] However, Sir Hamon, a nephew of Sir Henry, resisted this fate and, with the help of his wife, restored the fortunes of the family through the careful and innovative management of their estates.[3] How they achieved this outcome and secured the future of the Le Strange family, who still prosper at Hunstanton on their estates after 700 years, is the principal subject of this book.

So what was the secret of their success? A particular aspect of the strategy pursued by Sir Hamon and Alice was the way they tried, through their records, to ensure that their improvements endured and were sustained by their successors. Fathers often wrote books of general advice for their sons, but the Le Stranges' approach was specifically directed to passing on management skills and a detailed knowledge of the estate.[4] In effect, Hamon and Alice created a prototype knowledge economy which

---

1   NRO, LEST/P10. See chapters 3 and 7 for further discussion of Alice's summary of their financial affairs. From this note onwards, the prefix NRO (Norfolk Record Office) to documents in the Le Strange Collection (LEST) has been dropped.

2   See chapter 4.

3   See esp. chapter 6.

4   Sir Edward Coke drew up a list of 'Precepts for the use of my children and their Posteritye'; for a selection of his wise advice, which had minimal impact on his sons, see C.W. James, *Chief Justice Coke, His Family and Descendants at Holkham* (London, 1929), pp. 78–81, Appendix VI. More generally, Felicity Heal and Clive Holmes, *The Gentry in England and Wales, 1500–1700* (London, 1994) cite many examples of this aspect of gentry culture, notably that of Sir John Oglander of Nunwell: pp. 20–3.

Figure 1.1 Engraving of the portrait of Sir Hamon Le Strange by John Hoskins, 1617. NRO KL/TC 13/1/18.

Figure 1.2 Engraving of the portrait of Alice Le Strange by John Hoskins, 1617. NRO KL/TC 13/1/17.

they successfully handed down to their children, grandchildren and most particularly to their great-grandson, Sir Nicholas Le Strange, who inherited the estate as a minor in 1669 and lived until 1724.[5] This activity produced an estate archive of exceptional range and quality; the documents illustrate, quite clearly, through instructions to readers and cross-referencing back to earlier documents, how knowledge was created, managed and transferred from generation to generation, and how the family believed that this procedure was essential if the estate was to be preserved for posterity.[6] Their understanding of the economic value of knowledge and the need to pass it on resonates strongly with modern management techniques, yet historians have largely ignored this aspect of estate management; this book is an attempt to correct the omission and cast light on the process of knowledge management in the early modern period.[7]

A striking feature of the documents is Sir Hamon's early awareness of what was required.[8] Memoranda books dating from 1605 are full of information on the estate concerning the titles and rights to his property.[9] In the same year he commissioned his first map and started on new accounts and field books.[10] He also built up a library of agricultural texts and management manuals.[11] In his work Sir Hamon was guided by his guardians, Sir Henry Spelman, Sir Henry Hobart and his father-in-law, Richard

---

5 See chapter 5.

6 P. Warde, *The Invention of Sustainability: Nature and Destiny: c.1500–1870* (Cambridge, 2018), pp. 90–101, includes a section on posterity in the context of woodland management with particular reference to the popularising of the concept by John Evelyn in his widely read book *Sylva, or a discourse of forest trees* (1664).

7 An exception is Ursula Schlude's work on the Electress Anna of Saxony and her creation of practical knowledge on the electoral estates in the sixteenth century, 'Diversity of media – diversity of gender and social strata. Agrarian knowledge and the written word at a sixteenth century princely court', paper for *Rural History 2013*, Bern. For a later period European historians, led by Paul Brassley, Yves Segers and Leen Van Molle, are working on 'Knowledge networks in rural Europe since 1700'; see also Eric H. Ash, *Power, Knowledge and Expertise in Elizabethan England* (Baltimore, MD, 2004); Peter M. Jones, *Agricultural Enlightenment: Knowledge, Technology and Nature, 1750–1840* (Oxford, 2016).

8 Elizabeth Griffiths, '"A Country Life"'.

9 Four memoranda books survive: LEST/Q34, Q36, Q37 and Q38.

10 Between 1605 and 1633 Sir Hamon commissioned maps for every part of his estate. The earliest for Holme in 1605 is missing, but they survive for Hunstanton, 1615, LEST/AO1; Ringstead, *c.*1625, LEST/OD; Ringstead Brecks, LEST/OB5, OB6; Heacham (in two parts) *c.*1623, LEST/OC2, OB2; Sedgeford (in three parts) *c.*1631, LEST/OC1; Gressenhall, *c.*1624 NRO Hayes & Storr, 72, MR 235, 242 x 1, and Brisley, 1622, repaired by Sir Nicholas (4th Bt) in 1706, NRO MR RO402/7. Sir Nicholas also made a list of 'Surveys and Plotts … and time when taken' in one of Sir Hamon's memoranda books, LEST/Q37, which is how we know about the map for Holme. Subsequently, these maps formed the basis of his books of field maps undertaken in the 1680s and 1690s.

11 Jane Whittle and Elizabeth Griffiths, *Consumption and Gender in the Early Seventeenth Century Household: The World of Alice Le Strange* (Oxford, 2012), pp. 26–48 for a discussion on the use of these manuals, which included C. Estienne, *Maison Rustique, or the Countrey Farme*, translated by R. Surfleete in 1616.

Stubbe,[12] but his greatest asset by far was his wife, Alice, who soon showed her mettle, taking over the household accounts in 1610 from her husband and reviving the family tradition of weekly kitchen books in 1613.[13] At the same time, she started receiving rents in place of her elderly father and, with his help, she bought sheep and kept tiny flocks for her five children.[14] After he died in 1619 she managed her own estate at Sedgeford and reorganised the accounts and farming regimes. Gradually she extended her role, drawing up sheep accounts for the entire estate in 1625 and assuming responsibility for all the estate accounts in 1632; this included updating field books and rentals and keeping a record of the family finances. Alice's documents are notable for their neatness and clarity; she clearly understood the need to educate her children in farming and estate management, as she had been, and to present the information in an accessible and easily transferable way for her successors.

The success of her strategy can be seen most vividly in the farming notebooks of her eldest son, Sir Nicholas. Soon after his marriage in 1631 he embarked on a new venture draining marshes at Hunstanton, Holme and, later, Heacham.[15] In these notebooks, drawing on his father's expertise in water management and building work, he provided a record of the drainage process, from the layout of drains to the cultivation of the marshes and the establishment of new farmsteads, with calculations of the costs and profits. Most significantly, he imitated the clear handwriting of his mother and designed these books as manuals for his successors. The final notebook includes a survey of what had been achieved, with fifty-five pages of notes and 'miscellanie observations' accompanied by instructions to the reader. In 1641, when the marshes at Heacham had become productive, the income from corn rose to £864 compared with £290 in 1621; this formed a substantial portion of estate revenues, which had increased from £1700 to £2650 per annum over the same twenty years.

Continuing success was not, however, a foregone conclusion. The Le Stranges suffered severely in the Civil War when their marshes, corn and sheep flocks were plundered by the parliamentary forces; it took them several years to restock, reinstate schemes and stabilise their finances.[16] However, the point is that they did recover, unlike some other families crippled by similar losses, fines, sequestration and high taxation.[17] The sheep accounts show Alice rebuilding the flocks from scratch, with relatives, friends and tenants placing sheep and paying her a small fee, which she

---

12   Sir Henry Spelman of Congham, 1563–1641, antiquarian and jurist, <www.historyofparliamentonline.org>; Sir Henry Hobart (*c*.1560–1625), see Griffiths, 'Management' and 'Sir Henry Hobart: a new hero of Norfolk agriculture?', *Agricultural History Review*, 46 (1998), pp. 15–34; for Richard Stubbe see chapter 7.

13   Whittle and Griffiths, *Consumption and Gender*, esp. chapter 4.

14   See chapter 7.

15   See chapter 8. Four farming notebooks survive: LEST/KA6, KA9, KA10 and KA24.

16   The Le Stranges, father and three sons, were actively engaged in the civil war, playing a leading role in the defence of King's Lynn against the parliamentary forces in 1643. R.W. Ketton-Cremer, 'Sir Hamon L'Estrange and his sons', *Norfolk Gallery* (1958), pp. 56–94.

17   R.W. Ketton-Cremer, *Norfolk in the Civil War: A Portrait of a Society in Conflict*, 2nd edn (Norwich, 1985), pp. 292–304; Heal and Holmes, *The Gentry in England and Wales*, pp. 214–26.

recorded alongside tiny sums for the tithe wool and lambs; every penny counted.[18] By 1650 receipts for corn, wool and sheep had almost recovered to pre-war levels, although debts remained a stubborn problem.[19] The greatest threat to their lasting recovery was not so much the war as the deaths of Sir Hamon and Alice, and Sir Nicholas and his eldest son, Hamon, between 1654 and 1656. Sir Nicholas's younger son, who inherited the estate in 1655, also died young in 1669, leaving a small child, Sir Nicholas, the fourth baronet, in the care of his aunt, Lady Astley.[20]

Not willing personally to undertake her duties, yet desirous that the infant 'might be educated and his estate managed with the best care and advantage', Bridget Astley assigned the guardianship to Sir Christopher Calthorpe and John Le Strange, 'neere relatives and friends' of the young boy.[21] This was a wise move. In a letter to his aunt in 1682 Sir Nicholas acknowledged his debt, 'having rec'd Sir C.C.'s accounts for the Guardianship [of my estate] wherein I find he managed all things to the best advantage & care'.[22]

Over the next forty-two years, armed with this education and upbringing, Sir Nicholas engineered a further revival of the family fortunes. His strategy included searching the 'Evidence House', where he found Sir Hamon's memoranda books, as he explained in a note:

> This booke I found in ye old evidence house with a decayed and worm-eaten cover thrown by and neglected. But upon perusal meeting with severall things relating to building and every material and likely to be of use, I put an index or table to that part of the booke, and such other observations as might possibly prove of service and convenience to refer to upon occasion.[23]

In his estate records he referred repeatedly to Alice's field books and rentals and used them as models for his own updated versions. He also commissioned a series of new field maps with notes explaining how they should be preserved: 'These books ought not to be lodg'd in the ye Evidence Room. For by reason of some fault in the past the moysture & damp of that room contracts so great a mould that it is apt to spott and deface ye draughts as may be discern'd in most of ye tables.'[24] In other words, Sir Nicholas rebuilt the knowledge bank created by Sir Hamon, Alice and his grandfather; with even greater awareness, he tried to ensure it was used and preserved for future generations.

---

18   Chapter 7.

19   Griffiths, '"A Country Life"', pp. 230–55. Receipt books have not survived for the period 1641–50, so it is difficult to assess the precise impact of the war.

20   See Figure 5.1. Lady Astley was Bridget Coke, d. of John Coke of Holkham, widow of Sir Isaac Astley of Melton Constable.

21   LEST/AA18.

22   LEST/KA11, Sir Christopher Calthorpe, son of Sir James Calthorpe of East Barsham and Catherine Lewkenor, the sister of Anne who married Sir Nicholas Le Strange in 1631. The letter to Lady Astley, LEST/P20.

23   LEST/Q38.

24   LEST/EH8 field maps of Ringstead, c.1690s.

I

The Le Strange profile of recovery and renewal in the seventeenth century was not unique. Other Norfolk families, notably the Hobarts of Blickling, the Windhams of Felbrigg and the Townshends of Raynham, radically improved their estates and their record-keeping in the early 1600s, with women often playing a prominent part.[25] However, the Le Stranges were different in the scale of their activity and the intensity of their approach; they also started from a lower base and suffered more acutely in the Civil War. What their documents show, unlike those of the other families, is a genuine grasp of modern management and what was required to be commercially successful in the long run. For example, Sir Hamon fully acknowledged his wife's accountancy skills and they worked together in partnership quite openly.[26] This in itself was unusual. Women were no strangers to estate management, but typically they became involved as widows or in the absence of their husbands; they rarely worked alongside and certainly not as equals.[27] Likewise, Sir Hamon and Alice encouraged their eldest son, Sir Nicholas, to pursue his own ventures, offering him support and guidance. From 1632 the Le Stranges effectively operated as a family management team, indicating a further awareness of the principles of managing human capital. But, above all, they understood that creating knowledge and transferring it to succeeding generations was a key factor in securing the long-term survival of gentry families and their estates.

This emphasis on knowledge and managing for posterity offers new insights into gentry life and estate management in the early modern period. Estate studies have a distinguished pedigree in economic history dating back to the post-war period when landed families, or the National Trust acting on their behalf, deposited collections in county record offices.[28] The initial focus was on wealth creation, agricultural innovation, moving rents, tenures and leases, the benefits of enclosure and increased productivity, all played out against

---

25 See chapters 9 and 10, and also Griffiths, 'Management'; with Overton, *Farming to Halves*, for a case study on the Raynham, Hunstanton, Blickling and Felbrigg estates.

26 Alice's role in the management of Sir Hamon's affairs was publicly acknowledged in the interrogations for the Chancery case between Robert Cremer and Sir Hamon Le Strange, 1647.

27 In their widowhoods, Eleanor Townshend at Raynham, 1493–9, Lady Frances Hobart at Blickling, 1647–65 and Katherine Windham at Felbrigg, 1689–1720 did sterling work, while Anne (nee Vaux) kept exemplary estate accounts for her husband Sir Thomas Le Strange during his absence at court in the service of Henry VIII. See B.J. Harris, *English Aristocratic Women, 1450–1550: Marriage and Family, Property and Careers* (Oxford, 2002) for Eleanor Townshend and Anne Le Strange and C. Moreton, *The Townshends and their World: Gentry, Law and Land in Norfolk, c.1450–1551* (Oxford, 1992).

28 P. Roebuck, *Yorkshire Baronets 1640–1760: Families, Estates and Fortunes* (Oxford, 1980), pp. 1–16 for a historiographical background on estate studies dating back to the seventeenth century and an extensive bibliography. The Townshend papers are still at Raynham; those for the Hobarts and the Windhams, after negotiations with the donor families, were deposited at the Norfolk Record Office by The National Trust from 1940 and 1968 respectively. The Le Strange archive arrived at the NRO after a huge fire at Hunstanton in 1951 and the family continue to make additional deposits.

a background of rising and falling landed families.[29] Sidney Pollard, clearly impressed by all this activity, cited the eighteenth-century landed estate as the model for large-scale industrial enterprises.[30] As he explained, these estates differed from other enterprises involving masses of men, such as organising armies or building fortifications, in that by the eighteenth century they were managed to make a profit. The Le Stranges, as we have seen, were fully aware of the concept in the early seventeenth century, as Alice listed the profits of her dairy between 1617 and 1634,[31] and her son Sir Nicholas compiled tables showing the cost and profit of his drainage schemes. These references are limited and Sir Nicholas's tables were clearly experimental; nevertheless, they recognised the need for more informative accounts and ways of assessing the real value of their enterprises.

These profit-making activities Pollard described as entrepreneurial management, as opposed to internal management, which involved the creation of management structures, the use of professionals and the organisation and incentivisation of labour. Research in this area has been notoriously deficient, with Hainsworth's work on estate stewards often cited as a notable exception.[32] The explanation for this neglect, according to Pollard, was that the British took such skills for granted and that such matters were not worthy of analysis. However, as industrialisation spread across the world, attention turned to these issues and the social and environmental context in which they existed. Reflecting these concerns, historians have worked on landowners' relationships with their communities; their impact on rural economies and the English landscape; the existence of a moral capitalism; and the role of women in estate management.[33] Estate studies continue to be built around these themes and issues.

---

29   Notable examples include M.E. Finch, *The Wealth of Five Northamptonshire Families, 1540–1640*, Northamptonshire Record Society 19 (Oxford, 1954–5); A. Simpson, *The Wealth of the Gentry, 1540–1640* (Cambridge, 1961); R.A.C. Parker, *Coke of Norfolk: A Financial and Agricultural Study, 1707–1842* (Oxford, 1975) and more generally the work of J.H. Habakkuk, G.E. Mingay, F.M.L. Thompson, J.V. Beckett and C.G.A. Clay on landownership, the gentry and estate management.

30   S. Pollard, *The Genesis of Modern Management* (Cambridge, MA, 1965), pp. 25–60.

31   LEST/P8.

32   D.R. Hainsworth, *Stewards, Lords and People: The Estate Steward in his World in Later Stuart England* (Cambridge, 1990); Francis Guybon, the long-serving steward of Lord Fitzwilliam at Milton, was related to Francis Guybon, the principal tenant at Sedgeford and first cousin of Alice Le Strange, p. 25. For an earlier period, Rowena Archer commented on the importance of administrative history and its unpopularity amongst historians: R.L. Archer, '"How ladies ... who live on their manors ought to manage their households and estates". Women as landholders and administrators in the later Middle Ages', in P.J.P. Goldberg (ed.), *Women is a Worthy Wight: Women in English Society, c.1200–1500* (Stroud, 1992), pp. 149–81.

33   C. Oestmann, *Lordship and Community: The Lestrange Family and the Village of Hunstanton in the First Half of the Sixteenth Century* (Woodbridge, 1994); J. Broad, *Transforming Rural Society: The Verneys and the Claydons, 1660–1820* (Cambridge, 2004); M. Cragoe, *An Anglican Aristocracy: The Moral Economy of the Landed Estate in Carmathenshire, 1832–1895* (Oxford, 1996). B. McDonagh, '"All towards improvements of the estate": Mrs Elizabeth Prowse at Wicken Northants, 1764–1810', in R.W. Hoyle (ed.), *Custom, Improvement and the Landscape in Early Modern Britain* (2011); Griffiths, 'Improving landlords or villains of the piece?'; B. McDonagh, *Elite Women and the Agricultural Landscape, 1700–1830* (London, 2017).

In the 1990s interest turned to the issue of sustainability and its application to historical situations. This has proved treacherous territory. Turner, Beckett and Afton made a promising start in their research project on 'Sustainability in English Agriculture, c.1550–2000', correcting a widely held assumption that sustainability was simply a problem of our times.[34] They drew attention to earlier crises, notably of the late sixteenth and early seventeenth centuries, when the open-field system designed for subsistence could no longer meet the demands for food from a rapidly rising population. Against a background of dearth, with escalating prices threatening social stability, landowners and farmers were forced to develop more market-orientated systems able to feed and 'sustain' growing and more diverse communities. In this context, responsibility for sustainable systems shifted from the community to individual landowners; this posed serious risks to the harmonious working of rural society. Turner, Beckett and Afton explained that, for harmony to be maintained, three core elements were required: ecology, economy and equity. These concepts, which encapsulated an enduring respect for good husbandry, an understanding of the needs of the market and access to the land and its outcome, had to be in balance for a genuinely sustainable system. This provides a model that can be applied to empirical situations, such as that of the Le Stranges at Hunstanton.

More recently, Paul Warde traced the 'invention of sustainability' through discourses on agricultural and forestry practices, while Ayesha Mukherjee, in her work on Hugh Platt, made a connection between dearth, knowledge making and resource management at the end of the sixteenth century.[35] These arguments include the idea that handing down knowledge generated sustainable solutions in rural communities.[36] The Le Stranges make a crucial contribution to this debate, providing an example and illustrating the activities of practitioners on the ground; but what, if anything, did sustainability mean to them?[37]

The link between knowledge, learning and sustainability is not a new idea. Jules Pretty, in his work on sustainability in modern agriculture, has explained how knowledge underpins sustainability by providing people with the skills and understanding to live and work in sustainable ways.[38] Others have emphasised that sustainability is not a simple package but a process of learning, with the use of knowledge as the main mechanism

---

34 M. Turner, J. Beckett and B. Afton, 'Agricultural sustainability and open-field farming in England, c.1650–1830', *International Journal of Agricultural Sustainability*, 1 (2003), pp. 124–40, reprinted in J.N. Pretty (ed.), *Sustainable Agriculture and Food 1: History of Agriculture and Food* (London, 2008).

35 P. Warde, 'The invention of sustainability? The issue of durability in early modern agronomy and forestry', paper for the Land, Landscape and Environment conference, Reading (2008). A. Mukherjee, *Penury into Plenty: Dearth and the Making of Knowledge in Early Modern England* (London, 2014).

36 Sustainable Households and Communities: Early Modern Discourses of Environmental Change and Sustainability: workshop, Exeter, 2011, organised by A. Mukherjee and N. Whyte.

37 E.M. Griffiths, 'Handing down knowledge and securing the future: the Le Stranges of Hunstanton, 1604–1724', paper for Sustainable Households and Communities; 'Managing water and water based resources: the Le Stranges of Hunstanton, Norfolk 1604–54', for Early Modern Water Symposium, Nottingham, 2011; 'Mapping and measuring: the key to modern management on a Norfolk estate, 1605–55', for Early Modern Conference, Reading, 2011.

38 Pretty, *Sustainable Agriculture and Food 1*.

for survival in periods of rapid change.[39] What is becoming increasingly evident is that these concepts were familiar to landowners and farmers in the seventeenth century. 'Sustain' was a word they used and understood. In the 1600s Sir Henry Hobart, on his newly acquired estate in Norfolk, required tenants to 'decentlie cherish, maintain, keep and sufficiently sustain' hedges, gates and buildings; and also to spread muck on arable 'to the bettering, susteyning and improveing of the same'.[40] Sir Henry, a leading land reformer and commissioner for the crown lands, clearly appreciated the need to promote and protect improvements; he may well have advised his nephew, Sir Hamon Le Strange, to that effect. But 'sustain' meant more than that. The OED lists twelve different meanings dating back to medieval times with fourteen pages of references; the definition 'to keep in being, to cause to continue in a certain state, to keep or maintain at a proper level, and to preserve the status of' is most relevant to an estate study. Landowners were driven by the overwhelming desire to preserve their status and sustain their families for the future: in other words, they managed for posterity. The modern criteria for 'sustainability', that development should meet the needs of the present without compromising the ability of future generations to meet their own needs, does not remotely do justice to what drove these landed families. Managing for posterity is a more pertinent title for what motivated them and shaped their policies.

II

The focus of this book is on the seventeenth century, when the Le Stranges effected and sustained, through much adversity, an astonishing turnaround in their fortunes. This period is extremely significant, but it represents only a slice of a much larger archive, dating from the fourteenth to the twentieth century, which also includes records of the highest quality; in fact, historians have paid far more attention to the medieval and sixteenth-century documents than those of Sir Hamon and Alice.[41] Before the project on Alice's household accounts, Sir Hamon was known principally

---

39 N.G. Röling and M.A.E. Wagemakers, *Facilitating Sustainable Agriculture* (Cambridge, 1998).

40 Griffiths, 'Sir Henry Hobart', pp. 15–34.

41 D. Gurney (ed.), 'Household and privy purse accounts of the Le Stranges of Hunstanton from AD 1519 to AD 1578', *Archaeologia*, 15 (1834), pp. 411–569; H.L. Styleman, 'L'Estrange papers from the Hunstanton Muniment Room', *Norfolk Archaeology*, 5 (1859), pp. 122–45; Hamon Le Strange, *Le Strange Records: A Chronicle of the Early Le Stranges of Norfolk and the March of Wales AD 1110–1310 with the Lines of Knockin and Blackmere continued to their Extinction* (London, 1916); H. Le Strange, 'Roll of household accounts of Sir Hamon Le Strange of Hunstanton, 1347–1348', *Archaeologia*, 69 (1917/18), pp. 111–20; C. Hussey, 'Hunstanton Hall I – Norfolk', *Country Life* (10 April 1926). B.J. Harris, *English Aristocratic Women, 1450–1550* (Oxford, 2002), pp. 63–76. For the first full-length modern account see Oestmann, *Lordship and Community*. Besides her work on Alice Le Strange, Jane Whittle has written a paper, 'Estate management and agricultural labour, 1328–1630: the case of Hunstanton, Norfolk', given at a meeting entitled 'Town, country and consumers – a bouquet for Margaret Yates', University of Reading (2014), and an article, 'The food economy of lords, tenants and workers in a medieval village: Hunstanton, Norfolk, 1328–48', in M. Kowaleski, J. Langdon and P. Schofield (eds), *Peasants and Lords in the Medieval Economy: Essays in Honour of Bruce M.S. Campbell* (Turnhout, 2015), pp. 27–57.

for his exploits in the Civil War, while Alice merited only a few passing references. Their immediate successors, including their great-grandson, Sir Nicholas, have been largely ignored. For the later centuries, despite the existence of an extensive archive and a general awareness of its potential, little has been written about the family and the estate.[42]

As the oldest surviving gentry family in Norfolk, the Le Stranges are probably the best equipped to explain how to successfully manage for posterity. They have been associated with Hunstanton since the early twelfth century and have lived there as resident landowners since 1310, albeit with a gap of seventy years in the late eighteenth and early nineteenth centuries. The Le Strange archive, covering seven centuries, raises the question of whether some landed families consciously fostered a culture of record-keeping that promoted their long-term survival. Why did the Le Strange family keep such meticulous records in the first place? What role did these records play in their management for posterity? How did their approach compare with the strategies of their relatives and friends in Norfolk?

The experience of the Le Strange family also reflects the more general concerns of landed families. The quality of the documents for all the estates under discussion shows a marked improvement in the 1600s as the inflationary crises deepened and landowners needed to pay greater attention to estate business; this was followed by a noticeable simplification of the documents in the early eighteenth century as stability returned, allowing estate business to be delegated to professionals. The effect was to create a distinctive period when a handful of Norfolk gentry families were fully engaged with the modernisation of their estates. The chapters which follow, led by the experience of the Le Strange family, illustrate how the process evolved, and how they tried to secure their estates for posterity.

---

42 S. Wade Martins and T. Williamson, *Roots of Change: Farming and the Landscape in East Anglia, c.1700–1870* (Exeter, 1999); see also K. Fryer, *A Fine Strong Boy: The Life and Times of Henry L'Estrange Styleman Le Strange* (Hunstanton, 2000).

Chapter 2

The medieval inheritance of
the Le Strange estates

By the time Sir Hamon inherited his estate in 1604 the Le Stranges had been in possession of their lands at Hunstanton for over 450 years and resident for almost 300 (see Figure 2.1). The precise origins of the Le Stranges' association with Hunstanton are largely a matter of conjecture. The traditional view, based on Sir William Dugdale's account and repeated by Francis Blomefield in his *History of Norfolk*, was that the family was descended from Guy L'Estrange, a younger son of the duke of Brittany, who had been granted lands in Shropshire and Norfolk at the time of the Conquest.[1] This illustrious notion was firmly discounted by the antiquarian Hamon Le Strange in his book on the early Le Stranges, published in 1916.[2] Influenced by the Rev. Eyton's work on Shropshire, he identified Rhiwillan Extraneous, sometimes called Roland Le Strange, as the first recorded link with Hunstanton, citing two Norfolk deeds from the reign of Henry I in 1112 and 1122.[3] Roland married Matilda Le Brun, daughter and eventual heiress of Ralph Fitz Herluin, alias Ralph de Hunstanton, mesne lord at Hunstanton at the time of the Domesday Survey. After the death of Ralph, the manor came into the hands of the Le Stranges.[4]

The early Le Stranges spent little time at Hunstanton, especially after they established their principal residence at Knockin, Shropshire, in 1189, where they prospered greatly in the service of the king. In 1310, soon after the death of Sir John Le Strange, first Baron Strange of Knockin, his eldest son John, the second baron, enfeoffed his younger brother Hamon with the manor at Hunstanton. As the first Sir Hamon Le Strange, he was the founder of the junior branch of the family. He built the original house round a courtyard on a moated site, thereby signalling his intention to make Hunstanton his primary residence. However, he did not live long enough to enjoy it. He died young in 1316 leaving an infant son, another Hamon, who survived until 1362.[5] He was responsible for the first series of household and manorial accounts.

---

1   Sir William Dugdale, *Baronage of England* (1675); F. Blomefield and C. Parkin, *An Essay towards a Topographical History of the County of Norfolk*, 2nd edn, vol. X (London, 1805–10), pp. 312–27; in fact, Blomefield was doubtful about Dugdale's claims, but his version is no less confusing.

2   Le Strange, *Le Strange Records*.

3   R.W. Eyton, *Antiquities of Shropshire*, vol. 3 (London, 1856) pp. 123–4.

4   This version also appears in W. Rye, *Norfolk Families* (Norwich, 1912) pp. 477–82; *Burke's Landed Gentry*, 18th edn, vol. 3 (London, 1972) and Oestmann, *Lordship and Community*, pp. 12–13.

5   Hamon married Catherine, d. of Sir John Camoys and related to Thomas, 1st Baron Camoys. The barony fell into abeyance in 1426. In 1839 Henry L'Estrange Styleman Le Strange, in his efforts to secure a title, tried to claim it, but it was awarded to the Stonor family.

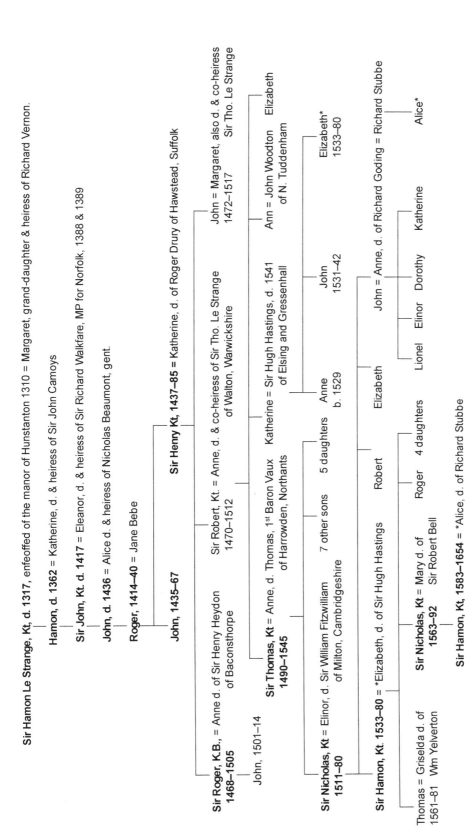

Figure 2.1 Family Tree: Le Strange of Hunstanton, 1310–1600.

Note: Lords of Hunstanton in bold type.

Sources: Blomefield, *Norfolk,*, vol. 10, p. 314; Walter Rye, *Norfolk Families* (1912) pp. 477–82; *Burke's Landed Gentry*, vol. 3 (18th edition, 1972); see also, J. H. Mayer, *Extraneus, A Social and Literary Chronicle of the Families, Strange, Le Strange and L'Estrange, 1082 to 1986* (1986).

These fourteenth-century documents have long been of interest to medieval historians and are the subject of several publications. Early research on the household accounts has been widely used by modern historians, while Bruce Campbell, in his important work *English Seigniorial Agriculture*, made extensive use of the manorial accounts.[6] More recently, Jane Whittle, working with both the manorial and household accounts, has constructed a unique study of a rural community in the early fourteenth century; this provides a glimpse of the world inherited by the Le Stranges as they settled down to life at Hunstanton.[7] Whittle has also compared these household accounts with those of Sir Thomas and Anne Le Strange in the first half of the sixteenth century and Alice in the first half of the seventeenth century.[8] The result is an overview of the social and economic relationships that lay behind the production and consumption of food and the commercialisation of the economy. These aspects include the buying, selling and gifting of food; the types of diet consumed by lords and workers and the various forms of agricultural labour used to produce and market different commodities, all of which influenced standards of living and the relationship between lord and village community. The picture that emerges is one of a diverse economy and community, flourishing on the eve of the Black Death, subtly different to the one presented by Campbell. He argued that, while landlords and peasants were generally prosperous at this time, those on tiny holdings without a surplus to sell were suffering, but there is little evidence for this at Hunstanton.

By all accounts, the Le Stranges inherited something rather special and quite unusual at Hunstanton. Geography played a significant role in their good fortune. Hunstanton lies in the north-west corner of Norfolk, facing the coast on two sides where the Wash meets the North Sea (see Figure 2.2).[9] With its long sandy beaches, brimming with shellfish, leading to rich fishing grounds beyond, Hunstanton has always offered its inhabitants the fruits of the sea as well as the land. The parish is relatively small, with about 1700 acres of medieval farmland divided into two great arable fields, West Field and East Field, where demesne land lay interspersed with that of the manorial tenants.[10] Rather than following a two-field system, Campbell found Hunstanton operated 'the most specialized and intensive cropping system' of medieval

---

6 Notably, Hamon Le Strange (1840–1919), 'A roll of household accounts of Sir Hamon Le Strange of Hunstanton, 1347', *Archaeologia*, 69 (1920), pp. 111–20 and G.H. Holley, 'The earliest roll of household accounts in the muniment room for the 2nd year of Edward III (1328)', *Norfolk Archaeology*, 21 (1920), pp. 77–96. See also C. Dyer, *Standards of Living in the Later Middle Ages: Social Change in England c.1200–1520* (Cambridge, 1989) and *Everyday Life in Medieval England* (London, 1994); B.M.S. Campbell, *English Seigniorial Agriculture, 1240–1450* (Cambridge, 2000).

7 Whittle, 'The food economy'.

8 Whittle, 'Estate management and agricultural labour, 1328–1630'.

9 J.C. Barringer, *Faden's Map of Norfolk* (Dereham, 1989). Although the map dates from 1797 much of the detail of commons, brecks, marsh and fens was the same in the sixteenth and seventeenth centuries: see A. Macnair and T. Williamson, *William Faden and Norfolk's 18th-Century Landscape* (Bollington, 2010). Ringstead Parva, south of the park at Hunstanton, was also known as Barrett Ringstead.

10 Sir Hamon commissioned Thomas Waterman to survey Hunstanton in 1615. Eastfield, forming the eastern half of the parish, was dominated by demesne land, and by that time the park had been enlarged and much enclosure had taken place; see below, Figure 3.2.

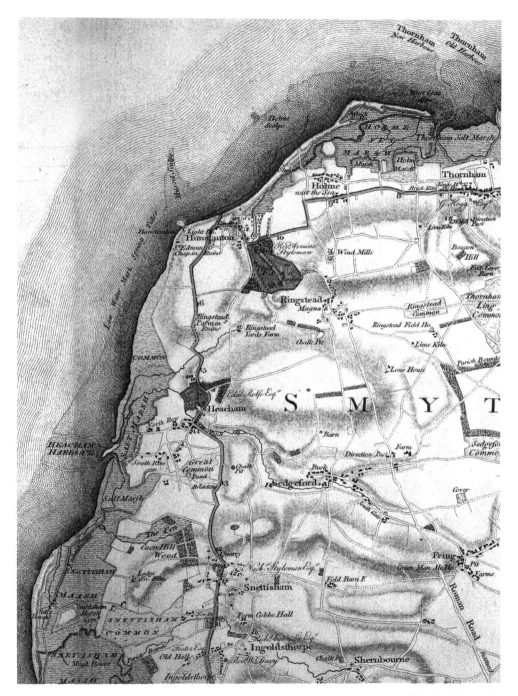

Figure 2.2 Faden's Map of Norfolk, 1797 – around Hunstanton. Image courtesy of Andrew Macnair.

England, his type 1, where wheat and barley were grown alongside legumes, which substituted bare fallows.[11] Unlike the parishes inland, where sandy soils dominate, most of Hunstanton's soil was highly fertile, farmed right up to the cliff edge of Westfield.[12] At the same time, the coastal location, with fishing and the crafts associated with it, offered additional occupations alongside agriculture. The coastal dunes and marshes also provided communities with plentiful pasture, besides the 100 acres of common land in the north-east of the parish. With this cornucopia of natural assets, Hunstanton was able to support a densely populated and prosperous community.

From an estate rental of 1335 Whittle identified 191 tenants for the manor of Hunstanton.[13] This manor, which also included land and extensive grazing rights on the marshes at Holme-next-Sea, formed the entire estate of the Le Stranges until the late fifteenth century.[14] Of these 191 tenants, 64 held less than one acre, while 128, or two-thirds, held less than four acres. It would be reasonable to assume that these small holders supplemented their income by working on the demesne lands of the lord, but in fact the Le Stranges relied on hired labourers and demesne agricultural servants or *famulii* to do 82 per cent of the work. Tenants performed the remainder of the work, but only during harvest time. The manorial accounts suggest that Hunstanton acted as a magnet, drawing hired workers, men and women, from the surrounding villages and from as far afield as the Fens. But this was not the cheap migrant labour we are familiar with today. Women were paid similar rates to the men and wages were higher than the average. In his index of farm wages Clark estimated the purchasing power of wages at 51 for 1330–49 compared with 61 in 1610, but Whittle shows that medieval workers at Hunstanton were significantly better off.[15] This was particularly the case with demesne servants employed as shepherds, swineherds and ploughmen; rates in 1342 of £7 a year were more than double the rate of £3 a year in 1621.

Tenants were rarely engaged as day labourers, but their families were sometimes employed as demesne servants. Tenants also sold food and made food gifts to the lord's household, but over half the food sellers were unconnected to the tenants' families and came from surrounding villages. Tenants often sold local produce – eggs, poultry, meat, apples, bread, candles and fish – to the family, while they gifted fish, poultry and eggs.[16]

11   Campbell, *English Seigniorial Agriculture*, pp. 269–70, 325, 337.

12   The inland parishes include Great Ringstead, Sedgeford and the eastern half of Heacham; see also Oestmann, *Lordship and Community*, pp. 88–9 with map of soils; Wade Martins and Williamson, *Roots of Change*, pp. 9–12.

13   The total of 191 tenants is after the duplicated names were eliminated. The figure, without amendment, was 213.

14   Oestmann, *Lordship and Community*, pp. 29–30, see below, pp. 18–22 for the consolidation at Hunstanton in the fifteenth and early sixteenth centuries.

15   Gregory Clark, 'The long march of history: farm wages, population and economic growth, England 1209–1869', *Economic History Review*, 60 (2007), pp. 97–135.

16   Gifting features prominently in all the Le Strange household accounts, with many from smaller tenants. The purpose is not entirely clear, but is it reasonable to assume that it was a method of currying favour or cementing social relationships. Whittle, 'The food economy', pp. 49–52; Whittle and Griffiths, *Consumption and Gender*, pp. 72–84.

Significantly, fish amounted to 71 per cent of the total gifted and was the most frequently purchased item by the Le Strange household.[17] Outside retailers also supplied these products, along with wine, vinegar, salt, spices, nuts, sugar, raisins and commodities not available locally. The Le Stranges played their part too, leasing out their dairy herd and purchasing the produce, as well as supporting other dairies.[18] In these ways, consuming, employing, fostering enterprise and promoting new ventures, the family acted as the pivot of a highly active and well-organised food market.

The main problem with fishing is the lack of documentation. Fishing rights, typically on the foreshore, 'are not maniorable' and consequently do not appear in manorial records, although transgressions of rules and regulations can be found in court rolls and details of 'profits of the sea' sometimes appear in manorial accounts.[19] This scarcity of records may explain why the significance of fishing has been underestimated by historians. Joan Thirsk, in her early work on the Fens, concluded that fishing was a subsidiary occupation to farming except perhaps among the poorest, and of limited importance as a full-time occupation.[20] Campbell, in his *English Seigniorial Agriculture*, based principally on manorial accounts, makes no mention of fishing or profits from the sea as a source of landlord income, although their rights to such assets are carefully itemised in charters for Hunstanton with Holme (1379), Ringstead Magna and Heacham.[21] The scale of the activity becomes apparent at Hunstanton only through the survival of household accounts with details of suppliers, the frequency and scale of deliveries, different types of fish and the nature of exchanges between buyer and seller. Unfortunately, for the two decades from 1328 to 1348 only forty-five months of these accounts are

---

17 Whittle and Griffiths, *Consumption and Gender*, p. 97 on the importance of fish in the medieval diet. Not only was it proscribed to be eaten for Lent, six and half weeks before Easter, but also on three days during each week as periods of abstinence from meat.

18 The dairyman paid a rent of 40–45s and in return received all the milk and half the calves; see also Griffiths and Overton, *Farming to Halves*, pp. 58–62.

19 For a discussion of this issue see <www.supremecourt.uk/cases/docs/uksc14–0191-judgement.pdf> for the judgement given on 13 April 2016 in the case between Lynn Shellfish Ltd and Loose (tenant of the Le Strange Fishery). The historical reference is M. Hale, *A Treatise Relative to the Maritime Law of England* (1888), which defines the boundaries of the foreshore up to the edge of the high tide, where the land is 'dry and maniorable': see p. 17 of the judgement. The case against Lynn Shellfish Ltd came to my attention on 20 June 2014, when a report in the *Eastern Daily Press* announced 'Cockle fishermen lose seven-year legal battle over historic fishery'. Mr Loose and Michael Meakin Le Strange won the case, but subsequently Lynn Shellfish secured a further right of appeal. For the judge's ruling and a brief history relating to the fishery see Loose v Lynn Shellfish Ltd & Ors [2013] EWHC 901 (Ch) (18 April 2013).

20 J. Thirsk, *English Peasant Farming: The Agrarian History of Lincolnshire from Tudor to Recent Times* (London, 1957), pp. 28–9, see also Oestmann, *Lordship and Community*, pp. 120–7.

21 Campbell, *English Seigniorial Agriculture*. Hunstanton, Barrett (Little) Ringstead and Heacham all occupy a coastal location and feature prominently in the book. Summaries and transcriptions of these charters can be found in LEST/Q37, fols 1–7; 37–85; 94–141. These documents have been used repeatedly since 1864 as the Le Stranges defended their right to their fishery.

available, while the court rolls are weak for that period.[22] However, in the first half of the sixteenth century the situation changed dramatically with the arrival of Sir Thomas Le Strange and his wife, Anne, and the household accounts they kept from 1518 to 1545.

I

By the time Sir Thomas Le Strange succeeded to his estate at Hunstanton in 1514 his grandfather Sir Henry (1437–1485) and uncle Sir Roger (1468–1505) had significantly advanced the position of the family and estate.[23] In 1470 Sir Henry acquired Lovell's manor, while Sir Roger purchased Mustrells in 1496 and the small manor of Snetterton's in the early 1500s, all of which were at least partly located in Hunstanton. Thus the Le Stranges built up their local base and secured complete control over the village and parish of Hunstanton. This process of consolidation is generally more associated with the early seventeenth century, but the Le Stranges had benefited from their long and unbroken residency at Hunstanton, which allowed them to exploit opportunities as they arose.[24] In this context, it is surprising that they did not make their moves earlier, but a changing political climate brought new opportunities. Soon after his marriage to Amy, daughter of Sir Henry Heydon of Baconsthorpe, Sir Roger built the impressive brick gatehouse at Hunstanton Hall and, with his wife's substantial dowry, purchased the larger manor of Mustrells.[25] He later secured a position at court as esquire of the body of Henry VII. His brother Robert similarly moved in courtly circles; it was his son Thomas who inherited the estate after the death of his cousin John, Sir Roger's only son. With his connections, Robert negotiated brilliant marriages for his two elder children: Katherine to Hugh, the eldest son of Sir George Hastings of Elsing and Gressenhall, 12th Baron Hastings, and Thomas to Anne, the daughter of Sir Nicholas Vaux, later Baron Vaux of Harrowden; she came with a dowry of 1000 marks, or £660.[26] In this way, the Le Stranges moved into the ranks of the leading Norfolk gentry.

Following in his uncle's footsteps, Sir Thomas soon found himself, as esquire of the body of Henry VIII, accompanying the king in his meeting with Francis I at the Field of the Cloth of Gold in 1520, but his sphere of activity mostly remained in Norfolk, where

---

22 Whittle, 'The food economy', p. 30.

23 See Figure 2.1.

24 Oestmann, *Lordship and Community*, pp. 29–30. This longevity and stability also explains why their archive survived intact, in contrast to that of other notable families, such as the Bacons of Stiffkey.

25 Oestmann, *Lordship and Community*, pp. 13–15. The marriage took place in 1491. Sir Henry Heydon of Baconsthorpe was a rising star in Norfolk politics. Amy's dowry of £280 covered the £200 for Mustrells.

26 Sir Hugh (1505–1540) succeeded his brother John as 14th Baron Hastings in 1514. Sir Nicholas Vaux (c.1460–1523) <www.historyofparliament.org.uk>.

he served on various commissions for the king.[27] He was knighted in 1529 and served as sheriff of Norfolk and Suffolk in 1530. After that appointment he obtained a royal grant exempting him from serving on juries and performing further onerous duties. However, in 1532 he was back at court attending the king on his visit to Calais in 1532 and at his marriage to Norfolk-born Anne Boleyn. At the same time, he struck up a close relationship with Thomas Howard, 3rd duke of Norfolk, and Thomas Cromwell, the king's secretary of state, working with them on the crisis of the Pilgrimage of Grace and the dissolution of the monasteries. Through these connections Sir Thomas secured some choice properties in Norfolk.

As with so many Norfolk families, the Le Stranges benefited greatly from the Reformation and the confiscation of ecclesiastical properties. Those secured by Sir Thomas Le Strange included a short lease in 1538 of several hundreds of acres of pasture at Godwick, part of Westacre Priory. In 1540 he was able to purchase the property and develop it as a profitable cattle ranching and dairy unit.[28] In the same year he clinched a ninety-nine-year lease of the cathedral priory manor at Sedgeford from the dean and chapter of Norwich at a rent of £61 7s 4d. It was subsequently renewed in 1637, but not in 1736.[29] However, by far the most valuable grant of ecclesiastical property was the manor of Ramsey Abbey at Great Ringstead in 1541, followed by a smaller manor, Bardolfs, and another, Baynards at Holme, both in 1545.[30] The acquisitions at Ringstead and Holme perfectly complemented the Le Strange's ancient holdings at Hunstanton and remain a central part of the estate.[31]

Prior to the Reformation Sir Thomas had purchased in 1527 the single manor of Barrett Ringstead and in 1529 the smaller manor of Calys at Heacham, continuing the policy of consolidation initiated by his grandfather and uncle.[32] Further east, beyond Ringstead and Sedgeford, he had inherited his father's estate at Docking and Fring.[33] At some stage in the early fifteenth century the family had also acquired two manors in Suffolk, Thorpe Morieux and Felsham, and a half interest in the manor of Oakley,

---

27   Apparently, Sir Thomas used his trips to London to arrange the legal documents for land purchases and sales: Oestmann, *Lordship and Community*, p. 16.

28   Oestmann, *Lordship and Community*, pp. 146–8; Sir Thomas had paid a rent of just £20.

29   See chapter 7. The lease was assigned to John Le Strange in 1562 by his father, Sir Nicholas; to Richard Stubbe in 1601 and then to Sir Hamon and Alice on their marriage in 1602, LEST/ A66–72. By 1736 the rental income was £696 a year, based on three flocks of sheep and great quantities of corn, so it was not surprising that the dean and chapter decided to break it up into more profitable portions. See Blomefield and Parkin, *Norfolk*, vol. X, pp. 385–90.

30   Blomefield and Parkin, *Norfolk*, vol. X, pp. 340, 343, 330.

31   See Faden's map, Figure 2.2, above.

32   Calys purchased from Thomas Wingfield, 1529: Blomefield and Parkin, *Norfolk*, vol. X, p. 309; Barrett Ringstead from Thomas Tilney, 1527: see Oestmann, *Lordship and Community*, p. 140, fn. 41.

33   Blomefield and Parkin, *Norfolk*, vol. X, p. 304. In his will of 1505 Sir Roger directed that if his son should die without issue all his possessions should pass to his brother Robert and his heirs male – i.e. Thomas Le Strange. See Oestmann, *Lordship and Community*, p. 14, fn. 5.

Table 2.1
The estate of Sir Thomas Le Strange, 1545.

Name	Acquisition and Description	Destiny
Hunstanton	With Holme, single manor estate, until consolidation in 1470 Lovells (in Heacham); 1496 Mustrells and 1500s Snettertons.[i]	Part of estate
Holme next the Sea	Lands with Hunstanton manor; Baynards as part of Gt. Ringstead, 1545; Holkham & Berrys by 1580.[ii]	Part of estate
Great Ringstead	Crown granted Great Manor of Ramsey Abbey 1541; Bardolfs in 1545.[iii]	Part of estate
Barrett Ringstead or Ringstead Parva	Purchased 1527 from Tho. Tilney – £241 4d – money from Sir Nicholas Vaux. 355 acres, mostly pasture.[iv]	Part of estate
Heacham	Purchased Caleys Manor from Tho. Wingfield 1529.[v] Lewes Priory manor, granted to Duke of Norfolk, 1537; 1608 re-granted to Thomas Howard, Earl of Suffolk; purchased by Sir Hamon LS, 1609 – £4400.[vi]	Sold in 1915[vii]
Docking	Sir John Le Strange and Eleanor, d. of Sir Richard Walkfare buying land in Stanhoe and Docking, 1406.[viii]	Sold by NLS 1569[ix]
Fring	Purchased by Henry LS in 1484, passed to Robert le Strange, inherited by TLS on his death.	Sold by HLS 1609 – £2140[x]
Godwick	Crown granted 21 yr lease 1538 – £20 rent – part of Westacre Priory; purchased 1540 – 100 ac arable, 40 ac wood, 623 acs meadow, pasture, heath & moor.[xi]	Sold by NLS 1557[xii]
Sedgeford	Cathedral Priory manor granted to Dean and Chapter of Norwich 1538; 1539 they granted 99-year lease to Thomas LS at £61 7s 6d p. an; confirmed to Sir Nicholas LS and assigned to his 3rd son, John LS, in 1562. His widow and new husband R. Stubbe assigned lease to their daughter Alice/HLS 1602. Renewed by HLS 1637; not renewed in 1736.[xiii] Sedgefords manor – in hands of John Le Strange by 1562, plus lands purchased by R. Stubbe.[xiv]	Returned to DCN – 1736 Sold 1915[xv]
Amner	Foldcourse, ref in Oestmann, but no details.	
Oakley, Bedfordshire	Moiety of manor Robt Le Strange IPM 1512.	Sold by TLS 1531[xvi]
Felsham & Thorpe Morieux, Suffolk	From the marriage of Sir John Le Strange and Eleanor, d. of Sir Richard Walkfare, mother, heir to Sir Thomas Morieux; son John Le Strange died in 1436 seized of manors of TM and Felsham.	Sold by NLS 1550[xvii]

Sources:

i   Oestmann, *Lordship and Community.*, pp. 29–30.

ii Blomefield and Parkin, *Norfolk*, x, pp. 330.

iii *Ibid.*, x, pp. 340, 343,

iv Oestmann, *Lordship and Community*, p. 140, fn. 41.

v   LEST/D2, Blomefield and Parkin, *Norfolk*, x, p. 309.

vi LEST/D5, LEST/Q37, fol. 18.

vii Sale of Heacham estate, 1915, Add. Deposits, 20/11/76, LEST/47, 49.

viii Blomefield and Parkin, *Norfolk*, vol x, p. 317.

ix LEST/Q34, fol. 46.

x   Blomefield & Parkin, *Norfolk*, vol x, p. 304; sale LEST/Q37.

xi Oestmann, *Lordship and Community*, p. 148.

xii Blomefield and Parkin, *Norfolk*, vol ix, p. 509.

xiii *Ibid.*, x, pp. 385–90.

xiv Henry Styleman's survey of his estate 1820 (on temporary loan to the Norfolk Record Office) shows the Styleman (Le Stranges) still in possession of 638 acres in Sedgeford, up from 490 acres in N. Kent's survey of 1784, LEST, R23 which shows two farms, Eaton and Magazine; see also, Griffiths, 'Her Price is Above Pearls', pp. 36–7.

xv It appears that both farms were sold to Sir Edward Green in 1915, who had purchased the Snettisham estate in 1877, but the record of the sale has not yet been found.

xvi Oestmann, *Lordship and Community*, p. 145.

xvii Sold to William Risby of Felsham in 1550. John A.C. Tilley, Notes for the History of Felsham, 1951 (unpublished).

Bedfordshire.[34] In the early 1540s, with the grant of lands at Great Ringstead and Holme, the estate reached its high watermark, but this level of progress was not sustained. In 1545 Sir Thomas died intestate, leaving his son and heir, Sir Nicholas (1511–1580), to provide for seven brothers and five sisters.[35] This involved the sale of the two Suffolk manors in 1550, followed by Godwick in 1557 and the manor at Docking in 1569 (see Table 2.1).[36] In 1562 Sir Nicholas also assigned both the Sedgeford lease from the dean and chapter and his own manor of Sedgefords to his youngest son John, thereby reducing still further the estate of Le Stranges of Hunstanton. In 1571 he sold the remainder of this estate to his son and heir, Hamon.[37]

As we shall see, the second half of the sixteenth century was a time of deepening and recurrent difficulties for the family; nevertheless, the inheritance from Sir Thomas Le Strange in terms of wealth, power and status was formidable. Looking out from

---

34 Blomefield and Parkin, *Norfolk*, vol. X, p. 317; Moiety of Reynes manor, Oakley; William Page (ed.), *A History of the County of Bedford* (London, 1904–14), pp. 149–53 for references to Robert and Thomas Le Strange, who sold it in 1531.

35 LEST/Q34; annuities listed in LEST/A48-A63.

36 Oestmann, *Lordship and Community*, p. 148; LEST/Q34, fol. 46.

37 Sir Nicholas (1511–80), following in his father's footsteps, pursued a successful political career, but his involvement with the Howards, and the proposed marriage to Mary Queen of Scots, led to his arrest and exile to Ireland in 1571. He returned to Norfolk in 1579, a year before his death in 1580: see Oestmann, *Lordship and Community*, pp. 21–4.

his portrait (Figure 2.3), he remains the star of the family, the model to follow.[38] It is no coincidence that Sir Hamon and Alice soon had their portraits painted in similar fashion.[39] As part of his legacy, Sir Thomas and his wife also left remarkable records, to which we will now turn.

II

The accounts kept by Sir Thomas and his wife Anne from 1518 to 1545 are perhaps the most treasured items in the Le Strange archive. While Alice's accounts, which are far more detailed and wide-ranging, received little attention until recently, those of the illustrious Sir Thomas and his aristocratic wife were the first to be analysed by the Victorian antiquarians and formed the basis of the first modern research project on the Le Strange family.[40] Alice herself recognised the importance of these documents in the 1600s, carefully annotating each account and using them as a model for her own, which she started in 1610 and continued until Sir Hamon's death in 1654. The early seventeenth-century Le Stranges clearly regarded these records as a most valuable part of their medieval inheritance. Their successors evidently thought so too. The annotations, made by different generations over the centuries, show the family using and learning from these documents.

In their original state, the accounts consisted of scores of paper books of different sizes. For their preservation, they were bound into volumes in the late nineteenth century and unbound by the conservationists in the late twentieth century.[41] Thus the first box, from 1518 to 1526, consists of eight books with a table of contents and an index provided by Hamon Le Strange in 1886.[42] Typically, each account bears an attribution by Alice on the front cover, a loose-leaf table inserted by Sir Nicholas (1661–1724) in the 1680s listing persons and points of interest in the text, and finally pencilled annotations throughout clarifying dates and highlighting items by Hamon

---

38 The portrait drawing of Sir Thomas Le Strange by Hans Holbein the Younger in the Royal Collection. Paintings survive in several versions: see cover of Oestmann, *Lordship and Community*.

39 See Figures 1.1 and 1.2, pp. 2–3.

40 D. Gurney, 'Extracts from the Household and Privy Purse Accounts of the Le Stranges of Hunstanton, from A.D. 1519 to A.D. 1578', *Archaelogia*, 25 (1834), pp. 411–569; Oestmann, *Lordship and Community*; Alice had to wait another twenty years for Whittle and Griffiths, *Consumption and Gender*; see also Harris, *English Aristocratic Women*, pp. 63–76.

41 The main part of the Le Strange archive was deposited in the Norfolk Record Office between 1950 and 1955 after a fire at Hunstanton Hall. Additional deposits were made in the 1970s and 1990s. More recently documents have been loaned for microfilming.

42 The present NRO catalogue is based on Henry Harrod's *Repertory of the Muniments in the Evidence House at Hunstanton*, commissioned by Hamon Le Strange in 1869; see also HMRC 11th Report, Appendix 7, 1888. Sir Thomas Le Strange's household accounts (1518–45) are listed under LEST/P1–P4, with miscellaneous accounts from the late sixteenth and late seventeenth centuries in P4 and P5; three other sixteenth-century accounts are listed with the medieval household accounts. These include LEST/NH13 for Sir Thomas Le Strange, 1530; NH14 for Sir Nicholas, 1578; and NH15 for Sir Hugh Hastings, 1531–49.

Figure 2.3 Drawing of Sir Thomas Le Strange (*c*.1490–1545) by Hans Holbein the Younger, *c*.1536. RCIN 912244. Royal Collection Trust / © Her Majesty Queen Elizabeth II 2021.

Le Strange in the late nineteenth century. His table of contents and index unlocks the Latin content for modern readers.

From Alice's attributions we know that Anne Le Strange took responsibility for the accounts from 1533, when Sir Thomas returned to London and spent increasing amounts of time in the king's service. Thus, in the third account in the second box Alice noted with emphasis: 'Sir Thomas Le Strange his Ladyes Expence Book in Her Owne hand 24 Henry 8'.[43] Anne's text is significantly better organised and more legible than the earlier accounts and continues to improve as the series developed

---

43   LEST/P2: weekly kitchen accounts for three years: 1519, 1527 and 1533.

from 1533 to 1545.[44] Her task included keeping weekly expense accounts for the kitchen, followed by general expenditure on wages, repairs, farming and brewing. In her books of receipts she recorded payments from her husband, rent from the bailiffs and income from the sale of timber, sheep, lambs and other items. The format was akin to the household accounts of the fourteenth century but increasingly sophisticated and comprehensive.

At the same time as Anne kept her accounts, her sister-in-law Katherine and her husband Sir Hugh Hastings were lodging at Hunstanton.[45] Accounts survive for several years in the 1530s and 1540s, recording their life as 'boorders' paying a weekly rent to Anne and receiving rents from Gressenhall and Elsing and annuities from Sir Thomas.[46] In 1536 Anne wanted to know precisely 'how many there be of them [boorders] and what they do pay by the weeke'.[47] From 1539, as Sir Hugh neared the end of his life, the accounts were kept by Katherine.[48] These accounts are less clear and complete, but follow a similar pattern to Anne's; they also include annotations by Alice and then by Sir Nicholas (1661–1724). Part of their interest lies in the sharing of knowledge and accountancy skills by elite women. However, the process of knowledge passing to the next generation was not guaranteed. There was a gap of sixty years before Alice started her own accounts, using Anne's work as a model.[49]

So what do the household accounts of Sir Thomas and Anne Le Strange tell us? Like those from the medieval period, they provide a mass of context and cast light on how the family lived their lives, but over a much longer time scale from 1518 to 1545.

---

44 LEST/P3: on the cover Hamon Le Strange [in 1888] corrects an error in 'Dan Gurney's Printed Extracts'. The index provided for P3 runs to thirty-four pages. Oestmann makes no reference to Anne's authorship of these accounts; she is referred to only in the context of marriage and children. However, Harris, *English Aristocratic Women*, corrects this omission on pp. 67–8, where she introduces Anne, along with the Countess of Rutland, as examples of 'two exemplary women'.

45 Katherine, sister of Sir Thomas Le Strange; see Figure 2.1.

46 LEST/NH15. Accounts survive for 1531 and 1535, when the Hastings started to lodge at Hunstanton; 1536, overseen by Anne Le Strange; accounts for 1539, 1540, 1544 and 1549 were kept by Katherine, Lady Hastings.

47 LEST/NH15. On the front of 1536 account Anne noted: 'Hastynge. The booke maketh mencon of all manor of Receipts and Payments for my brother in lawe Sir Hugh Hastings Knight Receyved and Payd by the hand of me Dame Anne Le Strange wiff unto Sir Thomas Le Strange Knight from [20 Nov 1536–same day 1537]'.

48 LEST/NH15. On the 1539 account Katherine noted in similar fashion, 'This booke maketh mencon of all manor of receipts rec by me Dame Katherine Hastings wiff unto Sir Hugh Hastings Kt.' Sir Hugh died in 1541 and Katherine stayed on at Hunstanton with Anne, who was also widowed in 1545; see Harris, *English Aristocratic Women*, pp. 68, 200.

49 Anne was the daughter of Sir Nicholas Vaux, 1st baron Vaux of Harrowden, 1460–1523, MP, soldier and courtier to Henry VIII and son of the Lancastrian Sir William Vaux, who was killed at Tewkesbury. Sir Nicholas grew up with strong and learned women, notably his mother Katherine, attendant to Margaret of Anjou, and Margaret Beaufort, mother of Henry VII; he was created a baron in 1523 <www.historyofparliament.org.uk>.

At a domestic level we learn what they ate and drank, how it was produced, where it came from, who they invited to celebrations, who comprised their intimate circle of friends, what visits they made, what networks they established and the vast amount spent on the children. The list is endless, offering plenty of scope for analysis, as with Alice's later accounts.[50] The term 'household' also included the farming undertaken by the lord on his demesne lands, with all its associated expenditure and income. The receipt books contain not only the income from farm rents but also sales of estate and farm produce, notably timber, sheep, wool, lambs, cattle and dairy produce. From this detail Oestmann was able to reconstruct Sir Thomas's new commercial farming activities at Godwick, Docking and Fring, as well as production at home for the family.[51]

The household accounts, as we anticipated, also provide a wealth of information about fish: the types on offer, the names and origins of the suppliers, and the amount purchased and consumed by the family over a relatively long period of time. However, they still tell us very little about fishing and the organisation behind it. Why, for example, did over 90 per cent of fish suppliers come from Hunstanton, when surrounding villages contributed in equal numbers to other basic commodities, such as eggs, butter and fowls?[52] How was the fishing managed? The answers to these questions lay in other records, such as wills and inventories, court records, subsidy returns and various deeds, used in conjunction with the household accounts. In this way, Oestmann built up a picture of how the fishing worked, who benefited and how the market operated, all of which challenged assumptions that fishing was a subsidiary and limited occupation.[53] From their wills, he identified fishermen and mariners involved in deep-sea fishing leaving their boats and nets to their successors, often holding a few acres of land. However, the critical observation was that fishing rights, owned by all sections of the village community, were also willed to successors. By the 1570s these rights were being traded openly between manorial tenants, which seems to explain the proliferation of inshore fishing among the villagers of Hunstanton.

III

So what were these fishing rights? How do they work? The key documents for sea lawers, as they were commonly known, are listed at the top of the title deeds for Hunstanton and Holme, reflecting their significance and status as freehold property.[54] They include a grant from the Duchy of Lancaster (1530) confirming the Le Stranges' rights to wrecks of the sea and fishing; papers about the fishery and sea lawers (1554–1606); and a lease of Hunstanton Manor Fishery (1857) that provides a detailed

---

50 Whittle and Griffiths, *Consumption and Gender, passim*.

51 Oestmann, *Lordship and Community*, pp. 132–52.

52 Oestmann, *Lordship and Community*, pp. 124–5. Of the 969 fish suppliers identified in the household accounts of Sir Thomas Le Strange between 1518 and 1540, 887 (91.5%) came from Hunstanton.

53 Oestmann, *Lordship and Community*, pp. 120–7; Thirsk, *English Peasant Farming*, pp. 28–9.

54 LEST/B1–3. NRO catalogue, *Le Stranges of Hunstanton*.

description of the geography and management of 'Sea Layers'.[55] By that time, the Le Stranges owned fishing rights stretching from Wolferton to Thornham and were about to embark on the first major defence of this property.[56] The grant of 1530 is a confirmation of an earlier grant in 1379 used as evidence in the trial.[57] The document is now missing, but it was summarised by Sir Hamon Le Strange in a memoranda book in the early 1600s.[58]

The sixteenth-century papers from 1554 to 1606 are of critical importance. They include two drawings or 'dragges' of the layout of the sea lawers on the foreshore, a list of sea lawers belonging to a particular property in Hunstanton and three legal documents recording the sale of sea lawers. Most of the information relates to the Peddar family of Hunstanton.[59] Roger Peddar listed 'the lawers perteyning to my house in Northgate called Snytt'tons' in 1554, indicating that lawers were originally attached to properties. The sale documents from 1579 to 1596 are linked to lawers owned or once owned by the family and show them being sold separately.[60] In 1606 John Peddar produced a dragge showing the ownership of the sea lawers at Hunstanton with a preamble explaining how they worked and the basis of their rights 'by the old ancient use, custome and lawe of the aforesaid sea'.[61] The other drawing, in the hand of Sir Hamon Le Strange, is a neat version of the original dragge of the Sea Lawers of 1554.

The drawings show how the system worked. The fishing rights were plotted out on the foreshore, the area between high and low tide, and staked out with nets, the idea being that they were drowned at high tide and at low tide fish were caught in the nets. The 'lawers' refer to the stakes that held the 'pokenettes'; each contraption was known as a 'birth'. The lawers, each containing several births, stretched eastwards from the

---

55 LEST/B3.

56 The linking of the Le Strange estate at Hunstanton and the Styleman's estate at Snettisham in 1762, following the death of Sir Henry Le Strange, 6th Bt, placed the foreshore under single ownership and led eventually to the creation of the Le Strange Fishery in 1879.

57 The Le Strange Fishery comprises the entire foreshore of Smithdon Hundred from Wolferton Creek (Snettisham) to Thornham harbour. Sir Hamon Le Strange Styleman kept the lordship of Smithdon when the Snettisham estate was sold in 1872. The Le Stranges still own the fishery, despite repeated legal challenges from 1864 to the present day. In the case of 1864, Le Strange v. Rowe, the Le Stranges produced a huge amount of historical evidence in support of their case.

58 LEST/Q37, fols 1–4 Charter of John of Gaunt, duke of Lancaster to Sir John Le Strange, 1379, confirming his occupation of the manor of Hunstanton with Holme and various rights, including wrecks of the sea, fish etc. The entry in the memo book LEST/Q37 is followed by notes on the 1531 grant, LEST/B1.

59 The Peddars were formerly lords of Snetterton's manor before selling it to Sir Thomas Le Strange.

60 LEST/B2, 4–6.

61 The first half of the preamble: 'A coppie of a Sea Dragge written in ye year 1554 of all the lawers within the sea of Hunstanton nominating their several places where they be sett with ye certain number of stakes and pooknette births that out to belong to each several lawer continying to be used each of them in ye same place & some of stake wth owt any alteration as they were first sett & each pson herin named & their predecessors … have peaceably possessed … tyme and tymes out of mind to them & to their heires … ' LEST/B2/1.

cliffs at Hunstanton to Holme-next-Sea, and outwards from the shore into the sea, and were named on the maps for ease of reference. The most useful drawing, sketched by Alice, complete with stakes and births, as well as the names of owners and lawers, dates from about 1630 (Figure 2.4).[62]

In the preamble to the 1554 dragge John Peddar noted that sea lawers had existed 'tyme and tymes out of mind'. Oestmann was unclear as to the origins of the system, but, with the benefit of a longer perspective, we can assume that they dated back to the twelfth century, when the Le Stranges were granted by the crown a private fishery off the coast of Hunstanton. This gave them exclusive rights to the fruits of the foreshore, including wrecks, whales and every type of shellfish. It is reasonable to conclude that sometime thereafter the fishing rights were divided up, attached to properties and let to their tenants. During the sixteenth century, with the rising population and demand for food, the sea lawers were separated from their properties for ease of sale. This would have alerted the Le Stranges, or at least Sir Hamon and Alice, to their intrinsic value and the need to protect their rights.

At some stage these sixteenth-century papers were assembled as if to prove the existence and status of these fishing rights.[63] It may have been in the mid-nineteenth century, as the Le Stranges gathered evidence to support their case, but it is more likely that, on the advice of Sir Henry Spelman, Sir Hamon intervened in the 1600s to establish full control of the Le Strange fishing rights. Renewed by Sir Hamon in 1616 and by Alice after 1630, the updated dragges show their determination to maintain and preserve their rights to sea lawers for posterity. Viewed from the perspective of the twenty-first century, the current family must be extremely grateful that they had this foresight. The fishing rights have proved to be among the most valuable parts of their medieval inheritance.[64]

IV

The ongoing battles to secure the medieval fishing rights and the modern Le Strange Fishery underline the need to preserve ancient documents and keep rigorous estate records. Sir Hamon was fortunate that his trustees understood this requirement and appointed Sir Henry Spelman to oversee the task.[65] The 'Order and Award of Sir Henry

---

62 LEST/B2/2. Sir Hamon renewed the dragge in 1616, followed by Alice sometime after 1630. It shows how her father Richard Stubbe left his lawers to his grandson, Sir Nicholas Le Strange, Bt, 1630. LEST/Q36, fols 60, 459.

63 Significantly, there is evidence of an earlier numbering system dating back to the mid-nineteenth century, when King's Lynn fishermen started to challenge the Le Stranges' rights to their fishery, indicating the amount of research that was done by the family to counter and fend off this challenge.

64 See above, fn. 19.

65 Stuart Handley, 'Spelman, Sir Henry 1563/4–1641', *ODNB* (Oxford, 2004). Sir Henry returned to Norfolk from Cambridge University in 1590 and married Eleanor, the eldest daughter of John Le Strange of Sedgeford; see Figure 2.1. In 1592 he was appointed a trustee for the Le Strange estate.

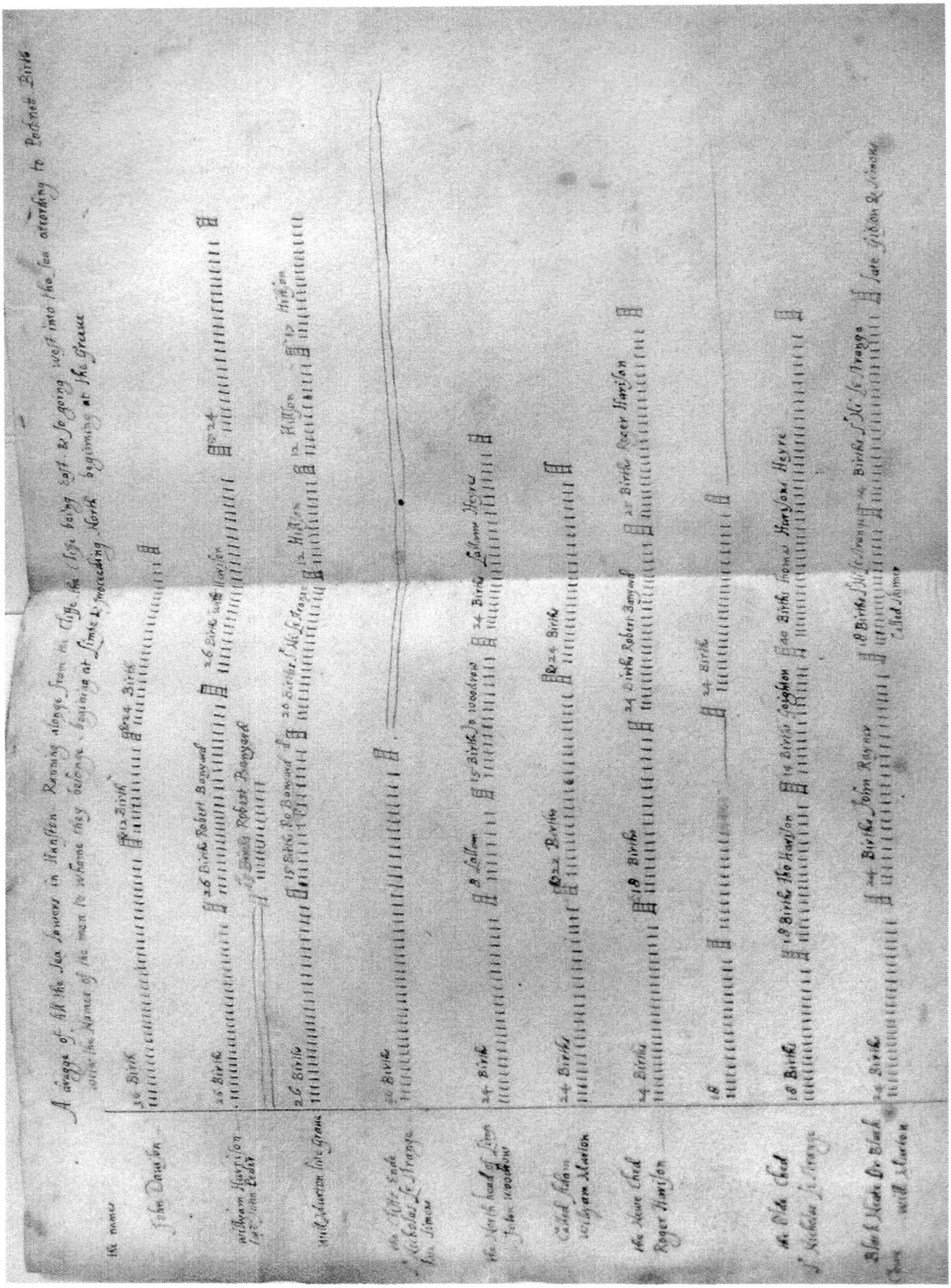

Figure 2.4 Dragge of Sea Lawers at Hunstanton, c.1630. NRO LEST/Q 36, fol. 459.

Hobart [assisted by others] between Sir Hamon Le Strange and Sir Henry Spelman, his Guardian', 1604, included the provision to deliver to Sir Hamon

> all evidences and other writings whatsoever which he hath or may conveniently come by concerning him and his estate. And shall also give him perfect note and information under his hand where any other are, and at whose hands they are to be required and had. And that shall be delivered unto him such remembrances as he hath concerning them.[66]

Spelman, a skilled antiquarian, who had clearly been collecting data and sorting out the Evidence House for some years, was awarded £200, allowed his arrears of £88 and paid £20 a year for five years for the loss of Fring foldcourse.[67]

Spelman wrote up his evidences in two paper books, bound in a leather volume in 1856 and titled 'Sundry Deeds at Hunstanton made in 1605'.[68] He started by providing 'An abstract of certain evidences of Sir Hamon Le Strange – in Queen Eliz[abeth's] time – taken 16 April 1605' and continued to deliver further writings to Richard Stubbe, Sir Hamon's father-in-law, concerning the Sedgeford estate until his death in 1619.[69] The book 'in Queen Elizabeth's time' covers a complex period when the Le Strange family had to deal with the outcome of a highly contentious marriage, the loss of three generations within a year, 1580–1, the death of Sir Nicholas in 1592 and the long minority of Sir Hamon.[70] Taken together, the notes help to explain the decline of the estate after the death of Sir Thomas Le Strange in 1545 and the accumulated problems facing Sir Hamon in 1604.

The first evidences list sales of land in Gressenhall by Hamon Le Strange (1532–80) and his immediate successors from 1573 to 1589. These entries relate to the highly contentious marriage between Hamon, son of Sir Nicholas (1511–80), and his cousin Elizabeth, daughter and co-heiress of Sir Hugh Hastings (1505–40) and his wife, Katherine, sister of Sir Thomas Le Strange (see Figure 2.1). On the death of their son John in 1541 the estate at Elsing and Gressenhall was divided between their two daughters, Anne and Elizabeth, wards of the courtier Sir Anthony Browne of Cowdray Park (1500–48).[71] When Browne died in 1548 he left the wardship of

---

66 LEST/Q37, fols 14–17. Sir Henry was assisted by Sir Edmund Bell, his brother in law and Thomas Oxburgh.

67 *Ibid.*

68 LEST/Q34. The books were bound and repaired by the steward A.L. Swatman, who assisted Henry L'Estrange Styleman Le Strange (1815–62) and Hamon Le Strange (1840–1919) in their cataloguing of the Le Strange MSS.

69 The second book, 'A catalogue or table of divers writings & deeds relating to the Sedgeford estate & Stubbes in particular', LEST/Q34. The deliveries continued until 1619, when Stubbe died and the estate passed to his daughter Alice, Sir Hamon's wife.

70 The three generations included Sir Thomas's eldest son Sir Nicholas (1511–80), his son Hamon (1533–80) and wife Elizabeth (1532–80), and their eldest son Thomas (1561–81).

71 On Sir John Hastings' death in 1541 the barony of Hastings fell into abeyance. W.B. Robison, 'Browne, Sir Anthony (c. 1500–1548)', *ODNB* (Oxford, 2004); Oestmann, *Lordship and Community*, pp. 24–6.

Anne with the Elsing estate to his second son William, and the wardship of Elizabeth with the Gressenhall estate to his youngest son Francis. The marriage of Anne and William went ahead, but Elizabeth preferred her cousin Hamon and broke the terms of her wardship.[72] The executors of Sir Anthony's estate brought a case against the Le Stranges for the loss of the value of the marriage which was settled in 1552 when Hamon's father, Sir Nicholas, agreed to provide security for 1000 marks as compensation. Spelman's notes show that the portioning of Sir Hugh's estate between his two daughters was not complete until 1571; this would explain the sales from 1573, presumably to pay off the award.[73] Sales also included land in Docking, Fring and Heacham, further depleting the estate built up by Sir Thomas in the first half of the century.[74]

A further complication, as we have seen, was that Sir Thomas Le Strange died intestate, leaving twelve children to provide for besides Sir Nicholas, his heir. In his notes, Spelman included an abstract of the unsigned testament citing the provisions for his wife and five daughters, and annuities to his seven non-inheriting sons.[75] This accounts for the sales of land recorded by Spelman, which far exceed the 1000 marks required by the Brownes.[76] There was an element of consolidation in these sales, with purchases at Hunstanton and Ringstead, but overall the picture was one of loss and decline.[77]

Spelman's evidences also pinpoint the emergence of Richard Stubbe of Edgefield, his acquisition of an estate in Sedgeford and how he came to be part of the Le Strange family. On the death of Sir John Le Strange in 1582 he married his widow Anne Goding and they had a daughter Alice, born in 1585. In the early 1590s Stubbe bought out the

---

72 During their childhood the Hastings spent much time at Hunstanton and kept their own household accounts (1531–49), which survive in the Le Strange archive, LEST/NH15. See above, pp. 24–5.

73 LEST/Q34, fol. 25; the sales in the first seven folios exceed £500; the remainder, which run to several pages, are not enumerated.

74 See above, Table 2.1.

75 LEST/Q34; LEST/A48–53. Oestmann, *Lordship and Community*, p. 21.

76 These properties do not include the Suffolk manors, Felsham and Thorpe Morieux, and the manor of Godwick, part of the jointure of Anne Le Strange, sold in 1550 and 1557 after her death.

77 In the event what was left of Gressenhall lands proved a useful asset until the estate was divided in 1784 between the co-heiresses of Sir Henry Le Strange, 6th Bt. In the valuation by John Claridge and Nathaniel Kent, LEST/R23, Gressenhall was listed under the 'Hunstanton Division' and the 'Gressenhall, Whissonset and Basham Division'. The marriage also made Sir Hamon's descendants co-heirs of the ancient and prestigious barony of Hastings. In 1841 Henry L'Estrange Styleman Le Strange (1815–62) succeeded in his claim to the extinct title. However, the crown found in favour of the youngest heir, Sir Jacob Astley, 6th Bt of Melton Constable, the descendant of Lucy, the younger sister of Sir Henry Le Strange, 6th Bt. Henry was descended from the elder sister, Armine, who had married Nicholas Styleman of Snettisham. See Figure 5.1. Walter Rye, in his *Norfolk Families* (1911), p. 481, noted that the title 'ought to have been determined in favour of the Hunstanton Le Stranges'. With its social cache and a seat in the House of Lords, the title would have been a spectacular addition to the Le Stranges' medieval legacy.

interests of John Le Strange's three daughters with Anne Goding, Eleanor, Dorothy and Katherine.[78] In 1601 he secured the lease of the dean and chapter and paid off debts to the other trustees, notably Sir John Peyton.[79] With this settlement he secured the betrothal of his daughter Alice to Sir Hamon Le Strange in 1602.[80]

Stubbe also played a part in securing the finances of the Spelman family. He not only bought out Eleanor's portion of the Sedgeford estate but arranged for the purchase of Holme Parsonage for them to live in. He subsequently bought the house back in 1606 and conveyed it to his son-in-law, Sir Hamon. In these ways, Richard Stubbe underwrote the Le Strange family and their close connections. Without his intervention, support and practical management skills it is unlikely that the Le Stranges and their estate would have survived. Quite simply, there would have been no medieval inheritance for Sir Hamon.

Spelman's contribution to the family was also profound and far reaching. He not only researched, preserved and transcribed their ancient records at a critical time but added significantly to that body of work with explanations and commentary. In his capacity as a trustee he oversaw the estate accounts and leased several closes of demesne land.[81] Above all, he instilled in the family a culture that recognised the value of these documents and the need to keep careful records. This understanding helped the family fend off challenges to their lands and rights throughout the seventeenth and early eighteenth centuries.[82] As we have seen, since the mid-nineteenth century their knowledge has yielded substantial benefits, notably as they faced repeated claims to their fishing rights based on ancient royal grants and their lordship of the Smithdon Hundred.

A by-product of Spelman's work on the medieval records was the huge interest it generated in the early history of the family. This appetite became particularly evident in the 1830s, when Henry L' Estrange Styleman Le Strange (1815–62) moved back to a refurbished Hunstanton Hall, eager to assume the mantle of the Le Stranges, lords of Hunstanton. He and his son, Hamon Le Strange (1840–1919) were both absorbed in the history and documentation of the family. Following in his father's footsteps, Hamon completed the cataloguing of the Le Strange MSS[83] and produced the definitive work on the early Le Stranges, which overturned traditional accounts of the origins of the family.[84] In this way, Spelman was instrumental in creating a family passion for their medieval inheritance which has been handed down from generation to generation.

---

78 Eleanor married Sir Henry Spelman while Dorothy married Roger Anderson of Lincolnshire, son of Sir Edmund Anderson, Lord Chief Justice. Katherine remained unmarried, while Lionel died young. See Figure 2.1.

79 £1000 for the release of Sir Hamon's wardship, LEST/Q34, fol. 2; Alice later complained that it was set against her marriage settlement, LEST/P10. See below, pp. 33–4.

80 LEST/A66–73; LEST/P10.

81 See below, pp. 42–3.

82 Examples mainly in LEST/Q37, refs to legal challenges. See chapter 5.

83 In 1872 with A. Horwood, but more successfully in the *Calendar of Papers at Hunstanton Hall*, 11th Report by Great Britain Historical Manuscripts Commission (1888).

84 Le Strange, *Le Strange Records*.

The inheritance comprised not only acres and buildings but also a culture of care and commitment to their estate and community that extended to the preservation of ancient documents and meticulous record-keeping. As we shall see in the next chapter, this approach and understanding could make the difference between success and failure, and a family's survival or disappearance, as landowners faced the wider challenges of the late sixteenth and early seventeenth centuries.

Chapter 3

The Le Strange estate in 1604

In her final book of disbursements, started in 1645 after the family suffered severe losses in the Civil War, Alice included what amounts to a history of the family finances. We do not know why she wrote these notes, but it was as if she needed to justify her management of the estate and explain to her successors their indebtedness after forty years of unrelenting effort.[1] At the end, where she summarised the sales, purchase of lands and losses in her husband's estate, she referred to the situation facing the newly married couple in 1604:

> my husband was left in debt by his fathers executors with mony due to his uncle Roger Le Strange, £1500; he was left neyther household stuffe nor stock & his cheife house halfe built, and all his farme houses in such decay so he hath built most of them out of the ground.[2]

Her principal target, as we see, was the trustees for the debts they left and their neglect of the estate during Sir Hamon's minority from 1592, but she was also aggrieved that the sum paid to Sir John Peyton for Hamon's release of wardship was set against her marriage settlement.[3] Significantly, the notes begin with a comparison of the settlements Alice and her half-sister Dionisia had received from their father Richard Stubbe.[4] Dionisia, who had married Sir William Yelverton of Rougham in the 1580s, was much older than Alice, being the daughter of Stubbe's first wife, Elizabeth Gurney of Ellingham.[5] Her settlement, neatly laid out on the left-hand page, itemised the lands and money paid to her on marriage and subsequently to Sir William and their two

---

1   LEST/P10, Alice kept the book from 1645 to 1654, when she handed over the accounts to her eldest son, Sir Nicholas, 1st Bt (1604–55).

2   LEST/P10. The executors, all closely related to Sir Hamon, included Sir John Peyton (1554–1630), Elizabethan soldier and administrator, married to Dorothy, heiress of Sir Edmund Beaupre of Outwell, widow of Sir Robert Bell and mother of Mary, Sir Hamon's mother (see Figure 2.1); Sir Henry Hobart of Intwood, who rose to be Lord Chief Justice of the Court of Common Pleas and was married to Dorothy Bell, sister of Mary; and Sir Henry Spelman of Congham, who married Sir Hamon's cousin and Alice's half-sister Eleanor, daughter of John Le Strange and Anne Goding.

3   Documents relating to the marriage settlement, LEST/A66–A73. See also Griffiths, *Her Price is Above Pearls*, pp. 67–9. Sir Hamon did not come of age until 1604 and Sir John Peyton had to be compensated for the loss of his wardship; he was also paid travelling expenses of £300. For a description of wardship, the burden it placed on families and the reforms proposed by the crown in 1608 see G.A. Metters, V. Morgan, E. Rutledge and B. Taylor (eds), *The Papers of Nathaniel Bacon of Stiffkey*, vol. VI, 1608–1613 (Norwich, 2017), pp. xl–xli.

4   Richard Stubbe, married to the widow of John Le Strange, was another of Sir Hamon's trustees.

5   Elizabeth Gurney married Richard Stubbe in 1561.

sons for the repayment of debts.[6] On the facing page Alice listed her own settlement, starting with £1000 'payd to Sir John Peiton upon his account on my marryage'. Both daughters received similar amounts in land, worth just under £500 a year, but Dionisia received considerably more in money, £6302 9s compared to Alice's £4669 13s 4d. She added a further £513 from her father in gifts, but remained resentful. As she concluded, 'So my sister had in land more than my selfe by the yeare, £26; my sister had in mony more than my selfe, beside Sherringham Parsonage, £1209 15s 9d', and this figure did not include the sum paid to Sir John Peyton. Her point is clear: they had been short-changed at the outset, first by the trustees and second by the unfairness of her marriage settlement.

In the notes that follow the settlement, which identify borrowings and levels of debt until 1654, Alice draws a contrast between the two families. While the Yelvertons plunged into further debt the Le Stranges managed their expenditure carefully, so that, by 1635, after £2600 was settled on their second son, Hamon, she could announce: 'Debt Remayne, 1634 – none'.[7] A dowry of £3500 for their daughter, Elizabeth, the following year entailed new loans, but with a rising income of over £2000 a year, their debt remained sustainable. Even after the disaster of 1643, with their huge losses of stock and corn, legal expenses and fines, they were able to structure a significant recovery.

From this information, so thoughtfully assembled by Alice, we discover that Richard Stubbe was supporting two ancient Norfolk families. However, while the Le Stranges overcame their difficulties and survived, the Yelvertons, even with continuing support from kinsmen, petered out in the seventeenth century. First, the male line failed in 1649 and the baronetcy became extinct, and finally the Rougham estate was sold in 1690.[8] The comparison between the Le Stranges and the Yelvertons typifies the subject matter of this chapter. Sir Hamon and Alice knew how to resolve their

---

6   LEST/P10. Griffiths, *Her Price is Above Pearls*, pp. 67–9. The Yelvertons were a family of great antiquity originally from Yelverton, in south Norfolk, where they held 'soon after the conquest'. In the late fourteenth century John Yelverton Esq. married Elizabeth, the daughter and heiress of Richard Read of Rougham, and bred a dynasty of eminent lawyers. Alas, Sir William Yelverton of Rougham (1559–1631), baronet in 1620, sheriff of Norfolk in 1622 and husband of Dionisia Stubbe, did not inherit these skills and neither did their sons. William, 2nd Bt (1590–1648), married Ursula, daughter of Sir Thomas Richardson; they had a son and two daughters. The son, another William, 3rd Bt (1621–1649), died unmarried and the title became extinct. Blomefield, *History of Norfolk*, vol. X, pp. 30–2. Sir Henry, Kt., the younger son of Dionisia and William, d.s.p. in 1648.

7   LEST/P10.

8   On the death of Sir William, 3rd Bt, in 1649, the Rougham estate passed to his elder sister, Elizabeth, who had married Thomas Peyton, esq.; he sold it to his kinsman Sir John Bladwell, who kindly left it to the fourth son of Elizabeth and Thomas, Yelverton Peyton. He sold the estate to Roger North in 1690, 'who made great improvements to the hall, and in the lands, by planting, inclosing etc'. Blomefield, *History of Norfolk*, vol. X, pp. 30–2; see also <http://www.historyofparliamentonline.org/volume/1660–1690/member/north-hon-roger-1653-1734>; <www.heritage.norfolk.gov.uk> for Rougham Hall and parish; N. Pevsner and Bill Wilson, *The Buildings of England: Norfolk 2: North-West and South*, 2nd edn (London, 1999), pp. 617–19. The North family still reside at Rougham.

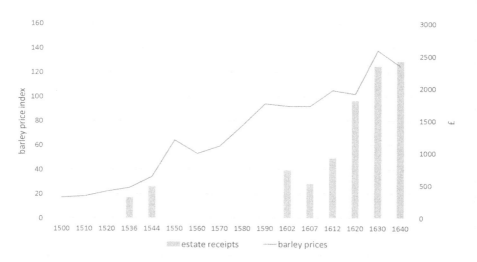

Figure 3.1 The movement of barley prices and receipts from the Hunstanton estate, 1536–1640.

problems and understood the wider issues of the day, while Sir William and Dionisia appear to have been completely oblivious to the challenges facing landowners at this time. This chapter will examine the state of affairs at Hunstanton and how the Le Stranges addressed the situation. We will then compare their experience with those of other Norfolk gentry families and consider the formula for enduring prosperity and the circumstances that invariably led to failure in the following chapter.

So what exactly was the situation facing Sir Hamon when he inherited his estate in 1604? How far can we trust Alice's version of events? A comparison of Hamon's position with that of Sir Thomas Le Strange in the 1530s and 1540s suggests that Alice's censure of the trustees was perfectly justified. Figure 3.1 shows a three-fold increase in the price of barley in the sixty years between 1540 and 1600, with receipts lagging behind; in other words, the estate suffered a serious decline in real income. In contrast, the figure highlights the extraordinary progress made by Sir Hamon and Alice over the next forty years in catching up with prices, which peaked in the 1630s.[9] So what happened between 1545 and 1604? Why did Sir Thomas's immediate successors fail to respond to the rising demand for food and capitalise on the high prices? We know that the sale of properties in the 1550s and 1560s, following his death, greatly reduced the size of the estate and their ability to raise their income, but how do we explain Sir Hamon's progress from the 1610s with similar resources?

---

9   Estate receipts do not include income from loans and sales of land, only receipts from rents and farming; see Oestmann, *Lordship and Community*, Table 14, p. 133, fn. 6; Griffiths, '"A Country Life"', appendix, pp. 231–4. Barley was the dominant grain crop on the estate and the prices were more relevant than those for wheat. At Sedgeford a substantial portion of the rent was paid in barley.

An analysis of the period from 1545 to 1604 is not easy. There is a significant lapse in the quality of the documentation during this period. A series of bailiff accounts for Hunstanton survives from 1542 to 1587, and includes other properties on the estate from 1587 to 1609, but there are no household accounts or receipt books with detailed information on demesne farming at Hunstanton before 1606.[10] Overall, the picture is patchy and incomplete; nevertheless, the bailiff accounts, accompanied by a few rentals, show the underlying unity between this period and Sir Hamon's reforms from 1606.[11] We know, from Oestmann's book, that Sir Hamon's father, Sir Nicholas (1563–92), raised the rent for the arable demesne land in Hunstanton in 1584 from 1s to 2s per acre, breaking a custom that dated from the 1490s.[12] But what was happening on other parts of the estate? The later accounts, which Oestmann did not consult, include records for Heacham, Holme and the Ringsteads that indicate similar changes, but they omit to mention Fring and Gressenhall. However, a browse through Sir Henry Spelman's papers yielded an abstract of accounts dated 1602 that did include receipts from Fring and Gressenhall.[13] This was a real breakthrough. The total figure of £735 for 1602 presents a very different picture to that conveyed by Alice. With this evidence it was possible to deepen the comparison of estate income over time, bearing in mind that the figure from 1602, as a statement from the trustees, still does not include any receipts from demesne farming.

The purpose of Table 3.1 is to compare receipts and estimates of income and to broadly gauge the productivity of the estate between the 1540s and 1650s; this is achieved by dividing the total receipts by the number of properties. By 1569, with the sale of Godwick and Docking and the two Suffolk manors, and the transfer of the Sedgeford estate to John Le Strange, the number of properties had declined

---

10   Bailiff accounts, LEST/R5 (1542–87); LEST/R7 (1587–1600); LEST/R8 (1598–1631); and LEST/R9 (1605–25). There is a gap between 1609 and 1614 followed by accounts simply for Hunstanton. The household accounts start with Sir Hamon's accounts, 1606–9, followed by Alice's first book of receipts and disbursements, 1610–13, and her first, third and fourth household books, 1613–21, are all bound together in LEST/P6; the fifth, sixth and eighth household books, 1621–33, can be found in LEST/P8; the ninth and tenth household books, 1633–42, are in LEST/P9, while the second book, 1614–16, and the seventh book, 1627–9, are missing. There is a gap between 1642 and 1650. A household book, not in Alice's hand, survives from 1650–53: LEST/P11. The disbursements are contained in LEST/P7 for 1613–33 and in LEST/P10 for 1645–54; this book is bound with the accounts of the Flocks and Foldcourses, 1618–54 and other miscellaneous items: see Griffiths, *Her Price is Above Pearls, passim.*

11   Hunstanton rentals: LEST/BI 32 (1559), LEST/BI34 (1569), LEST/BK1 (1575), LEST/BK 2 (1580, Holme); Sir Hamon's rentals: LEST/BK3, 4 (1611–12), LEST/BK5 (1613), LEST/BK6/1, BK6/2 (1618); Alice's rentals: LEST/BK7 (1634, 1640), LEST/BK8 (1647) and LEST/BK9 (1655), which support LEST/BK15, her combined estate account and rental from 1632–53. Further rentals survive from 1661–1720.

12   Oestmann, *Lordship and Community*, p. 62, fns 58, 59.

13   LEST/Q34, fol. 99.

Table 3.1
Income from rents and farming on the Hunstanton estate, 1540s–1650s.

	1539– 44	*1602*	*1607– 09*	*1610– 11*	*1612– 13*	*1617– 19*	*1620– 26*	*1630– 39*	*1640– 41*	*1650– 52*
Average receipts £	467		616.3	385	729.5	1085	1813	2100	2422	2278
Abstract of bailiff accounts £		735								
List of values £				905						
Note of revenue £						1247				
Landed possessions	10	6	6	6	6	6	7	7	7	7
Average income per property £	46.7	122.5	102.7	64.1	121.5	180	259	300	346	325.4

Note: As in Figure 3.1, the receipts exclude new loans, sale of lands and marriage portions to avoid distortion.

Sources: These include the household books from the 1540s, LEST/P3; abstract of accounts in Sir Henry Spelman's papers, LEST/Q34 fol. 99, and the records of Sir Hamon and Alice.

to five.[14] However, from 1571 Sir Nicholas (1511–80) also enjoyed the remaining rents from Gressenhall alongside Hunstanton, Great Ringstead, Ringstead Parva, Heacham Calys and Fring, bringing the number to six.[15] Within this number, there was an important change in 1607 when Fring was sold and replaced in 1609 with the great manor of Heacham Lewes, worth twice as much as Fring and with much more potential.[16] In addition, in 1620 the family regained Sedgeford, worth £450 a year, when Alice inherited the estate from her father, bringing the number to seven. So the quality of the properties improved, as well as the number, which helped to raise income further and contain the losses suffered during the Civil War. For our purposes, the most remarkable figure is the one for 1602 that shows that the increase in income dated from the late 1580s and dipped in Sir Hamon's early years.

The difficulty with comparisons over time is that we cannot be sure we are comparing like with like. The receipts for Sir Thomas and Sir Hamon exclude new loans, sale of lands and marriage portions to avoid distortion, but do the remaining receipts

14 The Suffolk manors, Felsham and Thorpe Morieux, had formed part of the jointure of Anne Le Strange.

15 In the 1602 abstract, the list of values *c*.1610 and the note of revenues 1617 the Holme lands are listed with Great Ringstead and Hunstanton. The possessions for 1539 to 1544, mapped by Oestmann, *Lordship and Community*, p. 19, map (c), list Holme next Sea separately. In Table 3.1 the figure has been adjusted to avoid confusion. Oestmann's map actually includes fourteen possessions; however, the properties at Snettisham and Anmer were not found in the text or catalogue and Oakley was sold in 1531.

16 Fring was sold to Edmund Richers for £2140; at twenty years' purchase price it was worth about £107 a year. Sir Hamon purchased Heacham Lewes for £4400; Alice valued it at £215 a year. See Table 3.2.

Table 3.2
Breakdown of receipts for the Hunstanton estate, 1602, 1610 and 1617.

	Abstract of accounts 1602			A list of values c.1610	A note of revenues 1617
Hunstanton	£122	19s	3d	£120	£331
Parsonage					£51
In my own use					£60
Ringstead Magna	£128	12s		£120	£111
Ringstead Parva	£119	10s		£100	£114
Heacham Calys	£77	7s	8d	£120	£124
Heacham Lewes				£215	£226
Fring	£63			Sold 1607	
Gressenhall	£223	11s	6d	£230	£230
Total	£735	0s	5d	£905	£1247

Source: Found in Sir Henry Spelman's papers, Alice's accounts and Hamon's memoranda book, LEST/Q38 fol. 10.

represent the entire income of the estate from farming and rents? Sir Hamon's receipts between 1607 and 1609 were erratic and certainly understated, raising questions about his accounting methods.[17] The situation becomes worse in the 1610 account, when Alice took over responsibility for recording the receipts and disbursements. The collapse in receipts coincides with a sharp increase in expenditure on building and repairs, amounting to £388, possibly associated with the pending renewal of leases in 1611.[18] It is conceivable that receipts were diverted at source for this purpose by Sir Hamon or Richard Stubbe, who acted as receiver of rents at this time.[19] In 1612 and 1613, with higher rents and much lower expenditure, receipts almost doubled (see Table 3.1). In 1613 Alice took over the role of receiver of rents from her father, and by 1617 the level of income had risen by a further 50 per cent. However, the figures for Hunstanton recorded by Sir Hamon in his note of revenues in a memoranda book far exceed Alice's estimate of values of 1610 and her receipts from 1617 to 1619 (see Table 3.2). Overall, this suggests that Hamon kept some receipts for his own use, sometimes indulged in creative accounting and was happy to hand over the whole task to Alice.

The figures for the abstract of accounts in 1602 are more straightforward. They include only the income from farm rents and manorial dues, which would have been scrupulously scrutinised by the trustees. The same cautious approach might explain their lack of expenditure on buildings and repairs, of which Alice was so critical. However, despite the limitations of the figures available, it is clear that Sir Hamon's

---

17   LEST/P6. Alice immediately picks up evidence of fraud in Sir Hamon's account.

18   In 1597 the trustees failed to enforce a rent increase agreed with the tenants; see below, p. 42.

19   In 1601 Alice set out a list of values (undated) amounting to £905 and expenses of £640, a third of which was payable to Sir Nicholas's widow, Lady Cope and Richard Stubbe, LEST/P6, fol. 158.

father made significant progress in raising income between 1583 and 1592 and that his initiatives were more or less sustained by the trustees. Thus Sir Hamon and Alice were able to build on reasonably solid foundations, but further improvement would require massive investment, a much more adventurous approach to estate management and rigorous record-keeping. In a nutshell, this is what they achieved.

I

To understand the nature and value of the reforms undertaken by Sir Hamon we need to examine more closely the geography of Hunstanton and the way it was managed prior to his taking possession. The map he commissioned from Thomas Waterman in 1615 shows at a glance the neat division between Westfield, with its dense network of open-field strips running up to the cliff edge, and Eastfield, dominated by the hall and park, with enclosed pastures and marshes leading to the sandy dunes of the common, the fishing rights on the beach and the sea at Holme.[20] The enclosures north of the hall and the remaining strips in front of the hall were the focus of Sir Nicholas's enlargement of the park in 1588, which was continued by Sir Hamon and his successors.[21] The north–south boundary between the West and East fields, or precincts, as they were known, started at Havengate, on the west side of the common, and ran along Northgate behind the hall and park to Southgate, where Sir Hamon planted acorns on newly emparked strips in the 1630s.[22] This line, which can be seen on Faden's map of Norfolk, marks a shift in the landscape, as the plateau of Westfield falls away to the valley of the River Hun, which rises in Ringstead Downs and flows northward through the park, around the moat system and through the pastures and marshes to the sea channel at Holme.[23] The map also shows that Holme, the Ringsteads and the eastern half of Hunstanton form a distinct geographical entity, which is evident in the documents and on the ground; this helps to explain the close relationship between these communities.[24] The inhabitants of Westfield were, more or less, a law unto themselves.

From chapter 2, we know that this geography played a crucial part in shaping the settlement, economy and culture of Hunstanton. In certain areas, principally Westfield, the soils were of exceptional quality and sustained a dense population and a diverse economy. The eastern half of the parish, which contained the less good arable, with pastures and marshes running up to the sea, was less fertile and ripe for

---

20   LEST/AO1.

21   The details listed by Sir Hamon in LEST/BK1, LEST/BH1 and Q38 fol. 5 record the process of enlargement up to 1618. Later field maps, LEST/IC68 and BH9, show the process nearing completion by the late 1680s.

22   LEST/BH1, Sir Hamon's field book of Hunstanton, 1618, supports Waterman's survey of 1615.

23   See Figure 2.2.

24   Later maps, LEST/A02 (1760) and LEST/A03 (1765) also emphasise the close links between the park and the Ringsteads; see also estate map of 1820, shown in Figure 6.13. This perspective becomes even more distinct after the building of New Hunstanton: see the Ordnance Survey map of 1905.

Figure 3.2 Sketch map based on Waterman's Map of Hunstanton, 1615, showing the division between West and East Field. NRO LEST/OA 1.

improvement. In Sir Thomas's time this area had been leased on terms of nine and ten years to groups of substantial tenants from Holme more familiar with the terrain and able to develop its potential. Sir Thomas initiated commercial enterprises further afield on newly acquired and well-established ecclesiastical estates, such as Godwick and Sedgeford. This option was not open to Sir Nicholas (1511–80), as he sold Godwick in 1557 and assigned Sedgeford to his youngest son John in 1562. Meanwhile, his eldest son Hamon (1533–80), resident at Hunstanton, turned his attention to Eastfield in the 1560s, taking in hand pasture for his own sheep enterprise. In 1571 his father conveyed to him the entire manor for his own use.[25] However, Hamon's intervention was not without risk.[26] By taking the pasture he upset the delicate balance of the leases, which included *en bloc* pasture, arable and marsh; the loss of the pasture made it a much less attractive option to the men of Holme. By 1559 they leased only twenty acres of Eastfield, with the remaining arable leased to smaller tenants from Hunstanton who paid 1s per acre, rather than 2s for the block holding with pasture.[27] In the absence of receipt books we have no idea whether Hamon's sheep made up the difference. However, in 1575 he was forced to reverse a rent increase for this land, from 1s to 2s per acre, that he had secured in 1569. So it was a fine judgement.

Hamon's attempts at improvement were abruptly terminated with his untimely death in 1580, followed by that of his eldest son, Thomas, in 1581.[28] His second son, Nicholas (1563–92), did not achieve his majority until 1584.[29] However, the bailiff accounts show that he was well prepared for the task, as he swiftly moved to reinstate the rise in farm rents initiated and rescinded by his father. The accounts are not complete and do not provide information beyond the remit of the bailiff; however, they contain detail of farm rents, the location and size of holdings, estate personnel, the role of the trustees, evidence of new initiatives and the interaction with tenants. Most significantly, they highlight Sir Nicholas's determination and reforming instincts.

II

The first set of accounts kept for Sir Nicholas dates from 1583 to 1587; it is the last item in a book of bailiff accounts for the manors of Hunstanton dating back to 1542.[30] The first point of interest is the change of personnel in 1583, when Firmin Gray replaced Thomas Spratt and John Pedder as bailiff. The Pedder family were the leading tenants in Hunstanton and feature in all the sixteenth-century accounts

---

25 LEST/A57. Sir Nicholas fled to Ireland in the 1570s, following his suspected involvement in the Ridolphi Plot.

26 For this section on Eastfield see Oestmann, *Lordship and Community*, pp. 58–86.

27 Rentals for Hunstanton for this period include LEST/BI 32 (1559); LEST/BI34 (1569); LEST/BK1 (1575); LEST/BK 2 (1580, Holme); bailiff accounts date from 1542–87, LEST/R5.

28 Apart from the disruption caused, early deaths proved expensive. Thomas made a will in 1580, leaving his household goods and jewellery to Griselda, his young wife, daughter of William Yelverton (LEST/AE6). After his death in 1581 she married Phillip Wodehouse of Kimberley; the trustees agreed to pay her £66 13s 4d twice a year (LEST/A60). In 1684 Sir Nicholas (1563–92) conveyed to them and their successors the manor of East Lexham, part of the estate of Thomas's mother, Elizabeth Hastings (LEST/A61).

29 After the death of Mary Bell, Sir Nicholas (1563–92) married Ann, daughter of Sir William Paston, as his second wife in 1590 (LEST/A65). After his death in 1592 she remarried as her third husband Sir Anthony Cope and continued to receive an annuity of £160 from the Le Stranges until 1637 (LEST/P7).

30 LEST/R5. The 'set of accounts' refers to the layout of the bailiff's account with date headings that run across the double page and bear the entries for a range of years.

and rentals as officeholders. John had performed the role of bailiff since the 1560s.[31] Gray had no apparent connections in Hunstanton. The appointment may have been a conscious decision to engage an outside professional to implement reforms that required breaking with tradition. Certainly, Gray had no qualms about raising rents. His first account shows a dramatic increase from £39 17s 2d in 1583 to £100 1s 1d in 1584, a two and a half fold increase. With a more rigorous collection of arrears, receipts soared to £184 8d in 1585 and £252 11s 2d in 1586, dropping back to £98 17s in 1587, while allowances remained at a few pounds. Over the same period rents for Mustrells manor rose from £10 11d to £19 1s 2d.

Gray was the proverbial new broom. In his next set of accounts from 1587 to 1592 rents edged further ahead, with the new seven-year leases, consolidating at around £128 per annum, while the layout of the account continued to improve, with more detail on individual holdings.[32] Gray also entered into an agreement with an older tenant for three closes of pasture, including Poole Close, amounting to 100 acres; in 1590 Sir Nicholas granted him a twenty-one-year lease of the parsonage of Fring for £20 a year as a base for his own farming activities.[33] At the same time, more land in Eastfield was taken in hand and 'enclosed to enlarge the park'.[34] These accounts appear in a new book alongside accounts for the manors in Ringstead, Sedgefords and Calys in Heacham, indicating a fresh start and a recognition of the need to organise information more carefully. The set ends abruptly in 1592 with the death of Sir Nicholas, leaving the trustees to deal with the renewal of leases due for 1594.

In the event the renewal of leases did not happen, but we have the agreement that the trustees, Sir John Peyton, Sir Henry Spelman and Sir Nicholas's brother, Roger Le Strange, made with the farm tenants. Dated 23 October 1597, the title refers to Hunstanton and the 'pcells of lands hereafter following set out and agreed to be demised to the psons hereafter named for the terme of vij yeres from Mich last'.[35] There is no sign of authorship, but the detail suggests Firmin Gray. The purpose was to raise the rent in Westfield from 2s to 2s 6d per acre to bring it in line with the strips in Eastfield. The list includes the name of the tenant, the location of the pieces and a summary stating the total acreage, the farm rent and the value of the 'task',[36] with the new rent inserted alongside; it involved twenty-four tenants and 187 acres. However, in the accounts from 1597/8 to 1600/1 the rents for Westfield were still set at 2s per acre, and remained at that level until 1611. There is no explanation of the trustees' failure to enforce this agreement, but it was probably linked to their failure to fund building projects, which may explain Sir Hamon's flurry of activity in 1610. With a rent increase after just ten years, tenants would expect something in return.

---

31   Oestmann, *Lordship and Community*, p. 46, Table 4. List of tenants of Hunstanton Manor, 1514, 1537/8 and 1559.

32   LEST/R5, Hunstanton with Holme account, 1587–92.

33   LEST/Q34, fols 97–8.

34   Further evidence of this enlargement, written up by Sir Hamon in the rental LEST/BK1 (1575) and in his new field book for Hunstanton, LEST/BH1 (1618–23).

35   LEST/R8, fols 44–51. The agreement is written in English rather than Latin.

36   The task was the value of the boon work they owed to the lord for the holding.

From this point the bailiffs' accounts are uneven, notably beyond Hunstanton, while no formal entries appear at all in the book from 1601 to 1604.[37] That is why the abstract of accounts for 1602 found among Sir Henry Spelman's notes is so valuable.[38] The accounts resume in a new book when Sir Hamon took control in 1605, but peter out in 1610. Gray had returned to his post, but appears to have left Sir Hamon's service permanently at this stage.[39] His absences may have been the result of a long-term dispute with the tenants. When the accounts reappear for Hunstanton in 1614 the bailiffs, Robert Harrison and Robert Banyard, were both drawn from established tenant families. The accounts for the Ringsteads and Heacham were always kept by tenants, namely Nicholas Reade and Thomas Gittings at Ringstead and the Skippons at Heacham. The experience with Gray may explain why Sir Hamon turned to Alice to keep his accounts rather than appoint another outsider or rely on a bailiff.

Above all, the bailiff accounts demonstrate the toughness of the tenants and the difficulty of imposing rent rises successfully. The rebuff in 1597 was not an isolated example or confined to the trustees; as we have seen, Sir Hamon's grandfather was forced to reverse a rent increase in 1575. These tenants were men of substance who farmed in a difficult environment and expected to be rewarded for their skills; therefore, they needed to be treated with respect. After 1597 Sir Henry Spelman became more prominent in the accounts, involved in the farming and working with tenants. Once again, he appears to have provided a lead, showing that collaboration, or farming to halves, was the way forward.

The first entry of Sir Hamon's new book of bailiff accounts, written clearly in English, refers to 'The profit of the tythes and halfes of the corne growing in the field of Barrett Ringstead in the yere 1605', with Sir Hamon sharing the costs of threshing, shepherds' wages and payments associated with managing sheep.[40] This account is supported by details of an arrangement in Sir Hamon's receipt book of 1606 that shows four tenants contributing to a fine of £20 in anticipation of a lease being concluded for Barrett Ringstead foldcourse and lands.[41] The principal tenant, Roger Browne, was responsible for Sir Hamon's contribution to the agreement. The lease for Barrett Ringstead farm expired in 1617 and was replaced by an agreement with a new group of tenants for a single year, 1617–18, when substantial building work at Barrett Ringstead was in progress.[42] The building of Ringstead Yards and Meadow Pitt Close in 1617 and 1618 was the subject of intense planning, with diagrams detailing the

---

37 It is quite possible these accounts were lost at the time, as they were between 1610 and 1614 (LEST/BG 43).

38 The bailiff account for Heacham Calys that survives for 1602 corresponds exactly with the abstract.

39 Firmin Gray survives in Sir Hamon's memoranda books (LEST/Q37).

40 LEST/R8. The bailiff's accounts make no reference to farming to halves. However, this account written in English appears on a separate page; the contents are confirmed in Hamon's receipt book in 1606 (LEST/P6). Ringstead Parva is gradually replaced by Barrett Ringstead.

41 A lease for expired in 1617 (LEST/Q38 fols 6, 8).

42 LEST/Q38, expiration of leases, front folio, followed by new leases for Ringstead severalls and Barrett Ringstead in 1616 (fol. 8).

specifications of barns, yards and watercourses.[43] The venture was the first example of heavy investment and collaboration with tenants designed to raise the productivity of a low-grade area of the estate; its principal asset was the location of the farm at the southern end of the park in Ringstead Downs.[44] In his first rental Sir Hamon recorded two similar but more limited agreements for farming 'to halfes' in 1613, first with Thomas Ketwood for producing a crop of barley in Upper Close and second with William Cobb for pease and vetches in Poole Close.[45] The ramifications of even these modest arrangements, where the inputs and outputs were shared with the tenants, underline Sir Hamon's deep and imaginative commitment to his task.

If Sir Hamon wanted to raise the income of the estate significantly, this was the type of approach he needed to pursue. The key to success was to increase profitability at every level. This meant more investment in buildings and enclosure, taking more land in hand, setting up new enterprises and raising rents as his father and grandfather had done. The next task was to radically upgrade their management techniques. This is where Sir Hamon and Alice excelled. In chapters 5 and 6 we will see how they consciously created a knowledge economy that embraced the needs of the new commercial environment, fashioned a more efficient management system and developed ways of using the information and human resources at their disposal more effectively. This was a gradual and experimental process, but it resulted in the modernisation of the estate and a three-fold increase in productivity by the early 1640s. The books of bailiff accounts ended in 1631, overshadowed by Alice's receipt books and finally superseded by her comprehensive reform of estate management procedures. However, before we turn to these developments, we examine how other Norfolk gentry families coped with unprecedented levels of inflation and tackled the erosion of their rental incomes.

---

43   LEST/Q38, fols 17–21.

44   Ringstead Downs is a designated SSSI and nature reserve, and one of the few surviving chalk grasslands in the county: <www.norfolkwildlifetrust.org.uk>; <http://designatedsite. naturalengland.org.uk>. The buildings, renewed in the eighteenth and nineteenth centuries, survive as a working farm on the estate; see Downs Farm, Barrett Ringstead, <www.heritage. norfolk.gov.uk>, and Ringstead Yards Farm on Faden's map (Figure 2.2).

45   LEST/BK3, assembled in anticipation of the rent review of 1611.

Chapter 4

Winners and losers: Norfolk gentry and estate management, 1590–1625

The purpose of this chapter is to provide context for the success achieved by Sir Hamon and Alice between 1604 and 1654, the year of Sir Hamon's death; this included not only the great increase in income by 1642 but the overcoming of the reversal of fortune they suffered in the Civil War. Many Norfolk gentry families failed in both respects. So what did it take to be a winner in this world of rising prices, falling incomes and a country divided?

In their approach to these issues Norfolk landowners can be roughly divided into five categories: great lawyers, such as Sir Henry Hobart and Sir Edward Coke, who knew precisely how to exploit and profit from the situation; established landowners like the Le Stranges, Townshends, Windhams and Bacons, who understood the nature of the problem and modified their strategy accordingly; ancient families with good contacts but poor management skills, who tried to augment their incomes by securing lucrative offices at court and in the county – notably the Cleres of Blickling and Ormesby and the Heydons of Baconsthorpe;[1] alongside these groups we find the recusants, such as the Southwells of Woodrising, excluded from office by their sympathy for the Catholic faith; finally, there were those such as the Yelvertons of Rougham and the Barneys of Langley, who were simply unwilling or unable to grasp the complexities of the situation and gradually disappeared from the scene. In this brutal battle for survival there were clearly winners and losers; this was the context of the warring factions described in Smith's *County and Court*.[2] Adding to this already potent mix, the crown and the Church were still significant landowners in the county with patronage and property to dispense, while the demise of the duke of Norfolk and the Howard family brought a string of estates and offices on to the market.[3]

Sir Hamon's uncle and guardian, Sir Henry Hobart (c.1554–1625), had links with all these groups through his extensive family network and in his professional capacity.[4]

---

1   A.H. Smith, *County and Court: Government and Politics in Norfolk, 1558–1603* (Oxford, 1974). These families hoped to fill the political vacuum created by the execution of Thomas, 4th duke of Norfolk, in 1572. The Cleres of Blickling and Ormesby, cousins of Elizabeth I, were in the frontline, and were opposed by the county faction – led by the sons of Sir Nicholas Bacon, the Lord Keeper, Judge Francis Windham and the Gawdys, and supported by other leading lawyers, including Coke and Hobart – which was eager to contain the crown and retain control of the county.

2   Smith, *County and Court*, pp. 47–53.

3   Elizabeth I's inheritance of half of Sir James Boleyn's estate in 1561 added to the crown's portfolio; see also Smith, *County and Court*, pp. 30–8; Oestmann, *Lordship and Community*, pp. 17–24 for the Le Stranges' relationship with the 3rd and 4th dukes of Norfolk.

4   Several branches of the Hobart family were recusants and rescued by Sir Henry.

He gave support and advice to relatives, friends and associates, including the crown and the Church, and benefited handsomely as a result. In fact, he provides a masterclass in how lawyers from relatively modest backgrounds could advance themselves and prosper greatly during this difficult time. He also casts a sharp light on those families that fell by the wayside. Unlike his contemporary, Sir Edward Coke, whose personal records were mostly scattered and lost, Sir Henry left a detailed archive of his acquisition process, so we have a well-focused picture of a real winner and several notorious losers in late sixteenth- and early seventeenth-century Norfolk. This provides a contrast to the more familiar accounts of the established families at Hunstanton, Raynham, Felbrigg and Stiffkey, who quietly took advice and successfully put the management of their estates on to a more commercial footing.[5] Sir Henry, given his background and the nature of his job, moved in more crisis-ridden circles. The emphasis in this chapter will be on his experience and that of those less fortunate. The period is from Sir Henry's marriage at Blickling in 1590, as a guest of Sir Edward Clere, to his death in 1625 as the owner and rebuilder of the Blickling Hall we see today.[6]

I

Although he was descended from an eminent lawyer, Sir Henry Hobart was the younger son of a minor gentleman and received no landed inheritance, so he was starting from scratch.[7] After studying at Cambridge and Lincoln's Inn he was called to the Bar in 1584 and worked his way up the legal ladder in his locality as under-steward to Lord Burghley and recorder of Great Yarmouth from 1588 to 1603.[8] He was appointed steward of the city of Norwich from 1595 and sergeant-at-law from 1603 to 1605; he also represented both boroughs in parliament – Yarmouth in 1596 and 1601 and Norwich in 1604 – and was knighted on James I's accession in 1603. Sir Henry's breakthrough on to the national stage came in 1605, when he was appointed attorney-general to the Court of Wards and Liveries

---

5 Griffiths and Overton, *Farming to Halves*, pp. 56–70; Griffiths, 'Improving landlords or villains of the piece?'; J.M. Rosenheim, *The Townshends of Raynham: Nobility in Transition in Restoration and Early Hanoverian England* (Middletown, CT, 1989). R.W. Ketton-Cremer, *Felbrigg: The Story of a House* (London, 1962); Griffiths, 'Management'; six volumes of *The Papers of Nathaniel Bacon of Stiffkey*, published by the Norfolk Record Society, 1978–2017.

6 This section is based mainly on Griffiths, 'Management', but includes new insights on the 'losers', notably the Cleres of Blickling and Ormesby, which brings a new perspective to Sir Henry's acquisition of Blickling in 1616.

7 Sir Henry Hobart was the great grandson of Sir James Hobart (1436–1517), attorney general 1486–1507, who migrated from Suffolk to Norfolk in the 1470s, established himself at Hales Hall, Loddon, and settled his younger sons on small estates in the vicinity; but his successors, apart from Sir Henry, made little impact, partly due to their recusancy. His father, Thomas Hobart of Plumstead, married Audrey, d. and co-heiress of William Hare of Beeston St Lawrence, where the family settled. Their eldest son, Miles, sold the estate to Sir Henry in 1624 to repay debts.

8 S. Handley, 'Hobart, Sir Henry', *ODNB* (Oxford, 2004); <www.historyofparliament.co.uk>. Neither source has any information about Sir Henry's estate building from 1596 to 1625.

for life and in 1606 attorney-general, a position he held until 1613, when he replaced Sir Edward Coke as Lord Chief Justice of the Court of Common Pleas. These promotions transformed his status and financial position, but, whereas Coke spent £100,000 buying estates 'in a hundred parishes across several counties', Sir Henry remained loyal to Norfolk, stating his desire to have his estate 'within the compass of one shire for ease of management'.[9] He spent about £60,000 on properties located mainly in south and east Norfolk, which gives us a rare insight into what was happening in that part of the county.[10] Most of the acquisitions are fully documented with surveys, Sir Henry's comments in the margins and details of their future management. In 1616, in succession to another celebrated Norfolk man, Sir Francis Bacon, he was appointed Chancellor to the Prince of Wales with responsibility for the estates of the Duchy of Cornwall, a further recognition of his expertise as a land manager and reformer.[11]

Sir Hamon Le Strange was indeed fortunate to have such a man protecting his interests during his minority. Henry Hobart arranged the settlement of his marriage with Alice Stubbe in 1602 and safely secured the transfer of lands from Richard Stubbe and assets from Sir Henry Spelman in 1604.[12] He also ensured that Spelman was properly rewarded for his role as the guardian resident at Hunstanton, overseeing the education of his charge and the day-to-day management of the estate.[13] This was typical of the role Sir Henry played within the family network. His association with the Le Stranges dated from 1590, when he married Dorothy Bell, the younger sister of Mary, the first wife of Sir Nicholas Le Strange (1563–92) and Sir Hamon's mother.[14] Dorothy Bell brought to the marriage a dowry of £500, which contrasts with the portion, estimated at £30,000, of Bridget Paston, who had married Sir Edward Coke in 1583.[15]

Reflecting his origins and circumstances, Henry Hobart proceeded cautiously in the acquisition of his estate. He made no purchase before 1596, when he secured the major part of Sir William Gresham's estate at Intwood, a few miles south of Norwich.[16] This prestigious estate, which Sir William had inherited in 1580 from his uncle, Sir Thomas Gresham, the renowned financier and founder of the Royal Exchange, came

---

9   James, *Chief Justice Coke*, appendix 2, pp. 304–6; see also C. Hiskey, *Holkham: The Social, Architectural and Landscape History of a Great English Country House* (Norwich, 2016), p. 14; Griffiths, 'Sir Henry Hobart', p. 19.

10 The exception being the purchase of lands in Lincolnshire at Bloxham, Stixwold and Halstead for his third son, Nathaniel.

11 By 1625 Sir Henry's income from rents amounted to about £6000 a year, while he earned at least £1250 a year from his legal activity.

12 LEST/A66–73; LEST/Q37, fols 14–17.

13 LEST/Q37, fols 14–17.

14 Mary (1561–85) and Dorothy (1575–1640) were the daughters of Sir Robert Bell of Beaupre Hall, Outwell, Norfolk (1539–77), Speaker of the House of Commons 1572–6 and Lord Chief Baron of the Exchequer 1577 <www.historyofparliament.org.uk>.

15 James, *Chief Justice Coke*, pp. 10–12.

16 Sir William Gresham (1555–1624), <www.historyofparliament.org.uk>.

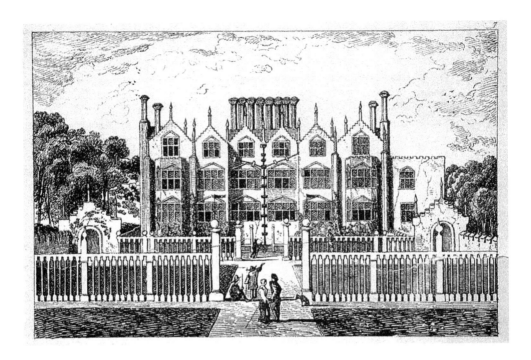

Figure 4.1 Sir Thomas Gresham's Flemish House at Intwood built in the 1560s. Image courtesy of Norfolk Castle Museum and Art Gallery, Norfolk Museums Service. NWHCM : 1954.138. Todd10.Humbleyard.38.

with a good house and was clearly appropriate to Sir Henry's new position as steward of the city.[17] Moreover, there was the prospect of buying further portions of the estate. The opportunity for purchase arose when Sir William, after an unsuccessful career in Norfolk, returned to the family's principal estate at Titsey, Surrey, in 1595.[18] The timing coincided with the end of a twenty-one-year lease for Intwood Hall and Farm, granted by Sir Thomas to his stepson William Reade in 1575. No sale documents survive, but a lease granted in 1606 by Sir Henry to his kinsman Roger Hobart of Morley shows that he acquired about 890½ acres in 1596 and a further 655 acres in Keswick and

---

17 Griffiths, 'Management', pp. 71–2, 91–100. Sir Thomas's father Sir Richard Gresham purchased Intwood and Keswick in 1537 and died seized of these manors with Swardeston, Swainsthorpe, Hardwick and Mulbarton in 1548. Sir Thomas inherited the estate from his elder brother, who died in 1560: see Francis Blomefield, *An Essay Towards a Topographical History of the County of Norfolk*, vol. 5 (London, 1806), pp. 39–46; A.J. Nixseaman, *The Intwood Story* (Norwich, 1972).

18 The family originated from Gresham, near Holt, in Norfolk; Sir John and Sir Richard Gresham migrated to London in the early 1500s. Sir John purchased the estate at Titsey, while Sir Richard returned to Norfolk. <www.historyofparliament.org.uk>, <www.titsey.org.uk>.

Swardeston in 1601.[19] This is confirmed by Sir Henry's view of accounts 1622–5 and a map of 1729, which gives the extent of the beautifully compact and mostly enclosed estate at 1545 acres. According to the schedule, much of the improvement at Intwood was achieved by 1606; the lease of 1575 suggests that the hall and its adjoining farmland had already been extensively reorganised by Sir Thomas.[20] No wonder Sir Henry pounced when the lease expired in 1596.

A comparison of the leases of 1575 and 1606 shows what could be achieved with a reformed landholding structure. In the lease of 1575 the Intwood estate was already divided into two commercial units: the hall with part of the demesne, leased for £20 a year, while 'the newe house called the deyrey house', with a 'new barn, stables, okeyard and 3 acres', included another 707 acres let for £28, which included 400 acres of heathland, 161 acres in four closes sub-let to a single tenant, 34 acres of enclosed pasture and meadow and 64 acres of arable strips sub-let to seven tenants. In addition, 48 acres of woodland was divided into four separate woods. By 1606 the total rent had risen from £48 to £230, or from 9d to 5s per acre, while the term of the lease was cut to seven years. The heathland had been reduced to 150 acres; the newly cultivated area with the existing four closes, the arable strips and felled woodland accounted for 620 acres divided into twenty closes. Only 1½ acres of woodland survived with 54 acres of meadow, while a further 57 acres was omitted from the schedule. With no documentation for the sale in 1596, we cannot be sure that all these changes were effected by Sir Henry. However, the most likely scenario is that Sir William felled the trees for a quick profit, leaving Sir Henry to enclose the heathland, reorganise the closes and capitalise on the rising price of corn, and to start the replanting.

The covenants in Roger Hobart's lease confirm this assumption. Sir Henry instructed Roger to replant with trees the two closes at the entry gate of the mansion, 'imedyatlie after two croppes'; he also included detailed husbandry clauses for the management of the new closes. The aim was to maintain a balance of arable and pasture, with restrictions on ploughing up certain closes and meadows or hardgrounds adjoining, and to ensure that the estate was left in good condition and adequately capitalised. Thus, at the end of the term, the tenant was to leave 'sufficient somerley of arable grounds' and to have ready money for tilth, tathe and seed. The lease provided for an October handover, so Roger had to compensate Sir Henry for the husbandry undertaken for the following year. The costings and cropping arrangements for 120 acres, divided into four closes, were specified in great detail and illustrate the link between enclosure, improvement and raising productivity. When a dressing of muck could almost double the cost of cultivation, a compact and enclosed space was a huge advantage and much more receptive to capital investment. These particular

---

19   Sir Henry paid Miles Branthwaite £2250 for Keswick and Swardeston; Branthwaite had acquired the property from Sir William Gresham in 1599; at the same time, Gresham sold Mulbarton to Sir Edwin Rich while Sir Henry was involved with the sale of Swainsthorpe, which Gresham sold in 1616: Blomefield, *Norfolk*, vol. 5, pp. 58–62.

20   In 1606 Sir Henry purchased Roger Hobart's estate at Morley, Deopham and Hackford, west of Wymondham, possibly to raise capital for the lease at Intwood.

closes were leased for 6s 8d per acre compared with the average of 5s per acre at Intwood. In 1622 the estate, with Keswick and Swardeston, was valued at £410 14s 6d (5s 3d per acre), which suggests that progress plateaued after 1606.[21]

The slowdown at Intwood can be explained by Sir Henry's appointment as Attorney-General in 1606, which required a residence in London and a caretaker for his Norfolk property. Hence the lease to his cousin Roger, who, besides farming the estate, kept the house 'sufficiently stuffed and furnished' and provided diet to his servant William Greene, while Sir Henry retained the right to use the mansion and repossess at two years' notice.[22] With Sir Henry's growing family, the arrangement was not ideal. The situation was resolved in 1609, when the Corporation of Norwich gifted Sir Henry a forty-one-year lease of Chapelfield House so that he could more easily perform his duties as steward of the city.[23] By this time Sir Henry also owned the Langley estate and included in a lease of the Abbey to another cousin, Edward Hobart, a requirement to send hay and wood to Norwich. Meanwhile, at Intwood, after Roger's death in 1612, the estate reverted to a more commercial structure with three holdings leased to local landowners. However, a degree of flexibility was retained there: the two holdings of 1575 were leased from year to year, while Keswick Hall was let for a twenty-one-year term. This structure closely resembled the layout of 1729 and illustrates the value of a strategy devised by two exceptionally able owners.[24]

During the early years, before his elevation to the Attorney-Generalship, Sir Henry also benefited from the patronage of the crown and the Church, which almost trebled his income by 1602. The properties were all concentrated in the Broadland area and reflected his personal and professional links. The first tranche came from the bishopric of Norwich in 1597 and consisted of ninety-nine-year leases of the rectories at Hoveton St Peter, Barton, Neatishead and Ashmanaugh. For these properties Sir Henry paid a rent of £33 18s 4d a year and sub-let them for £166 8s 4d. The royal grant of 1602 from Elizabeth I was significantly more generous. It included the manors of East and West Somerton, previously owned by the Cleres of Blickling and Ormesby, and several manors of the see of Norwich, namely Martham, Repps with Bastwick and Potter Heigham, for which Sir Henry paid a total of £177 4s 7d.[25] Of the bishopric manors, Sir

---

21 Sir Henry sold his interest in Swainsthorpe in 1616, and a manor at East Carleton he had acquired from Sir Edwin Rich in 1623: Blomefield, *Norfolk*, vol. 5, pp. 60, 103.

22 Sir Henry's personal and household accounts from 1621–5 show him paying rent of £10 15s for a house in Highgate, London, from 1621. It seems he bought a third of the house, which he left to his wife in his will. His eldest son, Sir John, made ample use of it in the 1620s.

23 Blomefield, *Norfolk*, vol. 4, pp. 169, 224. The position of steward of the city of Norwich was granted for life: W.C. Ewing, *Norfolk Lists from the Reformation to the Present Time* (1837), p. 73. Sir Henry surrendered the position in 1618, although the Hobarts happily hung on to the property until 1753.

24 Sir Henry left the Intwood estate to his wife and to his second son, Miles, but it returned to the main estate at Blickling when Phillipa, the daughter and co-heiress of Sir John Hobart, married her cousin, John Hobart of Intwood. The Hobarts retained Intwood and Keswick until 1793, when the estate was divided between the three daughters of Sir John Hobart, 2nd earl of Buckinghamshire.

25 Blomefield, *Norfolk*, vol. 11, pp. 189–92; NRS 13719 28 D.

Henry kept only Martham, which he leased with Somerton and the rectories for £742 by 1622. This was not the end of the largesse.[26] In 1610 the dean and chapter of Norwich cathedral duly obliged with a ninety-nine-year lease of Martham Rectory, for which Sir Henry paid £20 a year and sub-let for £98. From family and friends Sir Henry also acquired in 1597 a ninety-nine-year lease at Acle from his kinsman Thomas Clere of Stokesby and in 1624 the Hobart estate at Beeston St Lawrence from his elder brother Miles, bringing the total to £987 18s 6d.[27] The irony of these gifts and easy pickings is that Broadland was no longer Sir Henry's area of interest.

As a native, Sir Henry would have been fully aware of the limitations of the Broadland area for large landowners with an appetite for improvement, but the properties had been acquired sufficiently cheaply to make them worthwhile. In the open market there was much competition for this excellent land, which had been cultivated intensively for centuries. However, while the smaller properties held their value and were useful for settling younger sons, the larger holdings at Martham and Somerton were more problematic and less responsive to investment.[28] The farming practices on this exceptionally fertile soil were labour rather than capital intensive. In this context, the benefits of enclosure and farm buildings were not so apparent; large tenants struggled with labour costs and repair bills while small holders using the family as labour moved easily from strip to strip with their spades. The only real value of these properties was as a capital asset. The church leases at Acle and Beeston were set aside to support Sir Henry's two youngest sons, but when they died without issue in the 1630s Sir John Hobart sold them to purchase more land in the Blicking area.[29] Similarly, Somerton and Martham were sold on Sir John's death in 1647 to provide for his eldest daughter, Dorothy, and to pay off his debts.

From the amount of documentation that survives, it is clear that Sir Henry was much more interested in securing the future of the Langley estate, south of the river Yare on the marshes mid-way between Norwich and Yarmouth. The estate, a substantial and well-ordered monastic property, belonged to Richard Barney, who was married to Sir Henry's cousin, Elizabeth, the daughter of James Hobart of nearby Hales Hall.[30] Richard had inherited the estate from his father when he came of age in 1564, but he soon found himself in financial difficulties associated with the long leases granted in the 1540s and 1550s.[31] This proved to be an unwise strategy as prices rose

---

26 In 1606 the Great Hospital also granted a lease of Cringleford Mill for £10 a year, sub-let for £26 13s 4d.

27 Sir Henry paid £1100 for Acle manor, which yielded £71 2s 9d; he purchased the reversion from the earl of Arundel in 1622.

28 Griffiths, 'Management', pp. 101–12; Griffiths, 'Sir Henry Hobart', pp. 22–3.

29 The new land purchased by Sir John Hobart included fenland at Stow Bardolph from his cousin Sir Robert Bell and the Wood Dalling estate from the Bulwers, who were equally indebted; they had purchased it from the heavily indebted Sir Christopher Heydon in 1566.

30 The Premonstratensian Abbey at Langley, founded by the De Cheyneys in 1195: see Blomefield, *Norfolk*, vol. 10, p. 147. See W. Harvey, *The Visitation of Norfolk in the Year, 1562*, vol. 2, ed. Brig.-General Bulwer (1895) for the Barneys.

31 Notably, in 1547 John Barney granted a sixty-nine-year lease for the site of the monastery, Langley Grange, and the liberty of foldage at 12d per year; the premium is not recorded.

remorsely. In the late 1580s and early 1590s Richard purchased the remainder of these terms and relet the estate on a fully commercial basis. Given Sir Henry's status in the family, his later involvement with the estate and the type of reforms undertaken, he was probably advising them by this stage.

The movement of rents from 1537, which can be traced from the documents, highlights the devastating loss of income suffered by the Barneys in the late sixteenth century.[32] The earliest surviving particular, from the Court of Augmentations, 1537/8, records that the abbot leased the two principal holdings – the site of the monastery with its buildings and lands, and the Grange of Langley – to John Berney for twenty-one years at £23 9s 4d. With the rectory, other farmland, corn and assize rents, the total value of the estate was £60 18s 8d.[33] In 1539 Barney sub-let his tenancy, including the rectory, for £27 13s 4d, but when his possession of the estate was confirmed by the crown in 1546 he granted a long lease of the Abbey and Grange to Roger Mounteford for an undisclosed premium and 12d per annum. On Barney's death in 1559 the Inquisition Post Mortem stated that he died in possession of 'the said manor of Langley, the site of the monastery, 10 messuages and 970 acres of land'.[34] In a valuation of 1562, during Richard's minority, this acreage was scaled down to 800 acres and the estate valued at £36 17s 6, but it excluded the marshes and assize rents; when these rents are included, the value was almost identical with those of 1537 and 1539.

The breakthrough, at least for the two large holdings, came in 1592, when the Abbey was let on a seven-year term for £86 a year, followed by the Grange in 1599 on a three-year term for £100; this amounts to a total figure of £186 compared to £27 13s 4d in 1539, nearly a seven-fold increase. In 1609, when Sir Henry took possession of the estate, he raised the rents still further to £115 for the Abbey and £134 for the Grange, making a total of £249 a year, or a nine-fold increase over a slightly longer period. This compares with rents for the whole estate, which rose from £60 18s 8d in 1537 to £374 1s 5d in 1609, a six-fold increase.[35] These movements show that the potential for improvement lay in large, well-structured holdings receptive to investment and careful management. Significantly, the barley rent rose from £2 to £28 7s, a reflection of rising productivity.

The leases of the 1590s and early 1600s confirm that considerable progress, possibly with Sir Henry's help, was made during these years before he acquired the estate. The Abbey lease for 1592 included a dairy of twenty Northern cows and a bull with instructions on their welfare and penalties if they were not surrendered at

---

32   Griffiths, 'Management', pp. 129–32.

33   The rectory let for £5 6s 8d, farmland £16 12s 8d, marshes £12 6s 8d, corn rent £2, assize rents £13 3s 4d. The farmland included marshland leased to Sir William Paston on ninety-nine-year terms in 1518 and 1521.

34   Blomefield, *Norfolk*, vol. 10, p. 150.

35   The total figure for 1609 includes rents for parcels of marshland leased in the 1590s on twenty-one-year terms, indicating that Paston's long leases had been bought out. The total also included £30 rent for eighty acres purchased in 1602: see Griffiths, 'Management', p. 131. Smaller holdings were always leased on short terms for commercial rents.

the end of the term.[36] Excluded from the lease were Langmarshe and Oxmeadow, both 'newlie enclosed' by Richard Barney, which explains the lease in 1607 for a dairy on the marshlands 'with a house called deyryehill'.[37] This may have been a new venture, a revival of a decayed enterprise or a new location for the Abbey dairy; in any case, it represents an intensification of the dairying venture.[38] The Abbey tenant was also to perform the usual requirements to repair buildings and maintain dykes, hedges, fences and fleetes, while husbandry clauses included the provision to leave sufficient fodder and winter stover for the wintering of the cows and bull.[39] The lease for the Grange, lying further from the marshes, included more emphasis on timber and woodland management. The very short terms of the leases – seven years for the Abbey and only three years for the Grange, compared to twenty-one-year leases for the smaller holdings – suggest that the sale of the estate was anticipated and were designed to give vacant possession of the principal holdings. By this time Richard was in his late fifties, the couple were childless and the interests of Elizabeth needed to be protected.

In 1605 Sir Henry joined with Sir John Pettus, Sir Miles Corbett of Sprowston and Sir Thomas Berney of Reedham in taking a sixty-year lease of the Langley estate to secure an annuity of £180 for Elizabeth.[40] The heirs of Richard Barney – his three brothers John, Robert and George – were permitted to receive the rents and profits so long as this annuity was paid. If they failed, Sir Henry's heirs had to the right to repossess the property. The lessees paid Richard Barney £100 for the lease, but the arrangement did not solve the problem of Barney's debts. This was resolved in 1608, when Sir Henry finally concluded a bargain and sale with Richard for the recovery of a debt of £6000 that formed the basis of an agreement by which Sir Henry gained possession of the estate in 1609.

The acquisition of the Langley estate demonstrates Sir Henry's ingenuity and financial dexterity. With extreme care and foresight he secured one of the best estates in the county at well below market values and financed it entirely out of income. The agreement was based on a series of annuities payable to Richard, his wife Elizabeth and his three brothers. Sir Henry paid no capital until 1622 and needed to have only £4000 readily available; this sum he loaned to the earl of Arundel at 10 per cent interest, which yielded the income to pay the annuities. In 1622, when Sir Henry called in part of the loan, he was repaid with Methwold Parsonage and

---

36 The penalty was £52 10s, which corresponds to 52s 6d per cow.

37 Probably the marshes surrendered by Paston.

38 The herd does not appear in the lease of 1609; possibly the new tenant, Edward Hobart, purchased the stock or was subletting to a dairyman.

39 The tenants also supplied Richard Barney with six loads of hay, including a load taken to Norwich, the grazing of two horses and thirty-four qtrs of barley for the brewhouse, indicating that he resided in the city, like Sir Henry Hobart.

40 Sir John Pettus (1540–1614), tailor, freeman of Norwich, sheriff 1598, mayor 1608–9, MP 1601, 1604, <www.historyofparliamentonline.org.uk>. Sir Miles Corbett, JP, knighted 1598, d. 1607; Sir Thomas Barney, JP, knighted 1603, d. *c.*1618, Smith, *County and Court*. Barney alternates with Berney in the documents.

the reversion of Acle; he also granted Arundel a new mortgage on the manors of Fersfield and Lopham.[41] So, besides being a bargain, the agreement generated further acquisitions. At the same time, it provided the Barneys with a measure of dignity and security as the line died out in the 1620s.[42] In his 1614 Declaration of Trust Sir Henry commented that the transaction was 'not a mere purchase, but in part out of Barney's good affection a gift'. Sir Henry cemented the links with the family by granting a lease of the Abbey to Edward Hobart of Hales Hall, one of Elizabeth's brothers.[43]

The estate continued to prosper, with Edward Hobart performing a similar role to his cousin's at Intwood. The new leases, granted by Sir Henry in 1609 for the Abbey and Grange, reverted to the twenty-one-year terms, but at higher rents – £115 for the Abbey with 304¼ acres at 7s 6d per acre and £134 for the Grange, the capital house, with 444½ acres at 6s per acre. The lease also included more specific detail on the maintenance of buildings and the management of woodland, hedges, waterways and marshes, while the husbandry clauses paid particular attention to the protection of pasture. Significantly, the tenant of the Grange was required to survey all the woods so 'as the woods may not be cut down, stolen taken or carried away'. Holdings were amalgamated and rents continued to edge upwards, with small purchases of land assisting the process of consolidation. On his death, Sir Henry left the Langley estate to his eldest son to provide a reliable income; his judgement, as always, was pitch perfect. With its huge area of marshland and pasture, supporting livestock and dairy farming, the rental values at Langley were sustained when corn prices declined from the 1670s. However, probably out of sentiment or a desire to consolidate further in north Norfolk, the newly created Lord Hobart of Blickling sold the estate to Richard Berney, Recorder of Norwich, and kinsman of the Barneys of Langley, in 1729.[44] Berney soon exhibited a similar lack of aptitude with money; he built himself a grand Palladian mansion based on Holkham Hall and in a few years was bankrupt. In his will he described himself as 'weak of body', a condition which probably extended to his mind. On his death in 1737 the estate was acquired by George Proctor of Norwich.[45]

---

41   Griffiths, 'Management', pp. 118–19.

42   Richard d. in 1615, Elizabeth in 1622, George in 1624, John in 1625; no mention of Robert's death found.

43   Edward Hobart remained tenant of Langley Abbey until 1633; he was also Sir Henry Hobart's Receiver of Moneys and a trustee of his estate. His brother Sir John Hobart of Spital acted for Sir Henry on a regular basis.

44   Sir John Hobart, 5th Bt created Baron Hobart of Blickling, 1728; Richard Berney, 1674–1738, second son of John Berney of Westwick, <www.historyofparliamentonline.org>.

45   On George Proctor's death in 1744 the Langley estate passed to his nephew, William Beauchamp, created Sir William Beauchamp-Proctor, 1st Bt in 1745, who completed the unfinished Langley Hall. The house was requisitioned during World War II and subsequently sold by the Beauchamp-Proctors. It is now Langley School. Blomefield, *Norfolk*, vol. 10, p. 151, makes no mention of the estate ever being owned by the Hobarts.

II

By the time the agreement at Langley was finalised in 1609, Sir Henry's attention had turned northwards to the light loams and heathland that lay to the west of his native Broadland and offered more 'scope for improvement' (see Figure 4.2). His impressive legal career meant that he could now afford to set his sights on the estate of his old friend Sir Edward Clere, who had died in 1606 leaving huge debts and a widow in difficulties. Sir Henry and Agnes Clere soon developed a close friendship. In 1607 his eldest daughter, Dorothea, married her nephew Sir Robert Crane, so he became part of the family, which probably explains why Agnes got such a good deal with the sale of Blickling and Hanworth parsonage in 1616.[46] It was noted in the Declaration of Trust of 1620 that 'she yielded [her estate] to him out of her good affection, though it is more [her annuity of £400] than she did make of it or he can'.[47] This was the background of Sir Henry's purchases at Hevingham and Saxthorpe in 1608, the grant of crown lands at Cawston, Marsham and Hevingham Park in 1610 and the acquisition at Horsham St Faith from Sir Charles Cornwallis in 1612. After the Blickling sale was sealed Sir Henry acquired part of Sir Henry Clere's estate at Wymondham and a remnant of Agnes's personal estate at Weybourne in the 1620s.[48] In this section we will consider Sir Henry's policy on the 'northern heathlands' before the final masterclass, provided by Sir Edward Clere and his successors, on how to lose a great estate in three generations.

The move northwards appears to have been a conscious decision to acquire income-producing properties with a view to supporting the prestigious estate at Blickling.[49] As ancient demesne of the crown, Blickling had always been occupied by men of status and distinction, and formed part of scattered estates of owners, most recently the Boleyns and Cleres, who made little attempt to consolidate in the immediate area. However, in 1531 Henry VIII granted Sir James Boleyn lands of the bishopric of Norwich in Marsham and Hevingham Park, followed in 1539 by the crown's ancient manor of Cawston. On Boleyn's death in 1561, when the estate was divided between the descendants of his two nieces, Elizabeth I and Sir Edward Clere, Cawston, Marsham and Hevingham Park returned to the crown while Blickling came to the Cleres. Sir Henry may have had an expectation of a royal grant, but he needed to consolidate his holding. In his quest he engaged his cousins Edward Hobart and Sir John Hobart of Spitalfield. Gradually, they built up a hierarchy of properties

---

46   The bargain and sale of 1616 was between 'Sir Edward Clere [her stepson], the Old Lady and Mr Smith' and servants of Lord Hobart. John Smith was Agnes Clere's son from an earlier marriage, who had made purchases of land in Blickling for his mother. He received £1600 of the £5500 capital paid to Sir Edward Clere for debts.

47   In 1624 Sir Henry added his own comment on the annuity 'which I will have instanlie paid though it be a good deal more that her estate that I had of her, but it is her best livelihood'.

48   Sir Henry built the market cross that still graces the market place at Wymondham: Blomefield, *Norfolk*, vol. 2, p. 499. Weybourne formed part of her settlement with Agnes's third husband, Sir Christopher Heydon.

49   Blomefield, *Norfolk*, vol. 6, pp. 381–409; Griffiths, 'Management', pp. 172–84; Griffiths, 'The Boleyns at Blickling', pp. 453–68.

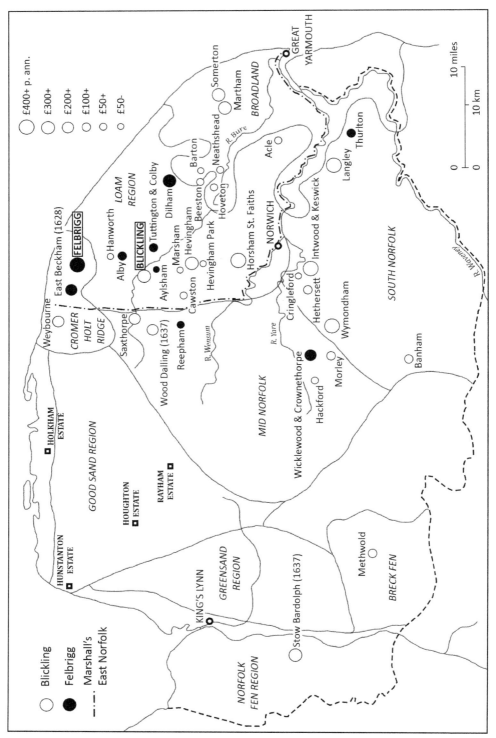

Figure 4.2 Location of the Blickling and Felbrigg estates, 1625.

with Blickling at the apex and satellites producing the income and supplies for rebuilding, furnishing and maintaining the hall, while Langley and Intwood, and later Wymondham, continued to support the family at Chapelfield, Norwich, with food, fuel and a reliable rental.

The first acquisition north of the city was Thomas Thetford's estate at Hevingham, Saxthorpe and Ketteringham Rectory. The Thetfords had been established at Hevingham since the fifteenth century, but acquired the manors at Saxthorpe only in 1588.[50] The reason for the sale was the need to repay loans to various landowners, including Sir Henry. He paid £8000 for the whole estate, valued at £573 a year, which was fourteen years' purchase, well below the market expectation of twenty years.[51] In the event, Sir John Hobart's valuation for Saxthorpe at £233 a year proved over-optimistic, but at £300 he underestimated the potential of Hevingham, and he was lucky with the £40 valuation for the rectory. Clearly, Sir Henry was not averse to a bit of asset stripping and taking a quick profit; Sir William Paston, as part-payment of his loan, had accepted the rectory at Ketteringham for £800.

So why did Hevingham succeed while Saxthorpe proved disappointing? At first glance Saxthorpe – with its consolidated holding, comprising both manors of Micklehall and Loundhall, leased to a single tenant – looks like a modernised estate, while Hevingham, with forty-nine holdings, resembles a medieval structure awaiting improvement. In a sense the impression is correct, but at Saxthorpe the process had gone too far and destroyed the balance of arable, pasture and meadow.[52] This was the handiwork of the Heydon family, who, having created extensive pastures for their huge sheep flocks, switched to arable as grain prices started to rise.[53] The switch to a more profitable enterprise was understandable, but it had long-term consequences for the fertility of the light soil and did not prevent the sale of their once great estate.[54] Saxthorpe was ripe for improvement, but in this case the need was to reinstate an earlier and more sustainable structure. The Hobarts consistently invested in buildings, management, reorganisation and planting, but with little effect, and rents never reached the valuation of 1608. The value of this property lay in its proximity to Blickling and the provision of barley and oats for the household.

At Hevingham the key to success was the survival of five manor sites and four medium-sized holdings, each with a core of permanent pasture and meadow, which served as centres of consolidation and improvement. Sir John's valuation shows that these nine holdings accounted for about 550 acres, while about 350 acres was divided between the remaining forty holdings. He had exaggerated the acreage

---

50　Blomefield, *Norfolk*, vol. 6, pp. 498, 376. The two manors in Saxthorpe were purchased by Sir Christopher Heydon in about 1562 and sold by Sir William Heydon to Andrew and Thomas Thetford in 1588. In 1593 the Thetfords acquired Catts manor in Hevingham.

51　Griffiths, 'Management', pp. 136–44.

52　Griffiths, 'Management', pp. 145–8.

53　Sir Christopher Heydon (1517–79), his son Sir William (1540–94) and his grandson Sir Christopher (1561–1623) were all likely to have played a part in this process.

54　Smith, *County and Court*, pp. 164–6 describes the descent of the Heydons and the weakness of temperament that marked these three generations.

by about 100 acres and there was repetition in the number of holdings, but the fragmentation was still severe. Rents ranged from 2s 6d per acre for arable pieces to 16s for enclosed pasture and 20s for meadow, and averaged 6s 6d per acre. When it came to reorganising and reletting the holdings in 1610, Sir Henry reduced the number to thirty by adding low-rated arable to the larger holdings. In this way he raised the average for arable to 6s per acre and the overall average to 7s 6d per acre. The over-estimate of the acreage meant that the total rental did not advance at this stage, but by the 1630s the benefits of Sir Henry's reforms were clearly evident. When leases were renewed in 1628 rents increased to £357 a year from nineteen holdings, a 19 per cent rise since 1610. In contrast, at Saxthorpe rents continued to decline to £172 by 1641 compared with £207 10s in 1610, a fall of 17 per cent, and 28 per cent less than Sir John Hobart's valuation.

As at Intwood and Langley, Sir Henry enforced his policy through detailed leases, seventeen of which survive. The covenants had settled into a standardised format designed to promote well-tended farmsteads, protect pasture and encourage good husbandry. As at Langley, the smallest holdings were not neglected. Significantly, these leases highlight the structural problem with holdings without adequate pasture to keep stock and provide sufficient manure. Tenants were required to 'muck well' at their own charge, an additional cost, which explains the very low rents and the need for consolidation. Creating and maintaining soil fertility, and the structures and conditions that promoted it, underpinned improvement, especially on these very light soils. The situation at Saxthorpe illustrated what happened when these principles were ignored.

The crown lands acquired in 1610 and 1611 at Marsham, Hevingham Park and Cawston provided a useful addition to Thomas Thetford's estate (Figure 4.2), but, as with the Broadland properties, they were a mixed bag and required different policies. The lands at Marsham, which included the foldcourse and a sixty-acre close, were relet at an increased rent with strict covenants. Later the holding was amalgamated with Rippon Hall, the largest manorial site in Hevingham, to create a substantial holding of several hundred acres.[55] In contrast, Hevingham Park, situated on the impoverished heathland soils, continued to be leased as a separate holding at a low rent with minimal management, awaiting a buyer.[56]

While Sir Henry received the lands at Marsham and Hevingham Park as a royal gift in perpetuity, he purchased Cawston for £1454 from 'certayne contractors' for his majesty's commissioners for the sale of lands, confirmed by Letters Patent in 1611.[57] He also successfully petitioned for the advowson of Cawston church as 'it lyes in the country where I was borne and neare my dwelling'. The grant was confirmed by 'R. Salisbury'. The royal gift and this transaction indicate that by this time Sir Henry's acquisition of Blickling was anticipated and James I was pleased to reward him. Likewise, in 1622 he granted Sir Henry a lease of the manor of Aylsham Lancaster in

---

55   Griffiths,'Management', pp. 149–51. The Rippon Hall estate still survives as a well-tended estate, with excellent hedgerow trees, owned by the Birkbeck family.

56   Hevingham Park was sold to William Marsham of Stratton Strawless in 1659.

57   Griffiths,'Management', pp. 151–8.

recognition of his service as Chancellor to the Prince of Wales and in 1625 he agreed in principal to Sir Henry's request to purchase the freehold.[58]

Sir Henry was not alone in his desire to acquire the royal manors in Cawston. In 1601 the neighbouring landowner Clement Herne of Haveringland made an assessment of the potential value of the property, which shows how these landowners competed for the crown lands.[59] The task was to calculate the scope for improvement on what was widely acknowledged to be heavily undervalued land. Thus, while the general rate of purchase was accepted as twenty years' rental value, Herne expected to pay double or even treble in purchases from the king, because 'the King's demaines for the most past have been demised at such an under rate that a very gainful improvement may easily be made thereof to countervaile the seeming high rate of purchase'. At that time, the crown received a yearly revenue of £54 from Cawston, which, at twenty years, meant the property was valued at £1080, and 'this being doubled' resulted in a valuation of £2160, which was regarded as 'a sufficient price for the manor'.[60] The demesne was 'in lease for 30, 20 and 10 years and at great undervalue' but the entry fines were fixed and there was no income from 'forfeitures of copyhoulders, wast of houses, fell of timber, demising for years, or any other causes of excheate usual in other manors'. In other words, the scope for improvement was confined to three rented holdings. Herne calculated that they would yield a further £105 over many years, which, added to £54, made £159; and at twenty years' purchase this made £3180. Against this figure £900 was deducted for the unexpired leases, which came to a final valuation of £2280. We don't know whether Herne offered this sum, but it was significantly greater than the £1454 paid by Sir Henry in 1611; even at this price, however, it was not a bargain.

The problem at Cawston, as Herne indicated, was a total collapse of control, which allowed the tenantry to encroach on the full range of ancient rights held by the crown or the lord in occupation.[61] These included the hugely profitable grazing rights across the heathland and the right of shack – grazing after harvest – over the open fields. Gradually, parcels of open-field strips and swathes of heathland were enclosed, thereby excluding the lord's sheep. The status of copyhold fines was also challenged. Clement Herne, a substantial copyholder in Cawston, went to law to prove that fines were 'certaine' rather than 'arbitrable'; his success greatly contributed to the augmentation of his estate in neighbouring Haveringland, and to the fragmentation of the crown's estate in Cawston. So, by the time Sir Henry purchased the property, the scope for improvement was severely restricted. The unexpired term of the lease on the main holding, Leeches and Baywoods, delayed any major reform.[62]

---

58 Griffiths, 'Management' pp. 179–81, 259–65. Sir Henry's death delayed proceedings and left his son to fight a long costly battle for the manor, which was not secured until 1647. Griffiths, 'Improving landlords', pp. 172–4.

59 A Particular of the manor of Cawston, 1601, NRS 27229 361 x 3.

60 Elizabeth I inherited the property from her uncle Sir James Boleyn in 1561; in 1562 she commissioned a survey widely used by historians: see NRO, MS 4521 Map Box E; Griffiths, 'Management', p. 153.

61 For a full description, Blomefield, *Norfolk*, vol. 6, pp. 254–68.

62 The £60 anticipated improvement on Leeches and Baywood was finally achieved in 1645.

Despite the constraints, Sir Henry effected improvement where he could. In 1612 he leased a wood for £6, with strict covenants as to its management, let the market stalls with the windmill and a few arable pieces for another £6, and relet a holding for £4 16s, way below the estimated improvement of £15. He had more success with the foldcourse and warren, which fulfilled the expectation of a £30 increase. Overall, between 1611 and 1625, the rents rose from £54 to £90, which, with a further £60 due for Baywoods, was still £9 short of Herne's estimate. However, as with Saxthorpe, this failure was offset by the proximity to Blickling. Consequently, the Hobarts persevered and even attempted to consolidate the fragmented estate, but, as with the manor of Oulton, which lay even closer to Blickling, Sir John Hobart and his nephew succumbed to attractive offers from Erasmus Earle (1590–1662), another lawyer on his way up the legal ladder, who had just purchased an estate at nearby Heydon.[63]

Sir Henry's final acquisition on the northern heathlands, the estate of the old priory at Horsham St Faith, was the most adventurous and rigorous test of his legal skills, which gave him a clear advantage in the market, as he noted: 'That it is fitt for me makes it less fitt for others'.[64] The initial transaction was straightforward, but Sir Henry needed to reunite the priory with its lands and extensive grazing rights in Horsford, from which the tenants had been excluded by Sampson Lennard, Lord Dacre of the South, the new lord of the principal manor of Horsford.[65] The dispute led to a protracted legal case and much documentation, which illustrates further the problems associated with the properties sharing the resources of the northern heathland.[66] At the same time Sir Henry entered into negotiations to buy the manor of Horsford, encouraged by Leonard Mapes, party to the original sale, who produced a meticulous survey in 1615. However, despite its obvious attractions, Sir Henry was not persuaded; at sixteen years purchase, as he noted in the margin, the price was too high. For Hevingham, Cawston and Horsham St Faith he had paid fourteen years' purchase and, by this time, he had a shrewd understanding of the risks involved in the area. Mapes was disappointed, as it would have resolved the issue of the shared grazing ground at a stroke, but deferred to Sir Henry's 'great experience by much buying can better direct you than my poor judgement'.

The close links between Horsham St Faith and Horsford date back to the endowment of the Benedictine priory by the de Cheyneys, lords of the manor of Horsford, in 1105. The gift included not only a substantial estate at Horsham St Faith but certain parcels of land in Horsford and the rectory.[67] In 1250 their descendant Hugh de Cressi added the grazing rights over Horsford Park around Castle Hill, which

---

63 The Cawston estate was sold in three stages: 1637, 1649 and 1662, while Oulton was sold in 1641.

64 Griffiths, 'Management', p. 164.

65 Sampson Lennard married into the Dacre family in 1594 and inherited the title through his wife, the sister and heir of Lord Dacre: see Blomefield, *Norfolk*, vol. 10, p. 433; the Dacres were linked to the 4th duke of Norfolk, when he married, as his third wife, the widow of Thomas, Lord Dacre in 1567: Smith, *County and Court*, pp. 23–4.

66 The documents survive among the Hobart MSS at the NRO; see also Blomefield, *Norfolk*, vol. 10, pp. 433–5, 441.

67 The de Cheyneys also founded the Premonstratensian Abbey at Langley: Blomefield, *Norfolk*, vol. 10, p. 147.

lies between the two parishes. At the dissolution Sir Richard Southwell of Woodrising, one of the greatest flockmasters in the country, was granted a lease of the priory with the lands in Horsford, while the grazing rights were specifically confirmed when the estate was settled on him 'forever' in 1542.[68]

The Southwells were another great Norfolk family whose fortunes rose steeply under Henry VIII but declined sharply in the second half of the sixteenth century. In this case, their influence waned with Sir Richard's support for Mary I, which excluded him from Elizabeth I's court and tainted his descendants with the charge of recusancy.[69] Sir Richard also lived an irregular life that brought further discredit to the family. Having no children with his wife, he produced two sons and two daughters by his mistress, whom he settled at Horsham St Faith in 1543.[70] His sons, being illegitimate, could not inherit the main estate, which passed to his nephew Thomas, the heir of his brother, Sir Robert Southwell.[71] Thomas's son Robert married Elizabeth, a daughter of Lord Howard of Effingham, a match that greatly enhanced his position at court and in the county and might have led to the full recovery of the family.[72] However, after securing several offices he died in 1599 leaving a baby son, another Thomas, who died in 1643 'having wasted most of his estate which he sold to Sir Francis Crane'.[73] Likewise, the illegitimate descendants of Sir Richard Southwell failed to prosper and sold their estate at Horsham St Faith in 1598 and 1601 to Sir Charles Cornwallis and his associates.[74] The sale documents show that Sir Henry was already involved with the property in the 1590s, had dealings with the principal tenant, Richard Whall, and was party to a number of transactions.[75] So, when Cornwallis with Sir Thomas Richardson and Leonard Mapes decided to sell in 1612, Sir Henry was the obvious buyer.

---

68 Sir Richard Southwell (1502–64), a favourite courtier of Henry VIII and a commissioner for the dissolution of the monasteries, acquired monastic property in Norfolk on a scale second only to the duke of Norfok and Sir Thomas Gresham: see T.H. Swales, 'The redistribution of monastic lands in Norfolk at the dissolution', *Norfolk Archaeology*, 34 (1966), p. 22. In 1545 his estate amounted to thirty manors in Norfolk: Blomefield, *Norfolk*, vol. 10, pp. 276–7.

69 Smith, *County and Court*, pp. 4, 65–6; Blomefield, *Norfolk*, vol. 10, pp. 273–9.

70 For the details of this lurid tale see Sir Henry Spelman, *The History and Fate of Sacrilege* (1632, republished 1853), pp. 252–4.

71 For Southwell's pedigree see Blomefield, *Norfolk*, vol. 10, p. 275. Sir Richard's illegitimate family included his grandson, Robert Southwell, the Jesuit priest, poet and martyr, canonised in 1970 as one of the Forty Martyrs.

72 Smith, *County and Court*, pp. 65–6.

73 Blomefield, *Norfolk*, vol. 10, p. 278.

74 Sir Richard's grandson, another Richard, married Thomasina, a daughter of Sir Thomas Cornwallis, the father of Sir Charles Cornwallis; this may well be his link with Horsham St Faith's: see Spelman, *History and Fate*, p. 253. Sir Charles Cornwallis of Brome Hall, Suffolk (1555–1629), MP for Norfolk 1604 with Sir Nathaniel Bacon, leader of the County party: see Smith, *County and Court*, pp. 329–30; <www.historyofparliament.org.uk>. Blomefield, *Norfolk*, vol. 10, p. 441, does not mention Cornwallis, stating the purchaser as 'Sir Henry Hobart the judge'.

75 Griffiths, 'Management', pp. 161–2. Sir Henry paid £980 to Whall for lands in Acle at the same time as he purchased a manor in Acle from Thomas Clere.

The sale by three vendors and the subsequent management of the estate at Horsham St Faith is an indication of the complexity of the property and the various interests involved. Apart from the new leases granted to Richard Whall for the Abbey and the Guildhouse, Sir Henry accepted those granted by Cornwallis in 1604 and 1610.[76] From the particular of Horsford we find that Whall also leased the site of Horsford Castle and its lands, while Richard Green, the tenant of the warren and foldcourse at Horsham St Faith, rented the heathland and very large foldcourse at Horsford; so there was a desperate need to resolve the dispute over the grazing rights. This difficulty probably explains why Sir Henry secured the property at well below the market value.[77] More complexity was created by the management of a huge cattle fair, St Faith's Fair, held in the first week of October. This handled the traffic of 'Scots runts' from the Highlands to Norfolk graziers who purchased the stores for fattening on the lush Norwich and Yarmouth marshes.[78] So great was the trade that they not only supplied Norwich and Yarmouth but sent vast quantities to London every week during the winter months. To deal with the fair, one of the greatest in the country, the village required a tollhouse and a prison – and a trustworthy and competent tenant to manage them. For this task Sir Henry granted Richard Whall a sixty-year lease for a nominal rent of 6s 8d with the requirement to build a new prison at this own cost, allowing him to benefit from the proceeds. The profits of the regular market were leased separately for an annual rent of £20, compared to £1 6s 8d for the market at Cawston and £3 18s for the Fish Stalls and Butchers Shambles at Wymondham. So, overall, a property with huge potential, but it needed sorting out and careful management to realise the full value.

Sir Henry moved swiftly to resolve the dispute with Sampson Lennard. The legal process started with a Commission of Enquiry in 1613 that stated the basis of Sir Henry's claim, the grant made to Sir Richard Southwell of the priory of Horsham St Faith in 1542, the counter-claim and action taken by Lennard. This was followed by witness statements that supported Sir Henry's claim in terms of the location of the shared grazing and the evidence of it taking place; this included the summer grazing of twenty cows and one bull kept by Richard Southwell. Judgement found in Sir Henry's favour and he was compensated with four closes in Horsford amounting to thirty-five acres. He also secured a further twenty acres, known as the Manor Peece in Horsham St Faith, which he claimed the priory had acquired in exchange

---

76   In 1613 Sir Henry granted Whall twenty-one-year leases for the abbey and guildhouse for £94 3s.

77   In his Declaration of Trust (1620) Sir Henry noted that 'the manors of Wymondham cost more by £3000 than St. Faith's and Cawston together'. It is unlikely that he paid more than a purchase price of twenty times the annual rent for Wymondham, or £10,000, which, deducting £3000 and £1454 for Cawston, leaves a sum of £5500 for St Faith's. At the rental value in 1612 this amounted to fifteen years purchase price, but once he received the Horsford lands in 1617, which was the gamble, it became much cheaper, at twelve and a half years purchase price.

78   The fair was held on Bullock Hill and Calf Lane until 1872, <www.heritage.norfolk.gov.uk>; for the most graphic description see D. Defoe, *A Tour Thro' the Whole Island of Great Britain*, Vol. 1 (London, 1724), p. 97; Blomefield, *Norfolk*, vol. 10, p. 441 for the origins of the fair in 1105 and the prison built by Hugh de Cressi in 1256.

for sixty acres in Drayton in 1521. Judgement again found in Sir Henry's favour.[79] In this contest over legal titles the Dacres were clearly no match for Sir Henry. He was perfectly aware of his advantage and exploited it to the full. To rub salt into their wounds, Sir Henry then declined to buy the manor of Horsford, the value of which he had so skilfully comprised.[80] However, Sir Henry had just spent huge sums of money securing his life's ambition, the estate at Blickling. In particular, he needed to manage his resources judiciously to complete the rebuilding of the hall initiated by Sir Edward Clere.

III

In 1615 Robert Clere, the highly regarded son of Sir Edward and Agnes and heir to his mother's estate at Blickling, died unmarried in his early thirties, so it was time for Sir Henry to support Agnes in her old age and find a safe solution for Blickling. With its deep association with Elizabeth I, saving Blickling for posterity was his ultimate aim.[81] His marriage at Blickling suggests that his affection for the place was long held, perhaps dating back to childhood, when the family visited their friends, the Cleres of Ormesby, in their new and splendid inheritance. Whatever the reason, Sir Henry's feelings for Blickling were profound; as he said to James I, in his petition for freehold of the neighbouring manor of Aylsham Lancaster in 1625, 'I will give what pence they [the contractors] will sett upon it, for I seek it not for profytt but for ornament and convenyancye.'[82]

The Cleres, like the Le Stranges, were an ancient family. They had been lords of a huge estate centred at Ormesby, a few miles north of Yarmouth, since the thirteenth century.[83] In about 1508 Sir Robert Clere married as his second wife Alice, a daughter of Sir William Boleyn of Blickling; they had a large family and benefited greatly from the connections at court enjoyed by Alice's eldest brother Sir Thomas Boleyn. His meteoric rise was facilitated by his links to the Howard family, who were busily re-establishing their position with the Tudors, having supported the Yorkist cause.[84] By the early 1500s Thomas Howard, earl of Surrey, had recovered most of his lands in Norfolk and could look forward to the restoration of his father's dukedom. Thomas Boleyn, highly educated, fluent in several languages and an accomplished sportsman, entered royal service at the court of Henry, Prince of Wales. He continued

---

79 Sir Henry later purchased the sixty acres in Drayton.

80 The Barrett-Lennards survived as a much diminished family at Horsford until 1970.

81 Blomefield, *Norfolk*, vol. 6, pp. 389–95; Griffiths, 'The Boleyns at Blickling'; see also Griffiths, 'Management', pp. 172–84.

82 Griffiths, 'Management', p. 180 for full petition. Aylsham abuts the Blickling estate.

83 Blomefield, *Norfolk*, vol. 11, pp. 231–40. The entry for Ormesby and the pedigree for the Cleres is very sketchy, unlike that for the Le Stranges: Blomefield, *Norfolk*, vol. 10, p. 314; more detail of the Clere family history is included under Blickling: Blomefield, *Norfolk*, vol. 6, pp. 389–95.

84 R. Virgoe, 'The recovery of the Howards in East Anglia, 1485–1529', in C. Barron, C. Rawcliffe and J.T. Rosenthal (eds), *East Anglian Society and the Political Community in Late Medieval England: Selected Papers of Roger Virgoe* (Norwich, 1997); see also Griffiths, 'The Boleyns at Blickling', pp. 462–4, fns 78, 81.

to serve Henry as king in various capacities, notably as a diplomat and political fixer. Thomas also married Elizabeth, eldest daughter of Thomas Howard, by then 2nd duke of Norfolk.[85] But, as we know, Sir Thomas Boleyn overreached himself, as did his daughter, Anne, in her marriage to Henry VIII. We need not remind ourselves of the circumstances of their demise; suffice to say it had implications at Blickling, as the estate passed to his younger brother Sir James Boleyn, who died without issue in 1561. The estate was then divided between Elizabeth I and Sir John Clere's third son Edward Clere.

John Clere (1511–57) was a credit to the family, served as an admiral and received grants of monastic lands for military service to Henry VIII, but, unfortunately, died in action in 1557, leaving Edward (1536–1606) in charge. At about that time Edward married Frances (1540–79), the daughter and heiress of Sir Richard Fulmerston, and inherited his vast estate at Thetford on Sir Richard's death in 1567.[86] In this way, the Cleres became a great county family, second only to the duke of Norfolk. The problem was that Sir John's descendants had little appetite for estate management, preferring the high life and basking in reflected glory. This was always a risky policy, but potentially disastrous in period of high inflation.

Sir Edward Clere played a major role in Smith's *County and Court* as the leader of the court party that emerged to fill the vacuum created by the execution of the duke of Norfolk in 1572. By that time Sir Edward had established a significant power base in Thetford, in addition to Blicking, Ormesby and London, and was determined with others of similar persuasion – notably Sir Arthur Heveningham, the Heydons, Lovells and Southwells – to secure offices and advantages for those ancient families loyal to the crown.[87] With rising prices and a lavish lifestyle, these families, steeped in custom and tradition, often found themselves in financial difficulties. The duke's demise provided them with a golden opportunity to replenish their coffers. However, they were no match for the county party, led by the lawyers, the sons of Sir Nicholas Bacon, the Lord Keeper, Francis Wyndham, several members of the Gawdy family and at court by Sir Edward Coke, who sought to constrain the power of the Council.[88] Sir Henry Hobart, perhaps because of his association with the Cleres, kept a lower profile. In the subsidy book Sir Edward Clere was regularly rated above £100 and in 1588 Burghley included him in a list of prospective barons, describing him as 'a knight of great possessions', but he was 'not to be called thereto without some precedent *service* to *deserve* the same'. Sir Edward and his associates did not understand the new reality; they could no longer bribe, bully or bluster their way to fortune without challenge and incurring deep unpopularity. Working in their own interests, rather than that of the county, eventually excluded them from lucrative positions and sealed their fate.

---

85   Sir Robert Clere (d. 1529), Sir Thomas Boleyn (1477–1539) and Sir Thomas Le Strange (1490–1545) all attended Henry VIII at Field of the Cloth of Gold, 1520. Sir John Clere, an active soldier, d. in action in 1557: see Smith, *County and Court*, pp. 160–3.

86   Sir Richard Fulmerston (1516–67), treasurer to Thomas, 4th duke of Norfolk from 1558, <www.historyofparliament.org.uk>; see Smith, *County and Court*, pp. 32–9.

87   Dramatis Personae for the court party: see Smith, *County and Court*, pp. 157–67.

88   Dramatis Personae for the county party: see Smith, *County and Court*, pp. 167–80.

In graphic detail Smith describes the Cleres' ineptitude and hubris. Despite his wealth in land, Sir Edward lacked an income sufficient to sustain the dignity of a baron. The few letters and papers that have survived show him floundering with his estate management, frequently in debt, borrowing from friends, often involved in litigation, without funds to purchase cattle and sheep for his pastures and unable to pay for his son's rooms at Cambridge.[89] By 1594 he was in the Fleet prison, presumably for debt. As Sir Edward's son, another Edward (1563–1626), grew to maturity the family became more profligate and disreputable; by 1585 young Edward was 'in peril divers ways of imprisonment and shame'.[90] Even his father doubted his ability to settle down and manage the estate. However, he married in his mid-thirties and produced a son, Henry, in 1598, but this did not satisfy or placate Sir Edward. In his will of 1605, quoted in a later enquiry, he left a significant portion of his estate to his second wife Agnes and their son Robert, a gentleman 'of admirable temperance', and his brother Francis.[91] He also diverted the historic lands at Ormesby to his grandson, by means of a conveyance to trustees for fifteen years until Henry reached his majority in 1620.[92] On his death the estate would pass to Henry's heirs, bypassing his father, who lived until 1626.[93] Sir Edward's will makes no mention of the estate in Thetford, but scattered references in Blomefield suggests that the Howard family reacquired it between 1594 and 1604.[94] As if to signal a revival of the family, James I created Henry a baronet on his coming of age, but, alas, he died in 1622, leaving a baby daughter, Abigail; evidence of her marriage and living on parts of the Ormesby estate survive, but only for a single generation.[95]

The detail of Sir Edward's will suggests a new understanding and a genuine attempt to turn the tide of the family misfortune. The conveyance to the trustees

---

89   Smith, *County and Court*, p. 160.

90   Smith, *County and Court*, p. 161.

91   Smith, *County and Court*, p. 161. The will of 1605 can be found in NRO, COL/13/20 (c) as part of an enquiry instigated by his son in 1611, possibly after the death of his brother, Francis, in 1610. Francis received lands in Suffolk, Norwich and in the hundreds of Blofield, Walsham, Loddon and Clavering; Agnes, over and above her dowry, the manors in Weybourne from Sir Christopher Heydon; all other purchased lands and the increase of rents in Wymondham and Tharston, with other purchased lands in N. and S. Erpingham Hundreds, which included Blickling. After her death, Sir Edward stated that these would pass 'to my son Robert', who also received his lands in Freebridge Lynn. There is no mention of the Thetford estate in Sir Edward's will, but scattered evidence in Blomefield, *Norfolk* (vol. 2, pp. 57, 66, 70–5, 86, 93, 100) suggests that it passed to the Howard family between 1594 and 1604.

92   Blomefield, *Norfolk*, vol. 6, p. 303. fns 3 and 4: Henry (1598–1622) inherited an estate worth £1200, which passed to his daughter Abigail, who married John, a son of Oliver Cromwell.

93   Sir Edward lived on the original manors and the old rents with half the rent of the Ormesby lands, but without the remainder and right to sell it or the others manors, which were effectively shared with his stepmother and stepbrother – hence the sale of Blickling in 1616 after the death of Robert.

94   Blomefield, *Norfolk*, vol. 2, pp. 57, 66, 70–5, 86, 93, 100.

95   Henry married Muriel, a daughter of Sir Edmund Mundeford (1595–1643) of Feltwell, Norfolk. For Abigail, see Blomefield, *Norfolk*, vol. 7, p. 212, vol. 11, pp. 154, 247. Abigail and John Cromwell had two children.

instructs them to direct the profits 'to the good bringing up of [Henry] in learning and virtuous exercise', with the surplus spent on maintaining estate buildings and paying off debts.[96] There is a clear recognition that their problems were associated with inadequate education, poor guidance and a lack of morality. His dramatic decision to bypass his son Sir Edward may have been influenced by Agnes and the example of their admirable son, Robert. The granting of a baronetcy to Henry in 1620 suggests there had been a measure of success, but with his untimely death we will never know if it was sufficient to reverse such a steep decline. The longevity of his father and the continuing drain on the estate would not have helped the young man. As his grandfather seems to have acknowledged, the decline of the Cleres was not simply a matter of ineptitude but a failure of character passed down from generation to generation. His action was an attempt to break that succession. In the event the matter was resolved by the failure of the male line and the extinction of the family.

IV

The experience of the Cleres, as well as that of the Southwells and Heydons, illustrates the range of problems that could afflict gentry families and affect their ability to survive. As we have seen, it was not simply a matter of incompetence, adherence to the Catholic faith or failure of the male line. More corrosive was the 'weakness of character' that developed in these leading families.[97] It manifested itself in lavish lifestyles, high-handedness, feuding with families, tenants and neighbours, reneging on debts, taking bribes, violent behaviour and even spells in prison. These degenerate traits became the subject of jokes, as Sir Nicholas Le Strange, Sir Hamon's eldest son, described Sir Robert Crane, nephew of Agnes Clere and son-in-law of Sir Henry Hobart, 'as a gentleman very prone to venery and one that declined few that came his way fit for that sport'.[98] Less amusing was Sir William Heydon's threat to his son Sir Christopher in 1590 that he would fell all the trees on the estate and demolish the castle at Baconsthorpe to repay his debts. Sir Christopher raised money from friends to save the trees, but it required the intervention of the Privy Council to save the castle and prevent Sir William entering 'into an action so hurtful to himself & his posteritie'.[99] The ruins of the castle survive to this day, but the weakness in the family continued, as Sir Christopher developed a passion for duelling and astrology, rather than attending to his estate management.[100] As with the Southwells and the Cleres, the once great Heydons of Baconsthorpe petered out in the 1640s.

The irony is that the new estates assembled by the great lawyers were not immune to degenerative behaviour either. Sir Edward Coke thought a legal training

---

96   NRO, COL/13/20 (c).

97   Smith, *County and Court*.

98   H.F. Lippincott (ed.), *'Merry Passages and Jeasts': A Manuscript Notebook of Sir Nicholas Le Strange*, Salzburg Studies in English Literature; Elizabethan and Renaissance Studies xxix (Salzburg, 1974), p. 15; see also Sir Robert Crane (1586–1643), <www.historyofparliamentonline.org>.

99   Smith, *County and Court*, pp. 163–6.

100   Blomefield, *Norfolk*, vol. 6, pp. 502–13.

offered protection: 'a great lawyer never dies *improlis aut intestatus*, and his posterity continues to flourish to distant generations.'[101] However, his sons quickly acquired a notorious reputation for profligacy and hubris, with the notable exception of his fourth son John, who married a local heiress, Muriel Wheatley, at Holkham and built up his inheritance.[102] Throughout the seventeenth century, as male lines repeatedly failed, Coke's ambition of founding a dynasty often hung by a thread. But for the minority of Thomas Coke and the exemplary work of the trustees from 1707 to 1718, the 'great estate' might not have survived. As it happens, the early death of Thomas's dissolute son Edward and the passing of the estate through the female line probably saved the family and estate for posterity.[103]

Sir Henry Hobart's dynastic ambitions proved equally fragile. He had twelve sons compared with Sir Edward's eight, but only four produced families, so there should have been enough to go around. Sir John's daughter and heiress, Phillipa, married her first cousin, John, the heir of Miles Hobart of Intwood, in 1647. In this way they reunited the principal parts of the Norfolk estate.[104] However, by this time Sir John was heavily in debt, with properties having to be sold on his death to repay loans.[105] His son-in-law was similarly profligate. Thus, the Hobarts entered a downward spiral, rescued at intervals by lucrative marriages until they achieved relative security in 1717.[106] In their case, the demon was parliamentary politics, which proved financially disastrous. From the 1620s to the 1690s this passion, which affected three generations, required all the paraphernalia of a house in London, building a network oiled with much hospitability, fighting elections and often winning them, but not enjoying the perquisites and offices distributed by the crown. In the meantime, estate management was delegated to professionals; they were not incompetent, but the estate simply could not bear the strain imposed by unrelieved politicking and the high living that went with it.

The common thread between the Cokes and the Hobarts was that their families had been elevated to such heights, and married so well, that they seemed to require a lifestyle to match. The great estate was a means to an end, not an end in itself; it provided the wealth and support to advance their status and power and

---

101 James, *Chief Justice Coke*, p. 78, quoting Coke's words in a chapter on his spendthrift family.

102 James, *Chief Justice Coke*, attributes this failure to the early death of Coke's wife Bridget, leaving eight young children – six sons and two daughters – without a maternal influence. It probably affected Coke too, who was often described as hot tempered and avaricious; see also Hiskey, *Holkham*, pp. 13–43.

103 Following the death of Thomas's widow in 1775 the estate passed to Wenman Roberts, the son of Alice, his youngest sister, who had eloped with Phillip Roberts and produced the much needed heir: Hiskey, *Holkham*, pp. 71, 243.

104 Sir Henry's third son, Nathaniel, was settled in Lincolnshire, while James had a small estate in Suffolk.

105 To be fair, Sir John still had to cope with the rebuilding and furnishing of the hall, and other unfinished business left by his father, such as the purchase of the manor of Aylsham Lancaster.

106 Sir John Hobart, 5th Bt (1693–1756), m. Judith, d. and co-heiress of Robert Britiffe (1663–1749) of Norwich and Baconsthorpe, MP for Norwich 1714–34, Recorder of Lynn 1704–30 and of Norwich 1737–43).

to achieve the ultimate aim of a new dynasty and a permanent legacy. But, as we have seen, great ambitions could be thwarted in so many ways. Building an estate was one matter, handing it down successfully to your successors was another issue altogether. The Cokes were fortunate that John established himself at Holkham with a local wife and developed a deep attachment to the locality, at a distance from his overbearing father and quarrelling brothers. He soon settled into the coastal locality, populated with gentry families such as the Le Stranges and Bacons. In fact, John's youngest daughter, Mary, married Sir Hamon's grandson Sir Nicholas, 3rd Bt (1632–69), in 1657. Their son, Sir Nicholas, 4th Bt (1661–1724), we recognise as the reformer who picked up the threads for the Le Strange family after another long minority in the 1680s.

So, it seems to be that the key to longevity was to commit yourself to the care and management of your estate and community and to pass on that culture to your children. The Cokes settled into this pattern in the eighteenth century, while Sir Hamon and Alice reached that point in the first half of the seventeenth century, albeit with the benefit of a well-tended medieval inheritance and some good guidance. In the next chapter we will examine how they built on that inheritance and secured it for the future. From the notorious examples that littered the county, they had learnt the price of inactivity.

Chapter 5

The knowledge economy of
the Le Strange family

The idea of Sir Hamon and Alice creating a knowledge economy at Hunstanton in the 1600s might appear a presumptuous claim, but, if we consider the modern definitions of the term, this seems to be what they were trying to do.[1] The World Bank defines 'knowledge economy' in a way that Hamon would have readily appreciated: 'a knowledge economy is one that utilises knowledge to develop and sustain long term growth'. For this to happen, however, four pillars need to be built: first, an economic and institutional regime that is conducive to the creation, diffusion and utilisation of knowledge; second, a well-educated and skilled population that creates, shares and uses knowledge efficiently; third, a dynamic information infrastructure that facilies the communication and processing of information and technology; and, finally, an innovation system of research centres, universities and other organisations that apply and adapt global knowledge to local needs to create new technology.[2] All these factors, working in unison, raise economic productivity.

As the World Bank steers under-developed countries to move in this direction, we recognise that elements of these pillars were already in place in early seventeenth-century England. In James I the country had gained an enthusiast for reform, who not only launched his own projects, modernising the crown lands and draining the Fens, but called upon landowners to leave the court, return to the country and improve their estates, which is precisely what Sir Hamon did in 1604.[3] Thus, the crown promoted a culture of improvement that stimulated a need for institutions and a demand for information and education. Education at this time may not have been universal, but it was sufficient to provide leadership, governance and guidance even in the most remote rural communities, largely through the good offices of the principal landowner, enterprising farmers and the vicar, a literate figure with significant influence. Similarly, the information

---

1 Sir Hamon (1583–1654). To avoid constant repetition we announce his full identity at the start of the chapter, and then drop the title. More difficult is the treatment of several Sir Nicholases, father, son, grandson and great-grandson; in this case a date will clarify identity when it is not self-evident.

2 The Overseas Development Institute provides a handy introduction to the World Bank's Knowledge Economy Framework, designed to promote the creation of knowledge economies in a global economy. <www.odi.org/publications/5693-world-bank-knowledge-economy-framework>.

3 Griffiths, '"A Country Life"', pp. 207–9; R. Hoyle (ed.), *The Estates of the English Crown* (Cambridge, 1992); Eric H. Ash, *The Draining of the Fens: Projectors, Popular Politics and State Building in Early Modern England* (Baltimore, MD, 2017); James I, 'Counsel for Ladies and Gentlemen', in A. Fowler, *The Country House Poem* (Edinburgh, 1994), p. 101; L. Marcus, 'Politics and the Pastoral', in K. Sharpe and P. Lake (eds), *Culture and Politics in Early Stuart England* (Stanford, CA, 1994), pp. 139–59.

structure may not have had the radio, television or internet, but there were books a plenty, with developing networks of readers and correspondents.[4] Likewise, the innovation system was restricted, but nonetheless produced great writers and philosophers, notably Sir Francis Bacon (1561–1626), who analysed the concept of knowledge, coining the phrase usually simplified as 'knowledge is power', which remains the essence of our understanding about the value of knowledge.[5] So, developments may have been in their infancy, but the value and power of knowledge was clearly understood and there was no institutional or cultural impediment to further progress; in fact, under the leadership of James I the reverse was true. In their enthusiasm for knowledge management, Hamon and Alice were certainly unusual, but they were not operating in a vacuum.

In this context the quality of the mentors enjoyed by Hamon from his early years and later with Alice was vital. Principal among these, as we have seen, were Sir Henry Hobart and Sir Henry Spelman.[6] Both were contemporaries and associates of Francis Bacon, while the Le Stranges were neighbours of his elder brother, Sir Nathaniel Bacon, who had been settled by his father, Sir Nicholas Bacon (1510–79), the Lord Keeper, on an estate at Stiffkey in 1570.[7] However, Francis did not share his brother's interest in Norfolk politics, preferring a more scholarly life in London, where he had been born and was brought up by his mother, the Lord Keeper's second wife Anne, daughter of the humanist Sir Anthony Cooke. As the youngest son, Francis missed out on a significant inheritance and made his way as a lawyer, politician and senior office holder, but his real interest lay in philosophy. His public career ended in disgrace in 1621, when he was found guilty of corruption, but at least it left him more time to pursue his academic interests.[8]

In a vast array of philosophical works Bacon brought his ideas to bear on a wide variety of subjects, including religion, morality, literature, judicial reform and, most

---

4   Warde, *Invention of Sustainability*, pp. 102–27. In his will Sir Hamon donated surplus copies of books from his library to local clergymen (LEST/AE8 or, more accurately, TNA, PROB 11/238/248).

5   Markku Peltonen, 'Bacon, Francis, Viscount St. Alban (1561–1626)', *ODNB* (Oxford, 2004). There is a huge literature on Bacon and his works, for and introduction see P. Zagorin, *Francis Bacon* (Princeton, N.J., 1998).

6   Sir Henry Spelman did not enjoy a happy relationship with Francis Bacon. He was involved in the parliamentary petition against Bacon for corruption which led to his downfall in 1621. This may have been revenge for Bacon's judgement against him in a case involving Spelman's purchase of the leases of Blackborough Abbey and Wormegay Priory from the crown lessees in 1594: see Handley, 'Spelman, Sir Henry'; also <www.historyofparliament.org.uk>.

7   The location was determined by Nathaniel's marriage to Anne, natural daughter of Sir Thomas Gresham, who contributed nearby manors at Langham, Morston and Hemsby. A. Hassell Smith, Gillian M. Baker, Robert Wayne Kenny (eds), *The Papers of Nathaniel Bacon of Stiffkey*, vols I and II, 1556–1585, Norfolk Record Society 46 and 49 (Norwich, 1979 and 1983). Although the families shared an interest in house building and collecting books, they do not appear to have been especially close; they crossed swords, for example, over grazing rights on the marshes (LEST/Q37, fol. 19).

8   Bacon received his first significant office as solicitor general in 1607; he followed Sir Henry Hobart as attorney general in 1613, was appointed Lord Chancellor and created Baron Verulam in 1618 and, finally, was created Viscount St Alban in 1621.

particularly, the study of science and the organisation of knowledge for the promotion of learning. Sir Hamon acquired several volumes for his library demonstrating his range of interests, including Bacon's *Essays of Religious Meditations* (1597) in 1612; *A Collection of Apophthegms* in 1625; *Sylva Sylvarum* in 1627 and *The Advancement of Learning* (1605) in 1640.[9] His successors added *Omnia Philosophia Moralis* in 1665 and the *History of the Reign of King Henry VII* (1622) in 1675. These are the books listed in the catalogue, but it does not mean that others were not read or purchased, or earlier copies acquired and discarded; no doubt Sir Hamon was well acquainted with the *Advancement of Learning* long before 1640. Quite possibly, he acquired a new copy when he started corresponding with Dr Thomas Browne (1605–82) and buying his books in the 1640s.[10] Greatly influenced by Bacon's seminal work *Novum Organum* (1620), Browne published several arcane titles and is credited with being the inspiration behind John Evelyn's more practical work. At the same time, Browne practised medicine from his home in Norwich and advised families such as the Le Stranges and the Windhams on their health, while they adopted his classically inspired planting schemes for their parks and gardens.[11] Within these networks, the 'new learning', initiated by Bacon, influenced the Norfolk gentry.[12]

The principal feature of the new learning, expressed most forcefully in the *Advancement of Learning* and *Novum Organum*, was that it offered a new approach to the formulation of knowledge based on observation, experimentation and method, rather than the theoretical argument of intellectuals afflicted by 'false idols'.[13] To modern readers, this is a statement of the obvious that attests to the revolutionary nature of Bacon's thinking and enterprise. We can imagine that for a thoughtful landowner like Hamon these ideas presented an exciting way forward that was relevant to his practical concerns. Having inherited a complex geography, he would have understood Bacon's maxim 'nature is only to be commanded in obeying her', or, as Warde clarifies, 'nature could be enhanced, but also had to be

---

9   LEST/NE1. It is not entirely clear whether the dates in the library catalogue LEST/NE1 refer to publication or accession; a later date than the first publication date of a book, as above, might indicate a later edition.

10   Browne's works listed in the catalogue include *Religio Medici* (1643), *Psuedodoxia Epidemica* (1646–72), *Hydriotaphia, Urn Burial* (1658), and *The Garden of Cyrus* (1658).

11   The plans were based on *The Garden of Cyrus*, the inspiration for John Evelyn's *Elysium Britannicum*: Ketton-Cremer, *Felbrigg*, p. 62; see chapter 9 for William Windham's work on his park. See also Rosenheim, *The Townshends of Raynham*, p. 170 for Browne's approval of Raynham Hall; Warde's section on posterity in *Invention of Sustainability*, pp. 90–101, is concerned principally with tree-planting.

12   Warde, *Invention of Sustainability*, pp. 102–27. Warde is more sceptical of the contribution made by Bacon to 'improvement', but given Bacon's family background his influence among the more radical and learned Norfolk gentry might have been more significant, as perhaps seen, for example, in Sir Christopher Heydon's seminal work on astrology *A Defence of Judiciall Astrology* (1603), listed in the Le Strange catalogue.

13   Warde, *Invention of Sustainability*, p. 110.

wooed as she was found'.[14] Clearly, Hamon needed to create 'a rooted knowledge, a localized virtuosity' of his estate.[15] In a sense there was nothing new in Bacon's injunctures; farmers had always worked intuitively with nature, while agricultural writers such as Charles Estienne had been analysing the process and providing guidance to practitioners long before Bacon appeared on the scene.[16] However, Bacon advanced a much more complex idea, contained in a compelling and overarching philosophy, which amounted to a new way of thinking and learning. It was not enough to have knowledge; you needed to know how to organise and use it methodically, and to preserve it for posterity. Sir Hamon absorbed the concept and, with the advice of his mentors, applied the principles to his estate management with vigour and imagination.

I

In chapter 2 concerning Sir Hamon's medieval inheritance we saw that the conscious gathering of written material for his benefit started in 1604, when Sir Henry Hobart instructed Sir Henry Spelman to deliver to the young man 'all the evidences and other writings' he had in his possession concerning the family and their estate; he also had to make 'a perfect note' of other material and where it could be found.[17] Spelman had been accumulating data since his appointment as a trustee in 1592, and Hobart was determined that this collection was secured for Hamon and his posterity. At the same time the trustees continued to improve the new bailiff accounts initiated by Hamon's father between 1585 and 1592 and added items of useful information. Spelman's two books of evidences focused on the difficulties encountered by the family after the death of Sir Thomas Le Strange.[18] The purpose was to provide Hamon with an up-to-date knowledge of the family and estate concerning various settlements, wills, financial transactions, legal disputes and sales of lands mostly connected with the marriage of his grandfather, Hamon, and Elizabeth Hastings, and the eventual acquisition of the Gressenhall estate in 1571.[19] In this way, Hamon had the evidence to meet any challenge to this controversial inheritance. Written clearly and methodically, the books also provided Hamon with a model to follow.

Alongside this created knowledge Hamon inherited a significant library, which can be described as collected knowledge. The catalogue, possibly compiled by his youngest son, Sir Roger L' Estrange, provides a meticulous record of the 2659 books

---

14 Warde, *Invention of Sustainability*, p. 119.

15 *Ibid.*, pp. 107–10, 119.

16 C. Estienne, *Maison Rustique, or the Countrey Farme,* translated by R. Surfleete in 1616 and listed among other husbandry manuals in the Le Strange catalogue.

17 LEST/Q37, fols 14–17: The Order and Award of Sir Henry Hobart [assisted by Sir Edmund Bell and Thomas Oxburgh] between Sir Hamon Le Strange and Sir Henry Spelman, his Guardian, 1604.

18 LEST/Q34.

19 Discussed in chapters 2 and 3 above.

acquired by the family in the sixteenth and seventeenth centuries.[20] The volumes are all numbered and listed in classes under letters of the alphabet, although the selection of books does not appear to reflect consistent themes. However, it provides a useful code for the index of authors and may simply be a device for locating books on the shelves. Of these volumes, 440 were published and acquired before 1600.[21] A breakdown illustrates the growth of the Le Stranges' collecting habits: forty-two date from before 1545, 196 between 1545 and 1580, 114 between 1581 and 1592, and finally eighty-eight during the period of the trustees from 1593 to 1599. As a yearly average, the figures show that the number of books acquired rose from one during Sir Thomas's life to six during the lives of his son and grandson, to ten by the time of Sir Hamon's father and to fourteen under the trustees. A separate calculation, which might have been influenced by Sir Hamon's education at Cambridge, shows that a further sixty books were acquired between 1600 and 1603, raising the yearly rate to twenty. From 1604 to 1654 Hamon added a further 1170 books to the library at a rate of twenty-four books a year; his descendants from 1655 to 1698 were responsible for a further 585 volumes, averaging just under fourteen a year, while 404 books were undated. The figures suggest that the Le Stranges developed a keen interest in books from the late 1540s that gathered momentum under Sir Hamon's father and the tutelage of Sir Henry Spelman, peaked during Hamon's lifetime and fell back thereafter to more modest levels.[22] Without doubt, Sir Hamon was a serious bibliophile with interests extending from the deeply religious through the popular classical texts, modern history, politics and general literature to a more practical taste for music, mathematics, natural history and manuals for managing the estate, household and family.

Sir Hamon's enthusiasm for knowledge can be seen in the way he amassed the full range of information available, buying new books for the library, gathering historic materials relating to his estate, reorganising the court rolls and bailiffs' accounts in the 'evidence house', creating his own memoranda books, commissioning maps and surveys and, finally, instigating field books and modernising rentals and accounts with the help of Alice. Both were entirely committed to the process, which encompassed the household as well as the estate, but in this they were not unique. In their evolving system we see a structure that closely resembles that adopted by

---

20 In the catalogue, LEST/NE1, the earliest entry is 1511, the latest 1698. Loose leaf notes date from the 1700s. Sir Roger lived until 1704, so might well have instrumental in its creation. Sir Hamon's nearest rival in Norfolk was Sir Thomas Browne, whose library, with 2448 titles, was recorded in the sale auction of 1710. Other notable examples include Sir Thomas Knyvett, with 1400 volumes in 1618; Sir Edward Coke, with 1237 books in 1634; Sir Henry Spelman, with around 400 books in 1641; and Sir Roger Townshend, with fewer than 300 when the Townshend library was inventoried around 1625. My thanks to Clive Wilkins-Jones for these figures.

21 LEST/NE1.

22 The library was sold by Nicholas Styleman following the death of his mother, Armine, eldest daughter of Sir Nicholas Le Strange, 4th Bt, and co-heiress of his estate in 1768. Hunstanton Hall and its remaining contents were effectively abandoned until the 1830s, when Henry L'Estrange Styleman Le Strange came of age.

Anna, Electress of Saxony (1532–85), for the management of her husband's estates in the 1570s.[23] There are the same recognisable layers and categories of knowledge, ranging from the formal agronomic texts to the handwritten notes and evidence of oral communication.

In her work on Anna's archive Ursula Schlude provides a useful comparison and a slightly different perspective. She found that the knowledge created on the electoral estates of Saxony closely reflected gender and social stratification. Published texts were uniformly written by men, while the estate-generated documents were often associated with men of lower status and females of every social strata, from aristocrats to peasant women. Significantly, the practical knowledge produced by these neglected groups was invariably more valuable than that contained in the printed texts, affirming Bacon's maxim that agricultural knowledge needed to be rooted and localised. Schlude's prime example was the survey of the electoral estates commissioned by Anna and undertaken by a professional surveyor, whom she subsequently appointed the major domo of the estate. His advice was to dissolve the tenancies and administer farms directly from the electoral court at Dresden; this would allow the Elector, rather than the tenants, to benefit from the rising prices for corn. With farms in hand, court officials could exploit the market, introduce radical schemes to raise productivity and greatly increase estate revenues. The success of the scheme enhanced the prestige of Elector Augustus (1526–86) and provided an example to others. Schlude also argued that this practical work and dissemination of knowledge was effectively the bridge between the sixteenth-century humanist texts and the academic science of the nineteenth century, and showed that it was neither a male nor an elite preserve.

Schlude's research extended well beyond the boundaries of the electoral estates, where she found more examples of informal scientific activity often centred around household needs such as gardening, cleaning, cooking and health care, as well as the improvement of the estate, which entailed the study of soils, crops, cultivation techniques, equipment, fertilisers, the climate and natural history. These places she identified as 'sites of knowledge'. Over time, the associated families and communities developed 'cultures of knowledge' that they brought to bear on their various concerns, spawning related interests in building, architecture, mining, astronomy and pharmacy, thereby creating a virtuous cycle of useful information and a basis for further experimentation. In this way, miniature knowledge economies were formed.

Schlude also provides a framework and terminology for this discussion of knowledge management. Returning to Anna's archive, she identified several categories of knowledge and the relationships between them. Starting with the printed texts, she separated the electoral library, which included works of Antique authors, such as Columella, Cato, Varro and Pliny, from Anna's personal collection, where herbals, botanical works and natural history dominated. In addition, she listed the manuscripts with comments on the books, indicating that they were working libraries. These manuscripts sometimes described the local situation, but they were not authored or literary in their ambition, simply a compilation of information. The next

---

23   Schlude, 'Diversity of Media', see above, p. 4, fn. 7.

group comprised the documentation generated specifically for and by the estate, such as the survey commissioned by Anna with the notes and decisions made on its implementation. Finally, Schlude listed the everyday documents used to underpin and manage estate activity, such as accounts and manorial records. She explained how these handwritten records co-existed with the printed texts and 'pushing up from below' gradually displaced the old-style literary works.

Working a generation later, Hamon reflected this trend, acquiring fewer agricultural manuals than one might expect from an avid book collector. The bulk of his library comprised books and manuscripts on religion, natural history, philosophy, political history, law and science, with several manuals on health and housewifery. For advice on estate management he inherited Conrad Heresbach's *Foure Bookes of Husbandry*, translated by Barnaby Googe in 1586, but was clearly influenced by Charles Estienne's *Countrey Farm*, which he acquired when it was translated into English in 1616.[24] First published in French, before 1564, it might well have been the choice of Electress Anna, although Schlude makes no mention of it. Significantly, Estienne highlighted the role of the housewife, in contrast to authors such as Heresbach, who took their cue from classical literature aimed at elite gentlemen with large estates.[25] As a noted physician, Estienne had much to say about the processing of farm produce, the making of food and the creation of medicines for people and animals, activities dominant in Alice's household books. The theme was taken up by Gervase Markham, who drew heavily on the *Countrey Farme* for his two books, *The English Husbandman* and *The English Housewife*, published in 1615; later he contributed to the English translation of *Countrey Farme*, making it more relevant to English readers. In 1631 Sir Hamon duly acquired Markham's collected works in nine books, *The Whole Art of Husbandry*, but the *Countrey Farme* reflects their thinking most evidently. So, not a vast collection of manuals, but well chosen.

While Hunstanton qualified as a 'site of knowledge' and the Le Stranges developed a 'culture of knowledge', in certain respects their approach was different to that outlined by Schlude. Firstly, Hamon initiated the process of knowledge making and management, encouraged Alice's full participation in estate business and remained active with new ideas throughout his life, while the Elector Augustus accepted Anna's superiority in such matters, allowed her to work alongside the major domo and formally handed over the management of all his estates to his wife in 1578. Secondly, although Anna and Augustus had fifteen children there is no evidence of knowledge being explicitly handed down to the younger generation or any understanding that this policy was necessary and sensible. In other words, there was not the same unity of mind and purpose as existed between Hamon and Alice; nor do the Le Strange documents reflect the issues of social stratification and gender that Schlude identified at the Dresden court. Similarly, other 'winners' in Norfolk improved their management procedures but not with the vision and intensity of Hamon and Alice.

---

24 Sir Hamon, or his father, may well have acquired a French edition long before the English translation. The catalogue lists many books written in French and several French dictionaries.

25 Whittle and Griffiths, *Consumption and Gender*, pp. 36–43.

II

In the knowledge economy created by Hamon and Alice we have already identified a few strands of the process, which included the gathering, commissioning and making of knowledge, and we will reference Schlude's framework in the following sections. However, their ultimate goal was to stimulate a culture of knowledge that would descend the generations. Alice played her part, producing well-organised documents in her crystal-clear lettering, while Hamon made copious notes and drew carefully measured diagrams in his spidery court hand, but the real challenge was the survival of heirs. As the family tree (Figure 5.1) shows, the deaths of Hamon and his son and grandson between 1654 and 1656, and the early death of Sir Nicholas, 3rd Bt (1632–69), left another eight-year-old boy to be cared for by trustees.[26] By all accounts, Sir Christopher Calthorpe performed the role competently and may well have pointed young Sir Nicholas, 4th Bt (1661–1724), in the direction of the archive stored in the gatehouse.[27] The result, as we will see, was the masterly insertion of indexes, annotations and additions, with cross-referencing to other documents and instructions for their upkeep from the 1680s. The different handwriting may confuse researchers at first, but it represents layers of knowledge and communication between the generations. In this way, the culture and knowledge economy was handed down to the eighteenth century.

The documents that most vividly demonstrate this process of interaction are the memoranda books initiated by Hamon, based on the models provided by Sir Henry Spelman. Three of these books survive with a mass of specific and miscellaneous information dating from 1604 to the 1720s. There may well have been others, 'thrown by and neglected' as Sir Nicholas noted in the book containing details of Hamon's building projects, so they may not represent the whole picture. However, for each of them Nicholas constructed an index or contents page that help us, in the twenty-first century, to make sense of them.

The earliest book, now catalogued as LEST/Q37, was begun by Hamon Le Strange and dates from 1605 onwards. It has references to Spelman, who continued to advise Hamon, and provides transcriptions of ancient documents confirming the Le Stranges' ownership of the properties and the rights that went with them. They begin with the charter of John of Gaunt, duke of Lancaster, to John Le Strange in 1379 confirming in Latin his occupation of the manors of Hunstanton and Holme and various rights to wrecks of sea, fishing and so on, followed by another of 1531 listing the Liberties of Hunstanton and Little (Barrett) Ringstead with rights wrecks, anchorage and groundage; both were cited in the ongoing legal disputes over the historic claims to the Le Strange fishery

---

26 This sequence uncannily replicates the loss of three generations in 1580–1, followed by the tragic loss of Sir Hamon's father in 1592.

27 Sir Christopher Calthorpe (1645–1718), the son of Sir James Calthorpe and Catherine Lewkenor, sister of Anne Le Strange, married Dorothy, the daughter of Sir William Spring and Elizabeth Le Strange; one of their many daughters, Anne, married Sir Thomas Le Strange, 5th Bt <www.historyofparliament.org.uk>.

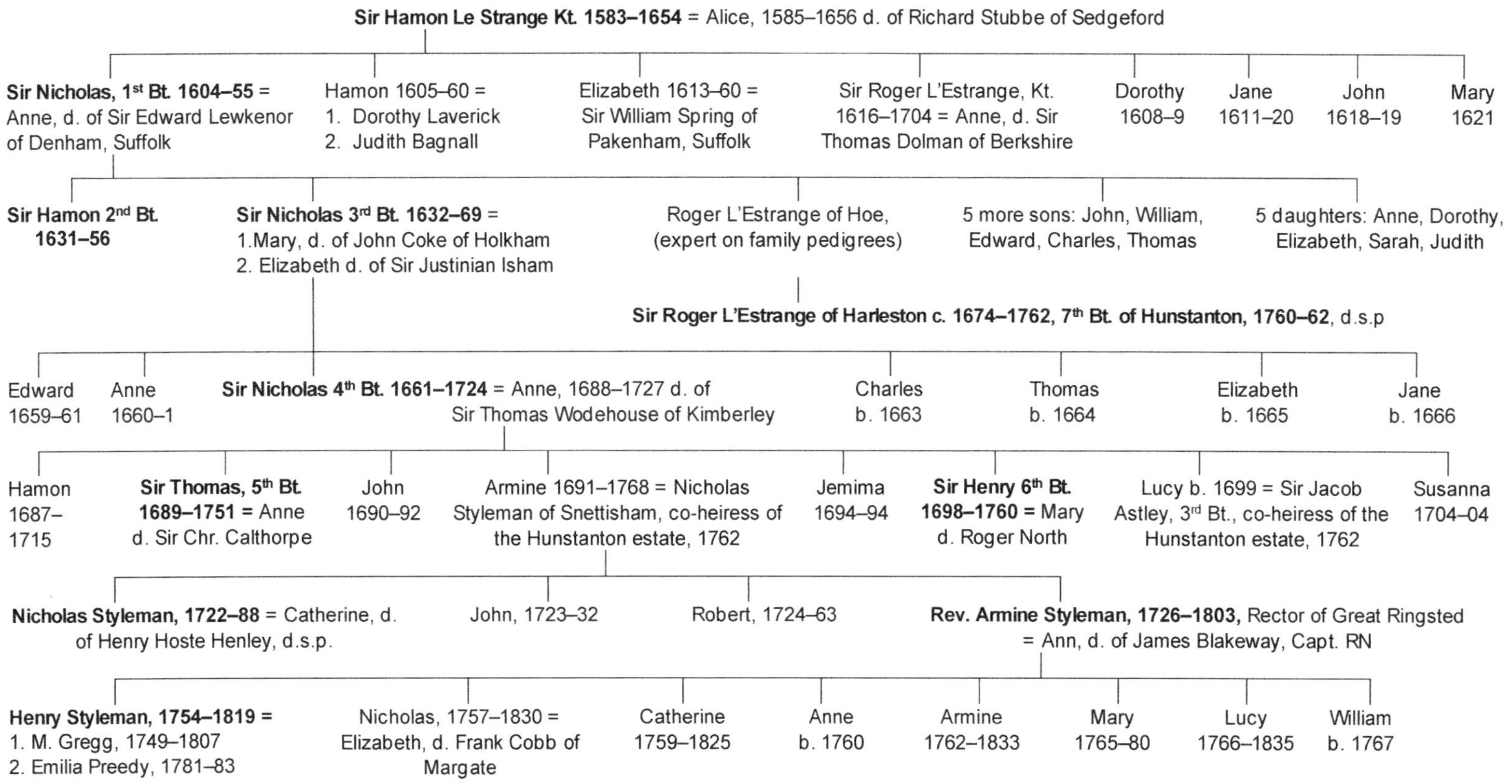

Sir Hamon Le Strange Kt. 1583–1654 = Alice, 1585–1656 d. of Richard Stubbe of Sedgeford

- **Sir Nicholas, 1st Bt. 1604–55** = Anne, d. of Sir Edward Lewkenor of Denham, Suffolk
- Hamon 1605–60 = 1. Dorothy Laverick 2. Judith Bagnall
- Elizabeth 1613–60 = Sir William Spring of Pakenham, Suffolk
- Sir Roger L'Estrange, Kt. 1616–1704 = Anne, d. Sir Thomas Dolman of Berkshire
- Dorothy 1608–9
- Jane 1611–20
- John 1618–19
- Mary 1621

Children of Sir Nicholas, 1st Bt.:
- **Sir Hamon 2nd Bt. 1631–56**
- **Sir Nicholas 3rd Bt. 1632–69** = 1. Mary, d. of John Coke of Holkham 2. Elizabeth d. of Sir Justinian Isham
- Roger L'Estrange of Hoe, (expert on family pedigrees)
- 5 more sons: John, William, Edward, Charles, Thomas
- 5 daughters: Anne, Dorothy, Elizabeth, Sarah, Judith

Sir Roger L'Estrange of Harleston c. 1674–1762, 7th Bt. of Hunstanton, 1760–62, d.s.p

Children of Sir Nicholas 3rd Bt.:
- Edward 1659–61
- Anne 1660–1
- **Sir Nicholas 4th Bt. 1661–1724** = Anne, 1688–1727 d. of Sir Thomas Wodehouse of Kimberley
- Charles b. 1663
- Thomas b. 1664
- Elizabeth b. 1665
- Jane b. 1666

Children of Sir Nicholas 4th Bt.:
- Hamon 1687–1715
- John 1690–92
- **Sir Thomas, 5th Bt. 1689–1751** = Anne d. Sir Chr. Calthorpe
- Armine 1691–1768 = Nicholas Styleman of Snettisham, co-heiress of the Hunstanton estate, 1762
- Jemima 1694–94
- **Sir Henry 6th Bt. 1698–1760** = Mary d. Roger North
- Lucy b. 1699 = Sir Jacob Astley, 3rd Bt., co-heiress of the Hunstanton estate, 1762
- Susanna 1704–04

Children of Armine Styleman and Nicholas Styleman:
- **Nicholas Styleman, 1722–88** = Catherine, d. of Henry Hoste Henley, d.s.p.
- John, 1723–32
- Robert, 1724–63
- **Rev. Armine Styleman, 1726–1803**, Rector of Great Ringsted = Ann, d. of James Blakeway, Capt. RN

Children of Rev. Armine Styleman:
- **Henry Styleman, 1754–1819** = 1. M. Gregg, 1749–1807 2. Emilia Preedy, 1781–83
- Nicholas, 1757–1830 = Elizabeth, d. Frank Cobb of Margate
- Catherine, 1759–1825
- Anne b. 1760
- Armine 1762–1833
- Mary 1765–80
- Lucy 1766–1835
- William b. 1767

Figure 5.1 Family tree: Le Strange of Hunstanton, 1600–1762 and Stylemans of Snettisham, 1722–1819.
Note: Lords of Hunstanton in bold type.
Sources: Blomefield, Norfolk, vol. 10, p. 314; Walter Rye, Norfolk Families (1912) pp. 477–82; Burke's Landed Gentry, vol. 3 (18th edition, 1972); see also, J. H. Mayer, Extraneus, A Social and Literary Chronicle of the Families, Strange, Le Strange and L'Estrange, 1082 to 1986 (1986).

dating from 1864.[28] Other documents include Sir Henry Hobart's instructions to Henry Spelman, details of tenures, leases, sales and purchases of land, more information on Gressenhall, all written in English, rather than Latin, and ending in 1610.[29] The next entry is the marriage settlement of Sir Nicholas Le Strange, 1st Bt, to Anne Lewkenor in 1631, specifying, among other issues, jointure lands apportioned to Anne and reserved for Alice.[30] (Figure 5.2 shows the index of this part of the book, later inserted by Sir Nicholas 4th Bt.) From that point folios are allocated to different properties, Ringstead, Heacham and Sedgeford with their relevant charters citing the possessions and rights enjoyed by the Le Stranges. Blank pages were left for additional information, such as the Tables of Brecks in Ringstead North and South Fields in 1665 presumably added by Nicholas (d. 1669).[31] So there was a clear purpose and structure at the outset, modified by Hamon and respected by his successors, including his grandson, who based his tables on 'a draught made by Sir Hamon Le Strange 1649'.[32] In 1647 Nicholas began his own memoranda book in the back of the same volume, mainly concerned with issues at Sedgeford.

With his particular interest in sheep, Nicholas may have been responsible for reversing the book and including a lengthy agreement between Hamon and Nicholas, his grandfather and father, and the inhabitants of Ringstead concerning the foldcourse in 1650; this is followed in the same hand by a long list of copyhold land held by the tenants of Holme lying in the field of Great Ringstead, highlighting the links between the two parishes (see Figure 5.3, the index to this section later added by Nicholas 4th Bt).[33]

In the subsequent pages Nicholas, 4th Bt, made contact with his great-grandfather as he neatly 'transcrib'd from a paper written by Sr Hamon's Hand': 'A Note of Sundry Matters to bee understood, to bee rectified maintained and preserved according to law and equity in the Estate of Sir Hamon Le Strange as the fitness of times shall invite and require.' The emphasis is on evidence that could be used to support their rights when challenged in a court of law. For example, he quotes a decree in Chancery of 1634 relating to the manor of Gressenhall and notes, with 'NB' in the margin, that copyhold fines were uncertain and at the will of the lord, and no felling of timber nor waste were permitted in copyhold houses. In Heacham the principal issues were the grazing rights, claims made by the Cremer family and disputes with the tenants on the composition of Caly foldcourse. Nicholas explains how the tenants in 1610 had 'misinformed and misled Sir Hamon' as to the rate of

---

28 There is no evidence that Henry L'Estrange Styleman Le Strange and his son Hamon consulted the memoranda books or any of the seventeenth-century documents so carefully conserved by Sir Nicholas. It appears that they worked from the originals.

29 The pause is associated with Spelman's move to London in 1612. Always short of money, he moved to the capital to better pursue his political and antiquarian interests: see <www.historyofparliament.org.uk>.

30 Principally, Gressenhall, Brisley and Stanfield for Anne, and Sedgeford for Alice.

31 The tables are dated but not signed by Sir Nicholas, d. 1669. However, he was a great favourite of Alice and features prominently in her sheep accounts, as discussed in chapter 7.

32 LEST/IC64.

33 LEST/Q37, fol. 1–25, pt 2; the fines were similarly arbitrable with similar restrictions on timber and waste.

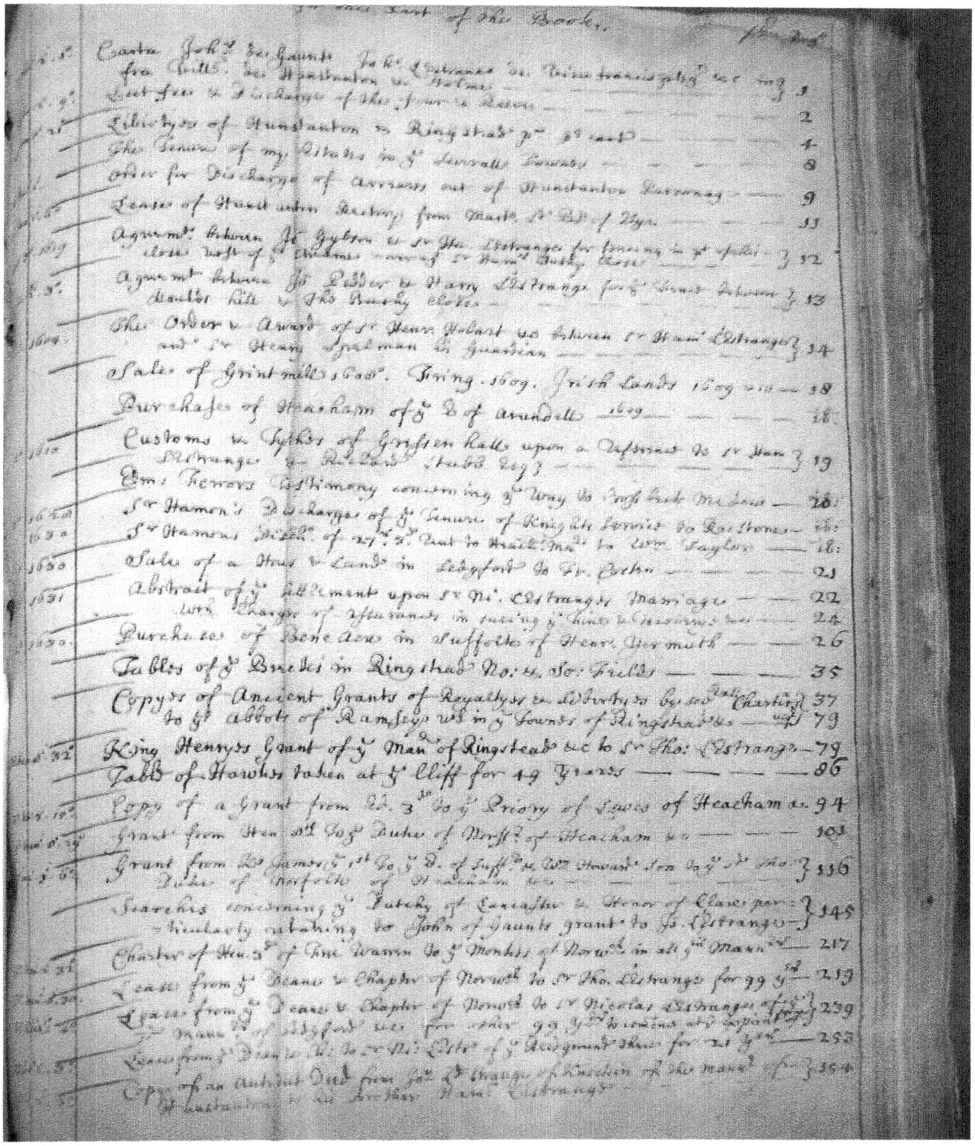

Figure 5.2 Index to Sir Hamon's part of LEST/Q 37, inserted by Sir Nicholas in the 1680s. NRO LEST/Q 37.

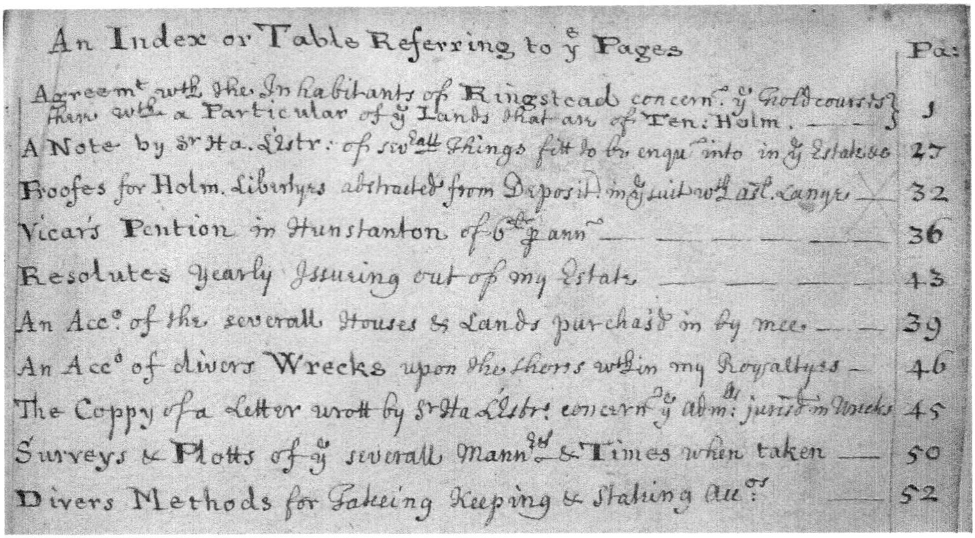
An Index or Table Referring to ye Pages — Pa:
Agreemt with the Inhabitants of Ringstead concern: ye Foldcourses there with a Particular of ye Lands that are of Ten: Holm. — 1
A Note by Sr Ha. L'Estr: of severall Things fitt to be enqu. into in ye Estates 27
Proofes for Holm. Libertyes abstracted from Deposit. in ye suit wth Ald. Langr. 32
Vicar's Pention in Hunstanton of 6li p ann — 36
Resolutes yearly Issuing out of my Estate — 43
An Acct of the severall Houses & Lands purchas'd in by mee — 39
An Acct of divers Wrecks upon the shores within my Royaltyes — 46
The Coppy of a Letter wrott by Sr Ha L'Estr: concern ye adm: jurisd in Wrecks 45
Surveys & Plotts of ye severall Mannrs & Times when taken — 50
Divers Methods for Takeing Keeping & Stating Accts — 52

Figure 5.3 Index to the pages at the back of LEST/Q 37, inserted by Sir Nicholas in the 1680s. NRO LEST/Q 37.

sheep to lay on the foldcourse, 'when his owne knowledge in ye matters of Heacham Towne was raw and imperfect'. This was a salutary lesson: landowners needed to be aware, watchful and well informed. The experience prompted Hamon to commission a new survey of Heacham and encouraged Alice to check the rentals and field books. The results provoked a challenge from the Cremers, which led to a fiercely contested legal case finally settled in Hamon's favour in 1651; Nicholas provides a summary of the settlement.[34] He also noted the nature of the fines, which were arbitrable, with restrictions on felling timber and waste in copyhold houses as at Gressenhall, but with the further stipulation that 'care needed to be taken that the p'sons lyable doe yearly scour and cleanse Caly Brooke'.[35]

The most heavily underlined section deals with the rights 'undoubtedly' held by the Le Stranges as lords of the manor of Great Ringstead and Holme. These relate mainly to the foldcourse at Ringstead and the beach and meeles (dunes) at Holme, which included lucrative rights to wrecks, whales and conies (rabbits). For the foldcourse, Nicholas (d. 1724) provided a summary of the 1650 agreement, but for the coastal issues he went into some detail. A bone of contention was the role of the sea-bailiff, appointed from copyholders of Holme, who for years had 'appropriated wrecks [of the sea] to themselves allowing the lord but half the value'. Apparently the Le Stranges had turned a blind eye to the smaller wrecks, but as they became 'more sensible of the abuse' they denied the rights of the copyholders to hold office and appointed their own water bailiff. In other words, landowners with knowledge were

34 See chapter 8.

35 LEST/Q37, fols 27–8.

able to assert their rights. Nicholas also noted that the fines for coyhold land in Holme and Ringstead were mostly certain, at 2s per acre for Holme and 12d for Ringstead, but for messuages 'they were uncertain & at will'. Similar customs prevailed for bond land and bond tenements at Hunstanton.

In support of the Le Stranges' rights at Holme, Firmin Gray assembled proofs for Hamon against Robert Stones and Aslack Lanye's farmers, who had committed various offences; this was followed by 'Searches and Proofs from Antient Court Rolls that Sr Hamon L'Estrange is Lord & owner of the Comons in Holme, and of the wreck of the sea & groundage there' dating back to the fifteenth century.[36] At the end of this section, as if to make the point, Nicholas noted in 1698:

> Mr Rogers upon the purchase of Mr Taylors Estate in Holm questioned my right of warren upon the Meeles. To whom I showed the decree in the Courts of Wards and the Depositions in that suit w[hi]ch are recited in the foregoing lease upon w[hi]ch he ceased the further Prosecution thereof.

At the bottom of the page, in a nineteenth-century hand, we find 'This note is written by Sir Nicholas Le Strange husband of Ann Woodhouse', confirming the continuing use of the book by the family. After listing purchases made between 1687 and 1704, Nicholas copied 'The transcript of a Pastboard table under Sr Hamon's Hand w[hi]ch hung up in ye Old Evidence House', which listed the manor courts, and concluded that 'these above written are Books and Rolls fitt to be produced at the courts'.[37]

Finally, as the index shows, Nicholas included a list of resolutes and rents yearly out of Hunstanton; a copy of a letter written by Hamon in 1637 concerning the administration and jurisdiction of wrecks; his own accounts of wrecks 'upon the shore within my royalties' from 1688 to 1705; an incomplete list of surveys and maps undertaken; and some advice on the keeping of accounts of an estate. All of this emphasised the need for knowledge and for it to be safely guarded. The entries are carefully collected, indexed and presented by Nicholas, no doubt in the expectation that the work would be continued by his successors. However, the entries peter out in 1718 and neither of his heirs made any contribution to the book. This may sound calamitous, but in fact they simply found more efficient ways of storing and managing knowledge. However, the book survived and was still being used in the nineteenth century.

The next memoranda book, LEST/Q36, is devoted to estate material for Hunstanton and Holme and is principally the work of Hamon with later additions by Alice. The book begins with a catalogue of hawks dating from 1604 'att the Park and cliffs of Hunstanton',[38] and includes two dragges of the sea lawers 'in Hunston shore', 1616 and *c.*1630, but it is mainly filled with early field books and renewals of rentals and firmalls up to 1654 (see Figure 5.4).[39] The field book for Hunstanton, which is undated,

---

36 LEST/Q37, fols 32–4.

37 LEST/Q37, fol. 41, pt 2.

38 The entries in the catalogue of hawks peter out in 1636; for an updated table, see LEST/Q37, fol. 86.

39 Rentals included manorial tenants; firmalls listed just farm rents. Barrett Ringstead is included as it amounted to an extension of Hunstanton on its south and west sides.

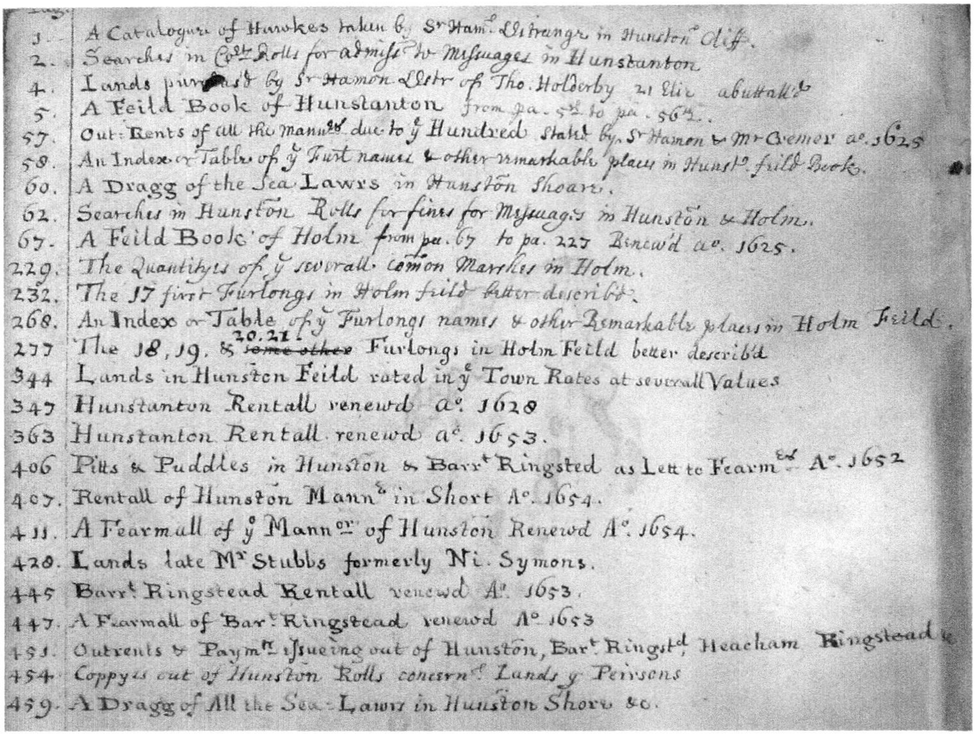

1. A Catalogue of Hawkes taken by Sr Ham. L'Estrange in Hunston Cliff.
2. Searches in Cort Rolls for admiss to Messuages in Hunstanton
4. Lands purchas'd by Sr Hamon L'Estr of Tho. Holderby 21 Eliz abuttall
5. A Feild Book of Hunstanton from pa. 5 to pa. 56.
57. Out: Rents of all the mannors due to ye Hundred stated by Sr Hamon & Mr Cremer ao. 1625
58. An Index or Table of ye Furl names & other remarkable places in Hunst. feild Book.
60. A Dragg of the Sea Lawrs in Hunston Shoare.
62. Searches in Hunston Rolls for fines for Messuages in Hunston & Holm.
67. A Feild Book of Holm from pa. 67 to pa. 227 Renew'd ao. 1625.
229. The Quantityes of ye severall comon Marshes in Holm.
232. The 17 first Furlongs in Holm feild better describ'd.
268. An Index or Table of ye Furlongs names & other Remarkable places in Holm Feild.
277 The 18, 19, & 20. 21. ~~some other~~ Furlongs in Holm Feild better describ'd
344 Lands in Hunston Feild rated in ye Town Rates at severall Values
347 Hunstanton Rentall renewd ao. 1628
363 Hunstanton Rentall renewd ao. 1653.
406 Pitts & Puddles in Hunston & Barrt Ringsted as Lett to Fearmed Ao. 1652
407. Rentall of Hunston Mannr in Short Ao. 1654.
411. A Fearmall of ye Mannor of Hunston Renewd Ao. 1654.
420. Lands late Mr Stubbs formerly Ni. Symons.
445 Barrt Ringstead Rentall renewd Ao. 1653.
447. A Fearmall of Barrt Ringstead renewd Ao 1653
451. Outrents & Paymts issueing out of Hunston, Barrt Ringstd, Heacham Ringstead
454 Coppyes out of Hunston Rolls concern. Lands & Persons
459. A Dragg of All the Sea Lawrs in Hunston Shore &c.

Figure 5.4 Table of contents for LEST/Q 36, inserted by Sir Nicholas in the 1680s. NRO LEST/Q 36.

appears to be experimental, with much crossing out, highlighting the difficulty of compiling a book with masses of ever-changing information.[40] The one for Holme, firmly dated 1625 and occupying 220 pages, is more carefully drafted, with additional information on the marshes and twenty-one furlongs 'better described'. This level of detail at such an early stage points to the importance of Holme and the difficulties the Le Stranges encountered in its management; they owned very little demesne land in Holme, only the grazing rights and manorial holdings, so they had no presence, making it difficult to exert control. In the first three pages of LEST/Q37, before Nicholas found a space to insert a table of contents, Hamon scribbled a list of the profits due to him as lord of the manor of Great Ringstead from the marshes of Holme; these grazing rights over hundreds of acres of marshland were extremely profitable and the subject of many disputes. As we have seen, to resist these challenges the Le Stranges needed to keep scrupulous records and monitor the situation carefully. Significantly, much of the information Nicholas transcribed from Hamon's papers in

40 Field books listed the holdings, furlong by furlong, strip by strip, identifying the demesne land, manorial tenants, type of tenure and acreage. In this early version there are no details of the park; these appear separately in LEST/Q38, fol. 5, and in the separate field book, LEST/BH1.

LEST/Q37 pertained to Holme.[41] This explains why Holme was the first property to be mapped, but it is also the only map not to have survived.[42] It is possible that its use in legal cases over disputed property rights is the cause of this loss.

These two memoranda books remained the reference point for Holme, but clearly they were not suitable for field books in general. For Hunstanton and Ringstead Hamon used separate paper books that were renewed at intervals in the 1640s by Alice and from the 1680s by Nicholas, who often made comparisons back to the 'old books'. The Holme field book was not renewed until 1700, when it was remapped along with Ringstead as part of the same geography and landholding structure.

The last memoranda book, LEST/Q38, begun by Hamon in about 1612, contains the most original and innovative information, including all his notes and diagrams on his building programme and the agreements with craftsmen and suppliers. At the back of the book Nicholas added details of his own work from the 1680s to the 1720s and concluded with a table of thirty pages summarising the building undertaken at Hunstanton from the late fifteenth century to 1731. Uncertain of the dates before Hamon's building programme, he resorted to lateral thinking: for the 'Tower or Gatehous[e]: I find not any mention of the Time of Building but believ[e] it to have been during the Match wth Heydon by reason those Armes are quarterd on ye North side of ye Arch',[43] and, for the 'Great Hous[e]: I find no mention of the Time of Building but for the figures cutt in the Hall Door 1577 & upon the chimney'.[44] From 1615, with the information from Hamon's entries, he was able to construct a dated list, with the first item re-covering the roof of the 'head house' with slate. However, earlier and further references to building work can be found in the books of general disbursements, before Alice accounted for building work separately.[45] While we have these comprehensive accounts from 1606 to 1654, for the later period no accounts survive; LEST/Q38 is the only evidence that we have of the building work carried out by Hamon's immediate heirs.[46] The layout of the book seems to have tested Nicholas's organisational skills. As with LEST/Q37, the book is in two parts, with Hamon's notes at the front and Nicholas's notes, diagrams and tables at the back. Hamon left no blank page for Nicholas to list the contents, so he included an index, improving on an idea devised by Hamon halfway through his

---

41   LEST/Q37.

42   LEST/Q37, fol. 50.

43   The marriage of Sir Roger Le Strange and Amy, d. of Sir Henry Heydon in 1491, brought a dowry of £280; see chapter 2.

44   This was the Elizabethan Wing started by Sir Hamon' grandfather in 1577 – with further progress made by his father – and completed in 1617. It is the structure with three high gables and chimneys shown on the cover.

45   LEST/P6 and P7.

46   In her description of the nineteenth-century farm buildings on the Le Strange Estate Susanna Wade Martins refers to a barn at Geddings Farm, Ringstead, bearing a datestone of 1630 but with no features from that date, while another building at Neat Lyngs Farm dated 1862 incorporated seventeenth-century arches and much older timber, all of which suggests an ongoing programme of repairs and modernisation rather than complete rebuilds. See her *Historic Farm Buildings* (London, 1991), pp. 132–7. We can confirm that the process dated back to the seventeenth century.

entries. At the beginning of his own section Nicholas provides an explanation of how he linked the two parts: 'An Index of ye severall Things contain'd in this Part of this Book. This mark * prefixt signifies the same to be found at ye other End of the Book under Sir Hamon's hand, referring to ye Index of that part, page 155.' In his text Nicholas also made repeated and highlighted references to Hamon and Alice; this interaction is particularly noticeable in his description of the Hunston Fishery, written on the pages before his table of the building work.[47] In the next chapter we will study the building work on the estate in greater depth, analysing how Sir Hamon worked with people and utilised knowledge on the ground, but for now we will turn to another aspect of the knowledge economy, where Hamon hired professionals to undertake specialist tasks, notably the surveying and mapping of the estate. This will be followed by an exploration of how Hamon and Alice modernised their management procedures so as to generate and preserve routine knowledge more effectively.

III

Our knowledge of the maps commissioned by Hamon is enhanced by a table, albeit incomplete, provided in LEST/Q37 by Nicholas, probably in the 1700s.[48] The title, 'Surveys & Plotts of the Severall Townes and Fields & w[he]n taken', suggests that the surveys and plots (maps) were listed in order of completion. Only three dates were recorded: Holme in 1605, Hunstanton in 1615 and Brisley in 1622; there is one reference to a surveyor, 'Willm Heyward', against Ringstead and no detail for Gressenhall, Heacham or Sedgeford, apart from the fact that there were two plots for Heacham and three for Sedgeford.[49] However, we know from inscriptions on the maps and payments in the books of disbursements that a map and survey of Gressenhall was undertaken by Thomas Waterman between 1623 and 1625 and of Sedgeford by John Fisher between 1631 and 1641.[50] Heacham was a conundrum, as only a single map was listed in the catalogue, showing the area north of the river Heacham; by chance, the map for the south was found among the Snettisham maps.[51] It bears the revealing attribution that 'The plotts of Hecham were made by William Heyward gt. Ao 1592 and exemplified Ao1623 by Thomas Waterman, clerk'.[52] Exemplified means to copy or transcribe a document, and, in this context, to form something after or in imitation of a particular prototype; this may explain how Waterman was able to complete the two

---

47   Sir Hamon's interest in fishing appears to date from 1626, when he ordered fishing nets to be made; he also analysed a whale beached on the shore at Holme and how sperm oil was extracted: LEST/Q37, fols 91, 101–4, 147–8.

48   LEST/Q37, Pt 2, fol. 50.

49   The Holme map has not been found; Hunstanton, LEST/OA1; Brisley, LEST/P7, MR RO/402/7; see Table 5.1, which fills in the detail.

50   The survey for Gressenhall costing £10, LEST/P7, has not survived, but the map can be found in a different collection, Hayes & Storr, 72; Sedgeford LEST/OC1, LEST/IC58.

51   Heacham north, LEST/OC2; south LEST/OB2 catalogued with Snettisham maps LEST/OB1, OB3, OB4, OB4/1.

52   <www.oed.com>. In 1592 Heacham Lewes was still owned by Phillip Howard, earl of Arundel.

Table 5.1
Surveys and maps commissioned by the Le Stranges, 1605–35.

Surveys & field books & references*	Date of map	Surveyor	Detail and references to Hamon and Alice's books of disbursements	Map & doc references**
Holme				
EH1 1509 EH3 1569 Q36 1625	1605	M. Spinke	1606 For the survey plot of the marshes and common at Holme £1. Map lost. EH3 Sir Hamon inserted an index.	LEST/P6
KA24 1633	1633	Jan van Hasdonck	'The Plotts of Holm Marshes' – survey of marshes.	LEST/FQ18
	1610	J. Fisher	Pd for a map to Mr Boston £1 16s – maybe associated with Haiward's map below.	LEST/P6
Ringstead				
EH2 mid-16th century EH4 1620 EH5 1621	1600–20	W. Heyward	Scale, name, but no date – range based on widowhood of Mrs Read and sale of Robert Read's estate in 1621. The table in Q37 suggests a pre-1615 date – see above.	LEST/OD
EH9 1645 EH10 1650 EH11 Alice & Tho. Crisp		John Fisher	Taken out of Mr Haiward's Platt of Ringstead by Jo. Fisher; date c.1645 and made for Alice's book on N & S Brecks; subsequent agreement, 1650; plan by Sir Nicholas, 1665.	LEST/OB5 LEST/OB6 Q37/ 2, 1–14 Q37/1, 35–36
Hunstanton				
BH1 1618–23 BH2 1648 KA24 1633	1615	Style of Thomas Waterman	Scale, date but no name – authorship based on comparison with Heacham maps.	LEST/OA1
		J. Fisher	Survey of marshes.	
Brisley				
	1622	T. Waterman	For surveying of Brisley £3. Later, 1706 repaired Sir Nicholas Le Strange, 4th Bt. identified J. Fisher as surveyor.	LEST/P7 MR RO/402/7
Gressenhall				
	1623–5	T. Waterman	1623–5 payments to men and boys for carrying the chain and instruments £2 17s 3d 1624 Mr Waterman for part survey £5 1625 Mr Waterman for finishing survey £5	LEST/P7 Hayes & Storr, 72
	1630s	J. Fisher	'A plott of my farms at Gressenhall', plus measured diagram of a 50-acre wood.	MR235, 242 x 1
Heacham				
DH1 1594 Q33 1596 KA24 1633	1623	T. Waterman North Plot South Plot	For exemplification of Heacham platt £3 'The plots of Heacham were made by William Hayward gt 1592 and exemplified in 1623 by Thomas Waterman Clerk'. Survey of marshes.	LEST/P7 LEST/OC2 LEST/OB2
Sedgeford				
IB83 1546 IC58 1582 IC58 1630s IB86 1652	1631–5	Jo. Fisher East Plot South Plot North Plot	Survey by Fisher, 1631–41, alongside maps, plus summary of Mr Shepheard's book, 1582.	LEST/OC1 LEST/IC58

Notes: *Current document references within the NRO LEST collection. **Sources of information regarding the creation of these maps and surveys.

Source: Based on the unfinished table by Sir Nicholas, LEST/Q37, Pt. 2, fol. 50.

Heacham maps alongside his lengthy work at Gressenhall. With this information we have been able to flesh out the table created by Sir Nicholas in the 1700s (Table 5.1).

The references to William Heyward at Heacham and Ringstead are significant.[53] In his work on land surveyors Peter Eden noted that William Haiwarde (fl. 1591–1637), alternatively known as Heyward or Hayward, was one of the most active surveyors in Norfolk before the Restoration and often worked with Thomas Waterman (fl. 1607–38).[54] However, he often left his work unsigned or undated, which was not uncommon at the time.[55] At Holkham, where he worked in the 1590s, there is only one signed map, that for Tittleshall (1596), out of several that on stylistic grounds could be ascribed to Heyward. We are fortunate to have two clear references. Although the map for Ringstead was missing, Heyward's authorship is confirmed by a small map of Ringstead Brecks, 'taken out of Mr Haiwarde's Map of Ringsted'; it has been attributed to Mr Fisher on the back, which suggests that he exemplified Heyward's map for Alice's reforms of the two Ringstead foldcourses in the 1640s.[56]

The breakthrough came when the large Ringstead map by Heyward was found among some nineteenth-century Le Strange records, with the inscription 'Guilielm Haiwarde Descriptio', but still with no date.[57] The estimate was *c.*1625, but on closer examination it seems that the map was concurrent with Sir Hamon's field book of 1620.[58] At that stage the principal tenant was Mrs Read, the widow of Robert Read, who appears on the map with her sons as 'heyres of Read'; their lands, amounting to 730 acres, were sold in 1621, probably on her death. The task book of 1624 lists the new owners as Cleare Francis (430 acres), with the remainder sold to Thomas Cremer, Richard Constable and Thomas Thurlow.[59] So, the latest date for the Ringstead map is 1620, but it may have been earlier. Significantly, Ringstead was listed in the table after Holme and before Hunstanton in 1615, while Maria Read was widowed by 1598, so the date range is from 1605 to 1615.[60] My hunch is 1610, when a small payment of £1 for a

---

53   P. Eden, 'Land Surveyors in Norfolk, 1550–1850', pt 1, *Norfolk Archaeology*, 35 (1970–2), pp. 476, 482, fn. 15.

54   The abbreviation 'fl.', short for flourished, is used by historians when dates of birth and death are unknown.

55   P.D.A. Harvey, 'Estate surveyors and the spread of the scale-map in England, 1550–80', *Landscape History*, 15 (1993), pp. 37–49.

56   These maps may be linked to Alice's field books 1645 and 1650 (LEST/EH9, EH10 and EH11), which underpinned the reforms of the management of the Ringstead foldcourses and the agreement of 1650. Heyward's maps of the Fens were also widely exemplified; see A.W. Skempton *et al.* (eds), *A Biographical Dictionary of Civil Engineers in Great Britain and Ireland*, vol. 1, 1500–1830 (London, 2002), pp. 308–9.

57   Ringstead map, LEST/OD. I knew what it was immediately, having assembled a full map of Ringstead from the field maps of the 1680s, and very little had changed.

58   LEST/EH4.

59   LEST/EH4.

60   LEST/R7. Maria Read appears in the Ringstead Bailiff Accounts, 1598–1600 a/c, paying 4d for 1r formerly paid by her husband Robert Read; Nicholas Read was recorded as bailiff of Ringstead Magna until 1596/7; NRO inventories DN/INV 12/121 and DN/INV 12/197 suggest that both men, identified as gentlemen, died in 1595.

map was made to Mr Boston, who may well have been one of Hayward's assistants.[61] A similar sum was paid to Mr Spinke in 1606 for the 'small survey plot of the marshes and common at Holme'. Given Hayward's expertise in the Fens and on the coastal marshes at Heacham in the 1590s it is possible that he was also responsible for the Holme map. It is even possible that he worked with Waterman on the Hunstanton map, which bears a date, but no attribution; it has been credited to Waterman only on the basis of his later ascribed work at Brisley, Heacham and Gressenhall.[62]

The likelihood is that Sir Hamon engaged Hayward following the example of the Cokes. These maps are of the highest quality; all bear a scale-bar, some with a pair of dividers drawn above it, denoting that each was created from a measured survey to a consistent scale.[63] In contrast, the maps of neighbouring Snettisham made for the Styleman family are significantly inferior, with no date, attribution or evidence of rigorous method.[64] Hamon clearly took mapping and measuring seriously; he wanted the best expertise and to be involved with the process. Between 1606 and 1609 he purchased not only books on mathematics and cosmography, including Robert Record's *Castle of Knowledge*, but measuring instruments, such as a pair of compasses, a quadrant and in 1610 a theodolite and geodital staff.[65] In this way he was able to participate in the activity, draw measured diagrams for buildings, watercourses and the courtyard walls, and sketch new drags for the sea lawers. He was not only commissioning professionals to undertake certain projects but learning from them and adapting their methods to smaller, more localised tasks. Likewise, Hamon's son, Nicholas, engaged Jan van Hasdonck to draw up Plotts for Holme Marshes in 1633 but wrote up all the notebooks, designed to instruct and inform his successors.

So why was there such a flurry of activity at this time? Estate maps came into existence in significant numbers from the 1580s, driven by landowners' need to upgrade and commercialise the management of their estates and made possible by a 'revolution in geometry' that transformed mapping techniques on the battlefield and were equally appropriate to the fields of Norfolk.[66] Maps were used to illustrate the information previously only contained in written surveys; they enabled landowners 'to know one's own' as McRae discusses, measuring their lands more accurately and

---

61 LEST/P6.

62 The Brisley map has no date or attribution. When it was repaired in 1706 Sir Nicholas noted that 'The survey of Brisley was drawn upon paper by Mr Fisher as I find in Sir Hamon Le Strange's acct book, 1622'. However, Alice's book of disbursements includes a payment of £3 to Mr Waterman for the task (LEST/P7). It is possible that both men were involved. Brisley is close to Gressenhall, where Waterman was employed for two years, 1623–5, while Fisher worked at Gressenhall in the 1630s: MR235, 242 x 1.

63 Harvey, 'Estate surveyors'.

64 LEST/OB1; OB3; OB4; OB 4/1. The maps became part of the Le Strange archive when the estate passed by marriage to the Stylemans in 1760.

65 Whittle and Griffiths, *Consumption and Gender*, p. 197, LEST/P6. The catalogue does not contain *Castle of Knowledge* (1556), only Record's *Urinal of Physic* (1546), but in 1650 Sir Hamon or his son purchased Oliver Wallingby's *Plano-Matria or Art of Surveying*.

66 Harvey, 'Estate Surveyors', p. 38.

assessing more easily the possibilities for improvement, notably enclosure.[67] Maps, supported by surveys, also proved useful in disputes.[68] It is likely that maps would have appeared at Hunstanton earlier but for the difficulties endured by the Le Stranges during the 1580s and 1590s. Ralph Agas, the noted surveyor, was presented to the rectory of Gressenhall by Hamon Le Strange in 1578 and served there until 1583; quite possibly he surveyed the estate during that period and may even have produced a map later exemplified by Thomas Waterman (see Figure 5.5).[69] The speed at which Hamon embraced mapmaking certainly suggests that the family were well familiar with the concept: witness the drag for the sea lawers on the foreshore in 1554.[70]

Despite the advent of the maps, written surveys and field books remained an essential tool of management. When he purchased Heacham Lewes in 1609 Hamon acquired an impressive written survey commissioned by the earl of Arundel in 1594. that followed the completion of William Heyward's map of 1592.[71] This was the ultimate arrangement and the model followed by the Le Stranges. As we have seen, Sir Hamon created new field books for Holme, Ringstead and Hunstanton in the 1620s to support the maps commissioned between 1605 and 1615. A generation later Alice updated those for Ringstead and Hunstanton, while Holme and Heacham were not renewed until Nicholas created his field map books from the late 1680s.[72] Sedgeford received the most lavish attention: a professional survey commissioned from John Fisher in the 1630s was accompanied by three maps, East, South and North Plots, reflecting the three foldcourses; the idea was to clarify their intricate operation and avoid the disputes that had plagued Richard Stubbe. Fisher also repeatedly referred to an earlier survey by Mr Shepheard in 1582, checking and correcting the measurements of closes and strips, which Shepheard frequently exaggerated.[73] The survey and mapmaking was part of a much wider review of the management at Sedgeford undertaken by Alice after the death of her cousin William Guybon in 1630. Subsequently, Alice renewed the Fisher's survey or 'breck book' between 1647 and 1650; this was followed by a further update conducted by Sir Nicholas in the 1700s.[74] Across the estate we find Alice consolidating and following the examples initiated by Hamon. No surveys or fields books have survived for Gressenhall and Brisley, reflecting their distance, detached management and separation from the principal estate in 1760.

---

67   A. McRae, '"To know one's own": estate surveying and the representation of the land in early modern England', *Huntingdon Library Quarterly*, 56/4 (1993), pp. 333–57.

68   At Heacham and Holme; see LEST/Q37 above, and chapter 8.

69   Eden, 'Land surveyors in Norfolk', pt 1, p. 482, fn. 13; Blomefield, *Norfolk*, vol. 9, p. 519; see also Harvey, 'Estate Surveyors', *passim*. With its figures on the common, the Gressenhall map is exceptionally beautiful. Agas's earliest survey and map was at West Lexham, a few miles west of Gressenhall, in 1575: NRO, MS 2118, 179 x 4; MS 20665, 308 x 2.

70   Dragge of Sea Lawers, 1554, and Sir Hamon's copy of the original, LEST/B2/1; B2/2. See chapter 2.

71   LEST/DH1 runs to 285 pages.

72   LEST/DH4; accompanied by a book of field maps, LEST/DH3.

73   Shepheard's survey was undertaken in 1582, probably on the death of John Le Strange; it was a renewal of an earlier field book of 1546, LEST/IB83, following the death of Sir Thomas Le Strange.

74   LEST/IB89, IB90, IB91; see also chapter 7. Alice's legacy at Sedgeford ran deep.

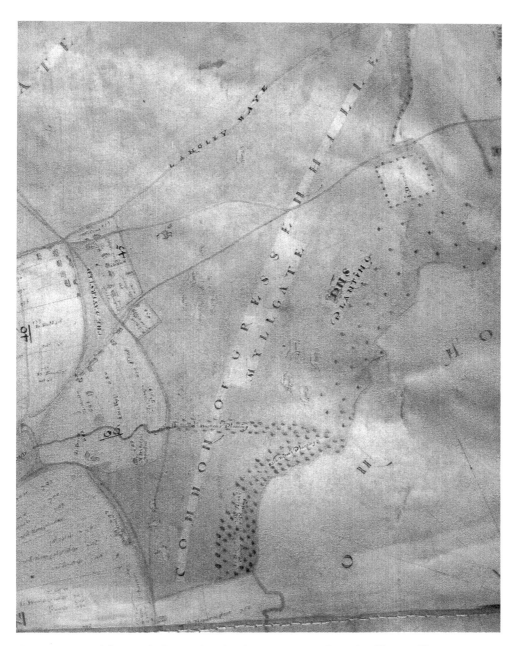

Figure 5.5 Part of Gressenhall map showing the common, attributed to Thomas Waterman, 1624. NRO Hayes and Storr map 72.

Table 5.1, based on the surveys and maps started by Sir Nicholas but completed with relevant dates, documents and references from elsewhere in the archive, shows above all Hamon and Alice learning from and building on the work of professionals. We now turn to the modernisation of routine records that underpinned day-to-day management. As we know from the situation in 1604, much thought and effort was required.

IV

Apart from the retrospective provided by Alice, our analysis of the situation in 1604 relied heavily on the bailiffs' accounts and a few rentals; there were no household accounts, no books of receipts and disbursements and no evidence of farming activities undertaken by the Le Stranges, all of which indicated a significant decline in record-keeping since the time of Sir Thomas and his energetic wife Anne. Sir Hamon's father made some progress, but with his early death the full task of modernisation had to await his son's coming of age. Alongside the memoranda books, maps and surveys, Hamon made a brisk start with a book of receipts and disbursements, but, as we saw, he showed less aptitude for accounts and urgently needed a competent, thoughtful and trustworthy assistant to perform this role. Fortunately for him, Alice possessed the necessary skills and qualities for the task; her ability with figures was comparable to that of her forebear, Anne Le Strange and of Anna, Electress of Saxony. These women were not simple book-keepers, but astute, strategic and imaginative accountants. If they were permitted, wives of this calibre could make all the difference to the management of their husbands' estates.[75]

Alice's involvement with the accounts dates from 1609, when she took over Hamon's book of receipts and disbursements. This may have been prompted by the increased size and complexity of the estate with the purchase of Heacham Lewes, but it also coincided with the death of her third child, Dorothy, and may have been a conscious move to busy herself and take her mind off her loss. Whatever the motive, the accounts improved markedly. She brought clarity to the task and a different approach to that of her husband. Most obvious is the way that she listed every single item, whereas Hamon relied far more on tradesmen, bailiffs and servants submitting their bills; he referenced the bills to numbered files, but this meant a lack of detail in the permanent disbursement account. Inevitably, Alice quickly found evidence of fraud.[76] For the years Hamon kept the accounts there is no consistent record of the payment of servants' wages or the purchase of food: two major items of expenditure.

Alice was much more systematic. She soon started grouping payments into categories using brackets and annotating items in the margin: wages to servants, corn and farm labour, expenditure on the various children, food for the household and building repairs. In time she siphoned off major expenditure, such as building and food, into separate accounts. This enabled her to exert closer control over detail and provided a framework for expansion which could then be cross-referenced back

---

75   For a full discussion of Alice's role as a household manager see Whittle and Griffiths, *Consumption and Gender*, pp. 26–48.

76   See chapter 7's discussion of the dismissal of Thomas Hogan.

to the main account. It was the beginning of a fully integrated accounting system covering the household and estate.

With these refinements, Alice gradually improved her management technique. The receipt accounts that recorded income from the estate, including farm rents, and sales of timber, corn, livestock and foodstuffs, were entered at the back of each household book, while half-yearly totals of receipts appear in the relevant book of disbursements. Separate building accounts were introduced in 1620, when Hamon's activities across the estate gathered momentum. These accounts consisted of two to four pages inserted at the end of each six-month section of the general disbursements, which could be cross-referenced to Hamon's memo book where he kept his notes on projects and contracts with builders and suppliers and jotted down his ideas and sketches.[77] With this arrangement, Alice paid the bills and itemised the expenditure, while Hamon concentrated on managing the building process. Her accounts meant that he could reliably predict his income stream and plan ahead with a degree of certainty. He could see at a glance the expenses and income, and the spare cash that he could allocate to various projects; this enabled him to carry out a rolling programme of building and repairs, which continued without a break, despite the financial setbacks of the 1640s, until his death in 1654.

The inheritance of the Sedgeford estate from Alice's father in 1620 increased the annual value of the estate from £1247 to £1720, but added greatly to the burden of management. Again the Le Stranges shared the task. Hamon supervised the building work while Alice kept the estate accounts and managed the sheep flocks. Her sheep and wool accounts are bound with the household accounts, demonstrating the growing range and interaction of her activities. These accounts, which start in 1617, represent Alice's first foray into farming, when she borrowed £73 from the father to buy sheep for herself and set up tiny flocks for her five children, Nicholas, Hamon, Jane, Elizabeth and baby Roger; these were augmented by her father's will, which directed that 'forty sheep a piece' should go to the three younger grandchildren.[78] With references to 'my father's book', Alice's intention was clearly to repeat the training that she had received from her father in sheep farming and estate management. The children's sheep were sold to Sir Hamon in 1627, but in 1634 Alice repeated the process with her grandchildren, including the younger Sir Nicholas (d. 1669), who became such a favourite.[79] This is the most graphic example of handing down knowledge, which we will examine more fully in chapter 7.

Alice's farming expertise came to the fore in 1620, when she purchased the Sedgeford flocks from her brother-in-law, Sir William Yelverton, who had been allowed to enjoy the profit for a year after Stubbe's death. In the first few pages of a new paper book for Sedgeford she listed the delivery and the division of 1333 sheep into three flocks: East, South and North. Her numbering system was a bit erratic at first, but she possessed a secure knowledge of the business and soon rationalised her methods.[80]

---

77 LEST/Q38.

78 See chapter 7; Stubbe's will, TNA, PROB 11/135.

79 Numbers limited the flocks to the eight sons of Sir Nicholas, 1st Bt.

80 See chapter 7 (sheep account, 1620–2).

By 1625 the management of their six flocks in Sedgeford and Ringstead had been streamlined, which prompted Alice to start the book entitled Flocks and Foldcourses. The family kept three flocks in hand at Sedgeford East Ground, Barrett Ringstead and the South Flock at Ringstead; they let the North Flock at Ringstead to a syndicate of tenants, and Sedgeford North and South Grounds to individual tenants. This structure survived and prospered until 1643, when the flocks were plundered by the parliamentary forces; they took 1715 sheep from a total of 1911, leaving Alice with less than 200 sheep.

At the same time as managing the sheep flocks Alice created a new estate account for Sedgeford, which she entered after the sheep account of 1620–2. It covered the period from 1621 to 1634, when the farming at Sedgeford was dominated by her cousin Francis Guybon, and the reorganisation that followed his death in 1631. We will discuss the situation in Sedgeford further in chapter 7; suffice to say that the knowledge and accounting system Alice built up as result of this process led to her taking over the accounts for the remainder of the estate in 1632. From the 1630s she also undertook the renewal of the rentals, which had been reformed by Hamon for the new seven-year leases granted in 1611. So we see Alice heavily involved in estate management in her own right from 1620, focusing on Sedgeford and building up a sheep flock for her children. Elsewhere, Hamon was the initiator of change, while Alice became the general accountant, consolidator and detailed organiser of his records. Her work on the Hunstanton records from 1632 demonstrates the point.

Traditionally, the estate at Hunstanton was managed through four different types of record. The field books provided a description of the landholding structure; rentals listed the manorial tenants owing freehold and copyhold rents; firmals listed those tenants leasing land from the Le Stranges; and the bailiffs' accounts gave a brief summary of the holdings, the allowances granted to tenants and the payments received. Before 1630 all these records were kept separately and it is very difficult to trace what individual tenants owed for their lands, which might be scattered across the estate, and the type of rents they paid. Hamon commissioned the maps which gave him a visual image of the geography and landholding structure and made a start on the field books, but much remained to be done. Alice, in her renewals of the field books, improved their layout and legibility so that they could be more easily cross-referenced to the maps and other documents. The rentals, firmals and bailiffs' account she drew together into a single volume. Every four years she listed each tenant's manorial and farm rents as an individual portfolio, noting changes in occupancy. Each year she entered a summary of the bailiffs' accounts. From 1638 she cross-referenced the receipts from each estate account back to the household accounts, attaching with a pin 'a note how this account was received and written in my Booke'; later these receipts were written more securely in the account book. In this way, Alice created a fully integrated system, linking estate and household accounts. Similar records survive for Ringstead, Holme and Heacham.

Thus, we see how Hamon and Alice consciously and systematically gathered, created and reorganised their knowledge of the estate, focusing on the need to facilitate access and safeguard it for the future. We will now move on to discuss how this knowledge was used and shared, and what it achieved within these local communities during their lifetimes.

Chapter 6

Using knowledge and working with people: building projects on the Le Strange estate

What did Sir Hamon and Alice do with all the knowledge they carefully accumulated? What was it for? How far and in what ways did it make a difference to the management of their estate? How did they benefit? Was it worth all the effort? To use knowledge effectively they needed to engage with people of every kind, including household servants, tenants and labourers, craftsmen, suppliers of goods and services and professionals such as surveyors, doctors, lawyers and the clergy. Those with specialist knowledge were often recruited from afar, while local families, involved with farming and fishing activities, provided a flexible labour force with a range of useful skills.[1] Success rested on Sir Hamon's ability to lead and manage this human capital, which included his wife and eldest son. Their enthusiastic contribution suggests that he possessed a particular talent for this type of role. By all accounts, he was sociable, public spirited, brave and sporty, all qualities likely to endear him to his fellow man, while Alice was similarly gregarious, told bawdy jokes and paid close attention to her female servants. Yet both were highly intelligent and firmly focused on the improvement of their estate, and they knew, like any paternalistic landowner, that it was in their interests to look after their employees. This was particularly the case with building projects, which required labour with knowledge and precise skills. These, along with aspects of water management, are the focus of this chapter.

Sir Hamon's ambition to complete 'his cheife house halfe built' and rebuild his farm houses 'out of the ground' was the most complex, knowledge-intensive and costly enterprise undertaken by the family. Both he and Alice left extensive documentation, stretching over nearly five decades, showing how they planned, financed and organised their building programme; this included not only radical work on the hall but every type of structure, functional and decorative, from farm buildings and hen houses to the Octagon in the park where Hamon played his viols. As we know, they worked as a team, with Alice keeping the accounts and Hamon managing the projects, making sketches and drawing up agreements with a host of craftsmen and suppliers in his memoranda book.[2] The process gained momentum in 1610, when Alice took over the accounts, with the construction of a dairy, brewhouse and malthouse to supply the household; this activity continued with escalating ambition until Sir Hamon's death in 1654.

Figure 6.1 shows the expenditure on building projects and repairs from 1607 to 1653.[3] The first two spikes coincide with Alice's growing participation in estate

---

1   See Whittle and Griffiths, *Consumption and Gender*, pp. 210–38.
2   LEST/Q38.
3   Based on Sir Hamon's accounts, 1606–9, followed by Alice's, 1610–54: LEST/P6, P7 and P10.

business from 1610, with work at Hunstanton, Holme, Ringstead and Gressenhall, and her creation of building accounts in 1621 to cope with substantial projects at Sedgeford and Heacham. The spike in 1632 reflects spending at Benacre, acquired for their second son Hamon, but it was sold after he decided to settle closer to home, which explains the additional outlay at Ringstead from 1636.[4] Expenditure slumped in 1643 when the sheep flocks were destroyed by parliamentary forces, but resumed in 1646 with more work at Heacham and Ringstead. In all they spent £8788 on construction over forty-five years; this included repairing all the churches on the estate, improving and extending Hunstanton Hall, building farmhouses and barns and erecting other structures, such as kilns, bridges, mills and watercourses, all of which required significant technical knowledge. Most of these activities were summarised by Sir Nicholas (d. 1724) in the memoranda book, alongside his own contribution, for the benefit of his successors.[5]

Before we immerse ourselves in the Le Stranges' building programme some context is needed. Sir Hamon's measured and holistic approach to estate building was very different to the activities of his relatives and friends, notably Sir Henry Hobart, who spent about £10,000 on rebuilding Blickling Hall between 1619 and 1629 and Sir Roger Townshend (1595–1637) at Raynham, who, in contrast with Sir Henry and Sir Hamon, chose a completely new site and built one of the first classical country houses in England.[6] The accounts for the new Raynham Hall are incomplete, so no overall figure can be obtained, but when Sir Roger died in 1637 he left the house unfinished after twenty years of building – and rebuilding. We can only guess at the cost, but it included the construction of foundations on a new site, a change of plan in 1622 requiring new foundations, recurrent problems with the water supply and a design for the house that needed constant modification. The new house at Raynham, wrongly attributed to Inigo Jones, was in effect an experiment and plaything for a wealthy landowner aspiring to be his own architect, with all the rethinking and the delays that invariably involves.[7]

---

4   The purchase of the Benacre estate was funded with Anne Lewkenor's dowry when she married Sir Nicholas in 1630.

5   Historic England and Norfolk Heritage Explorer appear to have no knowledge of these seventeenth-century sources, but they provide a useful technical description of the buildings: <https://historicengland.org.uk/listing/the-list/list-entry/1001006>, accessed 27 July 2021.

6   C. Stanley-Milson, 'The architecture and decoration of Blickling Hall up to 1629', PhD thesis (University of East Anglia, 1981); also 'Blickling Hall: the building of a great house', *Journal of Royal Society of Arts*, 135/5365 (1986), pp. 58–74; for a more recent perspective see Griffiths, 'The Boleyns at Blickling', pp. 453–68; For Raynham see L. Campbell, 'Documentary evidence of the building of Raynham Hall', *Architectural History*, 32 (1989), pp. 52–67; and 'Sir Roger Townshend and his family: a study of gentry life in early seventeenth century Norfolk', PhD thesis (University of East Anglia, 1990).

7   See Campbell, 'Documentary evidence', for a full discussion of Townshend's methods and sources of inspiration; also N. Cooper, *Houses of the Gentry, 1480–1680* (New Haven, CT, 1999), pp. 37–8.

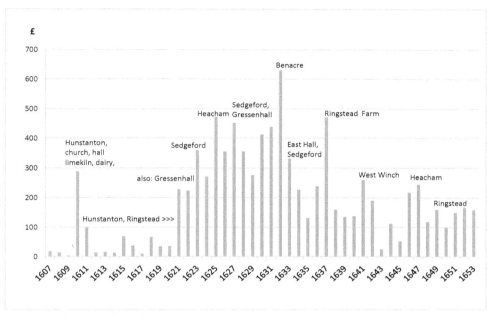

Figure 6.1 The cost of building projects and repairs, 1607–53.

Sir Roger clearly had ideas and ambitions different from those of his close friend Sir Hamon at Hunstanton, and much deeper pockets; he was also exposed to more varied influences. Like Hamon, he lost his father at an early age, but was brought up by his grandmother, Lady Jane Berkeley, principally in London, where she built several notable houses.[8] Roger spent little time at Raynham in his youth. When in Norfolk he lived with his mother, Anne, and grandfather, Nathaniel Bacon, who built a significant house at Stiffkey under the supervision of his father Sir Nicholas Bacon, the Lord Keeper and another compulsive builder.[9] So innovative building was in Roger's blood. Lady Jane died in 1617 leaving the young man a much improved estate at Raynham and the means to pursue his architectural interests, which he did with exceptional vigour and skill. A sketch by Edmund Prideaux (Figure 6.2) shows the new hall resplendent on a rise, cut off from the old hall, farm, village and church on the river, but exposed to the biting Norfolk winds, which remain a problem for the occupants to this day.

Besides being fatherless from an early age, Sir Hamon and Sir Roger shared another experience: both were influenced by Sir Henry Spelman over several years: he was Hamon's guardian and mentor from 1592 to 1602, while Roger was his pupil at

---

8   Notably at Ashley Park, Walton on Thames, Surrey: for an analysis of the influence of London designs and compact plans on the gentry see Cooper, *Houses of the Gentry*, pp. 131, 135–7, 155–7.

9   For Nathaniel Bacon's building projects at Stiffkey and later Irmingland see the six volumes of his papers published by the Norfolk Record Society.

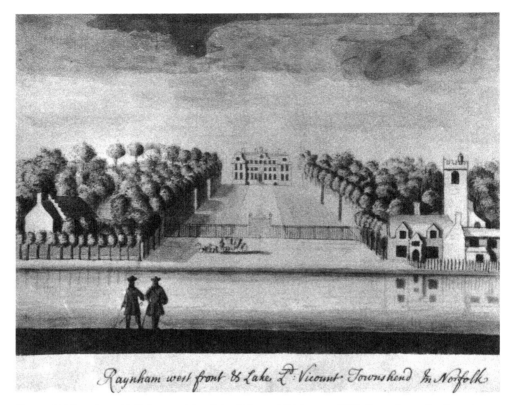

Figure 6.2 Raynham Hall, the west front, by Edmund Prideaux, 1724. From the collection of P.J.N. Prideaux-Brune Esq., Prideaux Place, Padstow.

Stiffkey before going to Cambridge in 1611.[10] In both cases Spelman instilled a deep interest in books, learning and knowledge, with a desire and the confidence to use it on the ground, working with professionals, but making all the key decisions.[11] As adults, both men acquired measuring instruments as well as books on architecture, mathematics and languages to facilitate the study of French and Italian texts. Roger is also credited with making a wooden model to assist the design process and promoting the use of perspective in drawings.[12] Their building programmes more or less coincided, with Hamon and Alice getting organised by 1610, while Roger started in 1618 on the death of his grandmother and the arrival of almost unlimited resources. He was a regular visitor to Hunstanton and no doubt they discussed their plans; they certainly shared skilled labour, notably the services of William Edge,

---

10   Sir Roger Townshend, 1st Bt (1595–1637), <www.historyofparliament.org.uk>.

11   On Sir Roger, see Campbell, 'Sir Roger Townshend'.

12   Cooper, *Houses of the Gentry*, pp. 37–8, illustrating 'Levels of Knowledge and Degrees of Involvement', but no mention of the Le Stranges at Hunstanton.

the mason who accompanied Roger on his travels through Europe to study the principals of classical architecture. Compared to Roger's radical approach, Hamon's upgrading of his medieval inheritance appears rather old fashioned, but he was no stranger to classical architecture – far from it. A closer look at the plans and elevation of the 'Elizabethan Wing' of Hunstanton Hall, started by his great-grandfather, Sir Nicholas, in 1577, suggests that the Le Stranges were actually pioneers of classical architecture in Norfolk – a more modest level than the Townshends, but knowingly radical nonetheless.

Unfortunately, the Elizabethan Wing was burnt down in 1853. However, we know about the building from the elevations and floor plans drawn by Jamesina Waller (1842–1912) in her recollections of the hall 'as it was before the fire of 1853' (Figures 6.3–6.6).[13] They show a compact double-pile house with a fully symmetrical front elevation, with the date 1577 on the door and the addition of an elaborate classical porch by Sir Hamon in 1618. The design with the three gables and three floors with symmetrical chimney stacks and windows is remarkably similar to a house in Shropshire dated 1578 and cited as being 'an extraordinarily early example of a house built to a deep rectangular plan'.[14] This plan was very different to the elongated medieval hierarchical plan with the great hall buttressed by service facilities at the lower end and amenities for the lord and his family at the upper end, often leading to private apartments accessed by a grand staircase. This gradation up the social scale is made firmly evident from the outside by the entry at the lower end of the hall, the separation of the services from the hall with a screens passage and, at the upper end, elaborate decorative motifs and ever-more splendid windows indicating status.

The Elizabethan Wing at Hunstanton, with its symmetry and centralised floor plans, downplayed the notion of hierarchy. However, a hall for communal activity was retained but reduced in size to fit a central entrance with a central staircase leading up to the first floor and the attics (Figures 6.4–6.6). The ground-floor plan shows the central front entrance into the lower end of the Tenants' Hall. The porch on the west front was added in the 1830s and survived the fire. The staircase, one of the 'glories of the Elizabethan building', led up to the Hall Chamber, an attendant bedroom hung with tapestries and two further generous bedrooms, all equipped with dressing room and fireplace.[15] The attic floor contained four more comfortable bedrooms, with a sunny room on the south

---

13   MSS book, *Hunstanton Hall, 1846–1853, My Recollections of Those Years, Jamesina Waller, 1910,* NRO MS 21219, T140 C. She was assisted with the plans by her nephew, Roland Le Strange (1869–1919).

14   This house was identified by Cooper (*Houses of the Gentry,* pp. 141–55). In his chapter 'Alternatives and experiments, 1550–1650' he describes how new ideas percolated from London to the provinces. As a career courtier, Sir Nicholas Le Strange, Kt (1511–80) may well have been influenced in this way; see also M. Girouard, *Robert Smythson and the Elizabethan Country House* (New Haven, CT, 1983), pp. 1–39.

15   The Hall Chamber had a good polished floor and was used as a ballroom, while the Tapestry Room was occupied by Jamesina's parents. See also the inventory of bedrooms at Hunstanton Hall drawn up in 1632 by Alice Le Strange in account book LEST/P10.

Figure 6.3 Sketch showing the east front of the Elizabethan Wing as it was before 1853. NRO MS 21219.

front used for drying lavender.[16] On the ground floor the south front rooms were similarly designed for family use.[17] Across the central passage from the Tenants' Hall, the family ate in the South Dining Room, which linked to the Library, with both rooms well heated and lit by large windows on the south and west fronts.[18] But where were the services? Jamesina does not mention a kitchen, buttery or pantry, but included several references to a wine cellar and an open courtyard to the north of the tenants' hall, to which the plan shows access. This suggests that the services were in the cellar and around that courtyard. The likelihood is that Sir Nicholas, when he built his new double-pile house, retained the service area of an earlier medieval house, leaving his successors to finish

---

16 Armine's Attic refers to Armine Styleman, 1691–1768, the eldest daughter of Sir Nicholas 4th Bt, who lived at Hunstanton Hall during her widowhood with her mentally disabled son, Robert. Jamesina described the attic rooms as light and sunny, with views over the north and south wings to the park.

17 John R. Mayer, *Extraneus: The Annals Quinquepartite of Strange Lives* (San Francisco, CA, 1993), pp. 123–6, 155–61, confirms that the south front and later the south wing were designed for family use. He seems to have had recent access to the hall, but not to have been aware of Jamesina's recollections on the Elizabeth Building; lack of references are a problem throughout.

18 The east front windows in the dining room were blocked, perhaps to give the family more privacy.

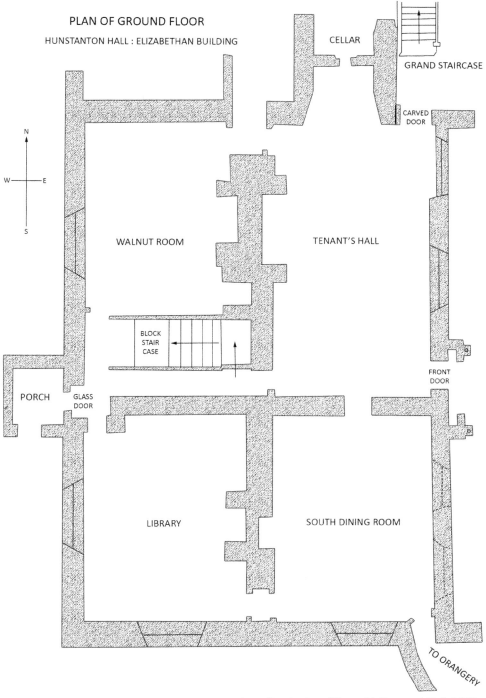

Figure 6.4 Sketch based on ground-floor plan of the Elizabethan Wing with Tenants' Hall. NRO MS 21219.

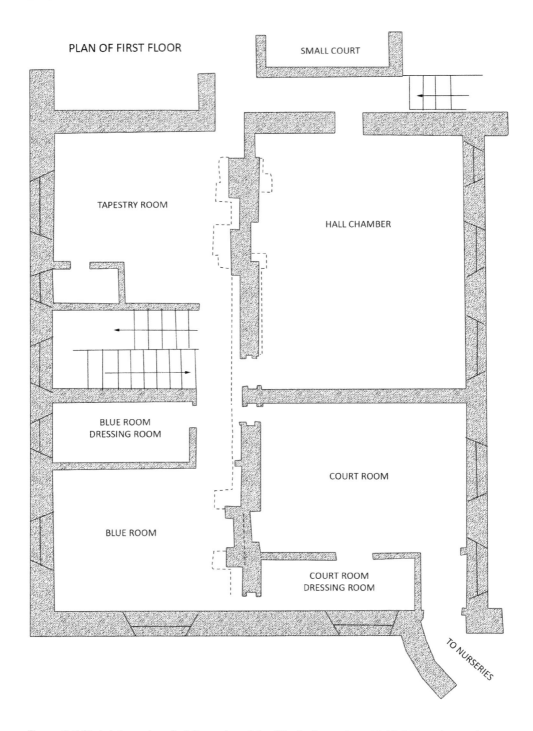

Figure 6.5 Sketch based on first-floor plan of the Elizabethan wing with Hall Chamber and family bedrooms. NRO MS 21219.

PLAN OF ATTIC FLOOR

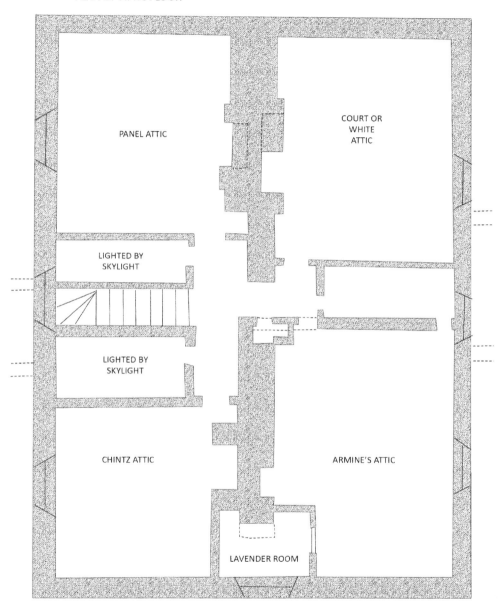

Figure 6.6 Sketch based on attic-floor plan with further bedrooms and the Lavender Room. NRO MS 21219.

the job. From Alice's accounts we know that improving these facilities was a priority in 1610, and continued to be throughout the seventeenth and early eighteenth centuries.[19]

Jamesina's plans also provide a tantalising glimpse of how the Elizabethan Wing was linked to the north and south wings built by Sir Hamon in the 1620s. The Grand Staircase on the north-east corner led off from the Tenants' Hall (shown in the bottom right-hand corner of Figure 6.4), while passages to the Orangery and Nurseries linked the family rooms on the south front (shown in the bottom left-hand corners of figures 6.4 and 6.5). Figure 6.7 shows the complete picture and the building phases from the fourteenth to the nineteenth century.[20] It illustrates how Sir Hamon closed the space between the Elizabethan Wing and the medieval gatehouse with two T-shaped wings and identifies the state rooms in the north wing and the open court, but does not explain the purpose of the black block described as dating from the fourteenth century. Historic England make no reference to any fourteenth-century remains, but their existence seems to be supported by an entry in Sir Nicholas's table of buildings that notes a date of 1396 against 'ye kitching chimney', which confirms that the services were located on the north side of the hall.[21] Finally, the plan shows that this area was the main focus of improvement in the early 1830s and indicates the unsatisfactory nature of the rebuilding undertaken after the fire in 1853.

The sketch of the Elizabethan Wing drawn just before the fire (Figure 6.8) illustrates a double-pile house facing outwards to the west and south, with nineteenth-century additions on the north side, extending service provision. It shows what a comfortable building this must have been and why the family were so distressed at losing it. The only comfort was the survival of Sir Hamon's porch, which, clothed in roses, 'forms a singularly beautiful approach to the gardens'.[22] So we begin to understand why Sir Hamon adorned the house with such a magnificent porch and why his successors in the 1830s, against professional advice, persevered with the old hall.[23]

The painting on the cover of the book, and Figure 6.9, shows the hall a few years before Henry L' Estrange Styleman Le Strange returned to Hunstanton in 1836.[24] It confirms the description in the *Excursions through Norfolk* (1819) that the hall was

---

19 LEST/P6, LEST/Q38, pp. 200–6.

20 Christopher Hussey, 'Country homes gardens old and new: Hunstanton Hall I. Norfolk. The Seat of Mr Charles Le Strange', *Country Life*, 59/1527 (10 April 1926), p. 559.

21 LEST/Q38, fol. 201. A marginal note questions whether 'it is not 1496'? This would bring it in line with the gatehouse. See Anon., 'Country homes gardens old and new: Hunstanton Hall, Norfolk, the Seat of Mr H. Le Strange', *Country Life Illustrated*, 8/189 (18 August 1900), p. 208: clearly influenced by the antiquarianism of Hamon Le Strange, referring to even earlier remains.

22 Anon., 'Hunstanton Hall', p. 210.

23 When the L'Estrange estates were valued for partition in 1784 N. Kent and J. Claridge estimated that the house was worth more for its materials and would not answer the cost of repairs; they recommended the family rebuilt on 'some pleasanter part of the park', in the 'Modern Fashion', away from the moat and the farmyard (LEST/R23).

24 Painting by John Westhall, 1823. The colours suggest that the Elizabethan Wing was built in carstone with freestone dressings; however, the colours of the east wing bear little resemblance to the black and white wings and the brick gatehouse we see today. Some artistic licence perhaps.

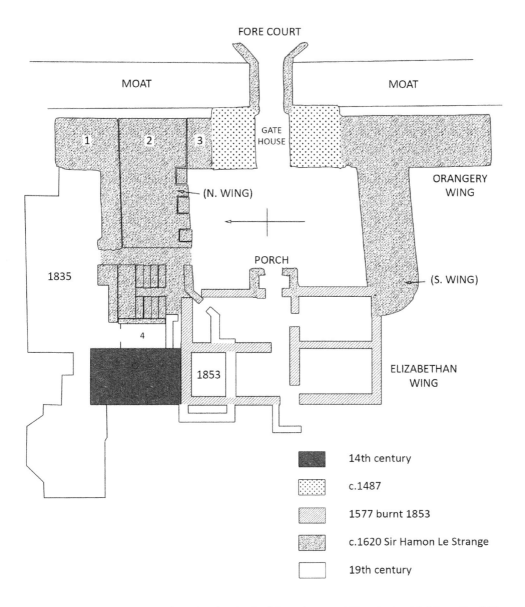

FORE COURT

MOAT   MOAT

1 2 3

GATE
HOUSE

ORANGERY
WING

(N. WING)

PORCH

(S. WING)

1835

4

1853

ELIZABETHAN
WING

	14th century
	c.1487
	1577 burnt 1853
	c.1620 Sir Hamon Le Strange
	19th century

Figure 6.7 Sketch based on plan showing the building phases at Hunstanton Hall from the 14th to 19th century. From Christopher Hussey, 'Country homes gardens old and new: Hunstanton Hall I. Norfolk. The Seat of Mr Charles Le Strange', *Country Life*, Vol. 59, Issue 1527 (Apr 10, 1926), p. 559.

Note: The numbers on the plan refer to 1. State Bedroom, 2. Drawing Room, 3. China Room, 4. Open Court. Note that the Elizabethan Wing is shown in reverse orientation compared to figures 6.4–6.6.

Figure 6.8 The Elizabethan Wing, *c.*1850 before the great fire of 1853 from 'Hunstanton Hall', *Country Life Illustrated* (1900), p. 210. NRO MC 1678/14, 896X7.

well on its way to becoming a romantic ruin with crumbling walls and a rustic fence struggling to keep sheep and yokels out of the outer courtyard.[25] As it happens, this is the only picture we have of the hall as it must have appeared to visitors after Sir Hamon finished his work in the 1640s. It shows the Elizabethan gables towering over his south and north wings and the medieval gatehouse, all fronted by his classical gateway and crenellated walls, with farm buildings still contained within the courtyard.[26] A family sketch of a long view of the park and east front, after the restoration of the 1830s, shows the gables, gatehouse and wings still intact but the classical gates nowhere to be seen – possibly a reflection of Henry's Gothic Revivalism (Figure 6.10). However, the same arrangement can be seen in a postcard (Figure 6.11), diverting attention away from the Victorian replacement of the Elizabethan Wing after the fire. Despite this unfortunate addition, Sir Hamon's work at Hunstanton Hall has withstood the test of time and taste.[27]

---

25 'Although the whole building has long been ruinous, this entrance (gatehouse) is still deserving of notice': T.K. Cromwell, *Excursions in the County of Norfolk*, II (London, 1819), p. 22; the sketch by J.S. Cotman highlighted the gatehouse and moat, but without the Elizabethan gables peering over the top.

26 Map for Hunstanton Hall in the estate survey of 1820, NRO MF/RO 597/5; Additional Deposits 2013/12/1.

27 Another fire in 1950 gutted the north wing, but this has been carefully restored.

Figure 6.9 Hunstanton Hall, by John Westall, 1823. © Le Strange Estate.

Figure 6.10 Hunstanton Hall, after the restoration, 1835. © Le Strange Meakin family.

Figure 6.11 Hunstanton Hall, *c.*1900 postcard.

Maps of various dates demonstrate how Hunstanton Hall's immediate environment was also altered over time. The enlarged section of Waterman's 1615 map (Figure 6.12) shows the manor site at Hunstanton surrounded by nine enclosures, bordering the park to the south, the open fields to the west and east and the village to the north. The double-pile Elizabethan building with the gabled south end and the two symmetrical chimneys can be seen, as well as a porch centred on the gatehouse, raising the possibility that Sir Hamon's porch of 1618 was an upgrade rather than a new build. Beyond the gatehouse and across the moat, the outer courtyard and entry to the hall was encircled by farm buildings, with a two-bay threshing barn, probably the Upper Barn, situated on the way to the village.[28] Two further closes, Lord's Close – formerly Jefferyes Yard – and Saffron Close, border the park boundary and the road to Holme. This arrangement in front of the house proved remarkably resilient. The survey of 1820, with maps of individual holdings (Figure 6.13) shows that the two farm buildings at right angles to the moat survived, as they do today, while the two long barns parallel to the moat framing the gatehouse have disappeared, replaced by Sir Hamon's courtyard walls and his classical gates in the 1620s.[29] But notice the development of the Upper Barn area. This work was probably initiated by Henry

---

28 No dates appear for the building of the granaries or the upper barn, suggesting that they preceded Sir Hamon's time and were part of an earlier medieval arrangement.

29 A survey of Henry Styleman's estate, by James Utting, 1820, with individual maps illustrating the farms and holdings and accompanied by a large folded map, NRO MF/RO 897/5; Additional Deposits, 2013/12/1.

Styleman following the advice given in the valuation of 1784 that the hall should be abandoned and a large farm developed on the site.[30]

However, his son had other ideas. Henry L'Estrange Styleman Le Strange, the arch Gothic Revivalist, followed up his restoration of the hall with a magnificent restyling of the gardens and an extension of the park. The final version and substantial nature of these changes can be seen on the Ordnance Survey map of 1887 (Figure 6.14), which shows the loss of the Elizabethan Wing in 1853 and the disappearance of the Upper Barn, as well as the retention of the dairy and accompanying barns within the courtyard walls. The map also shows the new gardens to the west of the hall, romantically fringed by turreted walls with the moats rearranged into decorative pieces of water.[31] Jamesina thought the Hall Gardens dated from the late 1840s, but Figure 6.15 suggests that the work started in 1859, possibly inspired by the fire of 1853, which opened up the internal courtyard to the west and the evening sun. Note that the axis of the new garden is based on the gatehouse and two surviving porches. The Upper Barn was still in evidence on the tithe map of 1844, but, as the park and gardens expanded, farming activities on the west of the park moved to Lodge Farm and on the east to Hall Farm, Ringstead, leaving the spirit of the medieval Le Stranges to flourish at the centre around the hall.[32]

I

How did Sir Hamon set about his massive task of remodelling Hunstanton Hall and other elements of the estate? What issues did he need to tackle? How did he develop his ideas? What systems did he put in place? But, first, in what state did he find Hunstanton Hall in 1604? Was it as bad as Alice made out? We are fortunate that Thomas Waterman included on his map of 1615 minute detail of the manor site that can be cross-referenced to the field books of 1618–23 and 1648, Sir Hamon's memoranda books and the household accounts from 1606 to 1654; all these sources indicate that the site was already a place of innovation and activity.[33]

---

30 Henry's father, Armine Styleman, rector of Great Ringstead, inherited the estate from his brother, Nicholas, in 1788 and Henry (1754–1819) took over the management. The survey of 1820 shows numbered sections of the park and closes, amounting to 348 acres, let to the steward John Carter, who lived at no. 1098, on the way to Hunstanton common and the beach (Caley's Hall, now a hotel), while Henry kept pieces in hand, but resided at Snettisham Hall. See E.M. James, 'The Old Hall, Snettisham and the Styleman family', *Norfolk Archaeology*, 38/2 (1983), pp. 343–57.

31 NRO MS 21219, T140 C, Waller, *Recollections*, pp. 118–24. Jamesina thought the development of the garden dated from the late 1840s; however, an annotated map above suggests the work dated from 1859, after the fire of 1853.

32 In 1820 farmsteads were located around the hall: Calys to the north, no. 1098; John Norton's holding to the east, based at no. 1061, in front of the hall; to the west John Hunn was based at no. 1006, in old Hunstanton – Cliff Farm on the modern OS map; while Robert Spanton's farmstead was absorbed by the new garden. This configuration can be seen more clearly on the large map of 1820: NRO MF/RO 597/5; Additional Deposits 2013/12/1.

33 LEST/OA1; LEST/BH1 and BH2; LEST/Q38; LEST/P6 and P7.

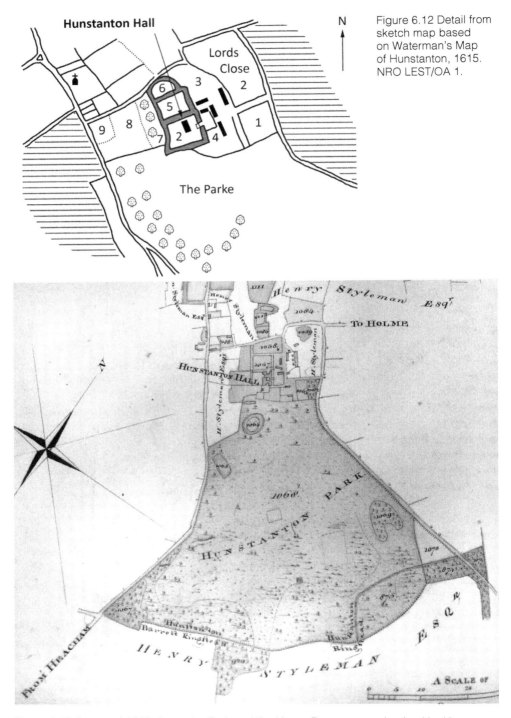

Figure 6.12 Detail from sketch map based on Waterman's Map of Hunstanton, 1615. NRO LEST/OA 1.

Figure 6.13 Survey of 1820 shows the Park and the Upper Barn area modernised by Henry Styleman. NRO MF/RO 597/5; Additional Deposits TD 2013/12/1.

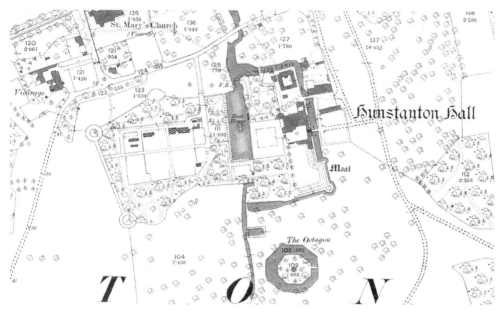

Figure 6.14 OS map showing the completed Hall Gardens and the domestication of the site. The hall and gardens were divided into lots and sold in 1952. However, the family repurchased the Hall Gardens because two members of the family had been buried there. A further fire happened in the north wing of the hall in the 1980s, but the wing has since been restored. OS 25" 1887 Norfolk VI.5. Reproduced with the permission of the National Library of Scotland, CC-BY-NC-SA.

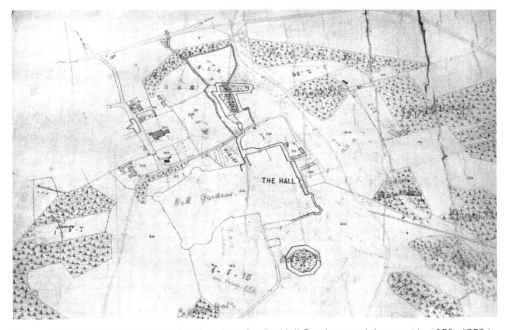

Figure 6.15 Annotated map showing the plans for the Hall Gardens and the moat in 1859. 1859 is the date of the only enclosure act relating to Hunstanton; it was for eighty acres. NRO LEST/OE 3.

Let us begin with the task Sir Hamon faced in the early 1600s. The positioning of the farm buildings in front of the hall, shown in Figures 6.12 and 6.13, appears an oddity, but development to the north, west and south of the hall was restricted by the complex system of moats fed by the river Hun, which rises at the south-eastern end of the park and flows northwards round the hall, through the mill pool and across the marshes and common to the sea.[34] At some stage, three islands were formed containing the hall and garden, an orchard and a swine yard, while, to the west, three more closes were acquired consisting of a further orchard and two crofts formerly owned by the Browne family.[35] In the field book of 1618–23 the closes and field strips are not numbered, as they are on Waterman's map (Figure 6.12). These were probably inserted by Alice when drafting the field book of 1648, which provides more detail of buildings, showing the progress made over the previous twenty years. For example, the Saffron Close, no. 1 on the map, had acquired a 'little house and a Bowling Ground'; no. 2 was by then known as the Limekiln Close, while the barnyards, no. 3, had stables and a granary in addition to the milking yard. The site of the manor, no. 4, now had a capital messuage, offices, garden and orchards, while the remaining closes, nos 5–9, remained as in 1623, although new functions appear in the memoranda book. Significantly, several of these functions, notably milking, pig keeping, slaughtering and brewing, required ample quantities of water, which might explain their proximity to the hall and their continuance into the nineteenth century. The moats were also burdened with the task of providing fresh water for the family and disposing of household waste. Needless to say, they were a health hazard and required constant attention and maintenance.

A striking feature of the documents was a growing awareness of the need to develop a strategy and the use of technology. This is illustrated in Sir Hamon's accounts of 1606–9 listing repairs to the chancel of Hunstanton church, for which as lay impropriator he was responsible.[36] The care of these ancient buildings was clearly a priority. Embellished over the centuries by the communities they served, their upkeep required an army of skilled craftsmen, including plumbers, masons, glaziers, painters, joiners, smiths, carpenters, sawyers, thatchers and carters, often working in teams with servers and labourers and using a wide variety of materials. The Le Stranges were fortunate in the availability of local stone, notably the red carstone and soft limestones from their cliffs at Hunstanton and their quarry at Ringstead Downs.[37] The chalky limestone was used in a variety of ways: in blocks as clunch, often in chequerboard patterns with harder stones, such as flint or carstone, as on the east front of Hunstanton Hall; and in a rougher form for barns and walls, as at Hall Farm, Ringstead. More generally, it was burnt in kilns to make mortar to fix the stones and

---

34   The source of the River Hun is just over the boundary in Great Ringstead at Spring Meadow Pit; see also chapter 8.

35   These three closes were those reconfigured as a formal garden in the late 1850s; see Figures 6.13–6.15.

36   Sir Hamon's remit also extended to Ringstead, Holme and Gressenhall, and later included the larger churches at Heacham and Sedgeford.

37   Layers of white and red chalk lie above the dark red carstone at Hunstanton.

limewash to cover the walls.[38] Sand from the beaches, notably at Holme, was also a vital ingredient for making bricks, tiles and pavements, while huge quantities of timber came from the Le Stranges' woods at Gressenhall for every type of structure. These local materials saved greatly on the cost of building and transportation. At this early stage, imports into the locality were confined to the purchase of lead for the roofs, gutters and pipes; decorative and plain glass for the windows; and freestone for sculptural pieces, quoins and dressing local stones.

Sir Hamon's plans gained momentum in 1610 when Alice took over the accounts, leaving him to organise the building work. His first venture was the construction of a lime kiln in front of the hall, beyond the courtyard, followed in 1611 by a brick kiln near the beach at Holme, used for repairs to the chancels at Ringstead and Holme.[39] For lesser houses and farm buildings in these villages, bricks were used to support and dress the softer carstone and clunch of the walls. The medieval gatehouse at Hunstanton Hall was built entirely in brick, with freestone quoins and dressings round the windows and gateway. It appears from the painting of 1823 that the Elizabethan Wing was built in block carstone with freestone dressings, similar to what survives at Snettisham Old Hall.[40] From these buildings we can identify a hierarchy of materials, with freestone used for gates, porches, battlements, quoins and windows, while local carstone, clunch, flint and bricks were used for the walls. In the 1610s, possibly with pressure from Alice, improvements focused on the dairy, brewhouse and malthouse at Hunstanton, while her father Richard Stubbe, resident at Holme, provided lodging for the extra carpenters, masons and labourers employed.

From 1613 Sir Hamon recorded his building plans and activities in his new memoranda book, consciously designed to inform and pass on knowledge to his successors.[41] He began with a biblical quote, 'If thou give any thinge by number & weight putt all in writing both that is given out & that is received againe', which was followed by a description of the various types of weights and measures, Troy weight, principally for silver and gold, Avoirdupois weights for the majority of other items, with separate measures for fish, paper, iron and lead.[42] Hamon's early notes included borrowing and buying lead from the churchwardens at Snettisham, Heacham and Sedgeford 'to cover my stayr case',[43] followed by contracts with Wilson of Lynn for oiling and colouring the stone bridge; with Dison, the joiner of Gaywood, 'for working with me'; with James Warner for his charges about the chapel at Gressenhall; and with John Steward for producing bricks, tiles and pavements at specified prices.[44] The first major scheme in 1616, itemised over four pages, involved two carpenters, William Costen of

---

38   Lime was also used as a fertiliser to reduce the acidity of sandy soils.

39   Sir Hamon also built a limekiln at Heacham (LEST/Q38, p. 25) soon after he purchased the great manor of Lewes Priory in 1609.

40   On the book cover.

41   LEST/Q38.

42   Ecclesiastes 42.7.

43   The main staircase in the Elizabethan wing.

44   LEST/Q38, pp. 1–2. These tasks included a range of other activities, such as agreements with London tradesmen for a splendid coach, and a new set of bows and arrows, pp. 9–10.

Snettisham and Francis Costen of Sedgeford,[45] for the reroofing of Hunstanton church and the sharing of the costs with the parishioners. Hamon agreed to pay a third, which probably covered the chancel and side chapels commemorating the family.[46]

The work on the churches stimulated Sir Hamon's building knowledge and helped to shape his overall strategy. With a local network of skilled labour and suppliers firmly established, he was able to proceed with his plans for completing the hall, drawing in specialists when required. His first agreement in 1617 with Hans Weller, a Dutchman and resident of Southwark, was for two pyramids to accompany the arms and escallop he had already finished on the porch (Figure 6.16).[47] For this task, costing a total of £35 4s 1d, Sir Hamon purchased freestone from Thomas Thorpe of Kings Cliffe, Northampton, for £19 and paid £3 10s for the shipping to Hunstanton and £9 18s 5d for lead for the fastening of the freestone.[48] Cheaper materials acquired for the church, namely wood and pavements, were also used, showing the interaction between different projects.[49] Weller carried out other work in the house and gave Sir Hamon useful tips, including 'howe to scoure & glosse ye black marble harth stone in my great chamber'.[50] In this way, we see Hamon tightly managing his resources, learning from specialists and recording their words for posterity.

An example of Sir Hamon's early technical knowledge is the scheme he drew up in 1617 for the drainage of Ringstead Yards, south of the park, and Meadow Pit Close, on the east side of the park near the boundary with Great Ringstead. The sites can be identified on the modern map as Downs Farm and Meadow Pits. Both have a spring derived from the chalk mass that includes the quarry at Ringstead Downs.[51] The outlet from Downs Farm runs south-west into the river Heacham skirting Manor Farm, the principal holding of the Le Stranges in Heacham, which may explain why Sir Hamon acquired the property in 1609. The other spring forms the source of the river Hun, which runs northward through the park at Hunstanton, round the moats and out to the sea at Holme.[52] Like many chalk areas, the watercourses are winterbournes and unreliable in the summer, when they become smothered in vegetation. This was a particular problem in Meadow Pit Close, to which Sir Hamon

---

45   On Francis Costen see Whittle and Griffiths, *Consumption and Gender*, pp. 226–7.

46   LEST/Q38, pp. 13–16.

47   LEST/Q38, p. 11.

48   The detailed payments, from 1616 to 1618, were listed by Alice in her accounts (LEST/P6).

49   LEST/Q38, pp. 22.

50   LEST/Q38, p. 23

51   Ringstead Downs is a dry chalk valley and an SSSI managed by the Norfolk Wildlife Trust. It has never been ploughed and is the largest area of chalk down surviving in the county.

52   The headwaters of the River Hun are submerged beneath an 'esker', a glacial formation, which runs from Meadow Pits north-west through woodland, past Park House and up to Kimberley Plantation: see P. Worsley, 'The Hunstanton Park esker, northwest Norfolk', *Mercian Geologist*, 18/2 (2013), pp. 119–27; and 'River Hun Catchment Plan', The Norfolk Rivers Trust with the Environment Agency (n.d.), <https://norfolkriverstrust.org/rivers/river-hun/>, accessed 27 July 2021.

Figure 6.16 Hans Weller's work on the porch, 1617–18. Author's photograph.

referred – hence the attention he gave to the structure and maintenance of these pits and streams, and why it took five pages to set out the agreements and explain his plans.

The agreements were mainly with Robert Johnson of Heacham and Richard Ransome of Snettisham for digging a network of dykes, drains and pits and building a sluice; each contract has a reference mark showing how the stretches were linked.[53] The plan was initiated in 1616, with three pits dug on the Common Fen at Ringstead Yards. However, they seem to have been too shallow – only eighteen inches deep, when they needed to be three or four feet. For the drainage at Meadow Pitt Close Hamon went a step further and produced a measured diagram with references to

---

53   LEST/Q38, pp. 17–21.

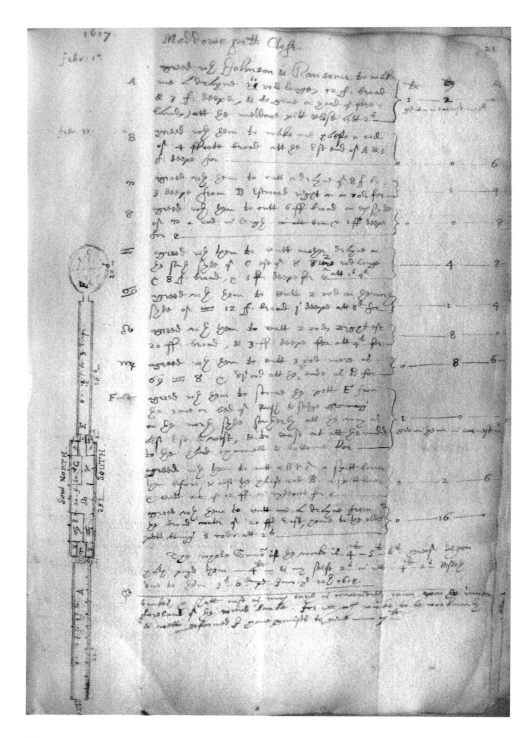

Figure 6.17 The scheme for Meadow Pitt Close, 1617. NRO LEST/Q 38, pp. 17–21.

the agreements clearly marked (Figure 6.17). In 1618, on a half-page between the two schemes, he inserted details of another contract with Johnson to clean the moats around the house, remove obstacles and create ponds at strategic points to help provide a regular supply of water. At the same time, Hamon drew up agreements for a new brewhouse, bakehouse and henhouse, with other contracts for the milking yard walls, the millhouse and barn, and more scouring of the moats and drains.[54] At Gressenhall in 1619 he followed a similar policy, completing a new sluice, stables and milking yards around the hall before embarking on work to the house.[55]

Sir Hamon's plans and building materials from 1620 reflect his growing prosperity and ambition for the hall.[56] The new orders of freestone from Thomas Thorpe included ashlars and corbels, sketched by Sir Hamon with measurements and costs, followed by the agreement of 1622 outlining the specification for the T-shaped wings that linked the Elizabethan building with the medieval gatehouse (see Figure 6.7).[57] At the same time, the Lower Barn was to be equipped with stables and individual saddle houses for Sir Hamon, strangers and the plowmen, followed by work on the millhouse and barn and the new granary, all carefully measured, costed and tiled by Bartholomew Mason. In 1623 Thorpe's work on the entry gates and in 1624 on the courtyard walls was set out in scrupulous detail.[58] The materials included expensive lead, glass and freestone, as with the chancels, but with more refined styles, decoration and furnishing, as one would expect for the residence of a leading gentry family. But where did the ideas come from? Who, if anybody, was advising Sir Hamon?

In recent accounts of the building of Hunstanton Hall much is attributed to Thomas Thorpe and William Edge, while the role of Inigo Jones, as architect of the entry gates, has been relegated to family myth, alongside the fable that he designed the new hall at Raynham.[59] New research confirms the influence of working men, notably masons, on the enthusiastic and highly educated owners. Of particular interest is a new study of mason's marks and the workshop of Thomas Thorpe.[60] Based mainly on Thorpe's work at Apethorpe Hall, a few miles from King's Cliffe, it includes a section on Hunstanton Hall and Blickling Hall. The authors knew that Thorpe was responsible

---

54 LEST/Q38, p. 50, work included the four moats round the house and three moats round the orchard.

55 LEST/Q38, pp. 34, 43.

56 LEST/Q38, pp. 54–61, 68.

57 See also Whittle and Griffiths, *Consumption and Gender*, p. 204.

58 LEST/Q38, pp. 70–3.

59 Historic England, 'Hunstanton Hall' (*c.*1999), <https://historicengland.org.uk/listing/the-list/list-entry/1001006>, accessed 27 July 2021; Pevsner and Wilson, *Buildings of England: Norfolk 2*, pp. 439–40. Inigo Jones is cited by Jamesina Waller and in the *Country Life* articles of 1900 and 1926. Sir Hamon is cited as the guiding force of the building project, and no other architects or craftsmen are mentioned in the text; likewise in the first edition of Pevsner, *The Buildings of England: North-West and South Norfolk* (London, 1962). For Raynham see Campbell, 'Documentary evidence', pp. 52–67.

60 J.S. Alexander and K.A. Morrison, 'Apethorpe Hall and the workshop of Thomas Thorpe, mason of King's Cliffe: a study in mason's marks', *Architectural History*, 50 (2007), pp. 59–94.

for the entry gates at Hunstanton in 1623, but discovered his marks on the porch dated 1618. Of course, if they had known about Sir Hamon's memoranda book they would have learnt more about Thorpe's involvement at Hunstanton.

The work on the porch predated Thorpe's association with Blickling, which suggests that Sir Hamon introduced him to Sir Henry Hobart rather than the other way round. The description of Thorpe's father, another Thomas, mason and Norfolk man, who came to Northamptonshire in the early 1570s, raises the possibility that the Le Stranges employed him to build the Elizabethan Wing in 1577 – the date on the door – with his son as an apprentice. After the deaths of Sir Nicholas and Sir Hamon in 1580 it is possible that Sir Hamon's father, Sir Nicholas (1563–92), engaged the young Thomas Thorpe to complete the building. However, the work ceased with Sir Nicholas's death in 1592, leaving Sir Hamon to finish the project in his own time. As we know, the map of 1615 shows the building with a porch, like the structure of 1618, suggesting that Sir Hamon completed rather than initiated it. This would explain Thorpe's early link with Hunstanton, why Sir Hamon engaged him and why he left so much detail of Thorpe's work in his memoranda book. The link with Thorpe might also explain Sir Roger Townshend's interest in the enterprise and the employment of William Edge and his team on the porch in 1618. Significantly, Sir Roger initiated visits to Hunstanton after Thorpe's death in about 1625.

The visits by William Edge in 1625 and 1626 to see the new building did not lead to more work until 1634, when building at Raynham was nearly finished. The first task, recorded by Alice, involved repairs to Heacham Chancel, followed by work at Hunstanton, which included installing a chimney piece in the Parlour Chamber in 1637, building the fire house and the falconer's chamber in 1638 and working on the 'little house', possibly the Octagon, in 1639. In 1641, still at Hunstanton, the Edges worked on the study and then moved outside to extensive work on the moat, which included 'cutting freestone and sawing it'. The Civil War reduced building activity on the estate, but in 1647 the Edges were employed at Calys house and Heacham manor, work that continued until 1653.[61] Only two references to the Edge family are recorded in Sir Hamon's memoranda book, suggesting an informal relationship.[62] From 1634 to 1653 the Edges helped the Le Stranges with great dexterity, but not at the specialised level of Thomas Thorpe and his team. They had accomplished their role at Raynham from 1619 to 1634, leaving Sir Hamon to engage other masons, notably William Goverson, to support Thorpe and complete the work after his demise.[63]

The principal work on the hall at Hunstanton did not start until the early 1620s. By that time Sir Hamon's finances had improved dramatically with the death of Richard Stubbe and Alice's inheritance of the Sedgeford estate; this explains the rise in expenditure and the creation of Alice's building accounts from 1621. The new work focused mainly on the hall and principal houses at Hunstanton and Sedgeford, and to a lesser extent at Gressenhall and Ringstead, followed by a significant programme

---

61 In LEST/Q38, Sir Hamon's entries end in 1645; Alice's accounts run until 1654 (LEST/P10).
62 In 1628 for repairs to stables at Ringstead for the use of Thomas Edge; in 1633 for work on Heacham Chancel (LEST/Q38, pp. 116, 142).
63 LEST/Q38, p. 68.

at Heacham from 1627, when the manor house was built, the chancel repaired and many other ancillary buildings constructed. Another boost arrived in 1630 with Sir Nicholas's marriage to Anne Lewkenor and her dowry of £3000. With these funds Sir Hamon purchased the Benacre estate and spent at least £168 11s 1 on improvements in 1632, before young Hamon decided to settle at Ringstead, hence the further rise in expenditure in 1637. At the same time attention turned to practical projects, such as more service buildings at Hunstanton and the creation of East Hall Farm on the brecks at Sedgeford. Activity slumped in 1643, after the attack by the parliamentary forces, but resumed in 1646 with the rebuilding of Calys manor and the mill at Heacham. Finally, in 1651, two shepherds' houses were built on the brecks at Ringstead.[64] The emphasis was on certain places at certain times, but ongoing work continued on every part of the estate, with considerable overlap, making it difficult to be precise about the expenditure on individual projects. While Hunstanton received the lion's share, with the extension of the hall, services, farm buildings and the moats, there is no sense that other parts of the estate were deprived of investment. Evidence of the building activities of Sir Hamon and Alice Le Strange survive not only at Hunstanton but also at Ringstead, Holme, Heacham and Sedgeford to the present day.

---

64   Later known as Neat's Lyng and Courtyard Farm. The idea was to intensify the farming management.

Chapter 7

Her price is above pearls: family and farming records of Alice Le Strange, 1617–56[1]

The huge archive left by Alice, the wife of Sir Hamon Le Strange of Hunstanton, forms part of one of the most important collections held at the Norfolk Record Office. In their scale and quality these records are exceptional; they include six bound volumes of general disbursements and household books dating from 1610 to 1654, Alice's sheep accounts from 1617, records for her own estate at Sedgeford from 1620 and accounts and field books for the entire Hunstanton estate from 1632.

The general disbursements and the household books have recently been the subject of a major research project on the organisation of an early seventeenth-century household.[2] This chapter examines Alice's life as a farmer, estate manager and guardian of the family finances. In many ways her performance in this field was even more remarkable than her management of her household, traditionally the province of gentlewomen. Women, of course, were no strangers to accounts or managing estates, but usually they assumed the role as widows or as single women, or in the absence of a male alternative. It was most unusual for a wife to undertake such a task alongside her husband. Over the years the Le Stranges created a family management team, with Sir Hamon providing strategic direction and masterminding the rebuilding programme, Alice acting as accountant and co-ordinator and their eldest son, Sir Nicholas, working on various projects, including the drainage of the coastal marshes.[3] By their joint efforts they rebuilt their estate 'out of the ground', as Alice noted in her summary of the family finances.[4] Sir Hamon had no doubts as to her ability and the value of her contribution to the management of his affairs. On the front of the fifth household book, concealed under a flap, he left a message, 'who shall finde a virtuous woman for her price is above pearls, the very heart of her husband trusteth in her … she overseeth the ways of her household and eateth not the brede of idleness'.[5] In his will he praised her 'incessant industry in straynes

---

1 This chapter is an abridged version of the introduction to Griffiths, *Her Price is Above Pearls*. The original documents referred to can be consulted in that volume.

2 Whittle and Griffiths, *Consumption and Gender*.

3 Sir Hamon left memoranda books full of details on his projects: LEST/Q36, Q37, Q38. For a perspective on Sir Hamon's activities see Griffiths, '"A Country Life"'. Sir Hamon was knighted in 1603; his son Sir Nicholas was granted a baronetcy in 1629. Sir Nicholas created at least eight farming notebooks, four of which survive: LEST/KA6, KA9, KA10, KA24, as discussed in chapter 8, below.

4 LEST/P10.

5 LEST/P8, based on the Book of Proverbs 31, v. 10, 27.

of knowledge above her sex to the just, faithfull and laudable advantage and advancement of my estate'.[6]

Alice's modernisation of the estate records and accounting system in the early seventeenth century is of the utmost significance. In this period of steeply rising prices it was essential for landowners to update their management structures and put their estates on a sound commercial footing. Norfolk was littered with examples of old gentry families, such as the Cleres of Ormesby and Blickling, and the Heydons of Baconsthorpe, who failed to do so; from the outset the Le Stranges were determined not to join their ranks. Soon after their marriage in 1604, Sir Hamon started compiling details of their titles and rights in his memoranda books, commissioning surveys of the estate, clarifying the content of rentals and firmals and keeping his own accounts.[7] Alice first became involved in estate management in 1613, receiving rents from the bailiffs and recording the receipts at the end of her household books.[8] In 1617 she set up individual accounts for the sheep that she and her father, Richard Stubbe of Sedgeford, gave to her children. On his death in 1620 Alice inherited the Sedgeford estate and assumed responsibility for its management. She took the job very seriously, gradually building up her knowledge, taking advice, creating new accounts, rationalising the complex field systems and organising new field books and rentals. From 1632 she used this experience to radically improve the records for the rest of the estate at Hunstanton, Ringstead, Holme and Heacham. Set out clearly and precisely, these records served as a reference work for succeeding generations. The estate, commended by Arthur Young as a model of improvement, owed much to Alice.[9] It would be no exaggeration to claim that her meticulous record-keeping secured the survival of the estate in the early seventeenth century and laid the foundation for its success in the eighteenth century and beyond.

Alice produced no single estate book, like William Windham of Felbrigg: evidence of her activities can be found in the scores of paper books that survive for every part of the estate.[10] Alice's particular contribution, however, is perhaps best understood from her work with sheep and on her own estate at Sedgeford. These records demonstrate her wide knowledge and deep understanding of farming systems in this part of Norfolk and explain why she came to play such an influential role in the wider management of the Hunstanton estate. With the expertise she learned from her father she was able to reorganise and keep the accounts for the flocks that the family farmed in hand from 1625 to 1654.[11] By the 1630s the sale of sheep, lambs and wool, and the associated production of corn, formed a significant part of their revenues. But it was not all plain

---

6   TNA, PROB 11/238/248; see also LEST/AE8 for a later transcription.

7   For Sir Hamon's early rentals, firmals and accounts see LEST/BK1, BK2, BK3, BK4, BK5, BK6/1, BK6/2 and P6. Rentals listed manorial rents; firmals listed farm rents.

8   LEST/R9.

9   A. Young, *The Farmer's Tour through [the East of?] England*, vol. 2 (London, 1770), pp. 23–9. In 1760, on the death of Sir Henry Le Strange, 6th Bt, the Hunstanton estate passed to Sir Nicholas Styleman of Snettisham through his marriage to Sir Henry's sister, Armine.

10 For William Windham see chapter 9.

11 LEST/P10. Alice's sheep accounts, see below.

sailing. From the sheep accounts we learn of the loss of Sir Hamon's flocks, corn and horses to the parliamentary forces in 1643.[12] Bravely, Alice started again, recording the painfully slow restocking process, with sheep supplied by sons, cousins, tenants and friends. This was not the only reversal they suffered at this time. Sir Hamon's later years were blighted by fines, sequestration and legal disputes, which may explain why Alice made a summary of their family finances towards the end of her last account book.[13] These notes provide a useful overview of their family and financial affairs.

Alice's farming records for Sedgeford are of particular value to the historian. They provide a unique picture of the working of an infield–outfield system in the early seventeenth century and the methods used to improve it. The system, a way of farming the light upland soils of west and north-west Norfolk, lies at the heart of our understanding of Norfolk agriculture and its development in the eighteenth century.[14] In 1631, on the death of her cousin Francis Guybon, the principal tenant at Sedgeford, Alice commissioned a survey of the estate.[15] This consists of three interlocking maps representing the three flocks and foldcourses of Sedgeford and a written survey explaining the organisation and use of the 'Sedgeford Brecks and Infield Lands'.[16] The book lists the rotations and the lands to be exchanged, while the maps provide a visual base for identifying the holdings at a glance. Later records show how Alice built on this method and how her successors developed the system.[17] Gradually the distinction between brecks and infields was broken down. By 1702 new farms had been created and fallows eliminated, with turnips and clover grown in rotation with wheat, barley, peas and vetches.[18] From this evidence, we can see that the process of improving the brecks and bringing them into regular cultivation, the cornerstone of the agricultural revolution, was underway on this estate from the early seventeenth century.

Before turning to these documents, however, we should briefly consider Alice's wider activities and assess her place in Norfolk history.[19] Just how unusual was she?

---

12 R.W. Ketton-Cremer, 'Sir Hamon Le Strange and his sons', *A Norfolk Gallery* (London, 1948), pp. 56–94; R.W. Ketton-Cremer, *Norfolk in the Civil War: A Portrait of a Society in Conflict* (London, 1969), pp. 206–17.

13 LEST/P10.

14 H.C. Darby and J. Saltmarsh, 'The infield-outfield system of a Norfolk manor', *Economic History Review*, 3 (1935) pp. 30–44; M. Overton, *Agricultural Revolution in England: The Transformation of the Agrarian Economy, 1500–1850* (Cambridge, 1996).

15 Francis Guybon's mother, Anne, was the sister of Richard Stubbe, Alice's father.

16 LEST/OC1, simplified in Figure 7.1; LEST/IC58.

17 LEST/IC55, IC64, IC65, IB85, IB89, IB90, IB93.

18 LEST/IB91.

19 Until the publication of Whittle and Griffiths' *Consumption and Gender*, little had been written about Alice, yet academics have long been aware of her archive. Ketton-Cremer briefly drew attention to her in *Norfolk Gallery* (pp. 64–5) and *Norfolk in the Civil War* (pp. 41, 190, 217–18). She appears in Hussey, 'Hunstanton Hall I', protesting against Sir Hamon's viol playing and insisting he build a garden house to practice in. References often attest to the bawdy quality of her jokes as recorded by her son, Nicholas Le Strange, in his jest book, *Merry Passages and Jests* (ed. H.F. Lippincott [Salzburg, 1974]). Her husband and sons all have entries in the *Oxford*

To answer this question we need to know more about Alice Stubbe, the girl from Sedgeford, who became Lady Le Strange. Born in 1585, Alice was the younger daughter of Richard Stubbe and his second wife Anne Goding, the widow of John Le Strange of Sedgeford.[20] Stubbe was not a native of west Norfolk. From a relatively modest background, his family came from Scottow and migrated to Bungay in 1534.[21] In 1561 he married Elizabeth, daughter of a local landowner, Anthony Gurney of Ellingham, and they had a daughter, Dionisia. Over the years he built up an estate across the county, which included lands at Harpley and Rougham, following the marriage of Dionisia to William Yelverton of Rougham, and in Sedgeford, Hunstanton and Holme, after he married Anne Le Strange in about 1583.[22] Trained in the law, Stubbe was active in county circles, resolving disputes and advising gentry families. He became closely involved in the affairs of the Le Strange family after the death of Sir Nicholas Le Strange in 1592. As the family lawyer he worked alongside the trustees, Sir John Peyton, Sir Henry Hobart and Sir Henry Spelman, guiding and securing the future of Sir Nicholas's orphan son, the eight-year-old Sir Hamon.[23] In 1602 the trustees arranged the marriage of Sir Hamon to Stubbe's daughter, Alice. For her settlement, he assigned his lands in Sedgeford and the leases and lands of John Le Strange that had passed to his widow, Alice's mother.[24]

Dictionary of National Biography, but Alice did not until Jane Whittle and I corrected the omission: 'L'Estrange, Alice, Lady L'Estrange (1585–1656)', *ODNB* (Oxford, 2005). The editors changed the spelling to that used for the men folk devised by their youngest son, Sir Roger L'Estrange, but modern authors tend to use Le Strange: see A. Moore and C. Crawley, *Family and Friends: A Regional Survey of British Portraiture* (London, 1992), pp. 84–6.

20 John (d. 1582) was the third son of Sir Nicholas Le Strange (1511–80) and uncle of Sir Hamon. In 1562 John was assigned, by his father, the lease of the two Sedgeford manors held by the dean and chapter of Norwich. By 1601 Richard Stubbe was the lessee: NRO, DCN (Dean and Chapter of Norwich) 59/30/10. Blomefield and Parkin, *History of Norfolk*, vol. X, p. 314 for the definitive family tree of the Le Stranges of Hunstanton; see also Whittle and Griffiths, *Consumption and Gender*, pp. 18–23; W. Rye, *Norfolk Families* (Norwich, 1913).

21 Rye, *Norfolk Families*, p. 859, see also W. and M. Vaughan Lewis, *See You in Court: The Potts Family of Mannington, 1584–1737* (Itteringham, 2009), pp. 572–4, for a background of the Stubbe family. Alice may have been named after Richard Stubbe's mother, Alice, daughter and co-heiress of John Richers of Bungay. References to Stubbe's land purchases include: Edgefield (Blomefield and Parkin, *Norfolk*, vol. IX, p. 303); Harpley (Blomefield and Parkin, *Norfolk*, vol. VIII, p. 455); Holme Parsonage (Blomefield and Parkin, *Norfolk*, vol. X, p. 333). Stubbe was involved in a dispute over the warren and chase at Castle Rising (Blomefield and Parkin, *Norfolk*, vol. IX, p. 56).

22 Sir William Yelverton of Rougham (1558–1631), baronet in 1620 and sheriff of Norfolk in 1622, married Dionisia, d. and co-heir of Richard Stubbe of Sedgeford. They had two sons: Sir William (1590–1648) married Ursula, daughter of Sir Thomas Richardson; their son Sir William (1621–49) was a royalist who was fined heavily and died unmarried; their other son Sir Henry married but d.s.p and the title became extinct. Blomefield and Parkin, *Norfolk*, vol. X, pp. 31–2.

23 See chapter 3 above for more details on the trustees.

24 LEST/AA66–73: documents concerning the marriage settlement of Sir Hamon Le Strange and Alice Stubbe, 1602.

The marriage was quite a coup. Sir Hamon was the scion of an ancient Norfolk family that had lived at Hunstanton since the twelfth century. Illustrious forebears included the first Sir Hamon, a hero of the battle of Crecy, who built the original medieval gatehouse, and Sir Thomas Le Strange, who served Henry VIII at the Field of the Cloth of Gold; he later greatly benefited from the dissolution of the monasteries and secured the most prestigious offices in the county.[25] However, in the second half of the sixteenth century the Le Strange fortunes were in decline, the family having failed to grasp the need for reform. By the time Sir Hamon inherited the estate in 1604, the rental and his income was a fraction of that enjoyed by his great-great-grandfather. He at once settled down to the task of reviving their fortunes, ably assisted by his guardians, principally Richard Stubbe and Sir Henry Spelman.[26]

When Hamon and Alice married they were still in their teens. The union lasted for over fifty years, a long time even by modern standards. During that period their relationship and the management of the family, household and estate went through several phases. Their first three children – Nicholas, Hamon and Dorothy – were born in 1604, 1605 and 1608, and, not surprisingly, Alice left no records from this time. Her involvement in Sir Hamon's affairs began in 1610, when he handed over responsibility for household expenditure.[27] Dorothy had died in 1609 and this may have been a tactful diversion for Alice, but it is more likely that Hamon needed her assistance so that he could concentrate more fully on estate management.[28] With Alice in charge the general disbursements immediately become more organised and rigorous. She itemised every payment, whereas Hamon had relied on the honesty of servants and tradesmen, paying their bills as submitted. For example, while he paid his groom Thomas Hogan 'his halfe yeares wages and 13s which he disbursed for me', Alice paid him for 'his diet 2s 6d and for 2 horses each of them 2 days in Norwich 4s 6d, so in all 7s'.[29] It is true that Sir Hamon often referred to bills kept in files, but his method left him open to fraud, as Alice soon found out, dismissing Hogan within weeks. Realistically, Hamon had little option but to trust his servants; his good fortune lay in having a wife able and willing to take on such a tedious task.

Alice soon started categorising entries in the accounts: wages to servants, expenditure on the children, repairs to buildings and food for the household. In time, food and buildings were siphoned off into separate accounts, giving her greater control over detail and providing a framework for expansion into new enterprises. At the end of her first book of disbursements, 1610–13, Alice jotted down an estimate of their estate income and expenditure. Of the £905 per annum income from rents she had to set aside nearly a third to pay annuities and another third for the household, leaving the family just under a third for everything else – so there was not much room for manoeuvre.[30] She clearly understood the idea of a budget.

---

25   Oestmann, *Lordship and Community*.
26   Griffiths, '"A Country Life"', pp. 203–20.
27   LEST/P6.
28   Sir Hamon had purchased the large manor at Heacham from the earl of Arundel in 1609, which added significantly to his portfolio (LEST/Q38).
29   LEST/P6.
30   LEST/P6.

The household books, sometimes described as 'kitchen books', provided a weekly record of food for the household.[31] In the first few weeks Alice experimented with the layout and arrived at a formula that remained unchanged. Every half year she started with a stocktake, followed by the weekly accounts recording items in store, items purchased and items delivered as gifts from tenants and suppliers. Then, for a standard list of staple foods, she noted the amounts received, bought, made, spent, sold and remaining. The limited range – beef, bread and corn – soon increased to include butter, cheese and different types of saltfish, beer, bread and prepared food. This routine provided effective controls over stock, was easily checked and could be used to predict consumption and expenditure from year to year. Payments for labour, mainly working on the home farm and in the gardens, concluded the weekly account; the half year ended with a further stocktake, including details of the piggery and dairy. The dairy first appears in the household books in 1620, although we know from the document 'A Reckoning of the proffit of my Deyrey' that it was a profitable venture from 1617.[32] The herd, milked by a succession of dairy maids, ranged in size from twenty-three to twenty-six cows by 1634; it produced huge amounts of butter and cheese for the household, often leaving enough for sale. Alice had no qualms about squeezing a profit from the household budget. The receipts from the estate, including farm rents and sales of timber, corn, livestock, wool, butter, milk and cheese were entered at the back of each household book.

The building accounts stemmed from Hamon's plans to rebuild the hall and the buildings on the estate, which gathered momentum in 1620 with Alice's inheritance of the Sedgeford estate. These accounts consist of two to four pages inserted in the general disbursements at the end of every half year; they can be cross-referenced to Hamon's memoranda books, where he kept notes of projects and contracts with suppliers, and jotted down his own ideas and designs. In this way, Alice paid the bills and itemised expenditure, while Hamon concentrated on managing the building process. His growing confidence in her meant that he could reliably predict his income stream and plan ahead with a degree of certainty. He knew at a glance his day-to-day expenses, his income and the spare cash he could allocate to various projects; this enabled him and Nicholas to carry out a rolling programme of building and repairs that continued without a break despite the financial setbacks of the 1640s.

Alice's involvement in farming and estate management increased greatly with the addition of Sedgeford. Prior to that date she kept the estate receipts and the children's sheep accounts with her household accounts. From 1620 she initiated a quite separate range of estate accounts and records for Sedgeford. In 1625, once she controlled all the flocks on the estate, she devised a more organised sheep account that gradually absorbed the children's accounts. In the early years at Sedgeford, Alice had relied on her cousin Francis Guybon, but on his death in 1631 she commissioned the survey by John Fisher of the estate that facilitated her programme of improvements. At the same time, the marriage of Nicholas opened up new possibilities. He and his wife Anne,

---

31 Whittle and Griffiths, *Consumption and Gender, passim*; nine household books survive: LEST/P6, 1613–21 (1st, 3rd, 4th), with a gap 1614–16; LEST/P8, 1621–33 (5th, 6th, 8th), with a gap 1627–9; LEST/P9, 1633–42 (9th, 10th), with a long gap 1642–50, followed by a book for 1650–3 in LEST/P11.
32 LEST/P8.

and their growing family, lived with Hamon and Alice at Hunstanton Hall, giving them every opportunity and incentive to develop the management of the family estates. As Nicholas embarked on his drainage schemes, Alice took on the accounts for the remainder of the estate at Hunstanton, Ringstead, Holme and Heacham.

The estate was managed through four different types of record: field books provided a description of the landholding structure in each parish; rentals listed the manorial tenants owing freehold and copyhold rents; firmals listed those tenants leasing demesne land from the Le Stranges and paying farm or leasehold rents; and, finally, bailiffs' accounts recorded the allowances granted and the payments made to the receiver. Before 1630 these records were kept separately, making it difficult to trace what each individual tenant owed for his lands, which might be scattered through several parishes, and the type of rent he paid. Hamon made some attempt to synthesise this detail, but it was left to Alice to modernise the system. She vastly improved the layout and legibility of the field books and drew together the rentals, firmals and bailiffs' accounts into a single volume; this is best illustrated in the Hunstanton estate account, 1623–53.[33] It starts with a combined rental and firmal, listing each tenant with his farm lands and manorial rents.[34] Against each item Alice noted the rents paid, distinguishing between types of farm land according to the rent paid per acre. Subsequently the rental and firmal were included at four-yearly intervals, noting any change of occupancy. Every year she entered a summary of the bailiff's accounts, recording the rent charge: customary and farm rents, profits of court, payments from rights and liberties; the amount allowed to the bailiff for repairs, expenses and outrents; and, finally, the sum received 'at several times by mee Alice Le Strange'. From 1638 she attached with a pin 'a note how this account was received and written in my [Household] Booke'; later these receipts were entered more securely in the account, and can be cross-referenced to the entries in the household book. In this way Alice created a fully integrated system, linking estate and household accounts.

From her estate accounts we can see a management strategy unfolding with attention focused on foldcourses, marshes and those areas of demesne where the Le Stranges exercised total control. Elsewhere, they accepted the fragmented landholding structure and worked with these large village communities, sustained by fishing and farming, to effect improvements on the estate. At the same time, the Le Stranges resolved to collect every rent due to them and to protect their own interests. This was Alice's achievement. By methodical accounting and record-keeping, she reduced the task to a simple routine, allowing Hamon and Nicholas to concentrate on improvement. The design of her account book as a work of reference also proved to be invaluable to future generations, notably Sir Nicholas, the fourth baronet, from the 1680s. By creating a modern accounting system Alice not only placed the business of the estate on a sound commercial footing but facilitated the improvements of the 1630s and 1640s and the substantial reforms of the late seventeenth and early eighteenth centuries.

From this brief description, Alice's activities can be compared with those of her relatives and other gentlewomen who kept household and estate accounts. To what

---

33   LEST/BK15.
34   LEST/BK15.

extent was she typical? Alice herself consulted accounts kept by Le Strange women in the sixteenth century and adopted a similar format for her kitchen books before adding her own modifications. Catherine Calthorpe, the sister of her daughter-in-law, Anne, married to Sir James Calthorpe, kept an account from 1652 to 1662 that remains in the Le Strange archive.[35] Slight variations in handwriting from the 1630s suggest that Anne may have assisted Alice with entries from time to time. Further afield, her cousin by marriage, Lady Frances Hobart of Blickling, was influential in reforming the accounts and finances of her husband, bringing clarity and control to existing methods and recruiting the right men to perform the various tasks involved.[36] Later, in the 1690s, Katherine Windham of Felbrigg kept the estate accounts for a while following her husband's early death, and supervised the family finances for the next forty years.[37] Clearly, these women were familiar with accounts. What is so unusual, possibly unique, about Alice is the scale of her activity, her enthusiasm for the task and her understanding of what was required for an effective accounting system. She never ceased perfecting her methods, showing a very firm grasp of accounting techniques. Her knowledge of farming and estate business was also exceptional. It allowed her to develop her role almost indefinitely, taking on the most intricate tasks. Most significantly, the benefits of her work outlived her, providing as they did a model for succeeding generations of improvers in this corner of Norfolk. She may not have been typical, but Alice shows what a woman could achieve in the first half of the seventeenth century with encouragement, training and support. The remaining sections of this chapter consider in turn three sets of documents: Alice's notes on family finances, her sheep accounts and her records of improvements at Sedgeford.

Family and finance

The details of the Le Strange family finances can be found with the final book of general disbursements, 1645–54.[38] We do not know when or why Alice Le Strange

---

35 The Calthorpes were a vast Norfolk family and closely related to the Le Stranges. Sir James Calthorpe of East Barsham (1604–52), married in 1641 his second wife, Catherine Lewkenor, d. of Sir Edward Lewkenor and sister of Anne Le Strange, wife of Sir Nicholas; see Moore and Crawley, *Family and Friends*, pp. 77–88, for several references to the Calthorpes, Le Stranges and Lewkenors, and see also LEST/BE6, LEST/P20. Catherine's son, Sir Christopher Calthorpe, Kt, 1661, acted as trustee for Sir Nicholas Le Strange, 4th Bt, between 1669 and 1682; he married Dorothy, d. of Sir William Spring and his wife, Elizabeth Le Strange. Their daughter, Anne, married Sir Thomas Le Strange: see Blomefield, *Norfolk*, vol. 7, p. 57.

36 Frances, d. 1664, daughter of the John Egerton, 1st earl of Bridgewater, second wife of Sir John Hobart, 2nd Bt 1593–1647; Sir Hamon's first cousin through their mothers, Dorothy and Mary Bell.

37 Katherine (1652–1729), daughter of Sir Joseph Ashe, wife of William Windham (1647–89).

38 LEST/P10 consists of two books bound together by Hamon L'Estrange Styleman in 1853. The first includes Alice Le Strange's final book of disbursements, followed by her notes on the family finances; the second, principally her sheep accounts, also contains Nicholas and Hamon's charges at Eton, Roger's expenses at Cambridge, a ship account and inventories of furniture and linen taken in 1620 and 1632.

wrote these notes but it was probably after the difficulties the family encountered in the early 1640s, as a way of explaining their indebtedness to their successors. What is noticeable is her aggrieved tone, first directed against her half-sister Dionisia Yelverton and her father, and then against anyone else who tried to do them down: principally those who challenged their rights and titles to their estate, and her husband's enemies during the Civil War. Alice compared the settlement made by her father on his two daughters. While her sister received lands worth £498 a year, Alice's estate at Sedgeford, with property in King's Lynn and Holme Parsonage, was worth only £473, 'So my sister had more in land than myself by the yeare £25'. On marriage, both sisters were given cash sums and continuing assistance from Stubbe until his death in 1619, but Alice's total of £4669 13s 4d was substantially less than the £6392 allowed to the Yelvertons. Even allowing for the £513 16s given to her family in gifts and legacies, this still amounted to a substantial difference: 'my sister had more in money more than myself £1209 15s 8d'. She also emphasised that much of the Yelvertons' money was used to pay off debts, while £1000 was deducted from her own account to pay Sir John Peyton's expenses.[39] The management of the trustees was another bone of contention. However, despite these grievances, Alice's early household accounts show a close relationship between father and daughter, with the old man taking a keen interest in her growing family, lending them money, giving them sheep and offering advice: her sister was also a frequent visitor and came to live at Hunstanton during her widowhood. Nevertheless, Alice's notes on the settlement, carefully documented for posterity, provide a striking picture of an assertive woman strong in defence of herself, her husband and her family.

After the sisters' settlement, Alice left twelve blank pages before listing the 'Sale of Lands and Purchases' from 1630. The date is significant, as it coincides with the marriage of their eldest son, the newly created Sir Nicholas Le Strange, to Anne, daughter of Sir Edward Lewkenor of Denham, Suffolk.[40] By this time Hamon and Alice had raised and educated four children: the three boys, Nicholas, Hamon and Roger, went to Eton, Cambridge and the Inns of Court, while Elizabeth was groomed for marriage by her mother. They had also made progress improving the estate, rebuilding Hunstanton Hall, increasing their income and reducing their debts. As their children achieved maturity and needed to be settled, their family finances became much more complex, with huge sums passing through the accounts. The impression is that Alice wanted to explain how this process was skilfully managed. Anne Lewkenor's dowry of £3000 was used not to repay debts, as was so often the case, but to purchase the Benacre estate in Suffolk. The estate was sold two years later to finance the marriage of their second son, Hamon, to Dorothy Laverick in 1634 – there is no evidence of a dowry. In all, young Hamon's settlement amounted to nearly £2600, with £1800 paid to Sir William Yelverton for an estate at West Winch and a further £800 in cash. By 1635 this transaction was completed, with Alice noting 'Debts Remayne 1635 – none'.

---

39   The assumption being that this charge, Sir Hamon's release of wardship, should not have been set against her estate.

40   Sir Edward Lewkenor of Denham, Suffolk (1587–1618), <www.historyofparliamentonline.org.uk>.

This happy state of affairs changed with Elizabeth's marriage in 1636 to William Spring of Pakenham, Suffolk, and the resulting need to raise a dowry of £3500.[41] The sum was raised principally by loans from relatives, such as the Lewkenors and Springs, friends, tenants, employees, including the Guybons and the Banyards, and more formal money lenders, such as Mr Simons, who loaned £800 from 1637 to 1648.[42] These borrowings might appear profligate but were sustainable against a background of rising estate revenues; the family continued to spend money on buying land, building, adventuring on Boston Fen and their own drainage schemes. From 1636 to 1654 Alice recorded the 'Debts Owing' and how they were financed from year to year, with loans repaid and new borrowings arranged. There is no mention of interest rates until 1654, when Alice paid the London money lenders 6 per cent; however, her books of disbursements record interest payments of 6 per cent and 8 per cent, with the higher rate often paid to relatives and tenants.[43] By 1642 the level of debt had been reduced from £3400 to £2100. But the downward trend did not last: it was brutally interrupted by the costs and losses incurred during the Civil War with Sir Hamon's dramatic intervention in the royalist uprising of King's Lynn.[44]

The crisis started on 13 August 1643, when the royalist faction of west Norfolk and King's Lynn, led by Sir Hamon, declared their support for the king. The earl of Manchester, newly appointed commander of the Eastern Association, responded by imposing a siege on the town, awaiting the arrival of relief forces and supplies.[45] Inside the town, John Percival and Thomas Toll, the puritan members for the borough, busily conspired against the royalists. Within a month resistance collapsed and terms were agreed, which included the payment of a levy to the besieging soldiers in lieu of plunder and, later, by parliamentary ordinance, compensation for any damage inflicted on 'well affected persons' of the borough. So, in addition to the loss of their flocks and corn during the siege, the Le Stranges were liable for the payment of their share of the levy to the soldiers and damages to Toll, Percival and others, and suffered the vigorous enforcement of the sequestration of their estates. Sums relating to these issues can be found scattered through the document from 1643: they amounted to over £3000, excluding the value of the sheep and corn.

---

41 Sir William Spring of Pakenham (1613–54), <www.historyofparliamentonline.org.uk>. Roger, the youngest surviving child, did not marry until the 1670s, but caused plenty of trouble and expense to his parents in the 1640s and 1650s: see H. Love, 'L'Estrange, Sir Roger (1616–1704)', *ODNB* (Oxford, 2004).

42 Reference to these kinds of loans can be found in *The Papers of Nathaniel Bacon of Stiffkey*, vol. 3, 1586–1595, Norfolk Record Society 53 (Norwich, 1987 and 1988), pp. 222–3.

43 LEST/P7 for 1631–45; LEST/P10 for 1645–54. For a similar variation of interest rates, see Elizabeth Griffiths (ed.), *William Windham's Green Book, 1673–88*, Norfolk Record Society 46 (Norwich, 2002), pp. 254–7. My thanks to John Broad for this point, and to Jean Agnew who suggested that the different rates might reflect the absence of a broker's fee.

44 Ketton-Cremer, *Norfolk in the Civil War*, pp. 206–17.

45 The first of these troops was led by Captain William Poe, who figures prominently in Alice's sheep accounts as the architect of the raid on the Le Strange flocks: LEST/P10.

Despite these reverses, the family continued as before, buying parcels of land and paying off debt; by the early 1650s it had fallen to £1300. In 1654, on Sir Hamon's death, the family borrowed £2000 to cover undisclosed sums, leaving a total debt of £3300. Given what they had suffered over the previous ten years, and the continuing high levels of taxation, this sum was not excessive.[46] Nevertheless, at the end of the list of debts Alice clearly felt the need to summarise and explain their position and perhaps to justify her management of their affairs.

The summary starts, after a gap of ten pages, with the final agreement of a longstanding legal case with the Cremer family, showing that it had been fully resolved. The suits against the Cremers and Styleman, over parcels of land in Heacham, had been an ongoing problem throughout the 1630s and 1640s. The principal issue was settled out of court in 1648, but it seems that Robert Styleman had exacted a payment from Sir Hamon in 1646, as Alice noted them 'being over powered by the times'.[47] She then listed the lands sold and purchased 'by my Husband' from the earliest years of their marriage. These included the sale in 1609 of the manor of Fring for £2140 to pay for the purchase of the manor of Heacham Lewis from the earl of Arundel for £4400.[48] She explains how the shortfall was met with the sale of Grint Mill, Holme Parsonage, Chappell Mill and South Linne, and the reversion of the Irish lands. As if to underline her financial rectitude, she noted that the expectation of improvement at Heacham would 'make the land bought as much as the land sold'; in other words, the improvement they expected to make at Heacham would cover the initial outlay. Alice then poignantly itemised the 'Losses in my Husbands Estate'. As a preamble, she emphasised the debts left by the executors and their neglect of the household and buildings during Sir Hamon's minority, which required them to rebuild 'most of them out of the ground'. This difficult inheritance was compounded by the 'many chargeable sutes' and 'unkinde losses', including the 'adventuring' in the East Indies and Boston Fens and the draining of marshes at Heacham. The section ends with an emotional reference to the 'Tirannical Oppression' of Mr Toll and his faction in Lynn, which cost them £1088, 'beside our greate Losse where we were plundered of all our Sheep and Corn'. Alice closed her summary on a calmer note, listing 'Lands and other guifts of Father', restating his contribution to their children; this is followed by an inventory of household stuff left to her by her father. The final item was a list of church repairs at Sedgeford and Ringstead in 1653: they amounted to less than £25, but they do indicate what Alice thought useful to include in this context.

Alice died in 1656, two years after Sir Hamon. Their wills tell us a great deal about the richness of their relationship: there was no lack of affection in this marriage.[49] Sir Hamon fulsomely acknowledged Alice's intelligence and her role in the education of their children and the advancement of his estate; she simply desired to be 'decently interred ... neere the Body of ... my late Deare husband'. Neither will is concerned

---

46 For an account of reckless borrowing see Sir John Hobart's experience at Blickling in Griffiths, 'Management', vol. 1, 1596–1654, pp. 248–53.

47 See Griffiths, '"A Country Life"', p. 230.

48 LEST/Q38, fol. 26; LEST/Q37, fol. 18; LEST/P6.

49 TNA, PROB 11/238/248; PROB 11/262.

with property, which had already been dealt with, but each provides a list of various bequests to family, friends, servants and the poor; these indicate the value attached to particular goods and people. By this time Alice had retired to Sedgeford and bequeathed all her brewing and dairy equipment to her favourite grandson, Sir Nicholas. At the same time, she ensured that her daughter-in-law, Anne, had enough bedding, curtains, furniture, kitchen stuff and tableware for her own widowhood at Sedgeford. Beyond small legacies and bequests to her own daughter, Elizabeth, and particular grandchildren, Alice singled out female relations, including her cousin Elizabeth Guybon, friends and servants. Francis Guybon, son of Alice's cousin and principal tenant, and John Fisher, the surveyor, appear as witnesses.[50] Both wills indicate a couple striving to ensure the future of their family and estate and living at ease with their servants, tenants and wider rural communities.

The sheep accounts, 1617–55

Alice Le Strange's sheep accounts are the first evidence of her working with farming records. Her initial purpose was to keep a record of her own sheep and those of her five children, Nicholas, Hamon, Jane, Elizabeth and Roger. She was continuing a family tradition, established by her father, whereby children were trained in the arts of sheep farming by allocating them ewes and allowing them the profit of lambs and wool. Richard Stubbe died in 1619, leaving each grandchild forty sheep.[51] Evidence of his enduring influence can be found in her description of the flocks on the estate, where she refers to folios in 'my father's booke'.[52] The sheep accounts are contained in a separate book bound with the disbursements and family finances.[53] The cover lists various accounts: the flocks and foldcourses by Alice 'for divers years'; the profits of a ship in which they had a share; her sons' charges at Eton and Cambridge; and inventories of furniture and bedding.[54] An entirely separate sheep account appears in Alice's first farming book for Sedgeford. This brief account will be considered first, as it illustrates Alice's development as a sheep farmer and her progression to managing all the sheep accounts for the estate in 1625.

The Sedgeford sheep account, 1620–22[55]

Alice's inheritance of the Sedgeford estate was not straightforward. In his will, Richard Stubbe had allowed Sir William Yelverton, his son-in-law, to enjoy the profits for a year.

---

50 There were in fact two John Fishers who both appear in both wills: John Fisher the surveyor of Heacham and John Fisher of Honing, gt. The latter is differentiated by his gentility; we may assume that when 'John Fisher' stands on its own it was the surveyor, who was also local.

51 Richard Stubbe's will TNA, PROB 11/135.

52 LEST/P10.

53 LEST/P10.

54 For a discussion of the last two topics see Whittle and Griffiths, *Consumption and Gender*, pp. 120–40; 174–83.

55 LEST/BK7, fols 3–15.

In 1620 we find Alice buying Yelverton's holding in the Sedgeford flocks, paying £355 14s 8d for 1333 sheep.[56] The short account provides much explanatory detail and a useful introduction to her system and sheep accounting methods. The first page records that 1239 sheep were delivered to three shepherds: 557 ewes to Woods at East Ground, 250 ewes to Rose at South Ground and 432 wethers to Corner at North Ground, leaving a shortfall of ninety-four sheep. In addition, tenants were allowed to put 'Joyce Sheep' into the flocks, amounting to 496 sheep.[57] The shortfall of ninety-four sheep highlights some of the difficulties with Alice's accounting system. For example, there is no consistency in her use of Roman and Arabic numerals, and some confusion in her use of the long hundred, 1C or 120, instead of 100 or vxx (i.e. five score), traditionally used for counting sheep. She refers to the 1C wethers she has exchanged and later refers to them as a hundred wethers. Frequently, her totals at the end of each account do not coincide with the actual totals: there is a discrepancy in the total for the South Flock in 1620, showing an excess of almost sixty sheep over the actual total of 502. This type of difference of twenty, forty or sixty sheep is a regular feature of the sheep accounts; a payment to Rose, the shepherd of the South Flock, in 1620 explains why. He was allowed two half-yearly payments of fifteen shillings 'for 60 sheep which we are to lay at 6d the sheepe which are not layd this year'. The inclusion of this allowance brings the total figure for the three flocks up to 1299, reducing the initial shortfall to thirty-four; this reflects fourteen morts (i.e. deaths) and possibly a hidden allowance of twenty for Woods or Corner. With this understanding of what was happening on the ground, Alice's accounts begin to add up, but they were not foolproof.

From the Sedgeford account it is possible to follow the cycle of sheep management. With the delivery of the sheep to the shepherds at Midsummer 1620 they were 'charged' with a certain number of sheep, which they had to account for at the 'clipping' the following year. Alice then itemised expenditure for the intervening months. The largest outlay was for the remuneration of shepherds, with wages at 16s 8d a quarter, livery (clothes and food) at 6s 8d per annum and the value of placing sheep in the flock at 6d a sheep.[58] In this way, Rose enjoyed an income of £5 3s 4d per annum. Payments were also made to nameless contractors for washing, dragging, clipping, greasing, branding and winding wool, and for necessities such as

---

56 LEST/P10. Richard Stubbe left the Yelvertons a year's profit from the estate at Sedgeford, which Alice recorded in the Sedgeford estate accounts 1621–35 (LEST/BK7).

57 Cullet or joyce sheep were sheep belonging to other people grazing with the flock of another person, usually the manorial lord, to whom they make a payment; see D. Yaxley, *A Researcher's Glossary of Words Found in Historical Documents in East Anglia* (Dereham, 2003) for all technical and local terms.

58 This package compares to 15s a quarter and 5s for livery, with a more generous allowance for sheep, albeit in a larger flock, at Sedgeford in the 1500s; see M. Bailey, 'The sheep accounts of Norwich Cathedral Priory 1484 to 1534', in M. Bailey, M. Jurowski and C. Rawcliffe (eds), *Poverty and Wealth: Sheep, Taxation and Charity in Late Medieval Norfolk*, Norfolk Record Society 71 (Norwich, 2007), p. 9.

pitch, tar and hurdles.[59] These expenses were set against receipts from tathe,[60] skins, the sale of lambs, crones, wethers and wool, payments for 'Joyce' sheep and rents for foldcourses when they were let. Following the clipping in 1621, Alice calculated a profit of £21 6s 2d made on the sale of sheep, with a further £57 12s on the sale of wool. The tithe paid on wool and lambs had been deducted at source from the shepherd. Crucially, the account provided information on the movement of sheep from flock to flock: for example, in 1621 Sedgeford wethers were shifted into Crisp's South Flock at Ringstead, as well as into Corner's North Flock. Crisp also received wethers from Barrett Ringstead, including those of the children.[61]

Alice's general sheep accounts do not, as a rule, contain the same level of information as these early notes. From 1625 they become in effect a centralised stock account incorporating individual shepherd's accounts, designed to keep a tally of numbers and the movement of sheep; they contain some references to prices received for lambs, wethers, crones and wool, but there is no attempt to strike a balance of profit and loss. Alice entered receipts in her receipt book at the end of each household book, while she noted expenses in her books of general disbursements. This is a more personal arrangement, tailored to fit in with her domestic accounts, than the traditional system found on large estates. For example, at Raynham shepherds submitted their own accounts to the sheep reeve, who kept a centralised stock account of the seven flocks under his control with a separate account summarising receipts, expenditure, profits and loss.[62] Between 1603 and 1617 these were presented to Jane, Lady Berkeley, grandmother of Sir Roger Townshend, who administered the estate during his long minority.[63] The structure at Raynham, noted for its long history of keeping large flocks, conforms to the practice of the Norwich Cathedral Priory as seen in the accounts of their flocks at Sedgeford, Gnatingdon and nearby Fring.[64] Alice's system was more idiosyncratic, reflecting her personal control of the flocks and their management; the accounts were designed not for an estate bureaucracy but to provide her with the information she needed, which varied from time to time.

The sheep accounts for Alice and her children, 1617–27

The start of this account is obscured as the top half of the page is missing, so we don't really know how and when Alice began her venture into sheep farming. The first entry dates from Midsummer 1617, when Page and Goodman, the shepherds at

---

59   Dragging usually means literally dragging unwilling sheep to the clipping.
60   Tathe was sheep dung, here used to fertilise the light sandy soil.
61   The Crisps were an old Sedgeford family; Richard was making payments for tathing in the 1490s.
62   The Townshend papers are still in private hands at Raynham Hall, but see Griffiths and Overton, *Farming to Halves*, pp. 56–132.
63   Jane, Lady Berkeley (*c.*1547–1617), married Sir Roger Townshend (1544–90) and in 1597 Henry, 7th baron Berkeley (1534–1613). On the death of her profligate son, Sir John Townshend, in 1603, she managed the Raynham estate until her death in 1617; see Campbell, 'Sir Roger Townshend'.
64   Bailey, 'Sheep accounts', pp. 1–96. Blomefield lists Gnatingdon separately, but it lies within Sedgeford parish and is also known as Eaton; see Blomefield and Parkin, *Norfolk*, vol. X, pp. 390–1.

Barrett Ringstead, took delivery of 204 wethers, lambs and hoggs, of which 194 were safely brought to the clipping at Midsummer 1618. This appears to be the sum total of Alice's holding, suggesting a new enterprise. In 1619 she repaid a loan to her father of £73 8s 2d, which would have covered the cost of buying these sheep, indicating that he was underwriting the project; she still owed him £30 when he died. The children's accounts start in 1618. In effect, Alice managed the children's sheep as an offshoot of her own, shifting animals around, selling crones and fatstock, replacing them with young ewes and wether lambs, organising the tasks that needed to be done during the year and keeping a record of numbers and movements. In her first account she bought Nicholas twenty ewes, which we find in his account for 1618, delivered to Page, who took responsibility for the children's sheep.

In these early accounts Alice recorded expenses and receipts in some detail. As at Sedgeford, the largest outlay was the payment of shepherds. As before, payments were made to contractors to carry out seasonal tasks: washing, dragging, clipping and greasing, branding and winding wool. Necessities included oil as well as the pitch and tar used to mark the sheep and protect them from diseases to which they were notoriously susceptible.[65] On the first page of Alice's account she 'Lost 25 sheep, bought of Mr Waters, which were stricken'; we note she quickly sold them off at a reduced rate, taking a loss of 12d per sheep. Large quantities of hurdles were also bought to fold the sheep on the arable. A further cost was the payment of the tithe on wool and lamb to the vicar, which was deducted directly from the shepherd. These expenses were set against receipts from the sale of crones, pooks (undersized lambs), fat lambs and wethers, and from wool. Income was also drawn from payments for cullett sheep and rents for foldcourses, when they were let.

As at Sedgeford, the annual life cycle turned around Midsummer, when shepherds were charged with a certain number of sheep that they had to account for at the clipping the following year. At the 'reckoning' the shepherd brought the skins of dead sheep, 'morts', to make up the numbers; if these did not tally, he had to 'make good' the difference. At the same time, crones and pooks were 'taken off' and sold with fatstock, while other sheep, mainly wether lambs, were moved to different flocks. From the small numbers involved in the early accounts it is easy to follow the natural cycle of the flock and to explain the terms used to describe the sheep at various ages. Lambs, born in the spring, were fattened and sold before the winter, or kept as hoggs until they were shorn the following year in May or June. Once clipped, they appear as shearlings or shorlins in Alice's accounts. The ewe shorlins were put to the ram, with the older ewes, in late autumn and lambed the following spring; the gestation period for a ewe is about five months.[66] When they arrived at the clipping with their lambs, they are counted as ewes or mother ewes. As they grew old and barren, they were croned or weeded out of the flock with the small lambs. The male lambs were kept as ram lambs or castrated as wether lambs, becoming wether hoggs, wether

---

65 Pitch, applied with a branding iron, was used for marking sheep; black tar was used to protect sheep against parasites and tick-born diseases; see J.A.S. Watson and J.A. More, *Agriculture: The Science and Practice of Farming*, 11th edn (Edinburgh, 1962), pp. 576–90.

66 That is 147–51 days; see Watson and More, *Agriculture*, pp. 576–90.

shorlins and wethers of two, three, four and even five sheare. This seems a great age, but wethers were kept for their wool and tathing as well as meat; their fleeces were heavier and more valuable than those of ewes. Wether lambs were taken from the breeding flocks at Sedgeford East Ground and Barrett Ringstead and kept in wether flocks, principally Crisp's South Flock at Ringstead. Later on, we find Alice selling more fat lambs in the summer and autumn, restricting the size of the flocks and the numbers over-wintered. The children were allocated ewes with the idea of building up little breeding flocks; once established, their wether lambs were sent to Crisp's flock or to Corner at Sedgeford North Ground before it was let in 1625.

The children's flocks varied in size, suggesting that there might have been an element of favouritism. Nicholas steadily built up his numbers, buying twenty more ewes, selling wethers and establishing a breeding flock of fifty-five animals by 1619. Hamon, a year younger, made a slow start in 1619, with just seven ewes and two lambs, and never caught up. Roger, on the other hand, received financial help from his grandfather in 1618, aged just two years, with twenty ewes and twenty-three lambs delivered to Page in that year. Jane started in 1619 with five young females, while Elizabeth received three in 1620; the forty ewes from Stubbe in 1620 were a significant boost to their numbers. When Jane died in 1621 Roger and Bess divided her forty-four ewes, while Dorothy Guybon received her twenty lambs. In 1622 Alice started diverting wether lambs and shorlins to the wether flocks. By 1623 the children held a total of 790 sheep in three different flocks. In 1627 they sold their entire holding of 924 sheep to their father for a total of £292 4s 8d, as shown in Table 7.1, possibly as a way of simplifying an increasingly complex system.

These little individual accounts are painfully repetitive, leaving us to wonder why Alice bothered. We can only surmise that their purpose was to educate the children and give them a sense of ownership over their ewes and lambs. But did the effort pay dividends? Certainly, Nicholas became an enthusiastic improver and worked closely with his mother at Sedgeford while Hamon farmed at Ringstead. From 1644 he helped in the recovery after the plunder of 1643, placing 120 cullett sheep in the flock at Barrett Ringstead with a further 200 sheep in Ringstead North Flock from 1648.[67]

Despite growing commitments elsewhere on the estate, Alice also kept sheep accounts for her grandchildren.[68] These start in 1634 with her providing twenty ewes for 'little Nicholas LeStrange' and '1 Lambe for little Ham'. In 1640 'little Jack' received two store sheep and four store lambs and 'little Wills' one store lamb in 1642. In 1643 Captain Poe 'tooke of the little Boyes' forty-five sheep, including '1 store lambe of little Neds'. In 1644 Goodman's charge 'after the plundering' included 'one [lambe] for little Roger' and in 1648 there were 'ewe lambes twinnes' for Charles Le Strange. By this

---

67 Hamon Le Strange (1605–60) married 1. Dorothy Laverick and 2. Judith Bagnall, and raised numerous children at Ringstead.

68 Sir Nicholas and Anne Lewkenor had thirteen children. Ham (Sir Hamon, 2nd Bt 1631–56) held fewer sheep than his younger brother, Nick (3rd Bt 1632–69); the elder son, who died prematurely in his early twenties, might have been mentally impaired, as he hardly figures in the documents. In 1652 Alice drew up a detailed sheep account for Nick but not for Ham. The younger boys were John, b. 1636, William, b. 1639, Edward, b. 1641, Roger, b. 1644, Charles, b. 1647, and Thomas, b. 1651.

Table 7.1
Sale of the children's sheep to their father, Sir Hamon Le Strange, 1627.

	Nicholas	Hamon	Roger	Elizabeth	Total	Prices	£	s	d
Mother ewes	120	72	121	50	363	7s	127	1	0
Ewe shorlins	25	16	15	12	68	6s	20	8	0
Rams	3	5	6	4	18	5s	4	10	0
Lambs	57	35	56	32	180	3s 8d	34	10	0
Wethers	60	55	84	96	295	6s 8d> 8s	105	15	8
Total	265	183	282	194	924		292	4	8

Source: LEST/P10.

time, the sheep allocated to the five younger boys were listed separately; in 1651 the youngest son, Thomas, joined them with '11 Ewes and 5 Lambes'. No provision was made for Sir Nicholas's five daughters, or for Hamon's children. Alice did not repeat the individual accounts, but simply accounted for them in Goodman's account for Barrett Ringstead. She did, however, draw up 'A Reckoning of the Sheepe of Nicholas le Strange my Grandchilde' in 1655.[69] This account started in 1652, when she bought a hundred ewes for him from his uncle Hamon for £48. She also calculated the profit he made of the sheep he held as a small child between 1634 and 1642 before selling them to his grandfather; alongside she listed the losses at Barrett Ringstead. Alice clearly believed that such methods developed the business sense of her children and grandchildren, and helped to instil the idea of profit and loss.

The sheep accounts for the Le Strange estate, 1625–55[70]

Alice's venture into large-scale sheep farming began in earnest when she inherited the Sedgeford estate and bought the flocks from her brother-in-law, Sir William Yelverton. We saw how she purchased 1333 sheep divided into three flocks located on the East, North and South Grounds. From 1622, with the South Ground let to Francis Guybon, Alice incorporated the two remaining Sedgeford flocks, the East Ground and North Ground, into her main sheep account. By 1623, with the sheep at Barrett Ringstead, she had a total of 2517 sheep under management. By 1624 all the shepherds, apart from Crisp of South Flock, Ringstead, had been replaced, with Allen at Sedgeford East Ground, Lennnard at Sedgeford North Ground and Pyper at Barrett Ringstead; these are the shepherds in Alice's new account, which begins with the shepherds' charge at Midsummer 1625, shown in Table 7.2.

Further insights into Alice's management policy can be obtained by working out the lambing rates. Do they improve over the course of time? How do they compare with those found at Sedgeford in the fifteenth and sixteenth centuries? Mark Bailey found a rate of 0.6 and 0.8 lambs per ewe in 1484–1534 and this is the range found among the

---

69   LEST/P10.
70   LEST/P10.

children's ewes at Barrett Ringstead in the early 1620s. There are instances of it rising to 0.9, but it never reached one lamb per ewe.[71] At Sedgeford East Ground the rate was slightly lower. In 1624 Alice noted 'of these 680 ewes I had 394 lambes', a rate of 0.57 per ewe; in 1623, with tithe lambs included, it was 0.53. From 1626 the rate at Sedgeford averaged 0.7, while at Barrett Ringstead it ranged between 0.75 and 0.9 per ewe. The explanation might be the reduced flock size, but also the improved ratio of rams to ewes. In 1623, at Sedgeford, nine rams were expected to serve 842 ewes, while in 1626 twenty-four rams served 674 – one ram to twenty-eight ewes. At Barrett Ringstead the ratio averaged one ram to twenty ewes. Even by today's standards this is generous.[72] From 1630, in the accounts, the ewes are counted at the clipping with ewe shorlins (yet to lamb) and rams, so the lambing rate is more difficult to calculate. However, it appears that Alice quickly achieved a measure of improvement. In 1641 she could look back on twenty years of steady progress, before disaster struck – of the 1911 sheep charged to shepherds in 1643, 1715 were taken by the parliamentary forces.[73]

The plunder left Alice with fewer than a hundred sheep. She quickly assembled a scratch flock for Barrett Ringstead, buying 143 ewes and 141 wethers to run with sixty-five sheep gathered from the park, the close, and the other shepherds. For the South Flock, the tenants laid on 311 sheep, '11 more than they ought for which they are to pay 2d a sheep', while the shepherd, allowed 100 sheep, appears to have placed only sixty in the flock.[74] In 1644, for stocking the North Flock, she sent wethers from Barrett Ringstead, while relatives, friends and tenants placed cullett sheep in these two flocks, raising numbers to almost pre-1643 levels. In 1653 Alice clarified the stocking rates for the North and South Flock.[75] In the new agreement of 1650 Sir Hamon and Sir Nicholas undertook to stock the North Flock, leaving scope for the tenants to place their 300 sheep in the South Flock.[76] At Sedgeford the East Flock was let to Robert Birch for £25.[77] During this period Alice also paid more attention to the collection of tithes on lambs and wool, recording the smallest amounts; for the first time, she summarised the sales of wool from 1643 to 1654, identifying quantities, prices and markets. The income from sheep and wool halved over the next few years, but by 1650, by working closely with their tenants and village communities, and by acting decisively, Alice and her husband were able to stage a relatively quick recovery.

Alice's wider task was to build up the income from sheep and wool on the estate, which through the management of the brecks and foldcourses had a direct impact on the income from corn. Before 1621, their income from sheep had been minimal, partly because Alice reinvested profits in breeding stock. With the acquisition of the Sedgeford flocks in 1622, income rose sharply and averaged between £200 and £250 a

---

71 Bailey, 'Sheep Accounts', pp. 12–18.

72 About forty ewes to a ram, Watson and More, *Agriculture*, pp. 576, 590.

73 Alice's figure is 1653, forty short of the actual total; she missed out twenty-two stolen from the park.

74 LEST/P10, 'A note of such sheepe as the Tenants layd on the South flock of Ringsted in 1643'.

75 LEST/P10, 'A note for laying of sheep in Ringsted before the Agreement with the Townsmen of Ringsted for laying the North flock Intire'.

76 LEST/Q38.

77 LEST/1B89.

Table 7.2
Sheep flocks in hand, 1626–43.

Charge	Sedgeford East Flock	Barrett Ringstead Flock	Ringstead South Flock	Total
Father's booke	Lord 940	Lord 700	Lord 400	
	Shepherd 120	Shepherd 100	Shepherd 100	
Charge				
1626	Allen: 912 [*952*]	Pyper: 674 + 40 [*694*]	Crisp: 409 [*429*]	[*2115*]
1627	Allen: 917 [*957*]	Pyper: 550 + 40 [*650*]	Crisp: 409 [*489*]	[*2096*]
1628	Allen: 812	Pyper: 586 + 40 [*606*]	Crisp: 404 [*424*]	[*1882*]
1629	Thistle: 879 [*890*]	Pyper: 599 + 40 [*619*]	Crisp: 419 [*434*]	[*1983*]
1630	Thistle: 906 [*926*]	Pyper: 600 + 40 [*621*]	Crisp: 418 [*463*]	[*2050*]
1631	Thistle: 908 [*928*]	Pyper: 548 [*568*]	Crisp: 408 [*448*]	[1944]
1632	Greenwood: 797 [*837*]	Cooper: 526 [*566*]	Crisp: 413 [*433*]	[*1836*]
1633	Greenwood: 713 [*763*]	Cooper: 418 + 10 [*438*]	Crisp: 367 [*387*]	[*1598*]
1634	Greenwood: 871 [*891*]	Cooper: 520 + 36 [*540*]	Goodman: 411 + 70 in North flock	[*1948*]
1635	Osborn: 771 [*791*]	Goodman: 457 + 56	F. Crisp: 346 [*366*] + 46 in N. flock	[*1716*]
1636	Osborn: 802 [*822*]	Goodman: 475 [*515*] + grandsons 64	Crisp: 324 [*344*] + 99 in North flock	[*1780*]
1637	Osborn: 807 + 21	Goodman: 536 [*556*]	Crisp: 393 + 101 [*121*] in North flock	[*1898*]
1638	Osborn: 807	Goodman: 472 [*492*] + grandsons 84	Crisp: 562 [*582*] with North flock	[*1965*]
1639	Osborn: 819 [*839*]	Goodman: 487 [*507*] + grandsons 101	Crisp: 462 [*482*]	[*1929*]
1640	Osborn: 817 [*837*]	Goodman: 586 [*606*]	Willis: 440 [*460*]	[*1903*]
1641	Osborn: 815 [*835*]	Goodman: 572 [*592*] + cullet 74	Willis: 482 [*502*]	[*2003*]
1642	Osborn: 726 [*780*]	Goodman: 590 [*630*] + 131 [*151*]	Willis: 410	[*1971*]
1643	Osborn: 774 [*794*]	Goodman: 553 [*573*] + 105 cullet/grandsons	Willis: 419 [*439*]	[*1911*]
Plunder	Osborn: 753	Goodman: 530	Willis: 410 + 22	1715

Note: Totals give Alice's total, followed by actual total in square brackets which include the extra sheep in flock (shepherds' own allowance, cullet sheep and sheep of other family members).
Source: LEST/P10.

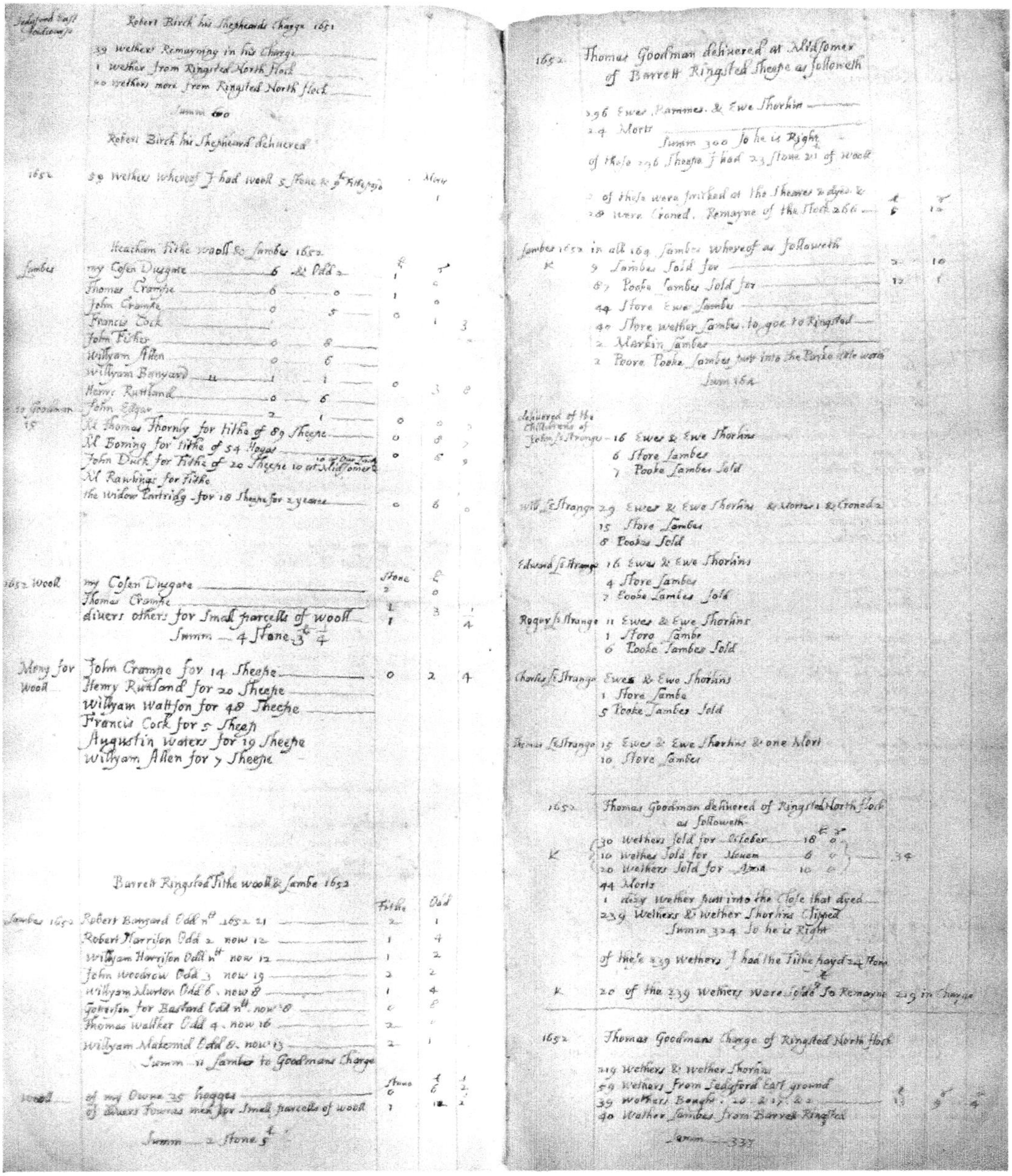

Figure 7.1 Alice Le Strange's Sheep Account 1651–2. NRO LEST/P 10.

year until 1641.The income from sheep partially recovered from the plunder of 1643, but not to the levels achieved in the 1620s and 1630s. The income from corn proved even more impressive and resilient, rising from an average of £315 between 1621 and 1626 to £550 between 1630 and 1641, principally due to the improvements at Sedgeford. By the 1650s, the family also benefited from the drainage of the coastal marshes, which produced quantities of marsh barley, notably from Heacham, but at a significant cost: in 1638 Alice noted a loss of £600 on draining Heacham Marsh. At Sedgeford income rose from £464 in 1621, with £287 paid in corn, to £690 in 1636, with £418 paid in corn. Sedgeford was a particular success story to which we will now turn.

The improvements at Sedgeford, 1621–56

Alongside the sheep accounts Alice managed her estate at Sedgeford, which she inherited from her father, Richard Stubbe, in 1619. Her purchase of Sir William Yelverton's sheep in 1620 was followed by her first set of estate accounts, which date from 1621 and end in 1633 following the death of her cousin, Francis Guybon.[78] When he died in 1631 she commissioned the survey of the estate comprising three maps, covering the extent of each of the three foldcourses, with an accompanying book explaining the use and organisation of the 'Sedgeford Brecks and Infield Lands'.[79] The surveyor, John Fisher of Heacham, frequently referred to an earlier survey, 'Mr Shepheards Booke', drawn up in 1582, a copy of which he included in his own book, indicating that Sedgeford had always been difficult to manage. By repeating the policy of engaging a professional, Alice showed her appreciation of the challenge and her determination to succeed. As with the sheep accounts, she clearly understood that her successors needed instruction and information on the estate if her improvements were to be sustained. The documents Alice commissioned or created between 1621 and 1635 laid the foundation for a new system of record-keeping which continued into the eighteenth century.[80]

The modern parish of Sedgeford extends to 4214 acres, which is close to the seventeenth-century estimates found in the documents.[81] The lands were divided between the two manors of the dean and chapter of Norwich, Easthall and Westhall, and a much smaller manor known as Sedgefords that came into the possession of John Le Strange, the second son of Sir Nicholas (1511–80), in the second half of

---

78 Francis Guybon's will: NRO NCC will register, Purgall 201, MF 91; and inventory DN/INV37/176.

79 LEST/OC1, LEST/IC58. The maps are not signed or dated by Fisher, but his references in his 'Breck Book' indicate that they were drafted alongside this work. Minor changes in the ownership of holdings in 1634 and further reorganisation of the brecks in 1641 suggest that the survey took several years to complete and in fact omissions can be found: some furlongs have no numbers, some strips no tenants.

80 E.g. Alice's later Sedgeford firmal and breck book: LEST/1B90; early eighteenth-century documents: LEST/1C64, IC65, LEST/IB85, IB89, IB91.

81 2001 Census. In 1619 the townsmen estimated Richard Stubbe's holding at 2300 acres and their own at 1800 acres with 100 acres of common, making a total of 4200 acres. In 1670 the balance was adjusted to 2400 acres and 1700 acres, reflecting the purchases made by the Le Stranges in the intervening period (LEST/1C64); Fisher's survey offers more precise calculations.

the sixteenth century.[82] In 1539 the dean and chapter had granted Sir Thomas Le Strange (c.1490–1545) a ninety-nine-year lease of their estate for a rent fixed at £61 7s 6d per annum, a fraction of what it was worth upon improvement.[83] This lease was confirmed to Sir Nicholas in 1562, who assigned it to John to make up his estate in Sedgeford.[84] On John's death in 1582 the lease passed to his widow Anne and subsequently came into the hands of her second husband, Richard Stubbe.[85] In 1602 Stubbe assigned the lease, with the manor of Sedgefords and other lands he had purchased in Sedgeford, to their daughter Alice as part of her marriage settlement to Sir Hamon Le Strange, to take effect two years after his death.[86] In 1637 the dean and chapter renewed the lease to Sir Hamon Le Strange at the same rent for a further ninety-nine years. However, it was not renewed to the family in 1736, being let on a twenty-one-year lease to a William Smith.[87] In 1733 Sir Thomas Le Strange had paid £75 a year for an estate valued at £696: no wonder the dean and chapter sought a more profitable solution.[88]

The lands of the dean and chapter formed by far the largest portion, estimated at 1734 acres out of the total 2232½ acres of demense land in Fisher's survey; Sedgefords amounted to 138 acres, leaving 360½ acres purchased by Stubbe. Of these 2232½ acres, Fisher classified 631¾ acres as infield and 1600¾ acres as brecks, sheep's pasture and furze ground.[89] The manorial tenants, freeholders and copyholders, dominated the infields, holding 1720½ acres with 213½ acres scattered through the brecks, making a total of 4166½ acres, excluding the commons.[90] These tenants, paying nominal fixed rents for nearly half the farmland in the parish, were a force to be reckoned with.

The infield–outfield system, devised to farm and utilise the sandy soils and heathland of west Norfolk, was made possible by the existence of river valleys that provided a core of fertile lands, the infields, where manorial tenants were able to grow their crops, keep their stock and sell their labour to the lords cultivating the brecks, the outfields.[91] Sedgeford was particularly favoured in this respect. Its lands rise

---

82   Blomefield, *Norfolk*, vol. 5, pp. 1322–6 (ed. 1736–95), where Sedgefords is known as Caston's Manor.

83   LEST/AA67; NRO, DCN 51/91. The parliamentary survey of 1649 of the dean and chapter lands estimated the improved value at £304 10s, but in fact the income from Sedgeford by this time was more than double that figure. The dean and chapter was abolished in 1649 and by act of parliament the cathedral estates were sold. At the restoration these sales were declared void.

84   LEST/AA67.

85   LEST/AA70–3.

86   LEST/AA67.

87   DCN 49/49.

88   DCN 59/30/1.

89   LEST/OC1, LEST/IC58.

90   Fisher's map for East Field suggests that part of the commons has been encroached and no longer amounted to 100 acres; this would bring his total figure closer to the modern estimate of 4214 acres. The parliamentary survey of 1649 says the common was 'about 100 acres'.

91   Wade Martins and Williamson, *Roots of Change*, pp. 10–11; Darby and Saltmarsh, 'The infield-outfield system'.

from the broad and fertile valley of the river Heacham to the light thin soils of the uplands, which become progressively less fertile to the east of the parish around the commons and the sheep pasture known as 'The Whins', named after the gorse and furze that flourished there.[92] The extensive infields enabled Sedgeford to sustain a large population located in the river valley mainly along the highway from Heacham to Docking. The lords, principally the lessees of the dean and chapter, concentrated their energies on improving the brecks, sub-letting their demesne lands to large farmers who drew on the labour of the village to plough the arable and harvest the corn. These farm tenants, principally the Guybon family, paid their rent in money and corn, with barley rents often exceeding money rents. By 1625 two of the Sedgeford flocks were leased to large tenants, while the large East Flock with its ground, which required the most attention, remained in hand until 1643.

The system was ingenious, but required careful regulation and management, particularly as it was combined with the organisation of three flocks and foldcourses: this explains the purpose of the three maps shown in Figure 7.2. Each map shows the extent and location of the eight brecks allocated to each foldcourse. Each breck was cultivated on an eight-year rotation: a first year of summerley and breaking up the land; three years of grain crops – rye, barley, barley and oats; and four years of grass.[93] When the brecks were out of cultivation manorial tenants had to be compensated with arable elsewhere. The purpose of John Fisher's book was to set out the rotations and specify these exchanges. This was done by matching brecks, so that Breck 1 was matched with Breck 5, Breck 2 with 6, Breck 3 with 7 and Breck 4 with 8.[94] 'The Parliamentary Survey of the Leasehold Estate of the Dean and Chapter of Norwich in Sedgeford in 1649' explained how these arrangements worked:

> There is a fouldcourse for 1200 sheep belonging to the Lord of the s[ai]d mannors [Westhall and Easthall] which are to be kept in this manner: viz partly upon the Common whereof there is about 100 acres and partly upon the shack of all the arable ground (whether they be customary, freehold or demesne lands of the s[ai]d mannors) and none else are to keep sheep there or the s[ai]d common butt the lords, and partly upon the lay or unplowed ground of the s[ai]d brecks whereof 5 parts (the whole being divided into 8 parts) are every year to be lay for the pastures of the s[ai]d sheep, and where it fall out in course that any of the copyhold or freehold lands are to ly for the purpose aforesaid, the Lord allows to the tenants in exchange & recompense for the same alike quantity of his demesne arable lands.[95]

---

92   Whins is a word for gorse or furze, used for fuel, making dead hedges and so on. Yaxley, *Glossary*, p. 235.

93   See Table 7.4 below. Summerley or summerland refers to land uncropped, but not necessarily unploughed, in the summer: Yaxley, *Glossary*, p. 207.

94   LEST/IC58.

95   NRO DCN 51/90, Parliamentary Survey of 1649. Note the compensation paid to tenants; see also Wade Martins and Williamson, *Roots of Change*, pp. 10–11.

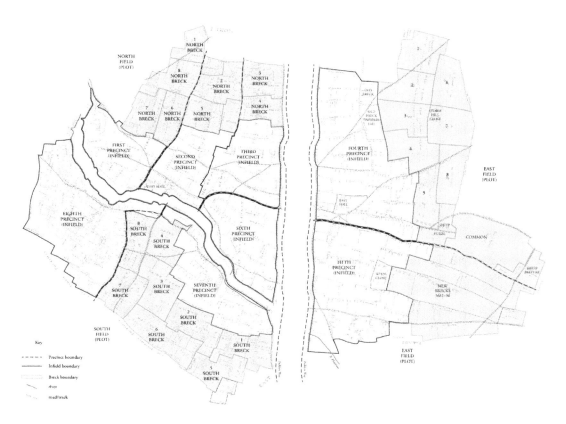

Figure 7.2 John Fisher's maps of Sedgeford, *c.*1631 (diagram). NRO LEST/OC 1.

The potential for disputes was ever present. Not only was the grazing restricted to the lord, but the issue of exchange of lands and compensation was constantly open to challenge. In a long-running dispute with Richard Stubbe, the tenants claimed grazing rights for their great cattle over the brecks. Stubbe conceded the right, but the terms of the agreement of 1619 show that the tenants were confined to The Whins and not allowed to graze their cattle on his severals.[96] This long-drawn-out dispute may well have persuaded Alice of the need for a full survey once Francis Guybon had departed the scene. Such a complex farming system depended on the collaboration

---

96   LEST/IC64 includes notes on the final agreement of this dispute. This farming book, started by Alice's favourite grandson, Sir Nicholas (1632–69), has much information on Richard Stubbe's estate in Sedgeford. References are also made to Fisher's survey of 1630, with a sketch of the commons, and Bradford's survey of 1653, indicating the continuing reliance on Alice's management techniques. 'Severals' means privately owned as opposed to common land: see Yaxley, *Glossary*, p. 185.

and the acquiescence of the entire farming community if it was to succeed. Having been brought up in Sedgeford, Alice was fortunate in the close ties and kinship she enjoyed with the community, but she still needed to be on her guard and act with firmness and clarity.

The maps show the extent of the brecks and the grazing regime of the three flocks and foldcourses in the 1630s, but they also show what existed before and what confronted Alice in 1621. The three maps, the north plot, south plot and east plot, fit together like a jigsaw and indicate an earlier structure based on 'precincts' and 'quarentena'.The north plot includes the lands of the first, second, third and sixth precincts; the south plot those of the seventh and eighth precincts; and the east plot those of the fourth and fifth precincts. The purpose of the precincts is not clear, but they seem to relate to the ecclesiastical origins of the principal manor of Sedgeford and the need to divide up such a large parish; it may even represent an earlier attempt at rationalisation. The term 'quarentena' corresponds to the more common furlong.

Fisher's maps are divided logically by Peddars Way and the river Heacham. On each map he superimposed the area covered by the eight brecks, making it easy to cross-reference to the breck books and identify the strips and parcels in cultivation or laid down to grass. The most congested area was in the north plot, dominated by the Guybons, followed by the south and finally the less fertile east. This was where the Le Stranges focused their efforts, reordering the East Brecks and building new farmsteads at Easthall and the Magazine which, with Stormhill and Whin Close, can still be seen on the Ordnance Survey map.[97] Here they began a gradual process of extending regular cultivation into the brecks.

The Sedgeford estate account of 1621–33 describes the situation facing Alice and shows how she gradually restructured the management of her new inheritance.[98] In the layout of the account we can see Alice developing her understanding and refining her methods; this particularly concerned the rotations employed by Francis Guybon on 'the great farme', based at the principal manor of Westhall. In the 1621 account she entered the details of his holding in two parts, distinguishing between 260 acres of infield land and inclosed ground and 279 acres of brecks. In 1621 Alice granted her cousin an abatement of 45s for the nine-acre Hall Bottom Close 'because the year was so hard, as the sheep had it for so longe he could reape no proffit from it', indicating her understanding of the need for improvement. In 1622 she started to clarify the rotation of the brecks, placing entries on different lines; by 1625 she had figures in the margin; by 1627, titles distinguishing between East Brecks and South Field; and by 1631 had adopted the rotation used by Fisher in his breck book identifying the first, second, last crop and summerley.[99] At the same time she started listing the holdings of tenants, noting the rents paid in money and barley. In 1633 the final account shows that Guybon's holding had been divided between his two sons, Francis and William: William occupied Westhall and had also taken on the lease of the

---

97 LEST/KA6, fols 185–213 for the building of the Magazine, 1639–40; it was used as a depot for military supplies.

98 LEST/BK7.

99 LEST/IC58.

North Foldcourse from John Cremer, and Francis was at Easthall, which was enlarged with the addition of 'the new farme' and the East Brecks.[100]

At the other end of the book Alice entered a rental of the Sedgeford manorial tenants for 1634.[101] This was a further part of the reorganisation following the death of Francis Guybon; it was probably devised to overcome the deficiencies of the account book and accommodate the new information arising from Fisher's survey.[102] Using the rental and the estate account for the year 1634, it is possible to reconstruct the farming profile of the Sedgeford tenants with their manorial and farm lands (Table 7.3). Underpinning all these developments was John Fisher's survey of 1631.[103] As we have seen, it was designed to clarify the landholding structure and to provide the information necessary for further reorganisation and improvement of the infield–outfield system. In the bottom left-hand corner Fisher set out the rotation to be followed; for how this worked across the eight brecks of 'Southfield' between 1631 and 1643, see Table 7.4.

The information in Fisher's written survey and on the maps illustrates the dramatic improvements undertaken in 'Eastfield'. The east map shows Easthall occupied by young Francis Guybon in 1634, extended with the addition of 'the new farm' and his responsibility for farming the East Brecks. Using the estate account for the years 1634 and 1635, we can trace the composition of this new holding carved out of the least fertile part of Sedgeford.[104] The section on 'Eastfield' in the breck book begins with a reference to the maps of Sedgeford made in 1631 and to the fact that the furlongs and pieces have been carefully remeasured and noted on the east map (see Figure 7.3). Clearly, Alice was trying to rationalise the East Brecks. At the end of the section on the brecks Fisher summarised the lord's holding in all three fields. He then provided a description of the new brecks in 'Eastfield', broken up in 1631, which can be identified on the east map as lying to the south of the Sedgeford–Docking road and Sedgeford Common; these were the newly broken grounds in East Foldcourse farmed by William Guybon in 1634 and 1635. Fisher concluded by setting out the redivision of the East Brecks into eight blocks of forty acres each and noting how they were farmed in 1641. The section on the brecks is followed by detail of the lord's infield lands in 1631, set out in a similar way, with references to Mr Shepheard's book. Fisher summarised the demesne lands let for money and barley, with half the brecks in cultivation.

Fisher's book of the brecks and infield lands became the model for management at Sedgeford, repeatedly referred to and updated over the years. In 1647 Alice started a new book reflecting the changes that had taken place in the intervening years, principally the termination of the Guybons' tenancies in the early 1640s.[105] Other farming books provide useful information as to what was happening in that period.

---

100 LEST/BK7.

101 LEST/BK7.

102 The most significant of these changes was the appearance of the new numbering system, listing the strips and closes from 1 to 1759.

103 LEST/IC58.

104 See also Table 7.3.

105 LEST/IB90.

Table 7.3
Farming profile of the Sedgeford manorial tenants and farmers, 1634.

	Manorial lands Manorial tenants paying manorial rents ½d to 4d per acre (fols 15–59)			Demense (farm) lands Let for money rent (fols 63–67) at 3s to 9s per acre						Let for barley rent (fols 66–73) at two bushels per acre					
				Infield			Outfield			Infield			Brecks		
	a	r	p	a	r	p	a	r	p	a	r	p	a	r	p
Robert Rose	242	1	10												
Rob. Banyard	211	0	0												
W. Guybon	169	3	15	144	0	0	252	0	0	36	2	0	149	1	20
Mr Gurling, clerk	162	3	35							1	2	10			
J. Lawes	155	0	20												
H. Cremer	104	0	0												
J. Ellgar	101	1	21												
R. Attwood	100	2	20												
R. Bird	81	3	0							0	1	30			
H. Minns	73	3	10												
W. Banyard	72	2	0												
H. Lawes heirs	64	2	30												
Rich. Banyard	63	2	30							17	2	10	4	2	0
G. Framingham	57	1	15										1	3	0
Allen Collen	44	1	0							1	3	0	10	2	20
Ellgars heirs	20	2	0												
F. Guybon	17	3	20	123	3	0	127	0	0	23	0	0	61	2	0
J. Lingey	13	3	30										2	0	0
R. Bankes, sen.	13	2	0										2	0	0
R. Dey	11	0	0												
Mr Waters, clerk	9	0	0												
E. Creamer	8	3	20												
E. Jenners	8	1	0												
R. Lawes	6	3	20												
J. Adams	4	0	0							8	1	20	6	0	0
J. Crisp	1	1	16								2	0	2	3	0
T. Spalding	1	0	0										2	0	0
9 tenants: 1–5 acres	27	1	36	H. Lawes, R. Hancell, W. Minnes, J. Roll, Mrs D. Redmans, C. Powley, W. Adams, W. Billament, T. Awdly											
6 tenants: 0–1 acres + barley rent	1	1	0	R. Bankes, junior, T. Bassam, G. Hargate, R. Gould, W. Byrd, T. Outlawe									1	0	0
	1850	0	0												
T. Longstreth				27	0	0				20	1	0	1	2	0
F. Costen				3	3	10				40	0	0			
M. Smith										69	1	0	2	0	0
Mr Loades, clerk										26	2	0	7	2	0
Widow Acres										14	1	20			
Widow Vickers, B. Crisp, W. Hill, W. Segon, G. Estrick, J. Sallter, L. Vile, T. Banyard, R. Crisp, P. Eade, Osburn										16	2	0	16	2	0
							Infield not let			9	2	20			
Total acreage	1850	0	0	295	2	10	379	0	0	276	2	20	274	2	0

Source: LEST/BK7.

Table 7.4
Cultivation of the South Brecks at Sedgeford, 1631–43.

	1st	*2nd*	*3rd*	*4th*	*5th*	*6th*	*7th*	*8th*
1631	last crop	2nd crop	1st crop	somerley	grass	grass	grass	grass
1632	grass	last crop	2nd crop	1st crop	somerley	grass	grass	grass
1633	grass	grass	last crop	2nd crop	1st crop	somerley	grass	grass
1634	grass	grass	grass	last crop	2nd crop	1st crop	somerley	grass
1635	grass	grass	grass	grass	last crop	2nd crop	1st crop	somerley
1636	somerley	grass	grass	grass	grass	last crop	2nd crop	1st crop
1637	1st crop	somerley	grass	grass	grass	grass	last crop	2nd crop
1638	2nd crop	1st crop	somerley	grass	grass	grass	grass	last crop

Source: LEST/IC58.

For example, the 'Corn Tithe and Farm Accounts' from 1643 to 1653 detail the corn received from different tenants for tithe and barley rent, the sale of the corn with prices and names of buyers, and the shipping of it to Newcastle, Norway and Dunkirk.[106] These accounts supplement the receipts paid directly into Alice's receipt book. There is no estate account for Sedgeford after 1633; expenditure and out-payments for Sedgeford appear in Alice's books of disbursements.

Alice's 'Sedgford Firmall and Breck Book 1647/8/9 & 1650' forms a comprehensive reference work that she drew up towards the end of her life.[107] The most striking aspect of the book are the names and dates inserted by Alice's successors, showing how they systematically used the document until the 1700s.[108] Creating a manual for posterity was clearly Alice's intention. The directions for using the Sedgeford Brecks show her trying to fit the relevant information on to a single page for ease of reference, with tables summarising the start of each rotation for the next twenty-five years. Unfortunately the acerage for each breck squeezed into the left-hand margin has been worn away. For Southfield brecks the figures have been inserted later above the acreage sold for barley. In the same hand, Alice's years for summerley stretching to 1670 have been extended to 1703. Likewise, in folio two, where she provided a full rotation for North Pasture, we can see her successors using the table, systematically crossing out and inserting the years down to 1702.

Alice's new breck book largely follows the format devised by Fisher. However, changes have been made to reflect the growing complexity of the holdings after the breakup of 'the great farme' leased to old Francis Guybon, the purchase of more land by the Le Stranges and the renewal of the lease from the dean and chapter in 1637. In contrast to Fisher's survey, the East Brecks, farmed entirely by the Le Stranges, occupy only a single page, while the North Brecks, with a host of manorial tenants

---

106 LEST/IC65, and Alice's ship account in LEST/P10.

107 LEST/IB90.

108 Sir Nicholas le Strange, 4th Bt; LEST/IB91.

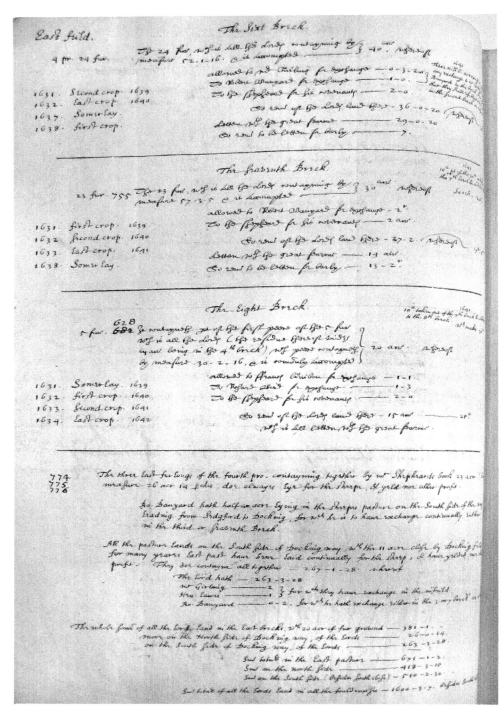

Figure 7.3 John Fisher's survey of Sedgeford showing East Field Brecks 6–8. NRO LEST/IC 58, East Field Brecks 6–8.

to accommodate, follow the old format and occupy ten pages. The firmals illustrate life in Sedgeford after the departure of the Guybons in 1641 and 1644, with demesne lands and foldcourses leased to a variety of tenants. It confirms the trend identified in 1641, with parcels of breckland being gradually drawn into the infields and regular cultivation.[109] Gradually, we see outfields being whittled away and rents being raised. Similarly, the area yielding corn rent was reduced. Tenants paid 'fearme barley' in 1653 for a total of 467 acres, compared with 551 acres in 1635.[110] The book ends abruptly at this point; Alice's involvement in farming more or less ceased in 1654 with the death of her husband.

The inserted names of the early eighteenth-century tenants that run through the firmals indicate quite clearly that Alice's book was still being used by her successors in the 1700s. In fact, it formed the basis of Sir Nicholas Le Strange's Sedgeford firmal of 1702, which was 'entered fayre and more perfect into a new book 1707'.[111] This book, in its format and frequent references to Alice's book of 1647 to 1654, attests to Alice's enduring legacy as a farmer and estate manager. The Sedgeford documents are not an isolated example. The pattern of innovation and meticulous record-keeping, with successors quoting her work, was repeated across the Hunstanton estate, notably at Ringstead, which shared many features with neighbouring Sedgeford. Alice's contribution to the family and the estate was not only the skilful day-to-day management of their affairs but the creation of exceptional records that, handed down from generation to generation, helped to secure the survival and future of the Le Strange family at Hunstanton. Her price was truly above pearls.

---

109 LEST/IC58.
110 See Table 7.3.
111 LEST/IB91.

Chapter 8

Draining the coastal marshes in north-west Norfolk: the contribution of the Le Stranges of Hunstanton, 1605–1724[1]

This chapter is about the reclamation of the coastal marshes in north and north-west Norfolk in the early modern period, an area almost entirely neglected by historians writing on drainage.[2] To be fair, their oversight is understandable. Compared to what happened in the Fens, the Norfolk Broads and the Halvergate Marshes, the drainage undertaken on this coastline was small in scale and of no great complexity; nevertheless, capital still had to be raised, risks assessed and the work organised, which sometimes even merited the services of a Dutchman.[3] And this was only the start; once completed, sea walls had to be maintained, drains scoured, new cuts made and farmsteads built. In contrast to the Fens, these piecemeal ventures are not associated with armed struggle and social dislocation, but rights and titles still had to be defined and disputes settled – not only between commoners and landowners but also between landowners of different status and with varying sizes of holding. Resolving their differences and managing this fragile landscape was the everyday burden of the coastal villages bordering the marshes from King's Lynn to Hunstanton and across the north Norfolk coast to Weybourne, as Piet van Cruyningen and Tim Soens have described, but we seem to have lost sight of their plight in our focus on the Fens.[4] Part of the interest in this area lies in the fact that it is now one of the most

---

1   This chapter first appeared as 'Draining the coastal marshes of north-west Norfolk: the contribution of the Le Stranges at Hunstanton, 1605 to 1724', *Agricultural History Review*, 63/2 (2015), pp. 221–42.

2   For discussion of drainage elsewhere see the classic works of H.C. Darby, *The Medieval Fenland* (Cambridge, 1940) and *The Draining of the Fens* (Cambridge, 1956); for more recent work, T. Williamson, *The Norfolk Broads: A Landscape History* (Manchester, 1997); H. Cook and T. Williamson (eds), *Water Management in the English Landscape: Field, Marsh and Fen* (Edinburgh, 1999); A. Reeves and T. Williamson, 'Marshes', in J. Thirsk (ed.), *The English Rural Landscape* (Oxford, 2000). Piet van Cruyningen has recently published a valuable overview of drainage in England, France and the Netherlands: 'Dealing with drainage: state regulation of drainage projects in the Dutch Republic, France and England during the sixteenth and seventeenth centuries', *Economic History* Review, 68 (2015), pp. 420–40.

3   Jan van Hasdonck, discussed below.

4   Bas van Bavel and Erik Thoen (eds), *Rural Societies and Environments at Risk: Ecology, Property Rights and Social Organisation in Fragile Areas (Middle Ages–Twentieth Century)* (Turnhout, 2013), pp. 15–45; see also, in *ibid.*, T. Soens, 'The social distribution of land and flood risk along the North Sea coast: Flanders, Holland and Romney Marsh compared, *c.*1200–1700', pp. 147–80, and P.J. van Cruyingen, 'State, property rights and sustainability of drained areas along the North Sea coast, sixteenth–eighteenth centuries', pp. 181–208.

heavily protected coastal sites in Europe, renowned for its birds, flora and coastal formations, with villages sustained by agriculture, fishing and, more particularly today, environmental tourism.[5] These sustainable outcomes indicate a long-term awareness of the requirements of managing a vulnerable landscape that included not only the marshes at the mercy of the sea but the light sandy uplands rising up behind the villages, susceptible to overgrazing and erosion. These local communities seem to have got it more or less right and for that reason alone it is worth exploring how they went about it.

I

As landlords, the Le Stranges of Hunstanton were very much part of this landscape. They were not new men with big money but an ancient gentry family who had lived at Hunstanton Hall by the coast in north-west Norfolk since the twelfth century. Their huge archive shows that from the earliest times they were embedded in the society, culture and geography of the area and wholly committed to the locality.[6] This distinguishes them fundamentally from their compatriots speculating in the Fens – and indeed Romney Marsh – who were noted for their absentee landlordism.[7] In 1604, when Sir Hamon Le Strange inherited his estate, he abandoned a promising career at court to tackle the accumulated problems that faced him at home. After half a century of lenient management by his forebears the family was in financial difficulties, having to pay off debts incurred by the trustees, complete the hall and rebuild the decayed farmhouses 'out of the ground', as his wife, Alice, noted.[8] Within a generation they had reversed their fortunes. In 1616 Sir Hamon estimated his revenue at £1247, which included rents from Hunstanton and Holme by the Sea, Great and Little Ringstead, Heacham and Gressenhall.[9] In 1620 Alice inherited an estate at nearby Sedgeford from her father, Richard Stubbe, raising their rental income to £1700 a year. From that date, with sales of sheep, wool and corn, receipts rose rapidly to £2000 a year, rising to a peak of £2640 in 1641, before their heavy losses of corn and sheep in the Civil War at the hands of the parliamentary forces.[10] Draining marshes was part of their

---

5   J.A. Steers, 'Scolt Head Island', *Geographical Journal*, 83 (1934), pp. 479–94; 'Some notes on the north Norfolk coast from Hunstanton to Brancaster', *Geographical Journal*, 87 (1936), pp. 35–46; *The Coastline of England and Wales* (Cambridge, 1946).

6   The Le Strange archive (LEST) is held at the Norfolk Records Office.

7   Romney Marsh was also noted for its absentee landowners, who leased their marshes to graziers; by the mid-seventeenth century only 16% of the marshes were owner-occupied: Soens, 'Social distribution of land', pp. 158–9.

8   As discussed in chapters 3, 5, 6 and 7 above.

9   Griffiths, '"A Country Life"', p. 210. Little Ringstead, lying south of Hunstanton Park, is more commonly known as Barrett Ringstead.

10 *Ibid.*, pp. 226–34. See also R.W. Ketton-Cremer, 'Sir Hamon Le Strange and his sons', in *A Norfolk Gallery*, pp. 56–94; *Norfolk in the Civil War*, 2nd edn, pp. 206–18. Sir Hamon, his wife Alice and his three sons, Nicholas, Hamon and Roger, all merit separate entries in the *Oxford Dictionary of National Biography*.

strategy to improve the estate and raise their revenues; it was undertaken principally by their eldest son, Sir Nicholas (1604–55), soon after his marriage in 1631.[11] By the early 1640s they were selling significant quantities of marsh barley and wheat, principally from Heacham, which greatly assisted their recovery after their losses in 1643.[12]

As a record of his work, Sir Nicholas left several pocket-sized notebooks of extraordinary detail and quality. In his knowledge and approach he owed much to his parents, combining his father's interest in science, mathematics and engineering with his mother's aptitude for accounting.[13] These notebooks, four of which survive, provide a record of the drainage process, from the layout and construction of drains to the establishment of new farmsteads with the costs and profits involved.[14] Most significantly, Sir Nicholas designed them as manuals with instructions and advice for his successors, following the example of his parents. We know this strategy worked, as his grandson, another Sir Nicholas (1661–1724), maintained the drains and introduced new initiatives, noting his progress in one of Sir Hamon's old memoranda books, which he updated by adding indices, tables, a system of cross-referencing and his own commentary.[15] So, not only do we find out what happened, but we begin to understand why the family avoided catastrophe. With their knowledge of the locality the Le Stranges knew the risks involved and were able to devise appropriate strategies to deal with them. They also understood the risks of adventuring on the Fens. Sir Hamon lost £500 on Boston Fen in the 1630s, which may explain why his son concentrated on the local marshes, which he knew and where he exercised more control.[16] The creation of the notebooks, a prime example of information management, was a vital part of Sir Nicholas's risk management strategy for himself and for future generations. Not for them the debacle of Hatfield Chase, South Yorkshire, in 1626, studied by Piet Cruyingen, or the reverses experienced in the Fens in the late seventeenth century and beyond.[17]

---

11 Sir Nicholas Le Strange (1604–55), 1st Bt, married Anne, daughter of Sir Edward Lewkenor (1587–1618) of Denham, Suffolk <www.historyofparliamentonline.org>.

12 Griffiths, '"A Country Life"', pp. 224–6.

13 Whittle and Griffiths, *Consumption and gender*, pp. 28–36; Griffiths, '"A Country Life"', pp. 203–5; and chapter 7 above.

14 LEST/KA6, KA9, KA10 and KA24 survive; four others, LEST/KA4, KA5, KA7 and KA8, are listed in the catalogue but not deposited. They almost certainly relate to the drainage at Heacham summarised in LEST/KA24, where entries refer to 'Heacham Marsh 4th booke'. A simple paper book, relating to costs and profits, has recently been found in a supplementary list, LEST/suppl. 25ii/xvi.

15 Sir Nicholas Le Strange, 4th Bt, 1661–1724. Sir Hamon's memoranda books, LEST/Q34, Q36, Q37 and Q38, include a vast range of information appertaining to the family and estate.

16 This 'loss' appears under 'The losses in my husbands estate' at the end of Alice's summary of the family finances, 1633–53 (LEST/P10). However, in 1636 she records expenditure at Boston Fen that is remarkably close to £500; it is possible that the 'loss' is not quite what it seems, as discussed below.

17 van Cruyningen, 'State, property rights and sustainability of drained areas', pp. 192–202.

In the final notebook Sir Nicholas provides a summary of the drainage work undertaken with fifty pages of his 'observations'; a reference to 'Heacham Marsh 4th booke' suggests that the four missing notebooks relate to Heacham. Overall, it appears that 245 acres of marshes at Heacham, Hunstanton and Holme by the Sea were drained between 1633 and 1653, with the marshes at Heacham accounting for 177 acres.[18] However, as responsibility for this enterprise was shared with his father, and Alice included his payments in her books of disbursements, we have a good idea of the scale of this venture and the problems associated with it; she also recorded the receipts for corn grown on the drained land in her household books. The earliest notebook covers the drainage of marshes at Hunstanton and Holme in 1633–42; it relates to only 67¾ acres, but includes the most minute detail of the processes involved, showing Sir Nicholas's grasp of the technicalities, organisation of the workforce and management of the finances.[19] The second book covers the next phase, ploughing and sowing the newly drained marshes, in 1643–53.[20] Another book deals almost exclusively with building work on the marshes and elsewhere on the estate, creating new farmsteads and housing for tenants and specialist labourers.[21]

The marshes in question lie in two distinct areas and can be seen most clearly on William Faden's 1797 map of Norfolk (see Figure 2.2 above).[22] Those at Heacham belong to the marshes bordering the Wash, technically an extension of the silt Fens, which stretch from King's Lynn to the chalk outcrop at Hunstanton. These marshes are not so exposed to storms and tidal surges and provide more opportunity for sustainable drainage projects. Faden's map shows an 'embankment' starting tentatively at Heacham and then running firmly southwards through the large estates at Snettisham, Sandringham and Castle Rising to 'Lynn Regis'; this embankment still survives, but lies well inland, as marshes have continued to be reclaimed from the Wash. Today, this area supports an intensive agriculture growing vast crops of corn and sugar beet – a stark contrast to the gentle livestock grazing along the north Norfolk coast. From Hunstanton, the marshes occupy a different formation, as the tides erode the chalk outcrop of Hunstanton cliffs and carry the debris eastwards to Weybourne, depositing it along the coast, creating sand dunes, lagoons, islands and spits.[23] At the same time tidal activity westwards brings more deposits from the eastern cliffs at Sheringham, adding to the silting up of the river estuaries and the creation of the extensive sandy beaches and marshland at Salthouse, Cley, Blakeney and Holkham. Figure 8.1 identifies the old cliffline, where the villages are situated, with its foreshore of accumulated marshland and sandy beaches. Faden's map also shows the light sandy uplands of Great Ringstead rising from the marshes at Holme, with patches of

---

18   LEST/KA24.

19   LEST/KA6.

20   LEST/KA9.

21   LEST/KA10.

22   Macnair and Williamson, *William Faden and Norfolk's 18th-Century Landscape*. Although the map dates from 1797, the authors note that much of the detail on commons, marsh and fen relates to what existed in the sixteenth and seventeenth centuries.

23   Steers, 'Scolt Head Island'; 'Notes from Hunstanton to Brancaster'; <http://www.jncc.defra.gov.uk>.

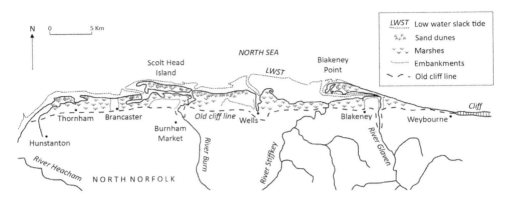

Figure 8.1 North Norfolk coast showing the old cliff line from Hunstanton to Weybourne. From V.J. May, 'North Norfolk Coast', Geological Conservation Rev., www.jncc.defra.gov.uk.

common land and lyng (heathland) clearly marked; these parishes lie near Thornham and Brancaster, studied by Angus Winchester and Eleanor Straughton in their work on lowland commons.[24] The whole landscape was part of a complex farming system, with regulated grazing rights on the common marshes and upland brecks, existing on either side of open-field arable, enclosed pasture and marshes.[25]

In his work on wool supply and the cloth industry in sixteenth- and seventeenth-century Norfolk, Keith Allison explained how these marshes were developed to meet the rising demand for wool and corn. Landowners such as the Howards of Castle Rising, the Cobbes of Sandringham, the Cokes of Holkham and the Bacons of Stiffkey, as well as the Le Stranges of Hunstanton, drained and improved their marshes in order to raise the quality and quantity of their summer grazing.[26] In this area, marshes formed an integral part of the foldcourse system, the foundation of sheep–corn husbandry in Norfolk. It involved the folding of sheep and cattle on the upland arable fields in the winter, where they fertilised the light sandy soils, preparing the ground for sowing. In the spring, when the crops were planted, the stock were moved to summer grazing; brecks, commons and heathland normally provided succour, but marshes, especially when they had been drained, were vastly superior. The presence of these marshes meant that landowners could increase their stocking regimes and bring more light land into cultivation. Allison's map of Holkham from 1590 shows two foldcourses that

24   C.P. Rodgers, E.A. Straughton, A.J.L. Winchester and M. Pieraccini, *Contested Common Land: Environmental Governance Past and Present* (London, 2011), pp. 163–88.

25   Brecks were the oufields in the 'infield–outfield system', cultivated intermittently, while the fertile infields were in permanent cultivation. Darby and Saltmarsh, 'The infield-outfield system'. The aim of improving landlords was to draw these outfields into permanent cultivation.

26   K.J. Allison, 'The wool supply and Worstead cloth industry in Norfolk in the 16th and 17th centuries', PhD thesis (University of Leeds, 1955); K.J. Allison, 'The sheep corn husbandry of Norfolk in the sixteenth and seventeenth centuries', *Agricultural History Review*, 5 (1957), pp. 12–30.

included large areas of saltmarsh; this was a common feature in all the villages along the north Norfolk coast.[27] An earlier map of 1586, from the Bacon archive, of the coast at Stiffkey and Blakeney illustrates this formation more graphically, with the villages along the old cliffline, the arable uplands behind and the freshwater marshes and saltmarshes towards the sea (Figure 8.2).[28] Sir Nicholas Bacon, the Lord Keeper, had purchased an estate in Stiffkey in 1571. Soon after, his son Nathaniel was constructing a sea wall and reporting to his father on its success; he also commented on the rising price of corn, especially wheat.[29] Later, in 1572, he told him of his plans to build a port at Stiffkey that was deeper and safer than Blakeney or Cley, and set out his specifications for a granary.[30] This economic activity gained momentum as prices rose from the 1580s; by the 1630s corn, as we have seen, was being grown on the drained marshes. However, landowners did not get it all their own way. These commercially driven initiatives by gentry landowners were often firmly resisted by village communities determined to protect their own rights and interests; if they were all to survive as functioning communities they needed to find a way of reconciling their differences.

II

One of the controversies generated by this heightened activity was noted by R.H. Tawney.[31] He was particularly interested in the corporate action taken by the yeomen, commoners and freeholders of the town of Burnham Overy against Robert Bacon[32] and Thomas Coke when they purchased marshes there in 1588. In return for walling, embanking and draining the marsh and making it suitable for pasture and tillage, the commoners agreed to sacrifice their grazing rights over three parts of the whole. In other words, they were prepared to surrender (property) rights for a *quid pro quo*. Tawney was impressed by their willingness to act as a single body:

> they buy land and they sell land and they can leave it to their heirs. Certain persons in the township act on their behalf, much as directors might act for a body of shareholders. Is it possible to speak of such arrangements simply in terms of individual rights? Are we not driven to think of the township as almost a landholding corporation?

Here Tawney gets to the heart of the issue: the distribution of property rights, the negotiated settlements and the common interests of these local communities. Disputes were frequent and hard fought, but ultimately all parties had to resolve their

---

27   Allison, 'Sheep corn husbandry', p. 17.

28   The map appears on the cover of V. Morgan, E. Rutledge and B. Taylor (eds), *The Papers of Nathaniel Bacon of Stiffkey, vol. V, 1603–1607*, Norfolk Record Society 74 (Norwich, 2010).

29   A. Hassell Smith, G.M. Baker and R.W. Kenny (eds), *The Papers of Nathaniel Bacon of Stiffkey, vol. I, 1556–1577*, Norfolk Record Society 46 (Norwich, 1978–9), p. 32.

30   *Ibid.*, pp. 41, 43.

31   R.H. Tawney, *The Agrarian Problem in the Sixteenth Century* (New York, 1912), p. 245, n. 1.

32   Robert Bacon was the son of the Lord Keeper's brother Thomas, and first cousin of Nathaniel.

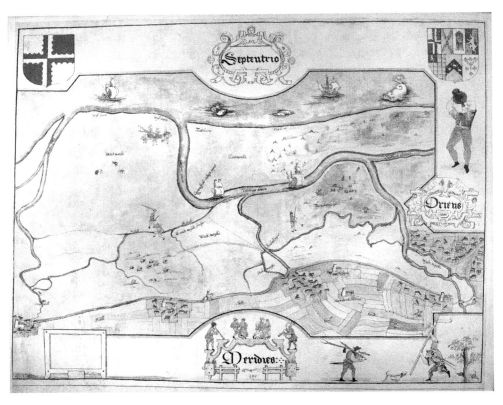

Figure 8.2: Blakeney Haven and the Port of Cley showing the marshes and villages at Stiffkey, Morston, Blakeney, Wiveton and Cley. A 19th century facsimile of the 1586 original, thought to have been surveyed by John Darby. NRO MC 2443/3.

differences. In the Fens adventurers could rely on the protection of the crown, but these coastal communities, more reliant on their own resources, needed to collaborate and create a system of 'sustainable governance', as Winchester explained in his work on Thornham and Brancaster.[33] For resident landowners, anxious to secure the future of the family, it was essential to find sustainable as well as profitable outcomes. They needed to work with their communities to find a way forward, but at the same time they had to protect their property rights.

Tawney's example is significant, as the Bacons and Cokes were relatively new to this part of Norfolk and possibly less familiar with the culture. In contrast, the Le Stranges, resident at the principal manor at Hunstanton since 1310, had long enjoyed a settled relationship with their tenantry. In the late fifteenth century they acquired

---

33   A.J.L. Winchester, 'Property rights, "good neighbourhood" and sustainability: the management of common land in England and Wales, 1235–1965', in van Bavel and Thoen (eds), *Rural Societies*, pp. 309–29.

two further manors, Mustrells and Lovells, leaving just the tiny manor of Snettertons, which they had absorbed by the time Sir Hamon inherited his estate.[34] Thus the family enjoyed unity of possession alongside their longevity and understanding of the area and its ways. From their records, it is evident that Sir Hamon and Alice worked closely and seemingly in harmony with their manorial tenants at Hunstanton.[35] However, elsewhere on their estates, where relationships were not so deep, they often found themselves fending off challenges and defending their rights.

The Le Strange archive is full of legal cases fought in defence of their property rights, particularly those relating to the marshes.[36] From a collection of legal papers on 'foldcourses and marshes of Holme by the Sea' a lease, cited in a case between various inhabitants of Holme in 1635, shows how these grazing regimes worked and the ever-present potential for dispute.[37] The lease, for twenty-one years, included a foldcourse for 480 sheep in the marshes, commons and shack of Holme.[38] The lessee, John Bass, brought a case against the tenants and farmers of William Taylor, lord of the manor of Holkham and Berrys, claiming they were 'so surcharging the common salt marsh' that he had 'no benefit from it'.[39] The principal farmer, William Holly, disputed his claim to any such foldcourse and asserted the rights of the inhabitants, who 'beyond memory had liberty of fouldcourse in all the Common Saltmarshes of Holme'.[40] The Common Marshes in Holme amounted to 408 acres.[41]

This case was simply the latest instalment of a long-running dispute over these grazing rights dating back to 1558, when an award specified the rights of William

---

34 Oestmann, *Lordship and Community*, pp. 29–30. Sir Hamon's field book of 1623, LEST/BH1, makes no reference to Snettertons, although there is a later insertion in the margin; Alice's field book of 1648, LEST/BH2, refers to these holdings as 'formerly Snittertons'.

35 Griffiths, 'Improving landlords', pp. 174–81.

36 Complex rights extended over the foreshore and the sea, which the Le Stranges have fiercely defended over the centuries. The most recent example is a successful case brought by John Loose, the tenant of the fishing rights owned by the Hunstanton estate, against King's Lynn Shellfish, a group of cockle fishermen, for infringing those rights. See Loose [2013] EWHC 901 (Ch) for the judge's ruling and a history of the legal cases relating to the Fishery. However, their research did not extend to Sir Hamon's memoranda books, which include much information on the management of the shore and sea (LEST/Q37).

37 LEST/FQ1. The NRO catalogue lists twenty-one separate documents and bundles in this box relating to disputes over the marshes and foldcourses at Holme, but some appear to be missing.

38 '4C' means a 'long hundred' – that is, 120 sheep. 'Shack', in this context, means the right of pasturage by the lord's sheep over the tenants' fields during the winter months; more generally, it meant the tenants' right of winter pasturage over the common fields. See Yaxley, *Glossary*.

39 LEST/FQ1. Surcharging means overstocking the marsh.

40 LEST/FQ1. The resolution of this case is not entirely clear, but it appears that the lessee, John Bass, exchanged his holding in Snettisham with Robert Riches, one of Taylor's farmers, for lands in Holme, with the stipulation that if William Taylor 'did not agree in time' the lessee would 'sowe the Holme lands to halfes with Riches'.

41 LEST/FQ1.

Aslack, then lord of Holkham and Berrys, and the inhabitants of the town.[42] In 1594 his descendant, Aslack Lany, let the estate to Giles Godfrey; a copy of the lease restates the contents of the award.[43] In 1607 the new lessee, Sir Nathaniel Bacon, armed with a similar lease, brought a case against the above-mentioned William Holly, who he similarly charged 'to have entered and fed with sheep upon Georges Marsh, North Holmes and West Marsh'.[44] The jury found for Holly 'as the marshes and meeles north of the said 3 parcels were comon and so fed by the inhabitants'. At about the same time Sir Hamon Le Strange brought a case against Aslack Lany himself, challenging the rights he claimed in the lease to Nathaniel Bacon.[45] These rights, he asserted, were due to the manor of Ringstead cum Holme, in the possession of his father, Sir Nicholas Le Strange (1562–92), on his death in 1592; this was proved by the fact that 'all offences of marshes and meeles (in Holme) have been punishable in the Courts of the said Manor'.[46] Lany, he claimed, had contrived to secure the freehold and inheritance of these marshes during Sir Hamon's minority. The court found in favour of Sir Hamon, confirming his position as lord of the manor of Ringstead cum Holme and his rights to the soil of the marshes and meeles of Holme.[47] A summary of this verdict was carefully copied down in a memoranda book by Sir Nicholas (d. 1724), Sir Hamon's great-grandson, alongside other items, which he noted could be understood and rectified according to the law.[48]

The survival of these legal documents and the later notes made by Sir Nicholas Le Strange (d. 1724) indicate a central plank of the Le Stranges' management policy: the assiduous study of their ancient documents to clarify their rights and titles to their property, and the meticulous keeping of accounts and records. Deeds, charters, depositions and judgements with annotations and notes fill the pages of Sir Hamon's memoranda books. With this knowledge, he and his successors were able to beat off several challenges. For example, in 1698 Sir Nicholas was able to refute the claim of Thomas Rogers, who had recently purchased William Taylor's estate at Holme, for the right of warren upon the meeles: 'I showed [him] the decree in the Court of Wards and Depositions in that suit w[hi]ch are recited in the foregoing lease upon w[hi]ch

---

42   Blomefield and Parkin, *Norfolk*, vol. X, pp. 328–30.

43   LEST/FQ2. Lany sold the manor of Holkham and Berrys to William Taylor in 1614, LEST/FQ4, document listed in the Norfolk Record Office catalogue, which cannot be found.

44   LEST/FQ1. In 1606 Martin Spinke was paid £1 'for the small survey plot of the marshes and commons at Holme' (LEST/P6). Sir Nicholas (1661–1724) later noted in LEST/Q37 that Holme had been surveyed in 1605, but the map has not survived. However, excellent Field Maps of Ringstead and Holme survive for *c*.1680 (LEST/EH8). See also below, n. 66, for Hasdonck's plot of Holme Marshes.

45   LEST/FQ3.

46   Listed under 'Searches and proofs of antient court roll that Sir Hamon Le Strange is lord and owner of the comons in Holme and of the wrecks of the sea and groundage there' in LEST/Q37. 'Meeles' are sand dunes.

47   LEST/FQ3.

48   LEST/Q37.

he ceased further Prosecution thereof.'[49] Sir Hamon's painstaking approach owed much to the advice he received from his uncle and guardian, Sir Henry Spelman, the antiquarian and jurist who lived at Holme from 1594 and specialised in the documentation of ecclesiastical estates.[50] The memoranda books include several references to documents borrowed from Spelman, indicating that he was closely involved with the researches into the manor of Ringstead cum Holme, formerly part of the estates of the Abbey of Ramsey.[51] Sir Hamon's acquisition of the manor of Heacham Lewes in 1609, where disputes also centred on the marshes, further tested their skills.

Heacham was particularly prone to disputes over property rights. With its extensive marshes, upland sheep courses and access to the sea through Heacham Harbour, it was a highly desirable asset for a landowner looking to expand, but fraught with the possibility of a legal challenge. The Le Stranges first acquired a foothold in Heacham in 1520, when Sir Thomas Le Strange (1490–1545) purchased the smaller manor of Calys Hall, whose lands lay mainly south of the river Heacham. The great manor of Lewes Priory, centred to the north of the river, was granted to the duke of Norfolk at the dissolution and was then leased to various local landowners, including the Le Stranges, and finally sold to them by the earl of Arundel in 1609.[52] This gave Sir Hamon the opportunity to consolidate his holding and effect radical improvements. However, by this time, benefiting from the absenteeism of the church and the Howard family, the tenantry had learnt to assert itself, vigorously challenging the status of their holdings and their grazing rights over the marshes. Sir Nicholas's (d. 1724) notes in the memoranda book include references to early disputes over Caly foldcourse, whose liberty extended across 'Old Field, Little Marsh, Great Marsh, Mayer Marsh and the Common Fenn and upon all the marshes and shackable lands on the south side of the river'.[53] With entries in the margin clarifying the stocking rate, he added for future reference:

> The rate for the sheep to be layd upon Caly Foldcourse made Nov. 13, 1610 by the power & persuasion of such as misinformed and misled Sir Hamon in the writing down of the same (and when his own knowledge in these matters of Hecham Town was raw and imperfect) is fit to be enquired into, altered and reformed in such manner as (upon full conference and deliberate consultation among the inhabitants) may be thought reasonable.[54]

---

49   LEST/Q37.

50   Sir Henry Spelman (1564–1641). In 1594 he purchased leases of Blackborough and Wormegay Abbeys from the crown, which resulted in lengthy, expensive and eventually unsuccessful litigation. The case led Spelman to research the charters and title deeds relating to Norfolk and Suffolk monasteries; his *Tract of the Rights and Respect due unto Churches* was published in 1613. Handley, 'Spelman, Sir Henry'.

51   LEST/Q37.

52   Blomefield and Parkin, *Norfolk*, vol. X, p. 309. Sir Hamon sold their estate at Fring for £4400 to pay for Heacham Lewes: *ibid.*, p. 304.

53   LEST/Q37.

54   LEST/Q37.

The language is unequivocal; landlords needed to be on their guard and know their facts, but also to be prepared to consult, negotiate and reach reasonable agreements with their tenants, however difficult and fractious they may be. This experience may have prompted Sir Hamon to commission a new survey of Heacham and encourage his wife Alice to check the rentals and field books.[55] Predictably, her initiative provoked a challenge from one of the principal manorial tenants. In 1638 Robert Cremer launched a petition at the Norwich Assizes accusing Sir Hamon, 'Dame Alice' and their steward of altering the court rolls for their own benefit.[56] The land in question concerned parcels that were required to complete the construction of a sea wall linking Heacham and Snettisham; as we have seen, the embankment is clearly marked on Faden's map and survives as a significant feature in the landscape. An earlier case had been brought against Sir Nicholas (d. 1655) when he started to build the bank. A meeting had been held between the parties at Heacham Marsh to resolve their differences, with Cremer, supported by his uncle Robert Stileman of Snettisham, threatening to petition if Sir Hamon did not meet their demands.[57] Matters reached such a pitch that Sir Hamon sued for libel in the Court of Chivalry, winning his case in June 1640; Cremer responded with a bill in Star Chamber.[58] The dissolution of these bodies in 1640 left the parties without a settlement. Cremer revived the case in Chancery in 1647, but after lengthy submissions and interrogations of witnesses, with much firepower aimed at Dame Alice, the matter was settled out of court and finally agreed in Sir Hamon's favour after Cremer's death in 1651; however, it was a long-drawn-out, expensive and close-run thing.[59]

These cases at Holme and Heacham show that the Le Stranges were vigilant and determined, even aggressive, in their defence of their property rights, but, as Winchester says, this was very much a contested landscape.[60] The real risks faced by landowners were not so much the inundations of the sea as unforeseen challenges to their property and capital investment. Even Tawney acknowledged as much, drawing attention to the organised toughness of the manorial tenants. Sorting out the property rights was a prerequisite to any expensive drainage scheme on the marshes. No wonder Sir Nicholas (d. 1655) started carefully, with the marshes at

---

55   Waterman's map of Heacham 1623 is in two halves: LEST/OB1 north of the river, LEST/OB2 to the south.

56   In the documents Alice is known as Lady Alice Le Strange, Lady L'Estrange and Dame Alice. Strictly speaking, she should be known as Lady Le Strange or Alice Le Strange, but I refer to her simply as Alice.

57   Robert Cremer was an absentee landlord; it is quite clear that Stileman of Snettisham made the running.

58   R.P. Cust and A.J. Hopper (eds), *Cases in the High Court of Chivalry, 1634–1640*, Harleian Society, new ser. 18 (London, 2006); for the full record, <http://www.court-of-chivalry.bham.ac.uk/index.htm>. The case was revived in the Court of Chancery in 1647: TNA, C 2/Chas1/C29/63; C 22/49/20, and, for the out-of-court settlement in 1648, LEST/DN1; see also Griffiths, '"A Country Life"', p. 230; Griffiths, 'Improving landlords', pp. 179–80.

59   Notes on Cremer's settlement follow those on Caly Foldcourse in LEST/Q37; see also LEST/DN1.

60   Rodgers *et al.*, *Contested Common Land*, pp. 163–88.

Hunstanton and Holme over which he had control or where tenants were less likely to launch a challenge. The notebooks, recording the drainage process and making salient observations, served as a further precaution for himself and his heirs, as well as providing us with a detailed insight into how these schemes were organised, managed and sustained in relative harmony.

III

The information in the earliest notebook, as we have seen, relates to the drainage undertaken at Hunstanton and Holme, which Sir Nicholas started in 1633. It concentrates on the closes and marshes along the valley of the river Hun, which runs northward through Hunstanton Park and then north-eastwards to the sea at Holme (see Figures 2.2 and 8.1).[61] Hunstanton Hall itself was built in a hollow facing towards Holme and Great Ringstead village, creating its own geographical unit separate from the village and West Field of Hunstanton, which lay on higher ground stretching westward to Hunstanton cliffs. Faden's map shows the north–south route neatly dividing the parish of Hunstanton. More precisely, Thomas Waterman's survey of 1615 shows West Field dominated by the strips of the manorial tenants and East Field, where the demesne strips were being enclosed, with further closes of pasture created to the north, and the marshes leading out to the sea.[62]

The marshes drained in this area amounted to just 67¾ acres, with Hunstanton Marsh, Clottons Marsh with 'Osyer Island', a 'peece next Hunstanton Common' and the 'Hopp Ground Osyer Island' comprising 24 acres, the Bogge 15¼ acres, the Meeles Walled Close 8 acres and the Whin Pasture 7¼ acres, leaving just over 13 acres in Holme.[63] These acreages are significantly less than those shown on the Hunstanton map of 1615, but clearly the marshes were not drained in their entirety. In addition, some of the names of the marshes have been changed. For example, the Whin Pasture does not appear on the map but as 'The Whinne Pasture New Close 1637' it is probably the northern part of the Clamp Close. The relevant field map of Holme of *c*.1680 refers to 'Clamp Close or The Whin Pasture' over the parish border in Hunstanton.[64] Likewise, the Meeles Walled Close, to the north of the Whin Pasture on the sand dunes, was new. Modifications were also made by Sir Hamon in the 1620s.[65] For example, Marsh Close was renamed Brimble Close and Bushey Close, south of Clamp Close, became Normans Close to distinguish it from the Bushey Close south of Clottons Marsh. This whole area on the east side of Hunstanton, almost exclusively demesne land, was subject to ongoing rationalisation and improvement; draining the marshes was simply part of that process.

The few acres in Holme, consisting mainly of two closes, Futters Close and Holme Marsh Close, lay adjacent to the north-east of the Whin Pasture on the east side of 'Sir

---

61 LEST/KA6.

62 See Figure 3.2 above. LEST/AO1; Griffiths, '"A Country Life"', pp. 218–26.

63 LEST/KA24.

64 LEST/EH8.

65 Griffiths, '"A Country Life"', pp. 218–21.

Nic. Stranges' banke'. This bank is marked on 'The Plotts of Holm Marshes' drawn by Jan van Hasdonck in about 1633; the bank is well established and almost certainly the same as the one mentioned in the award of 1558.[66] In the notebooks it is called 'the Procession Bank'.[67] The small amount of land drained in Holme may come as a surprise, but there was in fact little scope in Holme because, although the Le Stranges owned the grazing rights to the common marsh, they held very little demesne land. Holme was dominated by large manorial tenants who initiated their own drainage schemes and farmed much of the demesne lands in Hunstanton.

A significant aspect of these marshes is their proximity to Hunstanton Hall and their function as a playground for the menfolk. Sir Nicholas's earliest efforts were directed to improving the area for fishing, fowling and hawking.[68] He and his father, both passionate sportsmen, wanted to make places 'handsome to gunn and hawke in'; they created havens and pits for 'handsome flying', breast works and blinds 'to gaine shooes at the fowls' and 'handsome' riding passages along 'my new drains'. Note the word 'handsome' and the desire for an attractive amenity they could enjoy with their friends. This reminds us of the enduring association between field sports and natural landscapes enhanced by hedges, tree-planting and water. These cultural considerations, widely shared across the social divide, were clearly a priority and helped to shape the look and feel of these marshes; they also reinforced the common interests and purpose of the local communities. Despite his seemingly frivolous motives, Sir Nicholas managed 'the home marshes' with precision and commitment.

IV

From the outset, Sir Nicholas's notebooks are laid out methodically and designed to inform and explain. Written in a large and legible hand, each topic is named and dated with additional references; individual entries are itemised, costed and dated. In the first notebook the expenditure is seldom totalled, but relates to complex tables at the end of the book. The format suggests that Sir Nicholas assembled the notebooks at a later date, from concurrent notes, as a reference work.[69] He clearly understood the basic principle of information management – that knowledge, to be beneficial, has to be presented in a way that can be understood by and shared with others.[70] Similarly, the content demonstrates Sir Nicholas's genuine business sense, rational economic planning, technical knowledge and judicious management of labour – attributes not commonly associated with the gentry on the eve of the Civil War. As

---

66 LEST/FQ18 for Hasdonck's plots of Holme marshes; LEST/FQ12 and FQ13 include papers relating to an 'Inquisition into Hansdonck's claims 1633–34 for reclaimed lands'. Both documents are missing, but it shows that Hasdonck was involved at Holme at this time.

67 LEST/KA6.

68 LEST/KA6.

69 We now know this was to be the case, as a recently found subsidiary account was copied neatly into Sir Nicholas's final notebook, LEST/suppl. 25ii/xvi; LEST/KA24.

70 Websites on knowledge management abound, often quoting Francis Bacon's maxim 'Knowledge is power'. Several of Bacon's books are listed in the Le Strange's library catalogue, LEST/NE1.

this information is relatively rare, the following account offers a detailed description of aspects of his approach, particularly his understanding of the processes involved and his sensitive treatment of his tenants and workforce. From the first folios of the first notebook, we find Sir Nicholas thinking carefully. The project, the making of three osier islands in Hunstanton Marsh Poole, might seem trivial, but he painstakingly listed the labourers hired, the days they worked and the amount they were paid over six weeks from July to mid-August in 1633. Significantly, he noted that they were paid a higher rate in the second week, as the work was 'very bad', and a 'largesse' at the end; this acknowledgement of working conditions forms a central part of his remuneration policy.[71] Cross-references to further entries reveal the names of suppliers of the osiers, including Goodman Cave of Ely, who spent two days dressing and setting plants and 'instructing Kempe how to order them afterwards'. The idea of instruction, and passing on knowledge, runs through the text.

After the entry on osier management, Sir Nicholas sought to clarify the situation over wages by instigating a system that reflected different working conditions and ensured his labourers received a fair day's pay. In his 'Rates and wages in Draining' he specifies the 'rates which I allowed my workmen and at such proportions as they made good and competent earnings'. The calculations were based on the breadth and depth of the drain, the nature of the soil and the type of work, assessed at so much per rod, measured at twenty-one feet. For example, for a drain two feet broad and two feet deep, categorised as 'soyle and good scavel work', the pay was 2d per rod. At the other end of the scale, for a drain twelve feet wide and three feet deep, 'scavell work' was paid '11d, but if spade and mattock [with] clay and gravel 15d'. In the notes that follow Sir Nicholas defined the nature of good scavell work, ordinary scavell work and 'spade and mattock' work; for day wages, he specified the different rates for 'wett-work both summer and winter' at 12d per day and dry work at 10d; and, finally, he set out the terms for labourers who provided horses: 'old Greenrod for 2 horses, 6s a week (but I had to find him grasse) to tumbrell earth in the marsh and to himself 3s a week to follow the cart, in all 9s per weeke'. In similar fashion, under the 'Rates in Digging' he allowed 10s per rod for 'digging the rushy and toughest part of my marsh (which comes to 40s per acre) but for ground that was clean and easier I allowed 7s 6d, 30s per acre'. He based his calculations on Standard Measures: every rod was 220 yards or paces in length and 5½ yards wide, which made four rods to the acre.

In the notebook where Sir Nicholas summarised his strategy, 'rates and prices' are provided for every activity: bank work, wet and dry dikes, levelling with tumbrells and barrowing, digging and measuring, fencing, ploughing and harrowing, coleseed reaping, wheat, barley and oats, carriage of corn, and thrashing and dressing. He notes, 'In all these severall kinds of worke, being taken at the proportions and prices afore mentioned, they made very good wages, and I dare say, better cheape to me, then if I had used and employed them but at 6d per day.'[72] In this way he incentivised his workforce, improved their skills and secured better work at less cost

---

71   Osiers, or willows, were used to make a wide range of products, but were planted in this context
     principally to stabilise the newly raised banks and 'sconces'.
72   LEST/KA24.

to himself. For setting the rates and conditions he sought professional advice: 'I am experimentally assured that there will accrue to them [labourers] competent and faire earnings though these cautions and provisions following be members of the contract.'[73] Repeatedly, in his asides, he confirms his understanding of the need to establish good relations with his workforce, a concern unlikely to be found among the absentee landlords on the Fens.[74]

After setting out the wage rates, Sir Nicholas describes in the first notebook what had been achieved on Hunstanton Marsh between October 1633 and March 1634. For this purpose he listed thirteen drains dividing the area they served into 'Quarters', A to K. From this point, Sir Nicholas displays his virtuosity with the technicalities of draining: 'carrying stones and shingle to spring heads and their draines', 'stoning the spring heads', 'claying them in', making gutters and covering the gutters with planks. For carting the materials he constructed '2 raild cart passages'. He also started engaging specialists and groups of men under contract to perform specified tasks, such as constructing banks and sluices. For example, Scott, Awdly and Thomasin were engaged to build the Fence Bank, while Edward Goverson took responsibility for the sluices.[75] Sir Nicholas set out all the specifications, ending with the provision, 'A largesse given to my wett-workmen upon bargaines or working at unreasonable hours, in cases of necessity, for taking up dames and the like'. Extras also included the provision of drink to labourers.

In 1635 attention turned to 'ploughing and sowing at Hunstanton Marsh', with references to wheelwrights and blacksmiths mending equipment, seed merchants bringing coleseed and 'instruct[ing] my man how to sow it', and named individuals 'intending the work' of 'all other ploughmen'. Labourers were employed for 'sowing, harrowing, raking all the oates within my marsh', keeping vermin from the 'cole and oates', watergrupping, fencing, 'sheering and mowing and fitting all in the cart' and finally 'threshing and dressing these oates'.[76] As a specialist crop, the cultivation of coleseed received much attention. Sir Nicholas thanked Thomas Walker for his 'care and helpe about the sowing and reaping of cole', which required particular skills and equipment. In the final notebook he provides a sample agreement for the work, which was by then contracted out, rather like growing potatoes is today. Alongside this activity, work started on the infrastructure. Ship planks were bought to construct cartbridges, cattlebridges, footbridges, gates and styles, and post and rail fences. As before, Sir Nicholas provided the specifications and costings for each activity. The entries continue with detail on the Marsh Wall, the Common, Clottons, Cawkwell and Bushy Close, all around Hunstanton or Hall Marsh, before moving on to the Meeles, Bogge and Whin Pasture.

---

73 LEST/KA24.

74 Or on Romney Marsh in Kent. Soens, 'Social distribution of land', pp. 158–9. See also n. 7 above.

75 LEST/Q38. Goverson also entered into agreements to build the park wall at Hunstanton Hall. These arrangements are similar to those found at Stiffkey: A. Hassell Smith, 'Labourers in late sixteenth century England: a case study from north Norfolk [Part I]', *Continuity and Change*, 4 (1989), pp. 19–28.

76 'Watergrupping' means cutting ditches and drains; see also Yaxley, *Glossary*, p. 94 sub 'grup(p)'.

The Meeles, the Bogge and the Whin Pasture (as part of Clamp Close) were treated rather differently to the area around Hunstanton Marsh. Before 1632, all the marshes had been leased to tenants; in 1636 Sir Nicholas took over the tenancy of Hunstanton Marsh himself but continued to let the Bogge and Meeles to Woodrow and Murton until the 1650s, and Clamp Close, with the Whin Pasture, for the entire period to Richard Giles. These arrangements had a significant effect on their management. Sir Nicholas started the draining process in 1635, 'tumbrelling, barrowing and levelling' the Meeles and rebuilding the banks following 'sea breaches by the old haven'; typically, he took the opportunity to dig new pits, drains and havens 'for Flying'.[77] Similarly, at the Bogge, essential work was combined with making a 'handsome riding passage along Murton's bogge by my draines'. However, when it came to cultivating the Bogge in 1637, Sir Nicholas resorted to 'ploughing to halfes' with the Murton and Woodrow. This was a system whereby the landowner and tenant halved the costs of cultivation, each providing labour, seed and equipment, and halved the profit.[78] In other words, Sir Nicholas provided working capital at the early risky stages of the venture to help the tenant get established; instead of raising the rent to cover his own costs, he shared the risk by halving the crop. He also contributed to the venture a new Dutch plough, with the vendor, Charles Sands of Wisbech, who 'wrought with Mr Hasdonck, ploughing for five days in the Bogge and instructing Write how to use her'.[79] This is the earliest mention in the notebooks of Mr Hasdonck, although he was involved at Holme from 1633. He seems to have performed the role of a modern farming consultant, providing specialist knowledge and access to new technology.[80]

Similar agreements were made with Richard Giles at Whin Pasture New Close and between Sir Nicholas and his father for Holme New Marsh Close, both in 1637. In 1643 Hasdonck measured Holme Marsh Close and divided it between Sir Nicholas and his father. 'This ground set out by Mr Hasdonck as part of my father's proportion due to him upon the imbanking of Holme Marshes & used by my Fa[ther] and Me in a partible way of charge and profitt.'[81] On the same page Sir Nicholas noted the destruction of the first crop of winter corn by the rebels of Holme in 1643 as part of the plunder inflicted by the parliamentary forces in the summer of 1643. It appears they had accomplices in Holme: 'all this croppe was sequester'd and reap'd by some of the rebells of Holme (S.O. and R.C. [Simon Overman and Robert Crispe]) by vertue of a pretended ordinance of Parliament groun[ded] upon a most false and clamorous petition.'[82]

---

77   'Flying' refers to the wildfowl they wished to attract for sport.

78   Griffiths and Overton, *Farming to Halves*, pp. 60–2.

79   'Wrought' in this context means they created the plough together; see *OED* online edition.

80   Steers and Winchester also refer to Mr Hasdonck; it appears that he was a familiar figure along the coast, engaged in all sorts of enterprises at Thornham, Brancaster, Wiveton and Salthouse. Dutchmen working in this way, offering their services to individual landowners, were not uncommon. My thanks to Piet van Cruyningen for this point.

81   LEST/KA9.

82   LEST/KA9, fol. 98. A further reference in LEST/suppl. 25ii/xvi gives the names of the 'rebels' as Overman and Crispe.

The difficulties encountered by Sir Hamon and his sons in the Civil War may explain why these agreements with the tenants were terminated and why no further drainage projects were undertaken.[83] As with the adventurers on the Fens, war was not a risk they had anticipated, but with their management strategy in place the Le Stranges were better prepared to meet the consequences.[84]

The payments and receipts for Sir Hamon's share of Holme Marsh Close were recorded by Alice in her books of disbursements and receipts.[85] As it happens, they also reveal another share farming agreement at Heacham between father and son.[86] In her receipt book Alice recorded for April 1641: 'rec'd of my sonne Strange for the halfe of the Rushes and Whins and the fearme of the grasse of Heacham £10 8s 8d', 'Received of Sherringham for our halfe of the coleseed besides £70 before received and £106 0s 7d payd to my sonne Strange for his halfe – £36 0s 7½ d'.[87] From this entry it appears that the agreement dated from 1639, after the completion of the sea bank at Heacham in 1638. In her disbursement book Alice recorded for June 1643: 'Layd as appeareth by Heacham Marsh Reckoning the halfe of the charge for Bearne Farme stacks remooving, thrashing, looking at the cattle wintered there and the halfe of 2 earths ploughing 21ac 2r and 22 [combs] of seed beanes at 6s 8d – £20 14s 7d'.[88] The receipt book also includes a corn account that records the loss of the corn plundered by Captains Poe and Thorner between 1641 and 1643: 190 combs from Heacham, 51 combs from Sedgeford and 101 combs from Hunstanton. Despite these reverses, father and son continued to spend money on the marshes, paying 'for the mending of Heacham Marsh Bankes which were faulty' and in 1644 'for mending the Marshe Bankes [at Holme] after the Great Rage'.[89] Entries for expenditure on the marshes cease in 1645, when a new more simplified book of disbursements was created, but references continue to be made to other subsidiary books of disbursements that are now lost.

---

83   In July 1643 the family lost 1693 sheep, almost their entire flock, besides corn, wool and horses (LEST/P10). The sharefarming agreements for the Bogge and Whin Pasture ceased in 1642; the agreement for Holme Marsh Close was renewed in 1643, but no further reference is made to it after 1644.

84   LEST/P10. The flocks were restocked with cullett sheep from relatives and neighbours; see chapter 7, above.

85   For Alice's disbursements from 1613 to 1645, LEST/P7; household books with estate receipts, from 1613 to 1621, LEST/P6; from 1621 to 1633 in LEST/P8; from 1633 to 1642 in LEST/P9. There is a gap between 1642 and 1649, followed by a household book with estate receipts for 1650–3 in LEST/P11.

86   LEST/KA9.

87   LEST/P9.

88   LEST/P10. This entry follows an earlier one, for December 1641, on the cost of cultivating coleseed, winter corn, barley and oats at £122 18s 2d, but there is no reference to the cost being halved, just that it was 'payd as appeareth by my sonne Stranges Book of Reckonings for Heacham Marsh'.

89   LEST/P10.

V

Although the records are patchy after 1642, it is possible to estimate the cost of the venture and how the Le Stranges managed their finances, before and after the crisis of 1643. In the tables at the end of the first notebook Sir Nicholas attempts a calculation for the period up to 1642.[90] In the first two tables he set out the 'disbursements upon every particular ground' from 1633 to 1638 and from March 1638 to 1642. He then arranged the disbursements in tables to show 'The principall and uses calculated of the moneys which I have disbursed in Draining and improving Hunstanton Marish and other places … at 8 p. centum'. In columns he records the year, the ground, the principal [cost], the uses [interest] for one year, the uses for the whole term [of years] and the half uses of the whole term. Apparently, he is trying to assess the real cost of the draining by making a calculation for the interest lost on his capital; he adds a note 'I wrought all the uses by the table of interest in *Ponds Almanacke* for 1638'.[91] Finally, he tries to balance 'The principall and use monyes which I disburst, and the profits which I received of all the grounds'. Interestingly, he only includes the 'halfe uses of the principal', which suggests that the cost of the entire drainage operation was shared between father and son. At the end he provides 'Another way of calculation of principal and uses (differing from the former) from 1633 until 1643 with their totals'. This table shows that £1004 3s 11d was spent on drainage, which included £9 12s 6d at Ringstead Yards and Heacham Common, and £168 16s 5d on building, mostly at Sedgeford, with further calculations for the interest lost on the principal.[92] In this table he also includes a column recording half the principal, as well as half the uses, which seems to confirm that father and son were working in partnership; this may have been the purpose of these rather strange accounts. To avoid disputes, sharefarming agreements need to be completely transparent.[93]

The tables make no mention of the cost of draining Heacham Marsh, but on closer examination of Alice's accounts it is possible to arrive at an estimate. In her summary of family finances she records in 1638 spending £372 'on imbanking Heacham Marsh' and in 1640 a further £400. In her disbursements for 1641 she also entered a sum of £122 18s 2d for the cost of cultivating Heacham Marsh, which is not halved with Sir Nicholas; this makes a total of about £900. Working on the principle that father and son were in some kind of partnership, and that Sir Nicholas's share of expenditure would be recorded in his Heacham notebooks, the total sum would be about £2000.[94] This figure is not unreasonable given the costs at Hunstanton and Holme. However, a problem with this calculation is the 'loss' recorded by Alice at the end of her summary of the family finances, 'Lost by Heacham Marsh £600', under 'Losses in My Husbands Estate'. As we have seen with Boston Fen, this loss might not be quite what it seems; she might just be rounding up the expenditure on the marsh on her son's behalf.

---

90   LEST/KA6.

91   My thanks to John Barney for helping me with these tables.

92   The building costs date from 1638 to 1642 and mostly include expenditure at Sedgeford.

93   Griffiths and Overton, *Farming to Halves*, pp. 56–110.

94   The costs per acre based on 177 acres' draining in Heacham would be £11 6s 8d.

Alternately, she might be referring to the losses they incurred at Heacham during the Civil War, or the cost of the long legal case against Cremer and Stileman, although she recorded a 'loss' of £385 against Stileman 'in an unjust suite'.[95]

Returning to Sir Nicholas's tables in the first notebook, the downside of the format was the difficulty of accommodating receipts; the amounts listed look woefully inadequate. The answer was found in the subsidiary account, which sets out the profits against the charge for every ground from 1633 to 1644.[96] Most particularly, it shows the progress made by 1641, when receipts for corn peaked, followed by the slump in receipts during the war. For example, for Hunstanton Marsh from 1633 to 1638 the charges amounted to £368 5s 0d with profits (in reality receipts) of £129 2s 3d from the sale of coleseed, oats and hay. From 1639 to 1642 charges amounted to £99 4s 4d, while 'profits' rose to £156 17s 8d from wheat, barley, oats, meslin, osiers and grazing; so, a promising start. However, between 1643 and 1644 profits dropped to just £9 8s 0d, with sales restricted to grazing, hay and osiers. At the Bogge, for the whole period, charges amounted to £144 7s 10½d against profits of £85 17s 4d from the sale of coleseed, oats, meslin, barley and wheat; this was bad enough, but then in 1643 the wheat crop, valued at £9 3s 0d, was stolen by Captains Thorner and Poe. Similarly, for the Whin Pasture total charges amounted to £60 12s 6d against profits of £39 10s 5d, and then from 1643 'it was deserted and layde down to pasture as before'. At Holme Marsh Close profits of £49 6s 7d just exceeded charges of £48 2s 4d, which was promising, but in 1643 Poe and Thorner also stole the crop of wheat, valued at £7 5s 0d. The Meeles and Bank Fenne were the worst performers. Charges at the Meeles amounted to £65 10s 9d between 1640 and 1642, with profits of just £20 4s 0d. Similarly, at Bank Fenne charges amounted to £51 8s 11d and profits were £14 15s 9d; a small crop of wheat was stolen in 1643 and, like the Whin Pasture, Bank Fenne was left deserted and laid to grass. The entries for Heacham Marsh do not mention charges, but include the profits from 1640 to 1642: £138 15s 9d from the sale of coleseed and oats in 1640 followed by £133 4s 3d from coleseed, wheat and meslin in 1641.[97] These figures help to explain the sudden increase of corn revenues recorded by Alice, from £426 in 1640 to £864 in 1641.[98] With no receipt books from 1642 to 1649 it is not possible to calculate the depth of the crisis and how long it lasted. However, corn receipts were £619 in 1650 and £566 in 1651, so we can conclude that, although the recovery was slow, total disaster had been averted.

---

95 LEST/P10.

96 LEST/suppl. 25ii/xvi. The charge corresponds to the figures for 'disbursements' and the 'principal' entered in Sir Nicholas's neat books, LEST/KA6 and KA24. In other words, the 'charge' represents, in modern terms, his costs or expenses. The titles of the pages, on the RH side of the subsidiary book, actually refer to 'Expenses and Profitts', but, to add to the confusion, the sums he lists as profits are in fact receipts. In this way, Sir Nicholas experimented with the concept of profit but seems not to have fully understood the principle.

97 In 1644 Sir Nicholas sold the 1642 crop of Heacham barley to Mr Toll of King's Lynn for £38 6s 6d, almost certainly part of a fine payable after the collapse of the Royalist uprising in 1643. LEST/suppl. 25ii/xvi, a copy of which can be found in LEST/KA24.

98 Griffiths, '"A Country Life"'.

VI

The seeds behind the steady recovery can be found in the second and third notebooks, which record expenditure from 1643 to 1653, principally on cultivating crops and building farmsteads, but also on the maintenance and improvement of drains. In the second notebook the crop-growing schedules are neatly specified. For example, on Hunstanton Marsh in April 1646 fourteen acres of coleseed (having been eaten by doves in the hard winter) were ploughed in and barley was sown. This was harvested in August, together with three acres of wheat; the following March seven acres were ploughed for oats; in most years beans, peas and vetches also featured in the rotation.[99] Under 'miscellaneous charges' payments were made for 'easing and cleansing draines, planting trees and hedges, trimming the arbour and island and watergrupping'. There was no charge for mowing grass, as it was usually sold 'standing in the ground'. Substantial work was done on the Mill River, cutting new drains and bank mending – a task that involved building a horse bridge at the Bogge. The Procession Bank and the Great Sluice also received more attention. For the osier management, Sir Nicholas agreed in 1646 to bear 'halfe the charge of cutting and bunching wherein my share came to 5s 6d'; this agreement continued until 1652. At the Meeles the problem was drifting sand, so he planted hundreds of whins on the coastal side.[100] As ever, several entries relate to his passion for fishing and shooting; in fact, the overall impression was that it was business as usual.

Sir Nicholas's farm building programme also underlines his continuing commitment to the drainage project. In 1648 he started work at Hunstanton with the Marsh Wall House, the Meeles Close House, houses at Calkwell and Lawes House; even at Holme he built a Meeles House.[101] Each building merits up to fifty pages, with Sir Nicholas specifying every part of the process: foundations, carriage of materials, measuring up, masons' work, carpenters' work, ironwork, thatching, colouring and laying out the garden with fruit trees. For the Calkwell project he drew up a 'Prolegomena Calkweliana' (introduction to Calkwell) outlining the rates paid to different named craftsmen. For 'ordinarie labourers' he never paid more than 10d a day, but, as with the drainage work, good work, difficult conditions and unreasonable hours 'were motives to me to augment their wages'.[102] The entries are in no particular order, indicating, once again, that they were written up later, where space allowed. The latest entries date from 1653, which suggested there was a time lapse before they were written up neatly in the little books.

---

99   LEST/KA9.

100 'Whins' was the collective term for gorse, furze and broom. It was used for a variety of purposes; in this instance it was planted to stabilise sand dunes. See also Yaxley, *Glossary*, p. 235.

101 LEST/KA9 for Lawes House, everything else is listed in LEST/ KA10.

102 Without an archaeological survey these lesser buildings are difficult to locate; however, the Magazine in Sedgeford, also built by Sir Nicholas, survives as a holiday cottage, until recently let by the Vivat Trust: see LEST/KA6 fols 192–210. A more elaborate building, it was used to store military equipment; see also LEST/Q38, fols 85–9.

Sir Nicholas's death in 1655, a few months after his father in 1654 and a year or so before his mother and his eldest son, Sir Hamon, in 1656, was potentially far more damaging to the drainage project than was the Civil War.[103] Sir Nicholas's second son, Nicholas, inherited at the age of twenty-two but died in 1669, leaving a small child, yet another Nicholas, in the hands of trustees until 1682.[104] While the principal trustee, Sir Christopher Calthorpe, managed his affairs conscientiously, kept a good account and carried out minor repairs, by the time Sir Nicholas achieved his majority the drains – and the farm buildings – were in a woeful condition.[105]

Sir Nicholas (d. 1724) was the author of new field books and maps for every part of the estate from the late 1680s to the 1700s, but the most telling information comes from his work on one of Sir Hamon's memoranda books, which contains the extraordinary detail of the building programme carried out between 1619 and 1652.[106] Sir Nicholas noted:

> This book I found in ye old Evidence House w[i]th a decayed and wormeaten cover thrown by and neglected. But upon perusalls meeting w[i]th several things relating to buildings & every material & likely to prove of use, I put an index or table to that part of it writt by Sir Hamon & proceeded to putt down in writing at this part of ye Booke, such other observations as might possibly prove of service & convience to refer to upon occasion.

His notes mostly relate to buildings, by then in much need of repair, but they also include references to the marshes and drains from 1693 to 1720.

The strange aspect of these references is that Sir Nicholas refers only to Sir Hamon's work; he makes no mention of his grandfather, Sir Nicholas (d. 1655), or his drainage notebooks.[107] However, his notes indicate a familiarity with his grandfather's style and practice of making observations, which suggests the existence of subsidiary notes and accounts. As we have seen, the family increasingly adopted this approach after the crisis of 1643. Significantly, his first entry in the memoranda book in 1693 notes that 'the draines were very foul and overgrown'. In 1698 he cleaned the New River, which 'was so overgrown with sallowes and willow roots that the old passage was stopt and was become a stronghold for otters w[hi]ch haunted all my waters … '. The ditches between Whin Pasture and Holme Grounds, cleaned at 8d and 6d per rod, 'had been for a long time grown up and by that meanes very much injured both those pieces of ground'. This area also suffered from 'the extremity of storms' and 'great tides', first in 1714, when the river was choked with sand, and then in 1720, when large breaches were made over the meeles, filling up passages and flattening

---

103 Sir Hamon Le Strange, 2nd Bt (1631–56).

104 Sir Nicholas Le Strange, 3rd Bt (1632–69); Sir Nicholas Le Strange, 4th Bt (1661–1724).

105 LEST/KA11. Sir Christopher Calthorpe (*c.*1645–1718), <www.historyofparliamentonline.org>.

106 LEST/Q38.

107 In his table of building work Sir Nicholas (d. 1724) makes no mention of the houses built by his grandfather, Sir Nicholas (d. 1655), either; it seems fair to conclude that he had no knowledge of the notebooks.

the river to the sluices; this required him to make new cuts, raise banks and replace sluices built by Sir Hamon. Compared with the notebooks, these entries do not amount to much, but the likelihood is that routine information existed elsewhere. Of Sir Nicolas's understanding of the problems associated with drainage and the need for constant maintenance there can be little doubt. Steers quotes his description of the inundation of the freshwater marshes at Titchwell in the 1680s, when the meeles were flattened and the sea reduced the area to saltmarshes:

> The property being in the hands of Magdalen College, and the Fellows contenting themselves with the old rent, neither the principal tenant or his under servants will care to contribute towards the charge of Imbanking them afresh. Brancaster Bank being by this means exposed to the strong west winds suffers very much and t'will be a great expense to keep them in repair.[108]

These comments illustrate vividly the benefit of having a resident landowner, rather than an absentee or institutional owner indifferent to local concerns and reluctant to waste their money on such risky ventures. So, now we have arrived at the heart of the matter.

VII

What conclusions can be drawn from the piecemeal drainage projects undertaken in north-west and north Norfolk in the early modern period? How did they compare with the more familiar large-scale schemes of the Fens and elsewhere? Manorial lords, provided they could secure the cooperation of neighbours and tenants by negotiation, could undertake drainage at moments of their choosing. Drainage in the Fens was increasingly driven by external undertakers and the crown: both were less sensitive (and perhaps even indifferent) to local feelings. Of course, drainage on the Norfolk coast was largely drainage within a manor, whereas fen drainage was drainage across a whole range of jurisdictions and the property of a range of landholders. The key difference, then, seems to be the presence of resident gentry landowners prepared to work with rather than against local communities as they faced the challenge of a more commercial environment. This was particularly important on the marshes on the north Norfolk coast, which were notoriously susceptible to tidal surges and expensive to maintain and repair. Their value to large landowners lay in the sport they offered and the summer grazing they provided for cattle and sheep, which released the brecks on the sandy uplands for corn production; after reclamation, it seems corn was grown on the reclaimed marshes. From the profits of these crops landowners, notably the Cokes of Holkham, could afford to build and maintain sea banks extending the grazing marshes out into the North Sea. But beyond Holkham, on estates and in areas with fewer resources, the situation was patchier. Even the Le Stranges, resident at Hunstanton since the twelfth century and hugely committed to their estate and locality, neglected their marshes after the disruption

---

108 Steers, 'Some notes on the north Norfolk coast', p. 44, n. 2.

of the Civil War. Without the efforts of Sir Nicholas Le Strange from the 1690s to the 1720s, the reclaimed marshes at Hunstanton and Holme may well have suffered the fate of Titchwell and Brancaster. Both economically and socially, the defining feature of these marshes was the leadership, capital and commitment provided by these gentry landowners over many centuries.

Chapter 9

William Windham's Green Book, 1673–88: estate management in the later seventeenth century[1]

The Green Book: origins, layout and content[2]

In June 1673 young William Windham, recently married and preparing to settle permanently on his estate at Felbrigg, noted his intention to record:

> A particular of the yearly value of my manors, lands & tenements in Norfolk, Suffolke & Essex. And what farme rents, Quite Rents, Annuityes, Rent chages and other incumbrances are upon & issuing out of my estate & how they have been paid this last half yeare, & also what money is owing to me by Mortgages, Bonds & arrears or rent. With an account what moneys I have received out of the rents & profit of my estate what I have allowed for taxes, repaires & other incident charges from Our Lady to Mich 1673.[3]

His first attempt, based on the bailiff's accounts of the 1650s and 1660s, was not a success: the layout and accounting system did not yield the information required.[4] However, by October 1673, when he started afresh in a large paper book with green vellum covers, he had learned double entry keeping, which transformed the enterprise into a comprehensive and unique record of estate management. Windham probably acquired these commercial skills from his father-in-law, Sir Joseph Ashe, a merchant from Twickenham. Besides a dowry of £10,000, his daughter Katherine brought to the marriage in 1669 a keen eye for business.[5] Throughout her adult life she invested enthusiastically in stocks and shares, keeping a precise record of transactions and profits in her personal diary. She also undertook responsibility for the family and

---

1 This chapter is an abridged version of the introduction to Griffiths, *William Windham's Green Book*.
2 All archival documents cited in this chapter are located in the Norfolk Record Office: WKC 5/152 400 x. See also Griffiths, 'Management'.
3 WKC 5/151, 400 x 5.
4 WKC 5/442, 464 x 4.
5 WKC 6/12, 401 x 4. Sir Joseph Ashe provided an equally large portion for his daughter Mary Ashe, who married Horatio, Viscount Townshend, in 1673. Following Townshend's death in 1785 Windham acted as legal guardian to his son Charles, later 'Turnip Townshend', who was a frequent visitor to Felbrigg with his widowed mother and her young family in the 1680s. Mary Ashe died in 1687. Rosenheim, *The Townshends of Raynham*.

household, maintaining a parallel set of domestic and kitchen accounts.[6] On William's early death in 1689 she supervised estate business, making entries in the new Green Book until their eldest son, Ashe, assumed control in 1694. The Windhams were a genuine working partnership and the Green Book was at the heart of a system they devised to manage their family, household, estate and business affairs.

The Green Book appears to be a unique document. Certainly no other comparable work has been published or found for the seventeenth century. The nearest would be Henry Best's farming and memorandum books of 1617–45 and Robert Loder's farm accounts of 1610–20, but the Green Book is no mere account: the explicit motives behind its creation offer an extraordinary insight into the mentality of a young Norfolk landowner as he embarked on family responsibilities and the management of his estate.[7] He planned for the long term, designing the Green Book as a guide for his son. The tone is conversational, reminiscent of the dialogue format used by classical authors in similar manuals, with asides warning the son against certain courses of action. It had the desired effect on Windham's successors. In the eighteenth century Felbrigg became a byword for the excellence of its tree planting and the organisation of its farms; it was commended by Nathaniel Kent and William Marshall as an example for others to follow. Indeed, Kent may have used the Green Book for inspiration, as his own instructions for tree planting bear a marked resemblance to Windham's careful descriptions set out in the 1670s. Without doubt, the influence of the Green Book extended well beyond Felbrigg.[8] As a record of the management of a medium-sized estate in north-east Norfolk in the second half of the seventeenth century the Green Book comprehensively challenges the traditional assumption that agricultural innovation in the county was pioneered by the Cokes, Walpoles and Townshends on their large west Norfolk estates in the eighteenth century. It supports the alternative view, put forward by Marshall and Kent in the 1780s, that east Norfolk was the true area of agricultural innovation and that much had been achieved by the 1680s.[9]

A great deal of thought went into the layout of the Green Book. When Windham took possession in 1673 the affairs of the estate were in disarray and he determined to reverse the decline. He gathered together historic material – old accounts and leases – and devised a system that gave him easy access to all relevant records while keeping a current account of the estate. In his new estate book he numbered

---

6   WKC 6/13–18 401 x 5; for a history of the Windham family see Ketton-Cremer, *Felbrigg*.

7   D. Woodward (ed.), *The Farming and Memorandum Books of Henry Best of Elmswell 1642*, Records of Social and Economic History new series 8 (Oxford, 1984). G.E. Fussell (ed.), *Robert Loder's Farm Accounts*, RHS Camden 3rd series, liii (London, 1936).

8   N. Kent, *Hints to Gentlemen of Landed Property* (1775); *General View of the Agriculture of Norfolk* (1796); W. Marshall, *Rural Economy of Norfolk* (1787), vol. 2, pp. 356–71.

9   The most recent survey of Norfolk agriculture, Wade Martins and Williamson, *Roots of Change*, makes no reference to the Green Book. However, in their article 'The development of the lease and its role in agricultural improvement in East Anglia, 1660–1870', *Agricultural History Review*, 46/2 (1998), pp. 127–41, they recognise the importance of the heathlands of north-east Norfolk as an area of innovation.

every page and used a cross-referencing system that allowed the user to move easily from the Particular of the Estate at the front to the individual accounts and then to the leases entered at the back. In this way he was able to quickly build up a profile of each holding. In the centre pages he outlined his policy for the park, describing tree-planting schemes, plans for his deer and fish and the areas to be cultivated. He also included summaries of accounts, details of moneys on loan, family affairs and legal cases. The numbering system allowed further cross-referencing into subsidiary notebooks that record sales of timber, livestock and corn, providing a wealth of information on prices at that time. Throughout the book he modified his procedures, explaining his actions in the margins. In 1688 he started a new Green Book with a simplified format, abandoning the particular of every farm in favour of an alphabetical list of tenants – in effect a prototype of the eighteenth-century 'tenants' ledger' – thus reflecting his changing approach to estate management. These notebooks and accounts, with the Green Book as the centrepiece, show how Windham developed, through trial and error, a modern system of estate management.

The period covered by the Green Book, 1673–89, is of particular significance. For landowners these were years of unrelenting economic adversity, when they had to devise new strategies to make farming pay. Between 1664 and 1689, as corn prices continued to fall, they had to deal with bankruptcies, unlet farms and outstanding debts on a regular basis. Windham tried new contracts with his tenants, including share farming. 'Letting to halves', as it was known, was an unusual practice in England, and in fact no other evidence has been found of a landowner operating such an arrangement on a systematic basis. The difficulties Windham encountered may explain the rarity of the practice, and why he resorted to simpler methods by the late 1680s, placing his trust in large tenants rather than risking capital in partnership with small operators. In this way the Green Book offers an insight into the developing relationship between landlord and tenant, and may help to explain why in England that relationship became so sharply defined. However, we need to be careful. In a national context, Windham's energy and enthusiasm for experimentation may have been untypical, as no other document of this nature has come to light. Nevertheless, the Green Book stands as a working document, a tool of management, designed to facilitate improvement; it also offers a contemporary assessment of the relative success of different courses of action. Above all, it shows a landowner responding proactively, intellectualising his approach and applying commercial solutions to the management of his estate. He was not indifferent, inflexible or bound by tradition, as some historians have portrayed landowners of this period.[10]

---

10 Windham's enterprise contrasts sharply with the examples cited by M. Davies, 'Country gentry and falling rents 1660s and 1670s', *Midland History*, 4 (1978), pp. 86–96, who 'responded with little flexibility to losses in rental income'. See also H.J. Habakkuk, 'Economic functions of English landowners in the seventeenth and eighteenth centuries', *Explorations in Entrepreneurial History*, 6/2 (1953), pp. 92–102.

The Felbrigg estate: structure and topography[11]

The Felbrigg estate is situated in north-east Norfolk, about two miles inland from the coast, on the south-facing slope of the Cromer–Holt Ridge running down to a tributary of the river Bure (see Figures 9.1 and 9.2).[12] To the north of the estate are broad stretches of undulating heathland, which generations of owners have planted with trees to protect the house and park from the biting North Sea winds. South of Felbrigg Hall the parkland descends gradually to fertile meadow land, which extends into the tiny parishes of Sustead and Metton. Light soils dominate to the west, in the parishes of Aylmerton and Gresham and into East Beckham beyond. To the east of the hall lies Felbrigg church and the site of the earlier Felbrigg village, where open fields survived into the seventeenth century. With its highly valuable meadow land, enclosed pastures, easily worked arable land and scope for improvement on the light sandy soils, the estate offered its owners much opportunity for commercial exploitation. In the thirteenth and fourteenth centuries, at an estimated 400 acres, the demesne at Felbrigg was one of the largest and most productive in Norfolk; by 1616 this area extended to 732 acres, with just ninety-four acres in Felbrigg field awaiting enclosure.[13]

The success of the Felbrigg estate owed much to geography, but stability of ownership was a key factor, allowing the expansion of demesne lands to continue unimpeded. The estate has experienced only three changes of ownership since the Norman Conquest and each transfer was accomplished with little disruption. The medieval owners retained possession until 1450, when John Wymondham famously secured the estate by dubious means.[14] His descendants remained at Felbrigg until 1863, when the estate was sold to a Norwich feedstuffs merchant, John Ketton. The suddenness of the sale allowed Ketton to purchase the core of the estate around Felbrigg, with the hall and all its contents, and so it remained very much a 'Wyndham' house. His daughter married Thomas Wyndham Cremer of Beeston and their son inherited the estate in 1924, returning Felbrigg to the Wyndhams. Their grandson, the historian R.W. Ketton-Cremer, left the estate to the National Trust in 1968.[15]

The Felbrigg estate that appears in the Green Book was built up over several generations; by 1673 there were properties in east and central Norfolk, Suffolk and Essex (see Figure 10.1, below). Parts of the estate were treated differently and clearly enjoyed a different status, which helps to explain the policies pursued in individual cases. The estate that John Wymondham secured in 1450 lay in the Felbrigg area with portions in Banningham, Tuttington, Colby and Ingworth on the fertile loamy soils to the east of Aylsham. He had earlier established himself in the Wymondham area

---

11 Wade Martins and Williamson, *Roots of Change*, chapters 1 and 2.

12 *Ibid.*, pp. 13–16, 43–6 for Northern Heathlands specifically.

13 B.M.S. Campbell, 'Field systems in eastern Norfolk during the Middle Ages: a study with particular reference to the demographic and agrarian changes of the fourteenth century', PhD thesis (Cambridge University, 1975).

14 N. Davis (ed.), *The Paston Letters* (Oxford, 1983), pp. 10–13, 227, 257.

15 Ketton-Cremer, *Felbrigg, passim.*

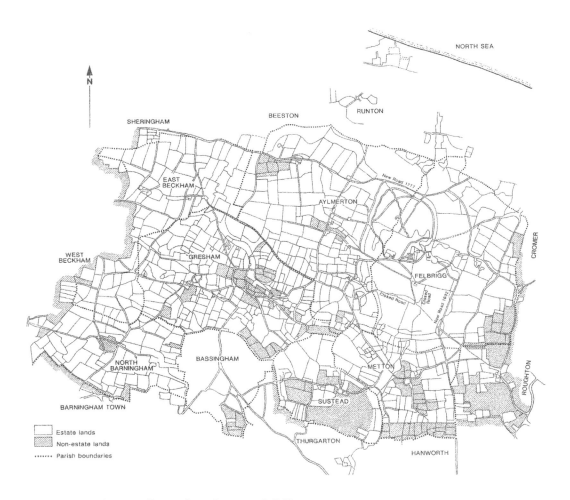

Figure 9.1 The Felbrigg Estate, from the map of 1830.

by purchasing a few hundred acres at Wicklewood and Crownthorpe.[16] As part of the Howard connection the family advanced, but in the early sixteenth century they suffered a severe setback when Sir John Wyndham supported Edmund de la Pole's claim to the throne, resulting in his attainder and the loss of estates. The attainder was reversed in 1512, but it served as a warning to the family, who henceforth avoided court life and concentrated their efforts in Norfolk. Edmund Wyndham added to the estate by purchasing land in Metton and Sustead from the Pastons and Dammes.[17] He acquired Beeston Priory at the dissolution and in the 1530s bought the estate

---

16 WKC 1/304, 392 x 6; 1/307, 392 x 6; 1/309, 392 x 6.

17 WKC 1/236, 392 x 2; 1/240, 392 x 2; 1/277, 392 x 4.

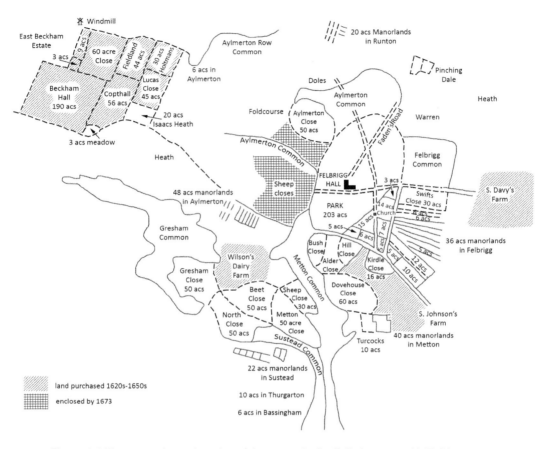

Figure 9.2 The approximate location of the estate in the Felbrigg area, 1615–73.

of the Ingloos family at Dilham.[18] At some stage the family also acquired a property at Thurlton and Toft Monks, on the marshes between Loddon and Great Yarmouth. The purchaser may have been Sir John Wyndham, who secured the reversion of the Felbrigg estate from his uncle Roger in 1599.

Sir John, descended from Edmund's younger brother, had married an heiress from Somerset and established a new branch of the family. He used his Felbrigg inheritance to endow his four younger sons, Thomas, George, Hugh and Wadham. He left Thomas the estate at Felbrigg with its lands in the Tuttington area. George, whose branch of the family eventually inherited the estate in 1924, he settled at Beeston, while Hugh and Wadham enjoyed the rents from Thurlton, Dilham and the estate at

---

18   T.W. Swales, 'The redistribution of monastic lands in Norfolk', *Norfolk Archaeology*, 34 (1966), p. 23. WKC 1/100, 391 x 4; 1/101, 391 x 5.

Wicklewood and Crownthorpe.[19] Henceforth, Thomas distinguished himself from his cousins by changing the spelling of Wyndham to Windham.

Thomas Windham was the founder of the modern Felbrigg estate. He came into his inheritance in 1616 and swiftly consolidated the existing holdings at Felbrigg, Tuttington and Dilham.[20] In 1628 he and his father purchased the East Beckham estate and, in the 1640s, following a second marriage, his new father-in-law assisted in the acquisition of similarly sized estates in Suffolk and Essex, and a farm at Reepham.[21] Between 1616 and 1654 Thomas increased the rental of the estate from £562 to £2400.[22] From the frequent references in the Green Book it is clear that William Windham modelled himself on his example.

Thomas Windham died in 1654 and left his estate divided between his eldest son John, from his first marriage, and his widow Elizabeth Mede, with her six young children. This second family enjoyed the £1200 annual income from the estates at Beckham and in Suffolk and Essex.[23] John produced no heirs and on his death in 1665 the estate passed to his much younger brother William. Neither John nor William added to the estate; indeed, no more acquisitions were made until Ashe Windham revived the policy in the 1700s.[24]

By 1673 William had recovered much of the property assigned to his mother and John Windham's widow, Frances. In 1669 he bought out her interest for £4500; in the same year he paid his mother £2000 'for debts incurred in my minoritye' and left her to enjoy the estate at East Beckham, with her new husband Richard Chamberlaine, until her death in 1679. Thomas Windham had also set aside a cash portion of £4000 for William's younger brother John and provision for dowries of £1500 for his two sisters. The details of these arrangements caused much rancour and occupy many pages in the Green Book. The estate in 1673 was worth £2114 a year, but in the adverse economic climate of the 1670s and 1680s actual income never reached this level.

---

19 WKC 3/16; 3/18, 399 x 4.

20 WKC 1/156, 391 x 8; 1/242, 392 x2; 1/172, 391 x 9; 1/153, 391 x 8; 1/260–3, 392 x 3; 1/290–2, 392 x 5; 1/8, 390 x 7; 1/116, 391 x 5; 1/115, 391 x 5.

21 WKC 1/47, 391 x 1; 3/17, 399 x 4; 1/354, 392 x 8; 1/342, 392 x 7; 1/183, 392 x 2.

22 WKC 5/420, 464 x; 5/442, 464 x 4.

23 WKC 5/442, 464 x 4.

24 Ashe Windham purchased the Palgraves' estate at Barningham and the Paston's property at Gresham. Further consolidation created the compactness which appears on the Felbrigg estate map of 1830, still hanging in a back passage at Felbrigg Hall. By 1854 the estate in the Felbrigg area extended to some 7000 acres, with a further 600 acres at Alby, Ingworth, Colby and Tuttington. A thousand acres at Dilham and the Hanworth estate of 1500 acres were purchased from the Doughtys in 1845. In 1863, following the bankruptcy of 'Mad Windham', John Ketton purchased 3000 acres in Felbrigg, Aylmerton, Sustead and Metton. Windham's estranged wife secured the settled estates for her son Frederick Howe Windham and the rest was sold to a Norwich banker, Robert Harvey. Felbrigg continued to decline under the stewardship of the Kettons. By 1968, when it passed to The National Trust, the estate amounted to no more than 1700 acres – the great demesne at Felbrigg and a couple of farms at Metton. See NRO Felbrigg Catalogue for references.

William Windham at Felbrigg, 1673–89

Plans and policies

From the outset William adopted a highly personal style of management, which affected every part and aspect of his estate. With the farms he clearly believed that with timely action and investment rent levels could be maintained despite the fall in corn prices (Figure 9.3). He conceded a reduction to the new tenants of Tuttington Hall in 1673, as 'I was loathe to take the farme into my hands not then living in the countye.' But when Mr Forby of Reepham made similar demands William terminated his lease and kept the farm in hand for four years. In 1674 11 per cent of the estate, including the park, was in hand; by 1683 the figure had risen to 35 per cent, and it remained at over 30 per cent in 1687. The policy required intensive management and proved costly, as large sums were lost supporting hard-pressed tenants, but in the long term his efforts paid dividends. He created a flexible, well-organised and fully capitalised estate capable of responding effectively to changes in market conditions. Moreover, the experience of the 1650s and early 1660s had shown that lack of intervention cost even more, as farms entered a downward spiral of debt, dilapidation and low rents. This had occurred at Tuttington, where John Crome had 'brought an ill repute upon the farme that I could not let it to able men for more'.

William's proactive approach to estate management reflected closely the advice of agricultural writers. In response to falling corn prices William increased his range of activities, placing his emphasis on livestock enterprises. He built dairies, leased out cows, improved neglected pastures, bought clover seed, bred herd replacements and experimented with agreements that shared the risk between landlord and tenant. Samuel Hartlib had recommended just this kind of assistance.[25] Utilising the park and land in hand, and working with dealers and local butchers, he also fattened hundreds of bullocks for sale at nearby markets. However, William reserved his greatest efforts for the remodelling of his park and woodland. In this he closely followed informed opinion, led by John Evelyn, that strongly advocated the planting of timber, the enlargement of parks and the creation of reserves for deer and game. It was a policy actively supported by the government, which passed a series of protective acts.[26] It made sense economically as well as aesthetically, as timber, venison and fish commanded high prices. William may well have been encouraged in his endeavours by the family physician Sir Thomas Browne, renowned philosopher and naturalist and a close acquaintance of Hartlib and Evelyn, who had lived in Norwich since the

---

25 'I only desire that industrious gentlemen would be pleased to encourage some expert workmen into the place where they live and let them land at a reasonable rate, and if they be poor and honest to lend them a little stock.' Sir Richard Weston's 'Legacie to his Sons', p. 10, printed in Samuel Hartlib's *His Legacie or An Enlargement of the Discourse of Husbandry Used in Brabant and Flanders*, 2nd edn (1652).

26 Joan Thirsk, 'Agricultural policy: debate and legislation', in Joan Thirsk (ed.), *The Agrarian History of England and Wales vol. v 1640–1750 pt II Agrarian Change* (Cambridge, 1985), pp. 325–88.

1630s.[27] Browne's essay, *The Garden of Cyrus* (1658), inspired John Evelyn to write his great work *Elysium Britannicum*, calling for the creation of an earthly paradise. This manuscript, never published, heralded more practical works. Evelyn's *Sylva, A Discourse of Forest Trees* (1664) clearly influenced William Windham's planting schemes. The care and effort he lavished on his young trees, deer and fish suggest a young man acting under guidance.

Park, woods and ponds

William's plans for the park, woods and ponds occupy a double page in the Green Book and continue in his Memo Book – the first discarded estate book – relegated to recording details on specific plantings, pond maintenance and the care of fish and deer.[28] The park was far from being a simple amenity area; William used it in several ways to support the various elements of his household economy. The park itself provided grazing for his 'sadle horses', for the sheep and deer that were consumed by the family in great quantities and for a few dairy cows supplying milk, butter and cheese. He fed his cart horses in Church Close and kept the meadow for hay. He also cultivated areas in the park, experimenting and noting the success of different rotations. In 1673 the thirty acres behind the house 'were sowne with severall sorts of Corne'; in 1674 he sowed part of Church Close; and in 1677 he broke up twenty-four acres of the Upper Parke, sowing it in a four-year rotation with buckwheat, or somerley, wheat and meslin, barley, and finally oats undersown with nonsuch. In 1679 he broke up the rest of Upper Park, which produced 'very good Winter Corne' the next year. He used the oats for his horses, buckwheat for poultry, wheat for bread and barley for malting; in 1681 he built a new brewhouse.[29] The park did not supply all their needs. William and Katherine purchased corn, meat, butter and cheese from tenants and paid various suppliers for fish, eggs and poultry, which Katherine records in her kitchen accounts.[30]

Woodland management interested William deeply. The entries in the Green Book and Memo Book show a man with a passion for trees, but his planting schemes were not purely decorative. He needed huge supplies of timber for a variety of purposes on the estate – for paling, fencing, building and repairs. Moreover, timber and topwood fetched a good price, which he noted carefully. Long before he tackled estate management he was selling and planting trees: 'in 1670 & 1671 I had planted the Oaks in the bottome by the Deer-house'. In 1676 he established a tree nursery, buying in thousands of seedlings – oak, ash, birch, beech, crab; combs of acorns, ash keys and haws; and bushels of holly berries, maple, sycamore, beechmast and some chestnut. He approached this task most professionally, noting the origin of seed

---

27 Hartlib Papers: folio 7/27/ 25 A–B dated 4 July 1643. Graham Parry, 'John Evelyn as Hortulan Saint', in M. Leslie and T. Raylor (eds), *Culture and Cultivation in Early Modern England* (London, 1992), pp. 134–5. See also D.D.C. Chambers, *The Planters of the English Landscape Garden* (New Haven, CT, 1993) pp. 32–49.

28 WKC 5/151, 400 x 5.

29 WKC 5/151, 400 x 5.

30 WKC 6/15, 401 x 5.

and seedlings. By 1679 these were ready for transplanting into areas enclosed for the purpose. From the 1680s his planting schemes show more concern for design as he experimented with different species, planting Scotch firs along the Pond Walk and 'in the Cross Walks in the Nursery'. In 1683 he planted forty-nine trees, including walnuts, chestnuts, oaks and limes, to 'stand square 7 every way', imitating the pattern of the 'Quincunx' described by Browne in *The Garden of Cyrus*. In 1687 he 'inlarged the Wood from the 3rd Cross-Walk to the Wall', planting out the seedlings of 1676, which amounted to several thousand trees. This final entry gives some idea of the scale and complexity of William Windham's achievement between 1673 and his death in 1689.

The management of deer and fish received much attention. He kept records of the type, age and number of his deer, inserting tags into their ears to monitor progress. He built a deer house and yard to protect them in winter, and in 1679 he planned a new nursery 'for Cops-wood to shelter deer'. In the Memo Book he used the terms fawn, pricket, sorrel and soar, which refer to the different ages of the male fallow deer, but the reference to a hinde, a knobler and brockets suggests that he was introducing some red deer into the herd.[31] These efforts, particularly the tagging of the castrated males – havers – and the keeping of 'paled' deer, indicate a serious interest in venison production. John Salman, the Felbrigg bailiff, recorded the purchase of six pots and 'hampers and holters' for venison. For similar reasons, William recorded details of his carp, noting when ponds were restocked, the numbers involved and the size and growth of the fish, which he measured from 'eye to tayle'. He moved carp from one pond to another to prevent overstocking, and tried to keep the same size fish in each location to ensure an even growth pattern. He enlarged existing ponds by removing gravel, and built extra ponds to accommodate the surplus. He was clearly fascinated by the mechanics of fish and deer production; no evidence survives of him selling these products on a commercial basis, but they supplied the household and made welcome gifts.

House and garden

Between 1675 and 1687 William added a new wing to the west side of the house, to the plans of William Samwell. In 1675 he 'felled all the Timber used about my new building at Felbrigg', and in 1684 he 'ordered all the trees in the two Upper Closes to be digged up [and] used about my Building Anno 1685'. Although the Green Book does not include further mention of this enterprise, which must have absorbed much energy and time, Salman's accounts refer to the making of huge quantities of bricks and tiles, the purchase of lead and the employment of an army of skilled workmen, including plumbers, tilers, carpenters, sawyers, painters, coopers and bricklayers, all supervised by a Mr Skerry between 1681 and 1683. Other buildings were being constructed at the same time, including the brewhouse, but the scale and quality mentioned in the documents suggests that most of the materials were destined for the west front.[32]

---

31   E.P. Shirley, *Some Account of English Deer Parks* (London, 1867).

32   J. Maddison, *Felbrigg Hall* (London, 1995), chapter 3, pp. 12–17, contains a detailed section on W. Windham's rebuilding, including Samwell's plans with his terse comments following William's modifications. Also Ketton-Cremer, *Felbrigg*, pp. 56–8.

When William inherited Felbrigg the house comprised only what is now the south front. Samwell planned three new wings to make a quadrangle, with service buildings neatly housed in an east wing, but much to his dismay William vetoed the idea in favour of the L-shaped house with just two fronts that survives today. His successors never satisfactorily resolved the jumble of service buildings to the east of the house. Only on the far side, walking away from the house, can Samwell's stylish west wing be appreciated. In this matter William's prudence in curtailing his architect's schemes is a matter of regret.

Land in hand and letting to halves

Throughout the period William kept land in hand that he managed as an extension of his enterprise in the park. These areas included the Sheep Walk, run by his shepherd Henry Bally, and the Dovehouse Close in Metton, where he fattened his bullocks; from these animals Thomas Sexton, the butcher, ensured Katherine a regular supply of butchered meat. William also kept a herd of sixteen cows at the Dairy Grounds in Gresham, which he leased to Michael Wilson, who supplied additional dairy products for the household. In his 'Account of the Stock of Beasts upon my Grounds' William noted the date of purchase and price paid for each animal, their location on the estate and how they were disposed of. From 1674, as farms failed, or under-performed, he drew them into this operation – notably Reepham, Crownthorpe and Keeble's farm in Suffolk. In 1680, as the business grew in complexity, he diverted these accounts to the Memo Book. The entries show that Salman co-ordinated the entire operation, using the grounds at Felbrigg as a clearing house for stock received from farms and for newly purchased beasts awaiting their destination. In this way William created a profitable business, building up a team of professionals skilled at farming and dealing in stock; this enabled him to experiment with different policies. His first attempt at a new strategy, fully recorded in the Green Book, was the management of Reepham Farm.

By the time he took Reepham Farm in hand in 1673 he had already invested heavily in the property. In 1668 he agreed 'to build a bakehouse and dairy with as much expediency as may be', so he had little sympathy when Mr Forby fell behind with his rent.[33] From 1673 Thomas Sexton worked the farm alongside his fattening enterprise at Sustead and Metton and in conjunction with Wilson's dairy. Salman supervised the operation, but, despite his efforts, William calculated in the bi-annual accounts that the farm in hand made a loss in 1675 and 1677. His expectation that the sales of corn, beef and sheep would pay a rent and cover the costs of production proved optimistic. The problem was that his costs, which included parish rates, tithes, purchase of stock, Sexton's wages and husbandry charges, were more or less fixed, while corn prices declined. Moreover, Sexton's accounts required the closest scrutiny by Salman, which was time-consuming. To reduce the level of management, William entered into a sharefarming agreement with Sexton: 'the trouble in looking after this farme made me let it to halves'. This was the first of a series of experiments

---

33   WKC 7/154, 404 x 8; 5/151, 400 x 5.

by Windham in sharefarming agreements in the Felbrigg area.[34] Difficulties with the agreement with Sexton led to further refinements.

William engaged Edmund Britiffe to draw up future agreements, which were copied in their entirety into the Green Book. The first of these, for 'hiring a Dairie of Cows' and 'plowing ground to halfes' in Felbrigg Park, he arranged with John Masters in 1678. His motive was 'to have the conveniencye of a Dairie near me, & bee free from the trouble of plowman'. Masters cultivated areas directed by William, while his wife ran the dairy. The scheme lasted until 1681, when 'Master's wife died, which made him not fit for imployment'.

The agreements still proved troublesome, however, and from 1681 William used letting to halves agreements only as a last resort. In 1682, when his tenant William Parke died at Alby, 'for fear I should not git a Tennant for the rest of Parke's farm, I agreed with Dan Shepherd to live in the house rent free'. William also laid on a small dairy herd of four cows and let the ground to halves. He retained the right to terminate the agreement at three months' notice, but in the event Shepherd stayed for three years and tried to dissuade the new tenant from entering the farm. William was forced to offer the new man more inducements to take the lease 'to avoid a sute'.

It is possible that letting to halves was established practice in the Dilham area. The earliest example on the Felbrigg estate was at Dilham Hall Farm in 1662, when, unable to find a replacement, John Windham broke up the holding and let several closes to halves for one year. This was the way the arrangement was more commonly used between farmers to overcome periods of sickness or widowhood; typically a neighbour would step in and sow the land to halves.[35] In 1610, for example, Robert Loder, when he entered his estates, 'put forth to halves' part of his 'mother's joynture'. An agreement from the Westwick estate, a few miles from Dilham, shows John Berney in 1698 letting to halves the farm occupied by Widow Westhorp for one year to John Ollyet, yeoman of Worstead.[36] These parishes lie close together in the fertile and intensively cultivated Broadland region where small landowners still predominated; in this type of area such a system of mutual support would have flourished. The likelihood is that Dilham was the source of the idea and William, probably on Salman's recommendation, adopted and developed the practice as a solution to his growing management crisis in the late 1670s.

The Windhams never let to halves beyond a fifteen-mile radius of Felbrigg, attesting to its experimental nature. At an early stage William was attracted to the idea and its possibilities. In fact, his first use of letting to halves was not as an alternative to direct farming but to effect the improvement of a neglected pasture, Rush Close, part of Wilson's dairy farm at Gresham. The agreement was for thirteen years. In the first seven years Waterson, the tenant, was to break up the pasture, level, drain, plough, muck and cultivate it. The rotation included, in year one, buck or summerley; in year two, wheat; in year three, barley; and in year four, oats, to be followed by five years of olland (i.e. fallow) – a true

---

34   This agreement is described in chapter 10, p. 209.

35   WKC 5/442, 464 x 4. For a fuller discussion see R.H. Hilton, 'Why was there so little champart rent in Medieval England?' *Journal of Peasant Studies*, 17 (1990), pp. 510–19.

36   Fussell, *Robert Loder's Farm Accounts*, pp. 1–4, 19; Pet. 159, 97 x 2.

system of up-and-down husbandry.[37] To encourage Waterson, William accepted half the corn and paid the parish rates for the cultivated area, whereas he charged 18s an acre for the remaining pasture. The arrangement ran its term, indicating that lettings to halves worked well within a limited application and a restricted time scale, but as an alternative to leasing farms for a negotiated rent for a term of years they were hazardous arrangements. Between 1690 and 1693 Katherine Windham, faced with mounting debts at Beckham Hall, revived the idea, but the agreement, the last at Felbrigg, cost her hundreds of pounds.[38]

Leased farms

William's primary objective was to have farms leased to reliable tenants for terms of years. In written leases, summarised in the Green Book, he specified their obligation to look after the woods, buildings and infrastructure, to follow beneficial husbandry practices and to pay their rents. In return he agreed to invest in new farm buildings, assist with repairs and ease their burden in times of difficulty. The latter often included generous treatment to widows or 'antient men'. In other words, he aimed for a stable framework in which improvement could be sustained despite the adverse economic climate. The idea of a mutually beneficial contract between landlord and tenant can be seen in the lease for Reepham Farm in 1668, where 'The Landlord Covenants' were followed by 'The Tennants Covenants'.[39] William's entries at the back of the Green Book merely note the essentials of the agreement, but he had a clear idea of the principle of mutual support and trust behind such contracts. When tenants reneged on the terms of their leases or behaved badly, he acted swiftly. In 1678 he did not allow John Kingsberry of Middleton Hall £10 'because he had been too long in the Wheelwright's companye'. In 1682 the relationship reached a crisis over Kingsberry's mistreatment of young trees – 'I am sure noe Tennant will take less care of the Timber & young stands than Jo. Kingsberry have done' – so he 'resolved to run the hazard of getting a new Tennant'. But his hasty eviction proved disastrous as Kingsberry's successor, Jeremiah Prance, was 'not able' and finally failed in 1694 owing £555.[40]

William's allowances for repairs, taxation and abatements averaged 20 per cent of estate income between 1673 and 1687, compared to 10 per cent in the 1650s and early 1660s. The most significant change was the increased expenditure on repairs. The full leases for Reepham Farm (1668) and Henry Grime's farm at Tuttington (1672) show that, when he inherited the estate, buildings and structures had been allowed to deteriorate. On both occasions he put the houses 'into good, tenantable and sufficient repair', provided wood to mend fences and gates and glazed the windows.[41] He allowed the tenants rough timber to maintain the property and repeated this

---

37   Up-and-down husbandry entailed ploughing up pasture for cultivation for a period of years, then laying it down to pasture once again. Adopted extensively by Thomas Windham in the 1620s, his leases for East Beckham include detailed clauses specifying its use.

38   WKC 5/158, 400 x 6.

39   WKC 7/154, 404 x 8.

40   WKC 5/158, 400 x 6.

41   WKC 5/154, 404 x 8.

concession in the majority of his leases. On building work he stipulated the contribution of the tenant: they had to provide so many days' work of a thatcher and dawber and often materials, but the time and the amount remained negotiable. Thus in 1683 at Scrivener's Farm, Dilham, the requirement for four days' thatching was reduced to three, and at Felbrigg-Gresham Farm in 1687 Thompson was relieved of all dawbing work. The summaries in the Green Book do not, however, accurately reflect the scale of William's expenditure. He invested in new buildings and other improvements, such as ditching and marling, as and when required and made special allowance for the upkeep of mills.

William tried to be constructive in his approach to rent reductions and abatements. Frequently incoming tenants paid a lower rent for the first few years of their term so they could establish themselves, but leaving the agreed rent intact. He often promised them new buildings, particularly on difficult farms like Crownthorpe, where in 1683 he agreed 'to make a new Plank threshing floor … Repayr the Barne floor … lay boards over the Calf House', shelve the cheese chamber, ditch the mowing meadow and 'give him £10'. From the early 1680s he accepted corn in payment of rent much more readily, a genuine concession as the price of corn continued to fall.

Beyond the requirement to leave the farm 'in a husbandlye manner' and 'in good heart', William rarely specified the farming practice to be followed, simply noting 'with other covenants how to use the ground', which clearly refer to more detailed leases. When counterparts of leases have survived they invariably restate, clarify or slightly modify husbandry clauses dating back to the 1620s and 1630s. Thus in 1632, Hubberds Close, Wicklewood was 'not be plowed any part which is not in Tillage, nor sowe any which is already plowed once more oftener than 3 yeres together, without somerlayinge the same'.[42] In 1678 the tenant 'shall not sowe more than 3 cropps of corne together and will somerlay and leave fallow every 4th year, as such grounds as are in Tillage; except such grounds as are new ploughed and then to somerlay the 5th year after 1st ploughing and every 4th year thereafter'.[43] Restrictions on overcropping and ploughing feature prominently. In Suffolk Houseman was not to 'plow above 40 A[acres] in any one year, nor Oats 2 years togeather; in one piece'; and in 1678 Gresham Close was not to be ploughed 'in payne of forty shillings an Acre'. As a general rule, William did not attempt to introduce innovative farming practice through leases, especially on established holdings, where he left the business of farming to the tenant. His main concern was that the ground should be used beneficially, mucked well – especially before winter corn – and left well ordered for the incoming tenant. Hence the requirements at Dilham to leave a third in wintercorn stubble, a third in summercorn stubble and a third olland, summerley or buck stubbe, with muck left in the yards. From the 1680s, reflecting his concern for the condition of the soil, he started to include clauses on marling. In 1683 he agreed with William Tower of Beckham 'that the said Wm shall lay on 200 Loads of Marle yearly the first 6 years. I diging and filling the same'.

---

42   WKC 5/136, 400 x 5.
43   WKC 5/61, 400 x 1.

Farming practices

Although William rarely used leases to promote innovative husbandry, other evidence in the Green Book shows that tenants had been experimenting with new crops for some time and that he encouraged their adoption, particularly the use of clover. In 1672 he paid for forty-two pounds of clover seed for Smith's farm at Dilham; in 1678 he paid £1 5s for clover seed for Reepham Farm; and in 1679 he directed that the closes on Aylmerton heath should be sown with clover or left olland, 'Mr Windham finding seed'. In 1674 he had reduced the rent for the Sheep Closes at Aylmerton because 'the Clovergrass decayed'. By the 1670s one of the large closes in Metton was called the Clover-grass Close. Turnips were also introduced into the estate quite early and used extensively to feed beasts and cows. In 1676 he had '3 Beasts at Turnops', and in several accounts he made allowances for turnips, including £10 for Widow Scipper's 'turnups'; £5 10s to William Frost at Gresham for a 'Close of Turneps' at Gresham; and to Plummer of Debney's Farm, Dilham for his 'Turnups'. The letting to halves agreement for the Park (1690–3) shows that turnips and clover were grown with grain crops, peas and vetches in what appears to be an informal rotation.⁴⁴ The use of clover and turnips was clearly well established by the 1670s, but not enforced as a matter of estate policy. In contrast, at Blickling, a neighbouring estate on the northern heathlands, leases for light-soiled farms at Horsham St Faith and Swardeston directed the tenant to grow turnips from the mid-1660s and included instructions as to their cultivation.⁴⁵ At Felbrigg, William preferred to leave these initiatives to the discretion of the tenant.

Manorial jurisdiction

William allotted several pages in the Green Book to manorial jurisdiction and clearly took these responsibilities seriously. His bailiffs collected the rents of assize and held court 'diners' and 'supers' for the tenants, while William pursued claims over copyhold land and asserted his rights over timber and game.

Rents of assize, the fixed rents payable on copyhold land, amounted to £141 11s 11¾d a year in 1673. Four bailiffs collected the rents: Robert Cooke for the Felbrigg, Beckham and Banningham area; Edmund Bale for Wicklewood and Crownthorpe; John Perry for Tofts and Thurlton; Henry Houseman for Suffolk. In Essex this duty fell to the Kingsberry brothers, where the tiny sums formed part of their farm rents. For Bale and Houseman, manorial duties occupied only a fraction of their time. In 1682, reflecting the declining importance and mechanical nature of this role, William terminated Robert Cooke's employment at Felbrigg, saving himself £5 by arranging for the rents to be collected by his 'menial servant'. Nevertheless, by collecting these seemingly trivial rents landowners asserted a legal right that others might have challenged. For a similar purpose, William recorded rents, fines and fees payable by him to other manors from which he held land.

The type of rent payable on parcels of copyhold land became the subject of several disputes in the 1670s and 1680s. The majority of copyhold rents on the estate

---

44   WKC 5/158, 400 x 6.

45   NRS 21135 74 x 2; NRS 11122 25 E 5; NRS 16023 31 F 10.

were fixed, but some were unfixed, leaving the landowner the right to raise them. John Blinman had carried out a survey of copyhold land between 1609 and 1615 to distinguish the different types of rent and ascertain the scope for improvement. Much had been achieved and Thomas Windham continued to increase rents where possible and keep a watchful eye on any attempts at evasion. John Windham and the family lawyer, Dr Robert Peppar, had been less careful and allowed payments to lapse, leaving William with the burden of reasserting his rights. He faced several challenges to either his title or his claim that rents were unfixed and could be improved. The most persistent litigant was Clement Herne, whose family had successfully pursued similar claims in the queen's manor of Cawston.[46] By winning judgements in their favour they had secured outright possession of a substantial acreage, which lay close to their estate at nearby Haveringland. The case started in 1672, when the family refused to pay the rent of £3 14s 0d, set by Thomas Windham in 1640, for nine acres one rood in Metton. William threatened the family with a Bill of Chancery, which had the desired effect, but when Widow Herne died in 1681 her son Clement reopened the issue by offering William the old copyhold rent of 9s 3d. The case went to court and the judges found in William's favour, but Herne did not pay any rent until 1685 and only after much pressure.

Thomas Doughty of Hanworth gained much encouragement from Herne's case. In 1673 William restated his claim to charge Doughty rent for one acre two roods in Metton. Doughty paid the 16s rent until 1681, but ceased when Herne's case came to court. William and Doughty were already in dispute over a right of way in Metton, which gave access to one of William's holdings. In the 1650s Thomas Windham had seized this parcel when the Doughtys failed to pay their copyhold rent. William settled the matter, with counsel's advice, by granting Doughty a ninety-five-year lease for a rent of £2 6s a year, and Doughty agreed to allow William access to his holding, but neither party was satisfied.

Another dispute erupted in Metton when the tenant refused to pay £3 13s 4d for eight acres in twelve pieces. The threat of legal action once more disciplined the tenant, but William needed to exercise constant vigilance. These cases all occurred in Metton, which suggests an element of copycat tactics among those tenants. William certainly thought so, and acted firmly to deter further challenges. In 1687 he went through his father's Audit Books noting the tenurial details and historic rent of several small holdings to equip himself with crucial evidence if the need arose.

William stipulated his rights over timber, game and access in leases for the larger properties, and a few of the summaries in the Green Book record such details, notably for Beckham foldcourse and Houseman's Farm in Suffolk. These clauses were no formality, as John Kingsberry learned to his cost in 1682, when William evicted him for maltreating young trees. William also retained payments in kind, in addition to the money rents, with tenants on several manors contributing a hen, capon or pullet. The miller at Ingworth had to provide '60 Roasting Eles' and half his fish.

---

46   NRS 27218 361 x 3; Also Griffiths, 'Management', pp. 153–5.

The estate community

A husband and wife team

On 9 June 1689 Katherine noted, 'this day my dear, dear husband left me, having made me hapy for 20 years'.[47] It was the final entry in her personal diary, after which she turned her attention to managing the estate and the family's financial affairs.[48] She was, however, no stranger to the task; her comments and initiatives, recorded in the new Green Book, indicate a longstanding involvement with a complex and diverse business. She had acted as manager, producer and consumer, co-ordinating a range of activities. Entries in the Memo Book show her receiving deliveries of meat from Thomas Sexton, selling hides and skins and paying wages to labourers engaged in work about the house and garden. Several accounts in the Green Book record her receiving rents and, from the 1680s, she supervised the Park Dairy. From the interlocking accounts kept by husband and wife we can see their procedures becoming steadily more proficient, with each learning from the other. From 1689 Katherine's domestic accounts, which were hitherto rather scrappy, resemble the layout of the Green Book, with a table of contents, numbered pages and double entry book-keeping. Together they created a management structure, organising their estate community to perform a variety of functions, adapting and modifying their roles over time.

The professionals

William employed a range of professionals to assist him in the management of his estate. The lowest layer of management consisted of a team of 'men on the ground', who received rents, made assessments for repairs, bought and sold stock and corn and ran the farms in hand. The most influential of this group was the John Salman who had supervised day-to-day business at Felbrigg since the late 1660s, a role that had brought him into conflict with Dr Robert Peppar, the family lawyer, who was nominally in charge of the estate from 1665 to 1671.[49] Peppar had complained bitterly of Salman's rudeness, but, as Judge Hugh Wyndham pointed out, the deficiencies invariably rested with the lawyer, who had neither the time nor the practical skills either to deal with farming matters on the ground or to establish good working relationships with tenants.[50] Wyndham solved the situation at Dilham by employing a local man on an annual salary and paying an attorney a fee to perform specialised services, such as holding the manorial court and auditing the annual account. William reorganised his

---

47   WKC 6/12, 401 x 4.

48   WKC 13–18, 401 x 5.

49   WKC 7/5 404 x 1. In his correspondence with William, Peppar complains 'I have been silent under somether of Salmon's affronts of this nature and pay let me have nothing to do with him. I am not so low a man to truckle under so rude and unmannerly a fellow!'

50   WKC 7/15, 404 x 1: correspondence between William and his uncle Hugh Wyndham regarding the management of the Dilham Estate, in which they shared an interest.

management structure at Felbrigg along similar lines, dispensing with Peppar's costly services, engaging Salman as his principal man of business and undertaking the overall supervision of the estate himself. Gradually, more names appear in the Green Book supporting Salman in various ways: Samuel Smith from 1679, Joseph Elden from 1682, John Barham and Edward Fairchilde in 1686. They received rents and in turn paid the 'weekly bills' and kept the supplementary accounts; disbursements included paying labourers' wages, building repairs, fencing, ditching and buying and selling sheep and cattle.[51] Salman kept his own accounts, to which the Green Book refers.[52] Stephen Legge, who became the principal accountant after William Windham's death, made his first appearance as a witness to a lease in 1678. Following Salman's retirement in 1688 he took responsibility for rent collection and negotiations with tenants and from 1694 kept the main estate accounts and assumed the title of 'Steward'.[53]

On the off-lying properties William relied on his bailiffs to look after his affairs, while Salman came over to receive rents and adjudicate on repairs and abatements. The bailiff, invariably, held one of the tenancies and bills for salary, repairs, fencing, ditching and manorial duties were set off against his rent. On occasion his duties were particularly onerous, as when Crownthorpe Farm failed in 1676 and William paid Edmund Bale £4 10s for 'his trouble in looking after my farme'. The Suffolk bailiff, Henry Houseman, had greater responsibilities, accounting for all the rents directly to William; this may well have contributed to the accumulation of debts and his failure in 1682. On the Essex properties the Kingsberry brothers paid their rents to William's financial managers in Norwich, Alderman Briggs or Mr Fowle, who either returned the money to London or sent it to Briggs in Norwich or even to William at Felbrigg. Alderman Augustine Briggs played a central role in William's affairs, managing his financial business. He had served as sheriff of Norwich (1660), mayor (1670), treasurer for Norfolk (1662) and MP for the City of Norwich in 1678, 1679 and 1681.[54] With his connections, he was well placed to receive payments, return sums of money to London for investment and pay election expenses and any outstanding debts.[55]

From time to time William appointed outside professionals for specific purposes. When he pursued the legal claim against Clement Herne he instructed counsel, Sir Robert Baldock, to draw a bill in chancery and ordered his attorney, Palmer, to prefer a bill against Herne. With his own legal training, William had no need to retain a lawyer to manage his affairs; he was quite able to direct the course to be followed. When he wanted advice on estate management he consulted Edmund Britiffe of Baconsthorpe, who drew up the letting to halves agreements with John Master and John Fincham and was retained as an intermediary in case of disputes.[56]

---

51   WKC 5/155, 400 x 6; 5/157, 400 x 6.

52   WKC 5/154, 400 x 6.

53   WKC 5/211, 400 x 6; 5/162–210, 400 x 6.

54   Moore and Crawley, *Family and Friends*, pp. 202–3.

55   Ketton-Cremer, *Felbrigg*, pp. 64–7, tells the story of the 1679 election when William Windham, with little enthusiasm, partnered Sir John Hobart at the polls.

56   Three generations of Britiffes appear in the records of several county families, including the Walpoles of Houghton, the Hobarts of Blickling and the Harbords of Gunton, as advisers on

William directed his management structure to achieve an effective relationship with his tenants and the efficient management of his farms, particularly if they failed and the farms needed to be taken in hand. He placed his emphasis on the level of management that would directly influence these matters, employing practical professionals, such as Salman, on a permanent basis and engaging lawyers and consultants as and when required. This strategy served his purposes, namely to maintain rent levels by intervention and positive management, but it was possible only because of his enthusiasm and the day-to-day control he exercised over estate business. As soon as Katherine Windham withdrew from this degree of involvement in 1694 Stephen Legge quickly emerged as the full-time professional estate steward, with a very different approach. Without the freedom and authority to experiment with risky options, he played safe; estate management became a professional business designed to reduce risk, simplify procedures and secure a reliable income for the landowner.[57]

The tenants

The farm tenants were a mixed group, socially and economically. A huge disparity existed between the Kingsberrys of Brunden and Middleton Hall who paid their rents in hundreds of pounds and dealt with William almost on equal terms, and those tenants who lived from hand to mouth and could not sign their names, like the share farmer Fincham, 'too poor to continue'. John Johnson of Felbrigg owned his own farm, in addition to renting Felbrigg-Gresham Farm, and in 1677 he left to 'live in his owne'. Some tenants William addressed with respect, such as Mr Harris of Roughton, but others he summarily dismissed: Crome of Tuttington Hall Farm was 'a lazy ignorant man' and Downing, the new tenant of Alby, was 'a sullen fellow'. Many families in the Felbrigg area, including the Abbs, Palls, Johnsons, Drakes, Powles and Lounds, had served the Windhams as tenants for generations and appear in Blinman's account of 1609 to 1615. William sometimes called on these men, whom he knew and trusted, to farm difficult holdings: William Frost and Richard Lowne (Lound) held the tenancy of Tuttington Hall Farm until 1680, when a local man, Richard Lilly, accepted a seven-year lease. William preferred local men, familiar with local conditions and practices. When Mr Harris of Roughton gave up his lease of the Sustead Closes in

---

estate business and family affairs. Identifed as yeomen in land transactions of the 1560s, they built up useful estates in the Cley, Hunworth, Baconsthorpe and Plumstead area. The first Edmund Britiffe advised Thomas Windham on his grazing agreements in the 1620s; his son drew up the sharefarming agreements for William Windham. Robert Britiffe served as Recorder of King's Lynn and MP for Norwich, and acted as Sir Robert Walpole's political agent. He was particularly skilful in the land and marriage market. Besides executing deals for Sir Robert, in the 1710s he arranged the marriage of his daughter to Sir John Hobart and his nephew to Hester Harbord of Gunton, contributing to the revival of two important county families. See Griffiths, 'Management', pp. 505–8 for further references.

57 Hainsworth, *Stewards, Lords and People*, pp. 251–64, discusses the inhibition of stewards and their reluctance to act on their own initiative in this period, when their role was still at a formative stage. The tendency was to err on the side of caution.

1681 after only a year that had 'proved so very dry and bad', he noted he had 'lately come into Norffolk'. He offered this as an explanation for his action because 'he lost nothing'. For tenants with particular skills he was often forced to look further afield. Gorse the Warrrener came from Haveringland and his successor Thomas Wegg from Banningham, both parishes ten miles or more from Felbrigg. In 1684 William made the comment that the new tenant of Ingworth Mill, although from Aldborough, had been 'bred in Ingworth' – clearly a point in his favour.

The specialist tenants, who included the limeburner, brickmaker, shepherd and butcher, as well as the warreners and millers, possessed skills that set them apart from their neighbours and meant they could negotiate their own arrangements. At Felbrigg the warren appears to have been very lucrative: in 1682 Gorse 'grew rich, married and would noe longer endure the hardship of a Warrener's Life'. The Sexton family were notably versatile. William the limeburner provided lime and marl; his brother Thomas supplied butchered meat to the house and hired Reepham Farm to halves; while Robert leased Ingworth Mill, with comparative success, between 1673 and 1682. With the falling price of corn, coupled with the high cost of maintaining buildings and equipment, millers led a precarious existence; Ingworth Mill changed hands six times between 1673 and 1686. In 1682 'William Greenacre brought me word his son was run away. And begged that I would release him', and in 1686 Sam Curril 'carryed away his goods in the night'. To secure a tenant William was forced to make substantial concessions; as he said, 'Corne is so low and Millers doe scramble for grist by fetching and carrying (which was not formerly done) 'tis hard to get a Tennant'. At Wicklewood in 1677 he laid out £27 11s 3d in repairs for the new tenant, and for Beckham Mill in 1683 he agreed to lay 200 loads of marl for the first six years of the lease. In Suffolk a struggle for business between Thomas Arteson of Lower Mill and Robert Keeble of Upper Mill led to disaster: 'Keeble desired to leave the Mill … because Arteshall had got many of his customers'. At Brunden Mill Francis Reynolds went bankrupt in 1674, resulting in a loss of £200. To attract a new tenant William had to spend a further £195 on repairs; he noted 'By his account one may see how little Mills are worth'. In 1683, in some desperation, he leased the mill to Robert Kingsberry: 'The Poverty and Knavery of Millers made me earnest to bring R.K. to the aforesd Agreement.'

Widows were another group who encountered difficulties, few surviving the season following their husband's death. Invariably, William made allowances and wrote off their debt 'more out of charity than reason'. However, there were exceptions and some women proved most capable. Widow Skipper continued for five years at Crownthorpe Farm before she was forced to a sale in 1676. The inventory shows a well-stocked and fully equipped farm growing a range of fodder crops, including £10 worth of turnips. Compassion extended to the old and infirm; 'Ransome is soe old & his son lame they can't order the ground as it should bee therefore I advise him to leave farming & tould him I would forgive him £10 arrears.'

The task of dealing with the arrogant, the whiners, the knaves, the lazy, the ignorant and the 'ill husbands' played havoc with William's nerves. The saga with the millers, in particular, helps to explain his growing frustration. The close relationship he conducted with his tenants was not easy, and probably inadvisable in the difficult economic circumstances. The situation called for a professional intermediary to stand between landlord and tenant.

The labourers

The Green Book is concerned principally with William's relationship with his tenantry. The labourers who did the felling, ditching, fencing, husbandry, marling and carrying appear mainly in the subsidiary accounts kept by Salman, Elden, Smith and Fairchild, who paid their wages and organised their work. But there is mention of Fox and Pye, who cut the flags, and several smaller tenants who ditched, thatched and carried in lieu of rent. In his weekly account Salman distinguished between daywork and those paid an annual wage. The former were paid 8d and 10d per day for a variety of menial jobs, such as gardening, looking after the ewes and husbandry work.[58] Other tasks included greasing lambs, catching rats, spreading molehills, cleaning ponds, dragging for carp, carting hay, glazing windows, coopering and brewing. More skilled workers were retained with an annual wage: Bally the shepherd and the keeper in the park earned £10 a year, the cooper £8 10s, Daryell the gardener £8, the tiler £7 and the husbandmen £4 10s. Joseph Elden's account of 1683 includes a few more names.[59] Fincham and Masters were paid for carrying, collecting and carting, Flaxman for pulling turnips, Pooly for mucking and Dix and his son for 'larth riving' (i.e. splitting laths). From Samuel Smith's account a cycle of seasonal tasks can be discerned. Winter jobs included threshing, stopping gaps, ditching, cutting drains, 'shulving' muck, brewing, cleaning the dovehouse, fetching hay, collecting coals, pulling turnips for the fat sheep, tying trees in the Park and killing cattle for Christmas. In the spring they harrowed, ploughed, worked in the nursery, mowed the walks, felled alders and fed turnips to sheep, and then moved on to weeding in the garden and nursery, mowing, turning and making hay, washing and clipping sheep, turning water into the grazing ground, spreading earth for turnips and watering trees. Harvest was accompanied by mowing and cutting brakes, making faggots, hoeing turnips, cleaning the ponds, moving fish, ploughing and muck spreading. All through the year they thatched roofs and repaired buildings and fences as and when required.[60] In addition to the labourers employed on the estate, the Green Book refers to personal and household servants: Jon Francis my Butler, Mark my Grome. In her personal account book of 1669–89 Katherine kept a record of wages paid to indoor servants, including £3 a year to wet nurses.[61]

The estate community formed a pyramid with William and Katherine at the apex directing and keeping a tight rein on estate and household business. Closest to them and employed on a permanent basis were the household servants, accountants and practical 'men on the ground' who ensured the smooth running of the estate. They provided the link with the tenants, who leased the farms by written contract. Below this managerial level were the labourers, indoor and outdoor, paid either wages or daily rates, who performed all kinds of menial tasks through the year. Like a modern landowner, William bought in specialist professional skills as and when required, but from the entries in the Green Book his relationship with these individuals always

---

58   WKC 5/154, 400 x 6.
59   WKC 5/157, 400 x 6.
60   WKC 5/155, 400 x 6.
61   WKC 6/12, 401 x 4.

appears more distant.[62] The estate generated a substantial economy and employed a huge number of individuals who interacted with William and Katherine in different ways, but they all expected the Windhams to provide them with a livelihood and to protect them in their old age or widowhood.

The wider context

Farming in adversity

Emphasis has been placed on the uniqueness of the Green Book, which raises the possibility that Windham may have been untypical in his interest and commitment to estate management. However, as we have seen, his strategy reflected the recommendations of government, the Georgicall Committee of the Royal Society and agricultural writers of the day.[63] Diversification from corn into stock and schemes for planting trees, rearing fish, fattening venison and developing a brewing outlet were the classic responses in this period of adversity. Historians often question whether landowners read the agricultural texts or paid much attention to the exhortations of agricultural writers. Certainly, if they had acted fully on the advice of Samuel Hartlib, Walter Blith and John Worlidge the concept of a seventeenth-century 'agricultural revolution' would not be in doubt. But the relationship between culture and action was more complex; economic inducements, the movement of prices and individual circumstances all played their part. Windham's strategy was clearly affected by his commercial connections, but he was also exposed to the deeply cultural influence of his friend and mentor Dr Thomas Browne, a longstanding member of the Hartlib circle. Already a scholar of European repute, Browne maintained a wide correspondence with other 'men of genius', including John Evelyn and the naturalist and historian Sir William Dugdale, exchanging the latest ideas and information. Such a man, serving as physician to the Townshends, Hobarts, Bacons, Pastons, Le Stranges and Windhams, was well placed to influence at least two generations of Norfolk gentry. The cultural climate in Norfolk may not have been the deciding factor, but it was certainly favourable to innovation, and there clearly existed a network for the dissemination of these ideas.

Price movements

Price movements may be a more reliable determinant of landowner action. The Green Book and subsidiary accounts include corn and stock prices for the 1670s and 1680s and from these we can create some rudimentary graphs (Figure 9.3).

---

62 Hainsworth notes the closeness of the relationship between landowner and steward, compared with the more distant relationship with the family lawyer. While the former was dependent on the family, the latter was a professional, often a gentleman, with other clients and independent interests (*Stewards, Lords and People*, pp. 251–64).

63 The Georgicall Committee on agricultural improvement set up by the Royal Society in 1664.

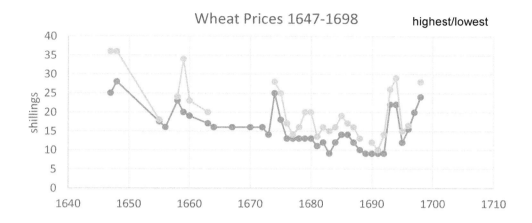

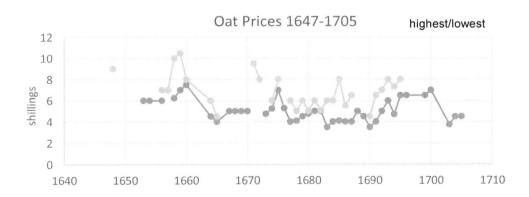

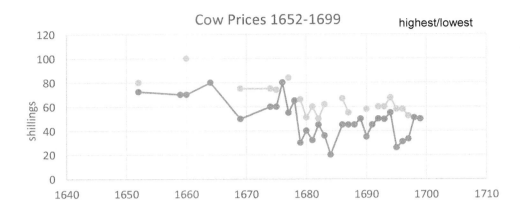

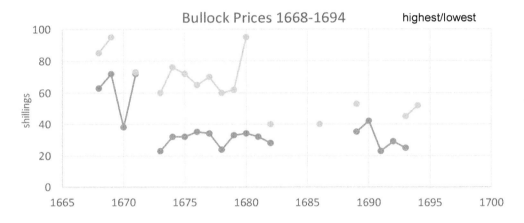

Figure 9.3 Agricultural prices on the Felbrigg and Blicking estates. Grain prices are per comb.

Unfortunately, the earlier accounts contain few prices for the 1650s and 1660s apart from 'rent barley' from 1655, so that a broader comparison of prices based on the Felbrigg material alone is difficult to formulate. However, by using Sir John Hobart's accounts for the neighbouring Blickling estate we can roughly trace the movement of prices between 1647 and 1707. The paucity of material from the late 1690s was due to the simplification of estate management policy and the curtailment of direct farming and interventionist policies on both estates. Prices for cows and fat bullocks disappear as interest shifted back to sheep and corn. The pattern identified at Felbrigg and Blickling compares closely to the cyclical trends outlined by Peter Bowden.[64]

Corn prices had been volatile since the early 1640s, but not until the early 1660s did they settle into a pattern of long-term decline. Figure 9.3 (a) shows that by 1664 wheat prices had dropped from a peak in 1647 of 36s a comb to a new low of 16s. In the years that followed they showed little sign of recovery, falling to 9s by 1683; a brief rally to 14s was followed by a further collapse to 9s between 1689 and 1691.[65] Figure 9.3 (c) shows that oat prices experienced a similar fate, falling from 12s per comb in 1661 to 4s 6d in 1664 and dipping to 3s 6d and 4s in the mid-1680s. Barley (Figure 9.3 (b)), sustained by the demand for malt, maintained its prices more successfully. Prices ranged between 8s 4d and 12s per comb in 1661 and edged lower in the late 1670s, but did not fall below 6s per comb until 1683. All corn prices staged a recovery between 1693 and 1699, only to retreat to very low levels by 1704.

Prices varied for each commodity at any one time. Seed corn, malting barley and oats specifically for riding and coach horses commanded the highest price in their range. Some prices were maintained artificially. John Talbott received 4s for his oats in 1684, but Windham allowed him 9s in 1685. Sir John Hobart followed a similar policy at Blickling, even devising Corn Agreements guaranteeing prices with tenants on struggling farms on light soils. Prices at Blickling tended to be at the higher end of the range; this might be explained by the proximity of many properties to the Norwich market and the amount purchased by Sir John to supply his households in London, Norwich and Blickling. Prices do not appear to reflect seasons; in July 1687 at Felbrigg wheat prices ranged from 12s to 16s and oat prices from 4s to 6s, which covered the full range of prices over the year.

Stock prices varied greatly, depending on the age, condition and quality of the animal (Figure 9.3). A cow in milk was worth double a dry or old one; heifers in calf were much more valuable than two year olds or barren heifers that were fattened for meat. Calves might be weaners or yearlings. Bullocks matured differently and were sold at different weights, and some breeds, such as Scotch runts, were particularly favoured. When bulls grew old and lazy they commanded little more than a mediocre bullock. Sheep prices include those for lambs, wether hoggs purchased and later sold fat, and old ewes, often called 'crones'.

---

64 P. Bowden, 'Agricultural prices, wages, farm profits and rents', Section D. Annual Price Movements, in Joan Thirsk (ed.), *The Agrarian History of England and Wales vol. v 1640–1750 pt II Agrarian Change* (Cambridge, 1985), pp. 41–54, Figs 13.2–13.10; 'Statistical appendix', pp. 828–84.

65 2 combs = 1 quarter; 4 quarters = 1 ton.

The graphs of corn and stock prices show that while the former fell steeply from the mid-1660s the value of stock and animal products remained relatively consistent throughout the whole period, after a downward adjustment in the 1670s. An estimate of crop yields on the Blickling estate, carried out in 1682, shows the expected return from wheat at two combs to the acre, meslin at three combs, barley at four combs and oats at five combs. At Felbrigg in 1687 William 'judged' wheat at 3.3 combs to the acre, and barley and oats both at three combs to the acre. Given the cost of cultivation and the likelihood of a fallow year, the return on corn compared unfavourably to the improvement possible on bullocks, with a stocking rate of one animal to the acre.[66] However, the high capital investment made bullock fattening and dairy farming a difficult option for tenants; few could effect the change without assistance from the landowner, which limited the scope for wholesale diversification from corn into cattle. Fat wethers and lambs offered a cheaper and more simple alternative, and landowners could avoid involvement in risky tenant-driven operations. Prices set the context for decision-making, but landowners and tenants had to consider other factors too.

Government policy

Government policy could also influence landowners' decisions. Tudor governments, with their anti-enclosure acts, intervened in agriculture to halt the conversion of open-field arable to enclosed pasture in order to ensure supplies of corn and protect employment.[67] These laws were never easy to enforce and highly unpopular with landowners, and James I relaxed their implementation and encouraged a more commercial approach to agricultural management; landowners won applause for cultivating waste and derelict lands, whereas twenty years before such an approach would have courted suspicion and possibly legal action.[68]

Land reformers directed their attention particularly to the improvement of pastoral areas and the creation of a more diversified agriculture: milk, cheese and meat were highly profitable. At Felbrigg in the 1620s Thomas Windham developed a huge bullock fattening enterprise based on the enclosed pasture and meadow of the demesne; he operated the system through grazing agreements with local butchers, overcoming the problems of disposing of the stock at the right time and price. In his leases he included clauses that either prohibited ploughing in certain areas or permitted it only for a stipulated number of years. In other words, he developed a carefully organised system of up-and-down husbandry. William Windham, following his father's example, was clearly receptive to ideas involving diversification into stockfarming.

In the late 1640s agricultural improvement became a national crusade. The Civil War, the need to supply troops, the possibility of social upheaval and high prices for food provided the stimulus for the Commonwealth to formulate a constructive policy towards agriculture as part of their wider plans for economic renewal and

---

66 T. Windham's Cattle Accounts: WKC 5/420 x. Also Bowden, 'Agricultural prices', pp. 9–10, on yields per acre, and Fig. 3.14, comparing the profitability of wheat against other commodities.

67 J. Thirsk, 'Agricultural policy', pp. 298–386.

68 Sir Richard Weston in Hartlib, *His Legacie*.

social reform. Through their publications the agricultural writers Samuel Hartlib and Walter Blith spearheaded the campaign.[69] Although few of their proposals reached the statute book, the debate attracted a wide audience among landowners and sowed the seed for future action. Moreover, the government had established a basis for developing policies and enacting laws. When corn prices slumped in 1653, after much deliberation restrictions were lifted on the export of corn to encourage landowners to maintain production. This decision, taken in 1656, paved the way for further manipulation of regulations governing the trade in agricultural products to the benefit of English producers and consumers.

With the recovery of corn prices in the late 1650s and early 1660s the incoming Restoration government resorted, at first, to traditional policies, prohibiting exports and acting against hoarders to ensure adequate food supplies. However, by 1663 the return of good harvests and the accompanying fall in prices brought renewed demands for the lowering of export controls; by 1670 these had been removed and imports suspended. At the same time they removed restrictions on the export of beer and encouraged distilling, greatly assisting Norfolk barley growers. Fearful of the continuing depression in prices, the impact on rent levels and the landowners' ability to pay increased taxation, in 1672 the government went further and introduced a system of bounties payable on corn exported. Bounties had a remarkable effect on production. Between 1660 and 1672 no British port exported more than 2000 quarters, but in 1674, the first year of operation, 23,000 quarters passed through King's Lynn alone. Bounties continued until 1681; the government renewed them in 1689, when prices fell sharply, and in 1693, when they imposed a new land tax. At Felbrigg William Windham eased the burden of taxation on his tenants by setting payments against their rent.

The Restoration government, like the Protectorate, preferred to regulate markets rather than direct landowners to particular courses of action. However, even this policy could prove controversial. In 1666 they encouraged diversification into stock breeding by prohibiting the importation of Irish cattle. However, not everyone benefited. Buyers of lean stock, like William Windham, saw the cost of beasts rise and profit margins narrow, as English and Scottish breeders could not meet the demand. Nevertheless, despite a temporary lifting of the ban between 1679 and 1681, the Cattle Act remained in force until 1759, to the benefit of graziers. From the mid-1670s calf prices appear more regularly in the accounts, suggesting that William took the initiative and increasingly bred his own replacements, particularly for his new dairies. The government encouraged dairy farming by removing restrictions on exports of butter and cheese in 1670; they also took steps to improve the marketing of dairy produce by tackling the problem of adulteration and deficient weights. They did not compel landowners to breed animals and move into dairy farming, but provided inducements that made these options attractive. In one area, however – sheep and wool – the government turned a deaf ear to the interests of landowners and farmers; the ban on wool exports imposed in 1614 remained until the mid-eighteenth century to protect the interests of the textile industry. At Felbrigg, despite the extensive area

---

69   Hartlib, *His Legacie*.

of heathland, wool features very little in the accounts; William noted the decline in the value of the foldcourse from £40 to £22, but the government would doubtless have argued that landowners in East Anglia were fully compensated by corn bounties.

The government also actively encouraged the development of parkland, tree-planting and game reserves. This policy made sense economically as timber, venison and fish commanded high prices, but possibly of greater importance was the intrinsic appeal such schemes had for landowners. In response to John Evelyn's investigation on woodlands for the Royal Society, the government passed a series of laws in the 1660s designed to protect timber and encourage new planting. They also acted swiftly against poachers, even giving gamekeepers the right to apprehend, and in 1670 they accepted the landowners' claim to reserve all the game on their estate. In this context, William Windham's enthusiasm for deer, fish and tree-planting can be fully understood. As far as possible, the government, by their regulatory policies, tried to look after the interests of landowners, forming a close and mutually beneficial relationship that continued until the repeal of the Corn Laws in 1846. From the pages of the Green Book William Windham emerges as a conscientious, thoughtful and enterprising landowner, responding in textbook fashion to the spirit of the times. He may not have been typical, but he certainly became a model for others to follow. The Green Book is the surviving testimony of his commitment to his family, Felbrigg and the estate community.

Chapter 10

Responses to adversity: the changing strategies of two Norfolk landowning families, *c*.1665–1700[1]

Ever since the late Sir John Habbakuk published his seminal article on English landownership in 1940, discussion of landed estates in the second half of the seventeenth century has taken place almost entirely within the terms he set out, namely the changing pattern of landownership in favour of great estates and the limited functions of landowners.[2] Little subsequent attention has been paid to the management strategies of landowners and their response to the depression in agricultural prices from the late 1660s. Margaret Davies, in her 1977 article on 'Country gentry and falling rents', attempted to correct this deficiency, but her conclusion more or less confirmed Habbakuk's view that landowning was primarily about landlordship rather than estate management. Gentry landowners responded to their difficulties, principally vacant farms, uncollected rents and declining incomes, with little flexibility. They granted refunds and abatements, but were reluctant to engage in commercial farming; this, she argued, was based on sound commercial principles and a recognition of the hazards of the market. Fundamental was the gentry landowner's lack of training not only for estate management but especially for farming.[3] Christopher Clay has been more generous in his assessment of landowners' priorities and responses, noting their willingness to invest in improvements, consolidate farms and promote new farming ventures. He also challenged Habbakuk's thesis that land was drifting remorselessly into the hands of the great proprietors. By concentrating on two counties, Northamptonshire and Bedfordshire, Habbakuk had failed to recognise the extent of exchange between landowners across the country; this process, Clay argued, was essentially a method of rationalisation rather than aggrandisement and an active response to economic adversity.[4] Two well-documented estates in Norfolk give us an opportunity to reopen

---

1   This chapter was first published as Griffiths, 'Responses to adversity'. It was based on a lecture to the Winter Conference of the BAHS in 1996 entitled 'A response to adversity: sharefarming in Norfolk in the 1670s and 1680s'. It continues the themes of an earlier paper, Griffiths, 'Sir Henry Hobart'. My thanks to Joan Thirsk, John Beckett and Richard Hoyle for their generous advice. All documents cited are in the Norfolk Record Office.

2   H.J. Habakkuk, 'English landownership, 1680–1740', *Economic History* Review, 10 (1940), pp. 2–17; idem, 'Economic functions of English landowners'.

3   M.G. Davies, 'Country gentry and falling rents in the 1660s and 1670s', *Midland History*, 5 (1977), pp. 86–93.

4   C. Clay, 'Landlords and estate management in England', in J. Thirsk (ed.), *The Agrarian History of England and Wales vol. v 1640–1750 pt I Regional Farming Systems* (Cambridge, 1985), pp. 119–245. See also J.V. Beckett, 'English landownership in the later seventeenth and eighteenth centuries:

the debate and test the different assumptions. We need, however, to bear in mind that Norfolk, or parts of it, were in the forefront of agricultural progress in the seventeenth century and that the experience of the families and their estates may not be typical. Despite these reservations, the management strategies adopted by the Hobarts and the Windhams on the Blickling and Felbrigg estates in north-east Norfolk are so clearly presented in the documents that they demand a re-examination of the responses of landowners to the depressed conditions of the second half of the century. Furthermore, the estates include substantial properties scattered across east and south Norfolk, and down to the Suffolk/Essex border, as can be seen in Figure 10.1 – areas that have received scant attention by historians. They offer a contrast to the traditional work on Norfolk agriculture, which concentrates on the great estates on the 'Good Sands' region of west Norfolk, namely Holkham, Raynham and Houghton.

The evidence from Blickling and Felbrigg estates supports the picture of landowners reacting energetically to the deep and prolonged recession of the 1660s and 1670s, but it takes the argument a stage further and suggests that they consciously modified their strategies over time. From the late 1660s to the mid-1680s, the Hobarts and the Windhams were closely involved with the management of their estates. Near to home, they intensified the exploitation of the demesne lands, carving out new farms from park and heath land, establishing livestock enterprises with direct labour and encouraging tenants and their wives to supply the household; all this activity had the added benefit of generating employment and local prosperity. They also reformed their management structures and accounting systems. However, the most novel aspect of their strategy was a willingness to co-operate and intervene in the farming activities of their tenants, which departs from even the most recent accounts of landlord behaviour.[5] Both landowners, principally to effect diversification into dairy farming, were prepared to provide working capital to tenants by leasing milking cows, and to subsidise, in slightly different ways, the costs of cultivation. William Windham went so far as to share the risk of farming by 'letting to halves', whereby he received half the corn crop as opposed to a fixed rent at the end of the year.[6] At Blickling, Sir John Hobart's steward avoided 'letting to halves' but instigated a system of contract farming, setting payments for cultivation against the rent for the dairy cows. In this way tenants built up capital and were eased into accepting large tenancies and leases. Sir John also directly subsidised production in corn agreements, offering a guaranteed price well above market values. However, by the late 1680s attitudes had started to change. Both families gradually abandoned their interventionist strategies in favour of simplified procedures that could be safely administered by subordinates. In the 1690s a new generation completed the process of withdrawal, firmly distancing themselves from estate business. In their absence, estate management assumed the familiar characteristics of eighteenth-century landlordship

The debate and the problems', *Economic History Review*, 30 (1977), pp. 567–81; idem, 'The pattern of landownership in England and Wales, 1660–1880', *Economic History Review*, 37 (1984), pp. 1–22.

5   R. Hoyle, 'Markets and landlords in the disappearance of the small landowner', paper given to the Colloque franco-britannique d'Histoire rurale comparee, at Le Mans, September 2002 (to appear in the conference proceedings edited by Nadine Vivier).

6   WKC 5/152 400 x; see also Griffiths, *William Windham's Green Book*, and chapter 9 above.

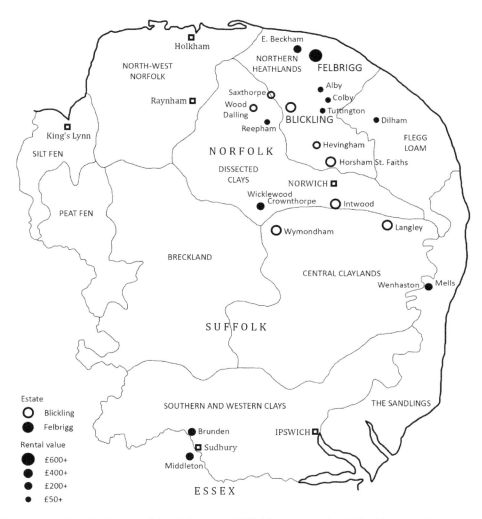

Figure 10.1 The distribution of the Felbrigg and Blickling estates in 1673 with approximate rental values. Landscape regions of East Anglia are taken from T. Williamson and S. Wade-Martins, *Roots of Change: Farming and the Landscape in East Anglia* (1999).

by which administration became the province of full-time professionals and farming the business of well-capitalised tenants. The relationship between landlord and tenant was standardised, their mutual responsibilities defined in written leases and mediated through the estate steward. However, this solution was not self-evident at the outset; it was shaped by the long and frustrating process of trying to make estates pay in a period of relentlessly falling prices.[7]

---

7   Bowden, 'Agricultural prices', pp. 41–5; also statistical appendix, pp. 828–84.

This process of withdrawal appears to be associated with a much wider cultural shift. Philip Jenkins and James Rosenheim have similarly identified the 1690s as a turning point in the political attitudes of the gentry.[8] Jenkins argued that the Civil War, and the years of trauma and instability that followed, cast a long shadow affecting not only the fortunes but the mentalities of landed families. Until 1688 landowners were preoccupied by the politics of the Civil War; their principal concern was to protect local authority against the centralising activities of the state. By the 1690s they had achieved those objectives and could turn their attention to foreign policy, business and leisure. From that time they created a distinctive gentry culture with its own rhythms. In his work *The Townshends of Raynham* Rosenheim drew attention to the withdrawal of the elite from county government. While the Civil War generation conscientiously attended local business and served on the bench, the next generation delegated local affairs to their nominees. Robert Britiffe, political agent to Sir Robert Walpole, was forced to appoint men of lower status, and commented on the 'great fault of Mr Ashe Windham and other gentlemen'.[9] Rosenheim singled out Sir John Hobart of Blickling as an 'exemplary father' followed by a 'less ardent son'.[10] What is argued here is that the changes in strategy evident in the 1690s, and indeed between 1665 and 1700, were driven primarily by economic forces but shaped, in significant ways, by these broader cultural issues.

I

National trends played their part, but any decision or strategy devised by a landowner at any time or in any period will ultimately be shaped by individual circumstances. Lifestyle, ambition, commitments, financial predicament: all create policies of infinite

---

8   P. Jenkins, *The Making of a Ruling Class: The Glamorgan Gentry, 1640–1790* (Cambridge, 1983); Rosenheim, *The Townshends of Raynham*. In his comparison between father and son, Rosenheim highlighted their different approach to estate management: Horatio, 1st Viscount Townshend, like his brother-in-law William Windham and close friend Sir John Hobart, was actively engaged in the minutiae of estate reform, while Charles, 2nd Viscount, adopted a more detached role, at least until his retirement from public office in 1730, when his enthusiasm for agricultural improvement earned him the sobriquet Turnip Townshend; Rosenheim, *The Townshends of Raynham*, pp. 64–104, 236–45. See also idem, *Emergence of a Ruling Order. English Landed Society, 1650–1750* (London, 1998).

9   Robert Britiffe Esq. (1661–1749), Recorder of King's Lynn 1704–30 and of Norwich 1737–43; MP for Norwich, at Walpole's behest, 1714–34. Son of Edmund Britiffe of Baconsthorpe, Robert gained wealth and influence as family lawyer, agent and adviser to several leading county families, including the Walpoles, Townshends, Hobarts, Windhams, Harbords of Gunton and Rants of Thorpe Market. See also J.H. Plumb, *Sir Robert Walpole: The Making of a Statesman*, vol. 1 (London, 1956), pp. 210, 310, 361; Rosenheim, *The Townshends of Raynham*, pp. 144, 266; idem, *Emergence of a Ruling Order*, p. 20.

10   J.M. Rosenheim, 'County government and elite withdrawal in Norfolk, 1660–1720', in A.L. Beier *et al.* (eds), *The First Modern Society. Essays in English History in Honour of Lawrence Stone* (Cambridge, 1989); see also Plumb, *Walpole, passim*; idem, 'The Walpoles: father and son', in J.H. Plumb (ed.), *Studies in Social History: A Tribute to G.M. Trevelyan* (London, 1955), pp. 179–207; idem, 'Sir Robert Walpole and Norfolk husbandry', *Economic History Review*, 5 (1952), pp. 86–9.

variety and no analysis can be made without consideration of these semi-independent variables. The Hobarts and Windhams were leading gentry families and neighbours in north-east Norfolk. Both families migrated from south Norfolk, the Windhams in the mid-fifteenth century and the Hobarts in the early seventeenth century, and both retained properties in that part of the county (Figure 10.1). However, whereas the Hobarts had, since the late 1620s, pursued ruinously expensive careers on the national stage, depleting the great estate amassed by Sir Henry Hobart between 1596 and 1625, the Windhams preferred the quiet life, building on Thomas Windham's modest inheritance from his father Sir John Wyndham of Orchard, Somerset.[11] By the mid-1660s both families enjoyed estates worth about £2000 a year. However, that picture of secure wealth is misleading. Sir John Hobart was deeply indebted, while William Windham enjoyed huge surpluses, bolstered by his wife's dowry of £10,000, which he loaned to his friends, including Sir John, at 6 per cent interest.[12] These sets of circumstances dictated certain strategies. Sir John Hobart's choices were severely constrained by the state of his finances, yet his political commitments required him to delegate his estate business to a trusted subordinate. He had to maximise his resources as far as possible, but he could not afford to take risks. Windham's position was the reverse. Permanently in residence, he could undertake day-to-day management, experiment and innovate, more or less free from financial worries. However, the Hobarts were not entirely disadvantaged. Absenteeism might be seen as a handicap, but over the years they had recruited professionals to conduct their estate business and their appointments were invariably shrewd, whereas the Windhams in this respect were less successful. As the recession deepened, personal management, however enthusiastic, proved to have its limitations and was not necessarily the wisest course.[13]

Geography and the structure of holdings also had a bearing on the possibilities. The two estates were centred on the northern heathlands, identified by Wade Martins and Williamson as areas of innovation and improvement, with off-lying properties on the claylands of south Norfolk and the Suffolk/Essex border.[14] Since the early seventeenth century, the heath and waste to the north and west of Felbrigg and Blickling had been steadily enclosed and drawn into cultivation, while detailed leases stipulated the use of up-and-down husbandry on the light soils at East Beckham, Saxthorpe, Hevingham and Horsham St Faith. The demesne at Felbrigg, consisting of a compact block of 750 acres, much of it enclosed pasture and meadowland, was a particular asset; it had long been used for large-scale commercial bullock fattening. More difficult were the holdings situated on the fertile loams of east Norfolk towards Dilham, regarded by William Marshall in the 1780s as the true home of agricultural

11   Griffiths, 'Sir Henry Hobart'; Ketton-Cremer, *Felbrigg*.

12   Sir John Hobart, 3rd Bt 1625–83, MP for Norfolk 1654, Cromwell's Upper House 1657; MP for Norfolk 1668–72, 1676–83; Griffiths, 'Management', p. 310; Sir John Hobart's sales and mortgages 1649–86, NRS, 10897 25D5; NRS, 16338 33C2; see also J.R. Jones, 'The first Whig party in Norfolk', *Durham University Journal*, 46 (1953), pp. 13–21; Rosenheim, *The Townshends of Raynham*.

13   Rosenheim, *Emergence of a Ruling Order*, pp. 47–88.

14   Wade Martins and Williamson, *Roots of Change*, p. 15.

innovation; these farms were highly productive but limited in scope by the prevalence of small landholders and fragmented ownership. The properties on the claylands of south Norfolk and Suffolk consisted of large flexible farms with a tradition of livestock and dairy farming. Notable is the lease for Langley Abbey in 1592, which included '20 northerne milche neat and one northerne bull'; this is the earliest reference to a leased dairy on either estate.[15] Both Sir John Hobart and William Windham could draw on a history of improved farms and diversified agriculture; both estates had the potential to develop their livestock farming.

II

By the mid-1660s the rent rolls of £2000 a year represented a nominal figure, as Sir John and William Windham faced a mounting crisis of unpaid rents, debt and vacant farms, compounded by poor accounting and inadequate management by bailiffs. At Blickling, John Tolke kept an estate rental and separate account books recording receipts and disbursements, but the periods do not correspond, no balance was taken and losses were not identified, so Sir John had little idea as to his real income.[16] Over the whole period from 1655 to 1666, the shortfall between actual income and anticipated revenues was £5500, the sum Sir John was forced to borrow to meet his expenditure; these figures suggest that he was, in fact, making strenuous efforts to live within his means. Inadequate procedures also deepened the crisis on individual farms. As corn prices fell Sir John made generous concessions to his tenants, forgiving rents, converting debts to loans and buying up stock, corn and equipment, but to little effect.[17]

Sir John solved his management problems in 1665 by recruiting the team who had successfully run his aunt's jointure at Langley, Wymondham and Wood Dalling between 1647 and 1665.[18] Robert Dey of Norwich and Wood Dalling handled legal matters, drew up leases and made agreements. Henry Gallant, tenant of Wood Dalling Hall, dealt with the practical side, buying and selling stock and corn, assessing repairs and surveying building projects, but kept rather scrappy accounts. To compensate for this deficiency, Dey recruited John Brewster of Fundenhall for his ability in all aspects of estate management, capitalising on his experience as a small landowner and farmer. Brewster combined exactly the right blend of professionalism and native wit necessary to manage an estate in an economic downturn. He could keep accurate accounts, negotiate confidently with tenants, devise new leases and agreements and supervise men on the ground to carry out repairs and make accurate returns. He also possessed an acute appreciation of the possibilities and limitations of alternative approaches, thus avoiding some of the expensive experiments made at Felbrigg. This

---

15   NRS 18346 33B4: The tenant agreed to yield up the same number of cows, or to pay a total of £52 10s, which indicates a rental of 52s 6d per cow. Griffiths, 'Management', p. 123.

16   NRS 10135 22F7, 14716 29D3, 11315 26B4.

17   Griffiths, 'Management', pp. 308–21.

18   Lady Frances Egerton, daughter of the earl of Bridgewater, married Sir John Hobart, 2nd Bt, in 1622.

shrewd and trustworthy man, who also served as Sir John's political agent, remained the linchpin of the Hobarts' estate management until 1714.[19]

William Windham approached the problems slightly differently. Younger than his neighbour by twenty years, he inherited Felbrigg in 1665 at the age of eighteen. During his minority the family lawyer, Dr Robert Peppar, had administered the estate, having promised to bring his affairs into 'method and order'.[20] However, Peppar proved no more successful than the bailiff Thomas Blofield, who had collected the rents and kept accounts between 1654 and 1665, as he possessed none of the practical skills necessary to deal with tenants in a time of economic difficulty; he complained about the tenants' failure to pay their rents and quarrelled bitterly with the Felbrigg bailiff John Salman.[21] The worsening situation at Felbrigg became the subject of a correspondence between William Windham and his cousin Judge Hugh Wyndham in the late 1660s, evidence that landowners were actively discussing new strategies at this time.[22] In a letter written in 1668, Judge Wyndham, who had inherited part of the Dilham estate, identified arrears as the principal problem: 'when tenants are suffered to run much in arrears it is inconvenient to the tenant as to the lord for thereby it grows heavier on ye tenant and renders him more unabell to paie.' His solution at Dilham was to replace his attorney with a local man, Mr Harris, who was able to negotiate with tenants, assess claims, formulate and enforce agreements and keep regular accounts. '[T]his I suppose be much better done by a country man in those parts than by an attorney whose imploiements in other affairs cannot afford him time and the opportunity.' Legal services were to be purchased 'at no great charge', while Mr Harris received an annual salary. Beside being more effective, this was a much cheaper arrangement. The inefficient and quarrelsome Peppar demanded £100 for his services, whereas the excellent John Brewster charged a mere £30 a year. Windham dismissed Peppar, preferring to undertake the day-to-day business of estate management himself with the support of a team of practical men, enlisting professionals when required; in this he followed the example of his father, Thomas Windham. However, influenced by his father-in-law, the merchant, Sir Joseph Ashe of Twickenham, he differed in his emphasis on accounting and record-keeping. Sir Joseph was a key figure at Felbrigg and Raynham in the 1670s and 1680s, encouraging both his sons-in-law, William Windham and Horatio Townshend, to reorganise their systems and manage their estates along commercial lines.[23]

---

19 Brewster neatly labelled bundles of very detailed accounts, with supporting information, for each property. The total receipts from the estate were paid into the household accounts. Not all Brewster's accounts have survived, so it is sometimes difficult to show the sequence of estate activity, as at Felbrigg.

20 WKC 7/5 404 x 1.

21 WKC 7/5 404 x 1, for example, 'I have been silent under some other of Salmon's affronts of this nature and pray let me have nothing to do with him … I am not so low a man to truckle under so rude and unmannerly a fellow.'

22 WKC 7/15 404 x 1.

23 Sir Joseph Ashe effectively underwrote these two Norfolk families with dowries of £10,000 a piece: his elder daughter Katherine married William Windham in 1669; his younger daughter

Common to all these solutions was the recognition of the need for professionalism and imaginative new strategies.

Windham expressed his enthusiasm and commitment in the Green Book, an estate book running to some 600 pages, in which he assembled all the information he required for the direct management of his estate. He started experimenting with a new structure and accounting system in 1671 and by October 1673 he had arrived at the definitive version, which included the adoption of double entry book-keeping.[24] The success of the Green Book lay in the system of numbered pages, which provided easy access from the particular of the estate at the front to the tenants' accounts, placed in the middle of the volume, and then to the relevant leases and agreements recorded at the back. The cross-referencing method extended to memorandum books and supplementary accounts, which note sales of timber and stock. It was designed specifically as a tool of management, able to provide quickly accurate and relevant data on each tenant and the overall performance of the estate; for example, Table 10.1 shows that in the first year Windham faced old debts and arrears totalling £4533. Windham supplied a running commentary, annotating his entries and reviewing progress; his express desire was that his son should learn from his mistakes.[25] He also included descriptions of tree-planting schemes, deer keeping and the management of fish as a reference for future generations. This instructional style, reminiscent of classical authors, reflects Windham's vision of estate management and his wider responsibilities to his family and local community.

Despite these lofty intentions, and before the pages of the Green Book were exhausted, Windham started a new account book, dispensing with the particular of the estate in favour of a numbered alphabetical list of tenants – in effect a simple tenants' ledger; only by casual reference or descent can the holdings be identified.[26] This simplified format, adopted in 1688, reflects a radical change of strategy, anticipating the delegation of day-to-day management to a full-time steward. Windham no longer required a detailed knowledge of individual farms; the tenants were dealt with through his steward Stephen Legge. Windham's relations with his tenants, illustrated so graphically in the pages of the Green Book, help to explain why he reached that solution. The series of estate account books at Felbrigg from 1673 to 1717 demonstrate quite clearly a underlying change in the philosophy of estate management.

III

Having reformed their management structures and accounting systems, the Hobarts and Windhams embarked on a range of strategies designed to maintain

---

Mary married the widower Horatio, 1st Viscount Townshend, in 1673. See Rosenheim, *The Townshends of Raynham*, p. 84.

24 WKC 5/152 400 x, see chapter 9 above.

25 He warned of the 'poverty and knavery of millers' and, when Crownethorpe Farm failed in 1677, he kept 'a strict account of it, yt my son may see the inconveniency of having farms come into his hands'.

26 WKC 5/158 400 x 6.

Table 10.1

The Felbrigg estate: summary of rental, arrears, lands in hand, rent charge, receipts and allowances, 1674–87 (£).

	1674	1675	1676	1677	1678	1679	1680	1681	1682	1683	1684	1685	1686	1687
Nominal rental	2114	2090	2090	2095	2105	2180	2280	2285	2300	2305	2300	2280	2250	2230
Park and lands in the Felbrigg area*	179	253	245	179	268	329	263	272	333	316	471	440	447	282
Farms in hand	52			127						265	265	255	255	350
Let to halves				62	62	100	100	100	216	216	74	10	10	10
Rent charge	1883	1837	1845	1727	1875	1761	1927	1913	1847	1498	1490	1575	1537	1498
Old debts**	440	440	440	440							715			
Arrears	4093	1757	2275	1533	1685	1766	2191	2892	2547	2476	1909	1805	1798	2354
Total due from rent & arrears	5976	3594	4120	3260	3560	3527	4118	4805	4394	3974	3399	3380	3335	3852
Gross receipts	4117	1200	2661	1680	1818	1438	1313	2226	1847	1266	1580	1524	1034	1577
Net receipts	3280	1058	1765	1569	1533	1096	943	1895	1609	1113	1411	1217	774	1212
Allowed***	837	142	896	111	285	340	370	331	238	153	169	307	260	365

Notes: * Closes taken in hand/farmed with park: dairying/stock fattening/arable/tree planting – flexible system, value estimated.

** Old debt was written off in 1678 and the Suffolk debt was written off in 1685.

*** Allowances averaged 18.5% of gross receipts: tax 1.5%; repairs 4.7%; abated 5.3%; paid in corn 2.5%; sales of goods and chattels 4.0%; lost 0.5%.

Source: Calculated from Griffiths, *William Windham's Green Book.*

rent levels. Some of these are familiar, but others – notably 'letting to halves' and contract farming, which show landowners participating in farming to the extent of sharing the risks with their tenants – have not been considered.[27] The reason is that sharefarming, while commonplace in Europe, is not associated with British practice. However, it is becoming clear that historians have occasionally come across these types of agreement without recognising their significance.[28] This ignorance, or lack of awareness, can be largely attributed to Arthur Young, who argued that the success of English agriculture, compared with the failure of French farming, where *metayage* was the dominant tenure, lay in the fact that such a system did not exist in England.[29] This may have been true in the 1780s, but even in well-known published sources there is scattered evidence of its use in the seventeenth century; for example, it appears on the first page of Robert Loder's famous farm accounts.[30] The practice remains elusive, as it invariably operated at an informal level between small landholders and husbandmen to tide them over periods of difficulty, sickness, widowhood or old age, so was rarely documented. It is significant that it first appears on the Felbrigg estate on the Dilham property in 1658 and 1662, an area dominated by small farmers, and was used as a temporary expedient for leasing a vacant farm.[31] This was also the context for the agreement between John Berney and John Ollyet at nearby Westwick in 1698.[32] The difference in the 1670s was that Windham, possibly acting on advice from his practical team, or perhaps influenced by the exhortations of agricultural writers, adapted it as a method for effecting improvement, particularly diversification into dairy farming, and concluded agreements for terms of years.[33] When his initial agreements were found wanting he enlisted a professional, Edmund Britiffe of Baconsthorpe, to draw up formal agreements, which Windham copied into the Green Book.[34] This is proof first that he was serious in developing the practice and secondly that professionals existed to give

---

27 Letting to halves is essentially a partnership between landowner and tenant, where the landowner takes half the crop as opposed to a fixed rent. See Griffiths and Overton, *Farming to Halves*.

28 From his work on the Verneys, John Broad has recently found a reference to letting to halves at East Claydon in 1651; Richard Hoyle has noticed farming to halves in the depressed years after the famines of 1622–3 on an estate in east Lancashire and Mark Overton reports that he noticed references to letting to halves in his work on Norfolk probate inventories.

29 A. Young, *Travels through France during the years 1787, 1788, 1789 and 1793*, ed. C. Maxwell (Cambridge, 1950), pp. xxvi–xxxv, 286–7, 296–9.

30 Fussell, *Robert Loder's Farm Accounts*, pp. 1–4, 19. In 1610 he 'put forth to halves' part of his mother's jointure.

31 WKC 5/442 464 x 4.

32 PET 159 97 x 2.

33 Sir Richard Weston, in his *Discourse on the husbandry of Brabant and Flanders*, published by Samuel Hartlib in 1652, desired that 'industrious gentlemen … to encourage some expert workmen into the place where they live … to let them land at a reasonable rate, and if they be poor and honest to lend them a little stock'. Windham enjoyed close friendships with members of the Hartlib circle, including Dr Thomas Browne, the eminent philosopher, resident in Norwich since the 1630s.

34 Edmund Britiffe of Baconsthorpe (1629–1715), father of Robert Britiffe.

such detailed advice; it was clearly not an unknown practice.[35] At Blickling Brewster pursued similar policies, but with crucial modifications. What follows is an analysis and comparison of the different approaches at Felbrigg and Blickling.

From the outset, Windham firmly believed that, despite the fall in prices, rent levels could be maintained through intervention and investment; the Green Book itself was the explicit expression of that policy.[36] In 1673 he conceded a rent reduction to the new tenants of Tuttington Hall Farm, from £47 to £37 a year, but only as 'I was loathe to take the farme into my own hands not then living in the countye'. But when the tenant of Reepham Farm made a similar demand William terminated his lease and took the farm in hand; the holding can be identified in Table 10.1, worth £52 under 'Farms in Hand'. He had already identified the farm for improvement, agreeing in 1668 in a lease for five years to build a bakehouse and dairy; similarly in 1670 he built a dairy at 'my house in Gresham'.[37] Diversification into dairy farming was an early objective and in several other parts of the country was recognised as a profitable venture at this time. Windham used Felbrigg Park and the demesne, with its extensive meadows, as a basis for this operation, receiving and holding animals before dispatching them to different farms, as their dairies – and bullock fattening units – were established. The value of the enterprise remained fluid as more farms were taken in hand, 'let to halves' or leased on a tenancy. In the Green Book Windham allocated several pages to listing 'The number of my beasts' and where they were 'held'.[38] John Salman, the Felbrigg bailiff, who co-ordinated the movement of stock, kept his own subsidiary accounts, recording hundreds of transactions.[39]

To ease the burden of managing these new dairies, Windham then resorted to letting to halves. The first such agreement was with Thomas Sexton for Reepham Farm in 1677: '[T]he trouble of looking after this farm made me let it to halves'. In the agreement, for five years, Windham leased a dairy herd of ten cows to Sexton at 45s a head, and the arable they 'plowed to halves': Windham provided the land, Sexton the labour, and they divided the corn crop at the end of the year. Windham calculated that the income from the cows and his half of the corn would equal the old rent of £52. However, for three years Sexton failed to pay the full rent for the dairy, while Windham's return on the arable declined with the falling price of corn. He noted at the end of each account, 'Lost for want of a tennant'. Nevertheless, he did not abandon the idea, suggesting that other reasons contributed to its failure. First, the agreement was poorly drafted with no clear division of responsibility, allowing Sexton to submit every kind of demand. Secondly, it made no provision for independent assessors to ensure that the Windhams received a genuine half. Thirdly, Windham may well have taken advantage of the clause that allowed him to graze additional stock 'for my own benefit', thereby reducing the pasture available for the cows. Finally, Sexton had

---

35 Rosenheim, *The Townshends of Raynham*, p. 94 refers to Stiffkey Hall being farmed 'to halves' in the early 1680s.

36 WKC 5/152 400 x, see also chapter 9 above.

37 WKC 7/154, 404 x 8.

38 Griffiths, *William Windham's Green Book*, pp. 171–4.

39 WKC 5/154 x 6. Griffith (ed.), *William Windham's Green Book*, p. 22, for further references.

no interest in the well-being of the dairy herd, as Windham took responsibility for all herd replacements.[40] Far from reducing the management burden, the arrangement required even closer scrutiny as so much depended on the honesty of the 'operator'.

To correct these shortcomings, Windham engaged Edmund Britiffe, a small but enterprising landowner who acted as intermediary and adviser to local gentry families. His meticulously drafted agreements were designed to avoid disputes. Crucially, the stocking rate was clearly stipulated, Windham's share of the husbandry costs defined and Britiffe retained as arbitrator.[41] In 1678 he arranged with John Masters the 'hiring a dairie of cows' and 'plowing the ground to halfs' in Felbrigg Park. Windham's motive was 'to have the conveniency of a dairie near me, and bee free from the trouble of plowman'.[42] Masters cultivated areas specified by Windham, while his wife ran the dairy. The scheme lasted until 1681, when Master's wife died, 'which made him not fit for imployment'. However, his successor continued until 1693, leasing the dairy and 'sowing to halfes' 67½ acres in the Park with wheat, meslin, barley, buckwheat, peas, vetches, turnips and clover.[43] Less successful was the agreement with John Fincham for 'Selfe's Farm'. Windham made no charge for the building, laid on a small dairy herd and gave Fincham a loan to set up his farming operation. However, the operation collapsed in 1681 with Fincham 'too poor to continue', leaving Windham to write off debts and buy up his stock.[44] This debacle, combined with Sexton's rising debts at Reepham Farm, probably explains why Windham leased both farms at a reduced rent.

Apart from the Park dairy, closely supervised by his wife, Katherine, Windham abandoned letting to halves in the Felbrigg area, preferring to take vacant farms in hand and develop his livestock enterprise with direct labour. A highly commercial business emerged, receiving stock from failed tenants and purchasing store cattle from local fairs, fattening them on the Beef Closes at Sustead and selling them to butchers. On the arable side, Salman paid men to carry out the husbandry and sold the corn to local millers. In this way Windham made a useful supplementary income and built up a network of local contacts. During the course of the 1680s he persuaded several of these local butchers, grocers and small landowners to accept leases; by that time he was prepared to concede strategic rent reductions to attract a well-capitalised tenant. Direct farming required intensive management, but it allowed him to keep control of the operation and his working capital. In other words, while letting to halves could work effectively in a controlled situation, particularly when strict commercial criteria did not apply, direct farming was less risky as a short-term expedient.

Windham did, however, continue letting to halves on more distant properties as a way of attracting tenants and supporting rents levels; used in this limited way it could prove successful. At Scrivener's Farm, Dilham, which he 'could not let ... without great abatement', Windham agreed with John Applebye 'to sow Mack's farm to halfes'. He kept control by renewing the agreement annually, which is the classic arrangement,

---

40 *Ibid.*, pp. 23, 150–2, 277.
41 See chapter 9 above.
42 Griffiths, *William Windham's Green Book*, pp. 283–5.
43 WKC 5/158 400 x 6: Griffiths, 'Management', pp. 388–98.
44 Griffiths, *William Windham's Green Book*, pp. 266–7.

and in 1683 he persuaded Appelbye to take a lease at a reduced rent in 1683, with an abatement for the first year.[45] Less wise was the agreement in 1682: 'for fear I should not git a tennant I agree[d] with Dan Shepherd to live in the house rent free'; he also leased him eight cows at a reduced tariff and they sowed the ground to halves. Windham retained the right to terminate the agreement at three months' notice, but in the event Shepherd refused to surrender his occupation and stayed for four years; in 1686 Windham bought him off with four cows and £2 worth of hay to avoid a legal suit.[46] This appears to have been the final straw. Tables 10.1 and 10.2 show that from 1687 letting to halves was phased out in favour of a uniform policy of rent reductions; the marginal recovery of corn prices in the mid-1680s made this strategy possible. However, when they slumped again in the 1688/9, the year of Windham's death, Katherine was faced with a clutch of vacant farms at Felbrigg, Reepham, Tuttington, Dilham, Beckham and Essex and was forced to review the strategy.[47] She concluded the most ambitious letting to halves agreement with John Lound at Beckham Hall, whose debts amounted to £210. To reduce his debts and enable him to continue farming, Katherine bought his cows, set them off against the debt and leased them back to him; she made no charge for the land and buildings, received payments in kind and allowed substantial sums for marling, repairs and tax. When she terminated the agreement in 1693 Lound still owed £34. With the rise in corn prices in the mid-1690s she took the opportunity to let the farms at reduced rents; never again did the Windhams enter into working partnerships with their tenants.

At Blickling Sir John Hobart's interventionist strategy was implemented by a team of professionals and illustrates the wisdom of employing intermediaries to conduct estate business.[48] They too supported tenants and invested heavily, but from the outset they exerted much tighter controls over expenditure and maintained a more even relationship with the tenantry. They were also acting under greater constraints. Robert Dey and John Brewster did not possess the same freedom to experiment and lose money. Sir John's indebtedness, in fact, left very little room for manoeuvre; his response to adversity had to be managed with foresight, firmness and efficiency. Brewster could not risk half the estate falling in hand; he needed to anticipate rather than react to disaster and to control costs at all times. Dey retained a guiding hand until 1671, but from 1669 Brewster initiated estate management policy, as becomes clear in the leases for Horsham St Faith, Langley Abbey and Swardeston Farm.[49]

The earliest evidence of their more sophisticated strategy is a plan for Langley Abbey in 1666, devised for the 'Aby to answer a profit in lieu of rent'.[50] They identified three enterprises. First, they leased the tithes for £60. Secondly, they allocated 127 acres with two tenements to maintain a dairy of thirty cows, leased at 45s a head, which they estimated to be worth £91 10s. The cows 'for their summer feed are to

---

45 *Ibid.*, pp. 16, 213–14, 249, 263.

46 *Ibid.*, pp. 206–8, 247, 249–50.

47 NRS WKC 5/158 400 x 6; Griffiths, 'Management', pp. 388–97.

48 Griffiths, 'Management', pp. 398–452.

49 NRS 16023 31F10; 11122 25E 5; 16017 31F10; 21135 74 x 2.

50 NRS 10379 25A6.

Table 10.2
The Felbrigg estate: summary of rental, arrears, rent charge, receipts and allowances, 1688–96 (£).

	1688	1689	1690	1691	1692	1693	1694	1695	1696
Nominal rental	2228	1780	1600	1594	1566	1543	1506	1494	
In hand	776	389	489	582	614	607	565	565	565
Let to halves			60	60	60	60			
Rent of stock			47	37	103	49		97	63
Rent charge	1462	1391	1051	952	892	876	921	907	453
Arrears	2638	2633	2490	2974	2533	2523	1074	955	1063
Arrears written off							1130		
Total due from rent & arrears	4100	4024	3588	3963	3528	3448	1995	1959	1580
Gross receipts	1466	1534	614	1428	1004	1243	1040	896	444
Net income in cash	1278	654	388	603	586	729	644	540	217
Paid in corn	102	98	104	276	112	110	163	59	199
Allowances	86	782	122	549	306	404	233	297	28
Written off								1096	
Percentage breakdown of allowances									
Tax	0.1	2.7	6.4	17.0	9.0	11.3	10.5	7.2	6.2
Repairs	4.0	8.3	12.8	9.0	18.7	9.7	6.5	8.6	0.1
Abatements	1.9	10.0	0.7	12.5	2.8	11.5	5.4	17.3	
Sales		12.2							
Lost		17.8							

Source: Calculated from Griffiths, *William Windham's Green Book*.

have 3 acres to a cowe, 12 acres of meadow ground for their hay for their winter feed besides straw'; 25 acres was let with the two tenements. From the remaining 258¾ acres they expected to make £78 10s, highlighting the superior returns from dairying. The 169 acres in tillage were divided into 30 acres of winter corn, 18 acres of peas, 33 acres of oats, 52 acres of barley, 16 acres of turnips and 20 acres of summerley. Finally, 90 acres was kept for mowing, 'keeping horses for ye tillage', young cattle 'or what else a good husband should think'. There was a 'full stock of cattle uppon ye ground and 12 beasts at stake with Turnepps', which would 'make ... compost against next seed tyme'; and 'in order to ye well disposing thereof there shall be a large sumerly left and ye other grounds left soe that they may fall in husbandly course to continue in tillage with several graines according to the qualities and nature of ye groundes'. This plan confirms the existence of farming regimes where the use of turnips in rotations was well established by the mid-1660s.

No accounts survive for this regime at Langley Abbey, but the arrangement lasted for three years, ending in 1669, when the holding was leased, with a 10 per cent reduction in rent, abatements for the first and final year, and Sir John assuming responsibility for repairs.[51] In 1666 a similar scheme was implemented at Langley Grange. Henry Gallant's accounts show that in 1668 the dairy was let to 'Henry Nott and his wife' at 40s a cow while Robert Horne cultivated the arable.[52] Horne, having acquired sufficient capital, took over the tenancy in 1675 and purchased the dairy of thirty-two cows.[53] These arrangements show, as at Felbrigg, the growing dependence of landowners on 'practical men' as agents and tenants, and also the importance of women when it came to the formal business of leasing dairies. In 1668, when the Little Park at Wymondham failed, Brewster leased the dairy of twenty-five cows at 55s a piece to Goodman Wakefield, blacksmith, and his wife Alice, who featured prominently in his accounts paying the rent and negotiating abatements.[54] The arable land was farmed by John Knight and John Cullyer on a contractual basis. In 1677 John Cullyer farmed both the dairy and arable on this basis at Intwood Hall Farm; in 1681 his son accepted a tenancy.[55] This progression from contracting to tenanting, and moving from one property to another, shows the rise of a class of enterprising tenants from modest backgrounds, vigorously responding to the demands of a difficult market and able and eager to take over prestigious tenancies previously held by men of quality.

Mr Drury, who had held Intwood Hall since the 1650s, was just such a man. Sir John had struggled to keep him afloat, but he finally failed in 1677 with huge debts; in time-honoured fashion Sir John agreed to buy up all his corn, stock and equipment. The independent valuer was horrified at the sums allowed for harness. 'I did say they were all too dear … I would not yield to £30, but if Sir John pleased to give it he might, but I dare not.' Drury's son thanked Sir John 'for his great favour and kindness in so generously passing by that great advantage w[hi]ch he might have of right made use of against me for breach of covenants'.[56] This interchange is instructive. It shows us, first, that if routine matters had been left to Sir John far less control would have been exercised; and, secondly, the advantage of employing professionals and intermediaries to deal with tenants. Sir John's and William Windham's position as landowners and leaders of society required them to be generous and charitable, but economic realities demanded firm action. Windham, by conducting his own negotiations, often found himself in a demeaning position, which made him lose his temper and placed him at a disadvantage. For Brewster and Allen, the hard-nosed professionals, driving a hard bargain on Sir John's behalf was a test of their skill. All parties accepted and understood their bareknuckled approach, which removed Sir John from the fray and allowed him to step in with gracious concessions if appropriate.

Brewster's astute management of Intwood Hall Farm between 1677 and 1680 demonstrates further the benefits of employing such a man. In this agreement John Cullyer leased twenty cows at 48s a piece and paid the rent for the cows by farming

---

51   NRS 3131 13B3.
52   NRS 181 33A3.
53   NRS 17416 32F13
54   NRS 18146 33A3.
55   NRS 11321 26B5.
56   NRS 11321 26B5.

the arable on a contract basis. Brewster specified the rates to be paid for ploughing, harrowing, sowing, reaping, carrying and laying corn into the barn, and for cultivating turnips, making hay, carrying and spreading muck and looking after cattle. The total cost of husbandry was valued at £22 10s. Brewster added to this figure allowances for repairs to buildings and the use of Cullyer's implements; the total sum was then set against Cullyer's rent of £48 for the dairy. Brewster reserved the right to review terms annually, which meant adjusting the farming rates and putting on more cows if the cost of farming the arable exceeded the rent for the cows. This happened after the first year, when Brewster made a small loss, but in the final two years, with five more cows and slightly reduced rates, he made a reasonable profit and Sir John still benefited from the sale of the whole corn crop. In this arrangement Brewster kept the initiative; the tenant knew that if his farming costs were too high Brewster would shift the emphasis to dairy farming. No sharing of the corn crop reduced the opportunity for fraud and left Cullyer with the incentive of making a profit on his cows. Nevertheless, the scheme still required careful management; Brewster's man on the ground, Francis Eagle, kept a record of work done, filling pages with minute detail that had to be checked by Brewster, a time-consuming and irksome task.[57] When Cullyer's son agreed to seal a lease, despite a 14 per cent reduction in rent, they terminated the scheme.[58]

Unlike Windham, Brewster never tried to maintain rents at artificial levels; from the outset he favoured negotiated concessions supported by written leases often containing directions to improve husbandry, notably the use of turnips on the light-soil farms. The 1666 lease for Abbey Farm, Horsham St Faith, is not unique, as Wade Martins and Williamson believed, but one of a series designed to improve this difficult farm.[59] Turnips had, in fact, been used at Abbey Farm prior to 1666; the sale of stock, corn and equipment by the outgoing tenant in that year included a crop of turnips. However, the inclusion in the agreement of detailed instructions as to their cultivation demonstrates an explicit intention to develop and extend their use on the estate. Sir John's agent, not Brewster in this instance, made several drafts before the terms were agreed; Brewster further clarified directives when he renewed the lease in 1673.[60] In 1679 Brewster concluded a corn agreement guaranteeing the tenant a market and price for his corn.[61] This was not share farming, but a straightforward subsidy controlled by Brewster. The net return at Abbey Farm, at 62.5 per cent of the rent charge, was the lowest on the estate, but better than the 50 per cent recorded in the 1650s and early 1660s; moreover, tenants survived and improvements were implemented. Brewster did not ignore the smaller holdings; for William Wix at Horsford he noted 'a dairy to be made'.[62]

---

57   *Ibid.*

58   NRS, 23513 Z105; see Griffiths, 'Management of two east Norfolk estates', pp. 429–37 (Brewster's accounts for Intwood Hall Farm 1673–97), and Table 5.21 (Movement of Rent at Intwood 1665–1701), also pp. 430, 436.

59   S. Wade Martins and T. Williamson, 'The development of the lease and its role in agricultural improvement in East Anglia, 1660–1870', *Agricultural History Review*, 46/2 (1998), pp. 127–41.

60   NRS 11122 25E5.

61   NRS 16023 31F10.

62   NRS 16017 31F10.

On the light-soil farms at Intwood a similar policy was pursued, directing tenants to leave a specified acreage 'somerlayed for Turnips'. At the Hall in 1676, among the sweeteners offered to Mr Drury, Sir John agreed to pay for the cost of cultivating twelve acres with turnips. On the cover of the lease for Swardeston Farm in 1669, requiring 'nyne acres somerlayed for Turnepps', is a reference to 'Langly Aby 1669' and a 'Turnepp Close'; yet none of the Langley leases stipulate the use of turnips, although we know they were cultivated. This suggests that the practice, well established on the fertile loams east of Norwich, was developed on the northern heathlands further west in a concerted effort to raise fertility and yields and effect a measure of diversification into stock farming. Far from being an isolated example, the lease for Abbey Farm, Horsham St Faith was part of a much wider strategy.

The nature of the intervention on the Blickling Estate changed noticeably after 1682. Leases included concessions, but these were directed to maintaining fixed capital, principally buildings and repairs, and increasingly marling, rather than involvement with farming activities.[63] As at Felbrigg, the priority was to find tenants with working capital and the right kind of expertise to operate in an increasingly difficult market; investment was directed to attracting and supporting these men.[64] What is clear, as Hoyle argues in his 2002 paper 'Markets and landlords in the disappearance of the small landholder', is that the movement towards larger tenancies was not the result of landlord coercion but driven by the market.[65] At the same time the exploitation of the estate at Blickling was intensified, with new farms carved out of the park and heathland and neighbouring farms drawn into a network supplying the household.[66] For these new farms, developed further after Sir John's death in 1683, young Sir Henry Hobart made available buildings close to the hall and paid for marling and fencing; the leases include no reference to building and repairs, for the responsibility of the landowner was taken for granted.[67]

The solvency of tenants was also assisted by the practice of employing them about the estate and purchasing their produce to supply the household. Brewster's household accounts reveal a complex local economy. Thomas Allen at Saxthorpe provided oats, hay and barley for brewing; William Trappet at Blickling kept the gardens, including the greenhouses, ran the dairy and took on several of the new tenancies at different times.[68] Some of the new tenants combined a variety of tasks. William Smyth at 'the Flash' collected rents, while his wife supplied milk, cheese, honey, peas, pears and apples. Goodwife Bongen kept sows and fowls, while her husband obtained plaice, soles, herrings and crabs. Goodwife Springall gathered 'hearbes for dyet drinks' and Mrs Jell supplied oatmeal. Richard Gay of 'the Park Grounds' reared bullocks, including ten steers at turnips, and provided butchered meat. Matthew Fairchild, the blacksmith, undertook ironwork and all sorts of repairs,

---

63   NRS 16019 31F10; 17184 32E6.

64   NRS 16333 32 C2; 23509 Z104.

65   Hoyle, 'Markets and landlords'.

66   Park Farm, Blickling bears the inscription JH; see also NRS, 23496 Z103; NRS, 12399 27D1.

67   Sir Henry Hobart 4th Bt 1660–98: MP for King's Lynn 1681; Norfolk 1688–90; 1695–8.

68   NRS, 16296 32B.

while James Grand, the tailor, repaired upholstery, including the interiors of coaches, made shoes and clothes for the children and taught them to read. Tenants also served as carriers, taking fresh food to the Hobarts' house in Norwich and surplus corn to Coltishall and bringing back wine, luxuries, coal and other household items.[69]

By the mid-1680s a new pattern had emerged on both estates. At the centre, the owners harnessed the economic power of the household to support tenancies, effect improvement and reduce their own expenditure. Both owners actively participated fully and enthusiastically in this process, generating prosperity for the wider estate community. Their tree-planting schemes in the early 1670s might be considered peripheral, but this form of diversification showed much foresight and paid handsome dividends in the 1690s and 1700s as prices continued to fall.[70] Beyond the centre, they tried to extricate themselves from involvement in tenant's farming activities, supporting them through investment in fixed capital rather than assisting with working capital. With tough professional management, this transition was more easily achieved at Blickling than Felbrigg.

IV

The deaths of Sir John Hobart in 1683 and William Windham in 1689 accelerated the process of withdrawal from active estate management at Blickling and Felbrigg. However, the turning point was the renewed slump in corn prices in 1689–93, coupled with the resumption of high taxation; the impact can be seen in Table 10.2.[71] The effect of the Land Tax on estate management has not been fully explored, but it is worth reminding ourselves that it was levied initially in 1689 at 1s in the pound and rose to 4s by 1691 – literally a 20 per cent tax on landed income.[72] The imposition on net profits did not deter investment in buildings, repairs and so on, but it did remove all incentive to maintain rents at artificially high levels. In fact, it made sense to let rents drift down, as taxes went down too. The Hobarts and Windhams, bearing the burden of taxation, curtailed risky enterprises such as the dairies; by 1706 even the dairy herd in the park had been sold. The test came in 1701, when prices fell sharply again, but this time the Windhams made no attempt to support rents by direct farming and letting to halves. They preferred to grant abatements, accept payments in kind and trim rents further; by 1707 Ashe Windham enjoyed an almost fully let estate and a steady, if slightly lower,

---

69 NRS, 12381 27C; 21437 39C; MS 4365 TI38B, Griffiths, 'Management', pp. 438–46, Table 5.22: Brewster's Household Accounts 1673–79, p. 451.

70 Griffiths, 'Management', pp. 455–6, Tables 5.24, 5.25 (Sir Henry Hobart's income and expenditure 1683–87; 1691–96) show receipts from timber sales in 1687 and 1691–3 amounting to £2066 in just four years. The likelihood is that the figure is far in excess of this sum, as there are no surviving accounts for the period 1688–90. Sales of timber at Felbrigg in 1707–11 amounted to £1819.

71 See also Griffiths, 'Management', Accounts for Intwood Hall Farm, 1673–97, p. 436.

72 Rosenheim, *Emergence of a Ruling Order*, pp. 55–6; see also M. Turner, 'The land tax, land and property: old debates and new horizons', in M. Turner and D. Mills (eds), *Land and Property. The English Land Tax, 1692–1832* (Gloucester, 1986), pp. 1–3.

income.[73] In this climate, sales of timber compensated for shortfalls in income on both estates. Sir Henry Hobart and Ashe Windham continued to invest heavily in their estates, but directed it more purposefully to their own interest.[74] Financing costly diversification schemes in partnership with tenants had proved expensive. Working capital had been lost, with little benefit to the landowner. Their long-term interest lay in improving the land and buildings to attract able, well-capitalised tenants rather than assisting impecunious ones. Land purchase, new buildings, enclosure and marling were a much more secure strategy for adversity, at least from the landowners' point of view.[75]

The withdrawal at Felbrigg, associated with Ashe Windham's coming of age and his taking possession of the estate in 1694, was particularly abrupt. The new Green Book, kept by Katherine Windham from 1688 to 1694, ends suddenly, as management passed to the accountant Stephen Legge.[76] Ashe took no initiative; his records are desultory and fragmentary until 1705, when he started a personal account book.[77] This book shows how sharply his life and concerns differed from his father; his severance from estate business was by that time complete. Alderman Briggs of Norwich organised his life, receiving rents from Legge, making cash payments to Ashe – wherever he was – and returning the surplus to business associates in London for investment in stocks, shares and mortgages. Ashe kept a record of wages paid to his butler, cook, gardener, groom, coachman, postilion, park keeper and husbandman and of his dealings with local tradesmen, including a glazier, a tiler, a blacksmith and a cooper. This was a man more interested in managing a lifestyle than an estate. Ashe Windham never participated in estate management; he engaged others and presided over their success. Likewise, Sir Henry Hobart remains a shadowy figure, rarely at Blickling, pursuing his political ambitions and public office and leaving Brewster with the task of funding high levels of personal expenditure.[78] However, Sir Henry's early death in a duel in 1698 provided Brewster with an opportunity for retrenchment.[79]

In the years after 1700 both families re-entered the land market to make their first purchases since the 1650s. At Felbrigg the Windhams, particularly after the South Sea Bubble, made substantial purchases in the locality, while at Blickling the marriage of Sir John Hobart, 5th Bt, to the daughter and heiress of Sir Robert Britiffe of Norwich restored the Hobarts' fortunes to the position they had enjoyed in the 1640s.[80] This new

---

73 Griffiths, *William Windham's Green Book*, Table 5, pp. 41–2.

74 WKC 5'162–210 400 x 6.

75 Several leases, from 1694–1723, contain references to marling: WKC 5'15 399 x 9; 5/95 400 x 3; 5/125 400 x see also Wade Martins and Williamson, 'Development of the lease', p. 130.

76 WKC 5/158 400 x 6.

77 WKC 5/2122 400 x 6; see also A.W. Moore, *Norfolk and the Grand Tour* (Fakenham, 1986), pp. 19–25; J. Black, *The British abroad. The Grand Tour in the Eighteenth Century* (Stroud, 1992), pp. 103, 204, 231, 264.

78 See Griffiths, 'Management', pp. 455, 456, Tables 5.24, 5.25.

79 *Ibid.*, p. 485, Table 6.10: Brewster's Accounts 1703–13. For the three years 1709–11 personal expenditure averaged just £222 a year; Brewster also repaid £1323 in loans.

80 With the marriage of his two daughters (Judith to Sir John Hobart, 5th Bt, in 1717 and Elizabeth to Sir William Harbord of Gunton in 1732) Britiffe effectively secured the future of both these

mood of optimism is captured in the maps commissioned by Lord Hobart in 1729, one showing plans to landscape the park with avenues and vistas and another identifying the principal seats of the gentry.[81] These, coupled with the twenty-five full-length portraits of his Whiggish friends, caricature the interests and attitudes of Habbakuk's landowners.[82] But these values and aspirations were not those of the generation of the 1670s and 1680s; the elaborate plans at Blickling overlay the enclosures and farms created by his grandfather, Sir John Hobart.

The withdrawal of the Hobarts and the Windhams from active involvement with the management of their estates signified a marked change of attitude that cannot be attributed wholly to economic forces. Seen from the cultural perspective offered by Jenkins and Rosenheim, their behaviour, and indeed the changes in strategy evident on the Blickling and Felbrigg estates between 1665 and 1700, make more sense. Clearly, neither Sir Henry Hobart nor Ashe Windham shared the anxiety or the concerns of their fathers; estate management did not have to be subordinated to the broader interests of securing peace and social harmony and could be organised along severely commercial lines to serve the long-term interests of a new ruling and leisured class. Their fathers, marked by their experience in the Civil War and influenced by the regenerative spirit of the times, had turned their attention to domestic matters and the management of their estates. Declining prices, the end of high taxation in 1664 and a government policy designed to promote the interests of landowners, provided every inducement to reform, but the supportive element in the reforms undertaken – the provision of loans, the shared risks of farming – suggest that both Sir John and William Windham were motivated by more than economic advantage. These landowners were clearly influenced by social considerations and regarded it as their moral duty to lead if not participate in the process of renewal, Sir John across the full spectrum of national politics and county government, Windham more narrowly focused on his estate and community. The cost implication of some of these policies, as prices continued to decline, led to their modification and phasing out by the late 1680s. What was different in the 1690s was the explicit desire of their sons to distance themselves from estate management. As Rosenheim argues, this was part of a much wider cultural shift associated with the resolution of political uncertainty and the emergence of a distinctive ruling order. 'The landowner who employed new men and methods was both adopting and announcing a different outlook and attitude toward his identity as a landowner.'[83]

Identifying these changing attitudes is vital to our understanding of agricultural change. As Mark Overton says, it offers a corrective to the view that change was an automatic response to the movement of prices and costs; in reality, the issues

---

leading gentry families. See also Plumb, *Walpole*, p. 311. Walpole was 'furiously eager to get his gains into the solid and indestructible fields of Norfolk'.

81   Sir John Hobart 5th Bt 1690–1750: cr. Lord Hobart 1727, earl of Buckinghamshire 1747.

82   The map of Blickling remains at Blickling Hall; that of the principal seats of the gentry, NRO, BCH 63; Moore and Crawley, *Family and Friends*, pp. 39–45.

83   Rosenheim, *Emergence of a Ruling Order*, pp. 87–8.

were much more complex.[84] The experience of these two estates bears this out. The priorities of landowners of the 1690s were very different from those of the late 1660s to the mid-1680s, and they expressed this change of attitude in their estate management policy. The conclusion must be that the picture presented by Habbakuk and Davies of English landowners in the second half of the seventeenth century, rarely challenged, does not penetrate deeply enough below the surface. Far from being inflexible and complacent, landowners approached the task of finding a workable and profitable solution to the problem of managing their estates during a continuing recession with ingenuity, energy and commitment. Moreover, they consciously reviewed and repeatedly modified their strategies in response to changing circumstances. Their eventual success in finding a solution that served both their financial interests and social needs was not a foregone conclusion. From the outset, landowners were involved in a protracted and difficult process; mistakes were made, valuable lessons were learned, but answers that were logical and fitted comfortably with the other trends of the time did emerge.

---

84   Overton, *Agricultural Revolution in England*, pp. 193–207.

Epilogue

The Le Stranges of
Hunstanton, *c.*1700–2000

By the early eighteenth century the tendency was for landowners to delegate their business affairs to full-time professional stewards. The Hobarts and Townshends had always used professionals to manage their estates, but the Windhams and the Le Stranges had made a point of their personal control. However, their heirs did not share their enthusiasm. The reasons for this withdrawal are not entirely clear, but the character of the Le Stranges' documents changes completely in the early eighteenth century, with no further references to Alice or comments and instructions to successors.[1] The timing differed, as Sir Nicholas Le Strange outlived William Windham by some thirty-five years, but the effect was the same. The impression gained is that, after decades of struggling with depressed prices, landowners were happy to relinquish the task rather than leave matters to disinterested or incompetent heirs. A sustainable and enduring future for the family was more likely in the hands of professionals who understood the intricacies of commercial estate management, family finance and legal issues, just as it is for large landowners today.

Between 1760 and 1762 the Le Stranges suffered the total failure of the male line, the ultimate catastrophe that could befall a landed family. Sir Nicholas's two surviving sons, Sir Thomas, 5th Bt, and Sir Henry, 6th Bt, both died without issue, leaving their two sisters, Armine and Lucy, co-heiresses of the estate in 1760.[2] On the death of Sir Henry the title passed to a distant cousin, but he also died without issue in 1762; thus the baronetcy granted to Sir Nicholas in 1629 became extinct. Armine, the eldest daughter, had married Nicholas Styleman of neighbouring Snettisham; their eldest son Nicholas inherited the Hunstanton estate on his uncle's death. Known as the Jolly Squire, he had no interest in his mother's family or property and sold precious items, including Sir Hamon's famous library, to finance an extravagant lifestyle. When Armine died in 1768 the hall was let and the ancient estate became an appendage of the newly formed Snettisham estate. By 1784 the hall was described as 'so ruinous as is not habitable' and would 'not answer repairing at any rate'.[3] In 1819 *Excursions in the County of Norfolk* explained that the hall had 'long been in a ruinous condition' but the gatehouse was still 'deserving of notice'.[4]

---

1   Griffiths, 'Responses to adversity'; Rosenheim, 'Country government and elite withdrawal'; Rosenheim, *Emergence of a Ruling Order*; see Plumb, *Walpole* (1956) and, more particularly, 'The Walpoles: father and son', in Plumb, *Studies in Social History*.

2   See Figure 5.1.

3   From the survey and valuation carried out by N. Kent and J. Claridge, 1784, for the formal division of the estates between the Stylemans of Snettisham and the Astleys of Melton Constable (LEST/R23).

4   Cromwell, *Excursions in the County of Norfolk*, pp. 24–5, illustrated by J.S. Cotman.

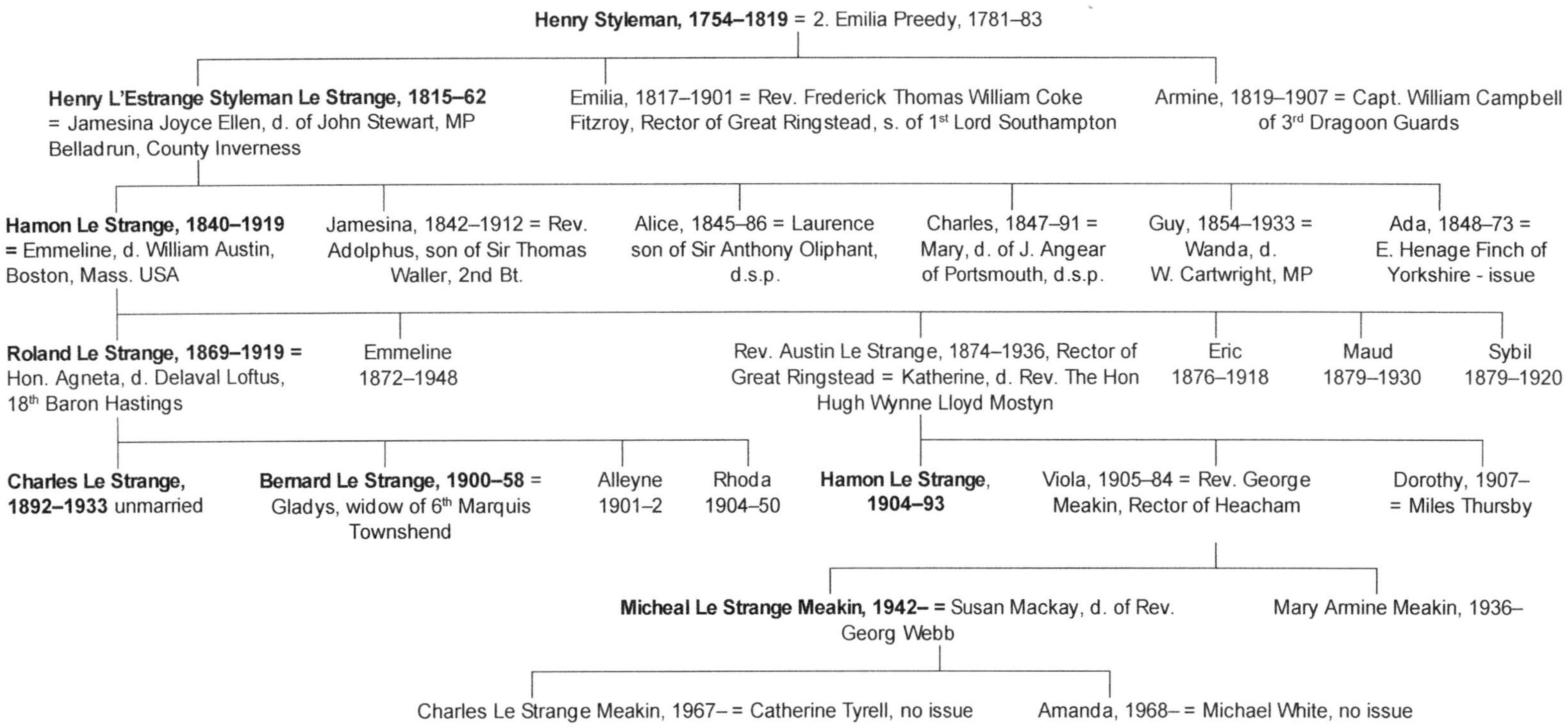

Henry Styleman, **1754–1819** = 2. Emilia Preedy, 1781–83

Henry L'Estrange Styleman Le Strange, 1815–62 = Jamesina Joyce Ellen, d. of John Stewart, MP Belladrun, County Inverness

Emilia, 1817–1901 = Rev. Frederick Thomas William Coke Fitzroy, Rector of Great Ringstead, s. of 1st Lord Southampton

Armine, 1819–1907 = Capt. William Campbell of 3rd Dragoon Guards

Hamon Le Strange, 1840–1919 = Emmeline, d. William Austin, Boston, Mass. USA

Jamesina, 1842–1912 = Rev. Adolphus, son of Sir Thomas Waller, 2nd Bt.

Alice, 1845–86 = Laurence son of Sir Anthony Oliphant, d.s.p.

Charles, 1847–91 = Mary, d. of J. Angear of Portsmouth, d.s.p.

Guy, 1854–1933 = Wanda, d. W. Cartwright, MP

Ada, 1848–73 = E. Henage Finch of Yorkshire - issue

Roland Le Strange, 1869–1919 = Hon. Agneta, d. Delaval Loftus, 18th Baron Hastings

Emmeline 1872–1948

Rev. Austin Le Strange, 1874–1936, Rector of Great Ringstead = Katherine, d. Rev. The Hon Hugh Wynne Lloyd Mostyn

Eric 1876–1918

Maud 1879–1930

Sybil 1879–1920

Charles Le Strange, 1892–1933 unmarried

Bernard Le Strange, 1900–58 = Gladys, widow of 6th Marquis Townshend

Alleyne 1901–2

Rhoda 1904–50

Viola, 1905–84 = Rev. George Meakin, Rector of Heacham

Dorothy, 1907– = Miles Thursby

Hamon Le Strange, 1904–93

Micheal Le Strange Meakin, 1942– = Susan Mackay, d. of Rev. Georg Webb

Mary Armine Meakin, 1936–

Charles Le Strange Meakin, 1967– = Catherine Tyrell, no issue

Amanda, 1968– = Michael White, no issue

Figure E1 Family tree: Styleman Le Strange, 1815–74 and Le Strange of Hunstanton, 1874–2000.
Note: Lords of Hunstanton in bold type.
Sources: Blomefield, Norfolk, vol. 10, p. 314; Walter Rye, Norfolk Families (1912) pp. 477–82; Burke's Landed Gentry, vol. 3 (18th edition, 1972); see also, J. H. Mayer, Extraneus, A Social and Literary Chronicle of the Families, Strange, Le Strange and L'Estrange, 1082 to 1986 (1986).

This sort of outcome was not unusual when estates changed hands through marriage; ancient family names and seats were often lost in this way as old estates were absorbed into new families.[5] The Gressenhall portion of the Le Strange estate was quietly assimilated by the heirs of Lucy, Sir Nicholas's younger daughter, who had married Sir Jacob Astley.[6] However, the Le Stranges and Hunstanton Hall staged an extraordinary revival. Such was the pull of lineage and antiquity that the Stylemans, within three generations, adopted the Le Strange name and reinstated Hunstanton Hall as their principal seat. In the 1870s Hamon Styleman Le Strange completed the process by selling the Snettisham estate and dropping the Styleman name, as it was 'unnecessary and inconvenient'; henceforth, he was known simply as Hamon Le Strange.[7] Thus the family continued until 1993, when the estate passed again through the female line to Michael Le Strange Meakin, the present owner (see Figure E1). Today, shorn of its later acquisitions, the estate bears a close resemblance to the one inherited by Sir Hamon in 1604.

The history of the eighteenth- and nineteenth-century Le Stranges and their relatives remains to be written. It is a story of loss and recovery. It would illustrate and explain the dramatic change of culture as the nouveau riche spendthrift Stylemans mutated into careful and committed Le Stranges, living in the old hall, suitably restored in the architecture of the Gothic Revival. Attention should also be paid to the management of the new estate, which stretched from Snettisham to Holme next Sea and embraced the entire coastline of the Smithdon Hundred with its ancient fishing rights. Although the Snettisham estate was sold in 1872, the new Le Stranges retained the Lordship of Smithdon, which has secured their control over the fishery to the present day. Defending the fishery became a major challenge from the 1840s, with massive research into the medieval records undertaken to support the Le Strange claims. Thus, Henry L'Estrange Styleman Le Strange and his son Hamon became experts in the Le Strange archive in much the same way as Sir Hamon was in the 1600s. The process generated a new interest in the sea and its resources, and led to the building of the seaside resort of Hunstanton St Edmund's. Today, the Le Strange estate survives as a substantial and successful commercial enterprise, with farmland, forestry, foreshore and fishing rights, commercial land – including the famous golf course at Hunstanton, recreation grounds, a caravan park, car park and beach – and six commercial properties comprising the old school, two village halls, two shops and the lifeboat house. The diversity of the business attests to the family's continuing steadiness and thoughtful management of their assets; it also reinforces the idea of an enduring culture of care handed down from generation to generation. The culture

---

5   C. Carpenter, 'The fifteenth century English gentry and their estates', in M. Jones and R.L. Storey (eds), *Gentry and Lesser Nobility in Late Medieval Europe* (Gloucester, 1986), p. 55.

6   Sir Jacob Astley, 3rd Bt 1692–1760.

7   LEST/NM2 for sale particular and map of Snettisham estate, 1871. Sale 1872 to Messrs W. & J. Brown raised £110,000 for the repayment of mortgages. The estate was sold on to Edward Green, a Yorkshire ironmaster, in 1877; he built the stylish Ken Hill as a shooting lodge: see M. Girouard, *The Victorian Country House* (New Haven, CT, 1979), pp. 366–74. See also Deed Poll Certificate, 1874, for dropping of Styleman name (LEST, Additional Deposits, 12/6/1976).

was so pervasive that it survived descent through the female line and reasserted itself in a later generation. The creation of this culture, with its long-term positive benefits for the family and estate, owed much to Sir Hamon and Alice and their successors in the seventeenth and the early eighteenth centuries, although its origins lay in the medieval period.

Index

Entries in **bold** refer to the Illustrations and Tables